THE PROFESSORS

Work and Life Styles among Academicians

Edited with Introductions

by

CHARLES H. ANDERSON

and

JOHN D. MURRAY

SCHENKMAN PUBLISHING COMPANY, INC.

Cambridge, Massachusetts

CONTENTS

Acknowledgments

We are pleased to express our special indebtedness to Professor Milton Gordon of the University of Massachusetts for his early and enthusiastic encouragement of our research on the academic life. Professor Charles Page, also of the University of Massachusetts, provided many helpful suggestions and active encouragement at an early stage in the project when encouragement was much needed. Dr. Allan Mazur of the Stanford University Laboratory for Social Research gave us specific and insightful criticisms of our analysis, and we are pleased to acknowledge our indebtedness to him as well. We are grateful also to Margaret Murray for her patient typing of several drafts and her advice on questions of style.

And, of course, our sincere appreciation goes to the authors and publishers who gave us permission to reprint their works for the creation of this book:

CHAPTER

1 Reprinted from *The Higher Learning in America* (New York: Sagamore Press, 1957), pp. 12-15, 110-114, 117-123.

2 Reprinted from *Academic Women* (University Park, Pa.: Pennsylvania State University Press, 1964), pp. 114-126.

3 Reprinted from *The Academic Revolution* (New York: Anchor, 1969), pp. 531-539.

4 Reprinted from *Men of Ideas* (New York: The Free Press, 1965), pp. 275-293.

5 Reprinted from *The American University* (New York: Harper and Row, 1968), pp. 34-47.

6 Reprinted from *The Public Interest*, Fall, 1965, pp. 37-50.

7 Reprinted from *The Public Interest*, Fall, 1969, pp. 60-77.

8 Reprinted from *The Nation*, Vol. 210, May 25, 1970, pp. 623-627.

9 Reprinted from *Social Problems*, Summer 1961, pp. 56-68.

10 Reprinted from *Sociology and Social Research*, July 1967, pp. 445-451 (revised and expanded).

11 Reprinted from *American Journal of Sociology*, Vol. 64, July 1958, pp. 25-35.

12 Reprinted from *Sociological Inquiry*, Vol. 39, Winter 1969, pp. 77-83 (revised).

13 Reprinted from *Assimilation in American Life* (New York: Oxford University Press, 1964), pp. 224-232.

14 Reprinted from *Sociological Quarterly*, Vol. 9, Spring 1968, pp. 210-227.

15 Reprinted from a doctoral dissertation, University of Massachusetts, 1969.

16 Reprinted from a doctoral dissertation, Johns Hopkins University, 1969.

17 Reprinted from a doctoral dissertation, University of Massachusetts, 1969.

18 Reprinted from *The Causes of World War III* (New York: Ballantine Books, 1960), pp. 143-151.

19 Reprinted from *American Power and the New Mandarins* (New York: Pantheon Books, 1969), pp. 323-333.
20 Reprinted from *The Dissenting Academy* (New York: Pantheon Books, 1968), pp. 3-12.
21 Reprinted from *Commonweal*, Vol. 89, January 31, 1969, pp. 552-556.
22 Reprinted from *The New Republic*, Vol. 154, May 28, 1966, pp. 17-20.

To
MILTON M. GORDON

I

INTRODUCTION

Work and leisure, for most men living in technologically advanced societies, are indeed distinct if not antithetical concepts. For the activities of men's lives are compartmentalized, although often at substantial cost to the individual. Perhaps there is, as Qoheleth professed long ago, a proper time for every happening under the sun; today, certainly, most men do see a time proper for work and another for play.

But the distinction that customarily is drawn between work and leisure does not, of course, mark the lives of all men. As a group, college professors form perhaps the most obvious exception to the general pattern. For quite unlike most occupational groups in post-industrial societies, a majority of academicians have difficulty in separating work from the rest of life. An economist spends his summer vacation gathering data in Africa, and a Spanish teacher travels to Spain to converse with the author of a novel that he plans to translate. An English professor works for a television network during the summer months, while a physicist attends a seminar at the other end of the continent. Where does work leave off and leisure begin? Few academicians are able to answer the question adequately. As a music teacher remarked to an editor of this book: "Vacations . . . usually find me acting in a professional capacity of some sort—composing, performing, or listening." And in the words of a political scientist: "I consider reading the newspaper part of my work. Then while socializing, shop talk is always at the surface or near it" (Anderson, 1966:95-96). As Gerstl (1961:48) said of the professors he studied a decade ago: "Their work *is* their life; their vocation is their avocation."

The nature of the academic's work has bearing upon more than simply his leisure time, however. Indeed, the quality of the intellectual life helps form every facet of the practitioner's personality. Not only the leisure style but also the self-conceptions, the ethnic group involvement and religious orientation, and the social and political attitudes of college professors are shaped to a substantial degree by the occupational environment. Thus, the relationship between job and personality appears and reappears, both explicitly and implicitly, throughout this book.

The influence of academic work upon the behavior and beliefs of college professors is most evident among teachers of the humanities and social sciences. Culture and society is the subject matter of these disciplines, and this, coupled with the very simple fact that humanities and social science teachers are members of the human race, means that these academics in particular cannot escape from being almost continually "on the job"—conjecturing, questioning, criticizing. Scientists and engineers, unless philosophically oriented, as a growing number indeed are, have greater mental distance between their work and the on-going life around them. Accordingly, it is no surprise that the scientist, in his social behavior and attitudes, differs less from upper-white-collar workers in general than does his arts and letters colleague.

Our examination of the impact of work upon the academic personality begins with a brief background commentary on the growth of the profession, followed by a number of general observations on the several areas to be explored in the text. The papers in Sections II and III concern strictly work-related issues, including the process of acquiring and keeping a teaching position and the tensions involved in teaching today at a college or university. The two short empirical studies in Section IV focus on the leisure style of college professors. Sections V and VI treat the academics' social world as a subcommunity within the larger American society: Section V describes the minority group character of this social world, and Section VI explores the role of ethnicity and religiosity in the subcommunal life of college teachers. Finally, the selections in Section VII center on the question of academic participation in the making of social policy.

A Changing Profession

Until quite recently, except during temporary crises, the American academic stood far removed from the discord and disagreements dividing management and workers, from the struggle for human rights and community, from the formulation of law and administration of public policy, and from the design and practice of war. Issues of societal welfare were not considered to be a part of the intellectual turf of men whose sphere of influence was limited to the college classroom. And commensurately little public support was received.

Before the beginning of the twentieth century, the real significance of higher education in America lay in the training of religious personnel and the cultivation of genteel life styles suited to the world of inherited business. Academic personnel consisted largely of ministers, classicists, and legalists. Professors lived precarious lives in economic terms, unless they enjoyed an independent source of income—a condition much favored by colleges in hiring, for independently wealthy teachers could be depended upon to present a cultured and respectable image to business interests and prospective donors. Because academics possessed basically impractical and nontransferable skills, reliance was placed upon the tenure system to assure economic security in a society which gave short shrift to scholarship and science for its own sake (see Chapter 6). Understandably, then, academic norms stressed polite convention rather than criticism and research; social and intellectual nonconformity was scarcely encouraged. Veblen's (1957:132) acrid comment that "Any inquiry which does not lead to corroboration of the opinions in vogue among the unlearned is condemned as being spurious and dangerously wrongheaded," although not without applicability today, is particularly descriptive of nineteenth century higher learning.

With the development of land grant schools after the Civil War, academics gradually began to play practical service roles in the emerging industrial economy. Teacher training, business programs, the industrial arts, and especially agricultural experimentation received increasing public support. The liberal arts struggled for their share of financial resources and began to expand because of the impetus of the already developing applied arts and professions. However, this new public support of higher education was rooted not in a change of heart concerning pure scholarship and science but, rather, in the needs of industrial capitalism. As Veblen (1957:138) put it, "the run of the facts is, in effect, a compromise between the scholar's ideals and those of business in such a way that the ideals of scholarship are yielding ground . . . before the pressure of business-like exigencies." Not until the twentieth century was pure (meaning unsolicited but not necessarily uncritical) scholarship and science to gain substantial public support.

By the first part of the present century academics had become rather well established in the advancing of industrial technology and the socializing of professionals. Even the liberal arts began to play a more active and practical role in the on-going society. Theodore Roosevelt, Woodrow Wilson (himself once a professor), Herbert Hoover, and Franklin D. Roosevelt each entertained the political and economic advice of the once isolated scholar (see Hofstadter, 1963). Presumed problems in national security, conjoined with the increasing complexity of economy and society, were to draw the academic once and for all out from his ivy-covered retreat. By the mid-twentieth century, it had become abundantly clear, at least to decision-makers, that technical knowledge and social information would be required on a reliable and massive scale, and the universities were seen as being well suited to lead the way in confronting such a task.

Thus, since World War II, and especially in the decade following Sputnik, academics found themselves in the midst of an astronomical growth in higher education. The field of college and university teaching and research was opened up to what appeared to be an unlimited number of qualified persons. Pure science gained greatly in capital and stature, while the social sciences came into their own with the promise of providing information on human behavior and solutions to social problems. With this development of the natural and social sciences within the universities and the massive government sponsorship of foreign language offerings, the humanities and fine arts were also to find themselves experiencing growth, although for the most part indirectly.

One result of the post-war boom in higher education has been the enlistment of about half a million persons in the academic profession. Whereas once only a select few from wealthier families could attend college, today nearly every other high school graduate goes on to college. And regardless of whether the felt need for colleges and universities as creators and repositories of indispensable information persists, and there is no reason to doubt that it should not, academic caretakers now perform the institutionalized service of occupying the time of steadily increasing millions of young men and women from seventeen until their early twenties whose energies, if released upon the larger society for twelve months a year, would precipitate a social and economic calamity of epic proportions. Consequently, although the serious shortage of college teachers that existed in the sixties has been alleviated and major institutions now appear to have a surfeit of

qualified job candidates in many disciplines, the overall demand for
Ph.D.'s on college faculties remains substantial. Job competition, as we
shall discuss later, is definitely on the upswing. But, like many other
professional occupations, that of college professor remains a career possibility for the many rather than a monastic order for a few.

Self-Examination

The spirit of inquiry which has contributed so very much to the
development of the academic profession has not until fairly recently
been turned upon the profession itself. Thorstein Veblen, in *The
Higher Learning in America*, was among the first to critically examine
his own vocation, and his insights into the definition of the academic
role remain pointedly relevant. And in his small classic, *Social Role of
the Man of Knowledge*, Florian Znaniecki incisively discussed several
common professorial types, including the Sage, that is, the man who is
expected to supply ideological justification for his group's interpretation
of social reality. But most prominent among the early contemporary
analyses of academics was Logan Wilson's 1942 publication, *The Academic Man*. Indeed, Wilson's study, which offered a rather well-developed
profile of the professor as a social type, although much outdated, remains
as the only attempt at a comprehensive treatment of the academician in
the institutional setting.

Since the late fifties an increasing number of scholars and researchers have delved into the multifaceted lives of academics, and much of
the description has been excellent. Stimulated by political controversies
over academic freedom and inquiries into the patriotism of academics
and intellectuals, Paul Lazarsfeld and Wagner Thielens in 1958 published *The Academic Mind*, the first major systematic survey of social
attitudes of one segment of the academic profession, the social scientists and historians. At the same time, Melvin Seeman (see Chapter
11) probed the self-images of a number of humanities and social science
professors and discerned a vocabulary of self-description similar to that
used by members of minority groups. The late fifties also saw the
publication of Theodore Caplow and Reece McGee's *The Academic
Marketplace*, an empirical investigation of the recruitment mechanisms
used in the profession. Following these landmarks in self-scrutiny,
additional studies of academics have been accumulating throughout
the sixties. And there is now emerging a picture of what modern
academic men are like—their work habits, job orientations, life styles,
social participation, ethnic ties and identities, religious and political

views, and public activities. The portrait, however, is incomplete. It resembles a painting in process: the sketch is there, but the color has yet to appear.

The main body of available empirical data concerns the arts and science faculties, particularly the humanities and social science teachers. Less information exists on academics in the professional schools and applied arts. But the nonacademic counterparts of the personnel of these schools—lawyers, physicians, medical scientists, agricultural scientists, technicians, engineers, and businessmen—compose much of what constitutes the upper middle class. And upper-white-collar people have been studied extensively. To the extent that academics in the professional schools do resemble the nonacademic professional and managerial class, then to that extent we understand them. Indeed, the same logic applies to liberal arts professors.

But a sizeable proportion of both academics and nonacademics have felt that professors are somehow different—even deviant. It is somewhat surprising, then, given the propensity of many students of society for observing the unusual or "deviant" case, that researchers in the universities have not thoroughly exhausted the study of academics, particularly so in view of their proximity. Perhaps because his gaze is fixed through training outward on society, the social scientist has been slow to focus upon the academic as a subject for inquiry. College students and higher education in general have received much more comprehensive treatment than academic personnel as such. Little can be added to Jencks and Riesman's *The Academic Revolution* in describing the evolution and contemporary status of higher education before the student unrest of the late 1960's. These writers also reveal much about the work setting of the academic, and we have included from *The Academic Revolution* a selection devoted to a critical analysis of classroom teaching (see Chapter 3).

Our basic aim in this book, then, is to focus attention on the academic man as a social type. As we have emphasized, and as shall become increasingly evident in the course of the reading, the academic's activities and attitudes both on- and off-the-job overlap and are tightly interconnected. A secondary purpose of the book is to raise some theoretical questions concerning group life and the sociology of the academic profession which might prove an incentive to further research, discussion, or simply reflection. For example, if the professor is different from persons in the middle classes around him, why is this so? Do social and intellectual deviants gravitate toward the academy as a way of life and thus lend to the profession its peculiarities, or do normal children of normal parents stumble into the academic world more or less by chance and then find themselves being transmuted by their work and environment into something quite different from what they expected to be as adults? That is, if the academic does stand apart in some respects from his middle class surroundings, did he arrive there by virtue of self-selection, or was he shaped, once there, by his work and environment? Available data cannot provide clear-cut answers to questions of this kind, although on the whole they indicate that the academic environment is a powerful influence in shaping its inhabitants. Most of the empirical studies included herein are of an exploratory nature and are largely suggestive of tendencies and general traits.

Beyond this, self-examination of the type being done here should heighten professors' and others' awareness of "the other side" of the American academic: college teachers live twenty-four hours a day like everyone else and have as many dimensions of personality as their white-collar neighbors. Technically, the off-the-job life of the academic occupies the major portion of the book. But again, the distinction between work and non-work is often nebulous.

Work as Income

Few people have been motivated initially to enter the academic life by the promise of economic reward. Although the paycheck of today's rank and file professor has considerably more purchasing power than it did a generation ago, his base annual salary seldom exceeds that of his former undergraduate students who have entered business. His standard of living approximates that of the book salesmen who frequent his office or the bricklayer who is his neighbor. Nearly everyone with a level of education similar to that of the college teacher easily outdistances even the full professor economically.

But what businessman, book salesman, bricklayer, or lawyer has, after a few years on the job, virtually a guarantee that he will never be fired for his job's equivalent of ill-prepared classroom presentations, ignorance of the new literature in his field, or intellectual lethargy? How many persons can add many thousands of dollars to their income by working in the summer while vacationing at the other end of the country—and add perhaps two thousand more by meeting with students one or two evenings a week to repeat what was recited earlier in the day? Or go into semi-retirement at age forty-five for writing a textbook? Or pocket $200 an hour for "consulting"? Or receive a

$250,000 grant and possibly create a spin-off business to market a resulting product? And as an alternative, a qualified professor may quit his job at the college (or take a leave of absence) and double his income by going to work for a "brain-trust," a corporation, or the government, or by setting up a "problem-solving" company of his own. To quote Ridgeway (1969: 11), "Professors once sneered at businessmen and the profit motive, but since they have been so successful in taking up the game themselves, the profit motive is now approvingly referred to as the 'reward structure'." The annual salary of many college professors, then, may be a misleading statistic, as their capacity for highly remunerative "moonlighting" grows, albeit the income of even the top echelon of professor-entrepreneurs remains well below that of the established physician, dentist, corporate lawyer, and executive.

Academic entrepreneurship takes time. And very often it is the students' time. So the students rebel as they witness significant portions of the universities, under the guidance of both professors and administrators, being transmuted into federal laboratories and grant stations for, ultimately, the increasing of corporate profits and power and the sustaining of the national and international status quo. Veblen's "instinct of curiosity" has already been dealt a serious blow by certain kinds of university research, specifically research sparked by the insatiable technological appetites of the defense wizards (well over half of all university research funds in America come from the Department of Defense, and these monies are amply backed up with Atomic Energy Commission and National Aeronautics and Space Administration funds), the social engineers,[1] and the market-manipulated consumers, a sizeable minority of which has moderate to severe—and unnecessary—shortages of goods and services and does not need to be artificially enticed into consumption. Indeed, today, "Veblen's test" (work that has a commercial value does not belong in the university) has been turned on its head. Thus, a single research facility at M.I.T. has received about $80 million a year from military and space agencies. Fully 80 percent of that university's budget comes from federal monies, as does 50 percent of Columbia's and Princeton's. Pump-priming money for research on missiles, atomic warheads, radar, com-

---

1. Huxley (1955) has written that "The most important Manhattan Projects of the future will be vast government-sponsored enquiries into what politicians and the participating scientists will call 'the problem of happiness'—in other words, the problem of making people love their servitude."

munication systems, counter-insurgency, and "social problems" flows
from the taxpayer to the government to the elite universities.

Nevertheless, in spite of these research ties with the military, the social status quo, and profit-oriented interests, there continues to exist considerable room for independent research. The university remains, as
Coser argues (see Chapter 4), the most favorable setting for the open,
inquiring mind. What, then, of the alleged conflict between pure scientific and scholarly research and teaching? As Jencks and Riesman (see
Chapter 3), and Hexter (see Chapter 7) argue, there is no intrinsic incompatibility between conducting research and presenting ideas in the
classroom. On the contrary, the art of teaching as practiced by professors, or men of knowledge (in contrast to teachers, or transmitters of an
orthodoxy, in Bernard's terminology; see Chapter 2) requires for its success the continual experience of critizing, probing, discovering, relating,
and synthesizing. Indeed, the latter constellation of traits form the authentic role of the professor, for it is through observing these activities
that the student learns intellectual craftsmanship. Professorial duties
are more a witness to a *style* of work than a dispensing of information.
Unquestionably, however, preoccupation with research endangers the
proper fulfillment of classroom responsibilities, especially if the research has a profit-motivated orientation. And if the function
of the professor is eroded by the dispensing of purchased information
to outside employers, then the university itself becomes a less favorable locale for the proper work of the academic as intellectual or
scientist.

The actual mechanics of recruitment have probably not changed
much since Caplow and McGee conducted their research in the 1950's,
but there has occurred at least one important change in emphasis.
A basic criterion used in recruiting at major institutions today is access to "outside funds" (see Chapter 5). An independent scholar
without either grant experience or a grant in hand is little competition
for the skilled fund raiser or the person with a moveable
bank account. As Klaw (1969: 107) has observed, "The most conspicuous symbol of the new order is the academic entrepreneur, who
is adept at thinking up big and expensive research projects and at
persuading the government to pay for them." In the day of the "edu-
cational-industrial complex," traditional independent scholarship faces
many challenges. "The univeirsity," Ridgeway (1969:1) argues, "looks
more like a center for industrial activity than a community of scholars." Or as even General Eisenhower remarked in his farewell address

to the nation, a government contract has become virtually a substitute for intellectual curiosity. Of course, there is another side to all of this: the overhead charges assessed by the university against these large grants often are funneled into departments lacking technological delivery systems, thus raising the economic and prestige level of not simply the grantsmen but the entire faculty, including the protesting (not against their higher salaries and six-hour class loads) poets, historians, philosophers, and other humanities professors.

But all of this applies primarily to the college and university elite, whose monopoly of the academic prestige system and trend-setting activities are well-known. What of the rank and file of liberal arts, state, and municipal college professors who compose the large majority of the profession? They are where they are for many different reasons. Either truncated graduate study or a graduate degree from a minor university may have relegated them to an unwanted position. Or they may have "deselected" themselves because of personal preference for a school of a certain type or size, or a particular geographic location. Possibly they perished after teaching at a major university (the reasons for such failure are many, but usually they have little to do with actual teaching performance). Or they may have been unable to find a teaching vacancy anywhere other than at a minor school. The problem of an excess of applicants for too few teaching jobs began to plague new Ph.D.'s in American history, foreign languages, and certain fields within the humanities during the latter part of the 1960's; it has now become a problem of major proportions affecting graduate students in most of the traditional disciplines within the nation's universities, and prospects for an early improvement in the situation are dim (see Chapter 8). Finally, if women, these teachers at the rank and file colleges may well have been victims of the rather substantial discrimination which is so often directed against prospective female teachers by chauvinistic male administrators in the colleges and universities. Many female graduate students, because of this discrimination, have been forced to take jobs at the least prestigeful and lowest paying colleges, and often at salaries lower than those of their male colleagues, and with increasing competition with male graduate students expected during the 1970's for a limited number of teaching openings, it is likely even at these schools that women will be experiencing increasing difficulty in securing a job.

Regardless of the reasons why a teacher finds himself at a less than top rank school, once down, the prospects for an ascent are dim. Pros-

pects are nil if down, unpublished, and over forty. Frequent moving
about from one teaching job to another occurs among young academics
who use what bargaining power they have for a change of scenery, a
raise, a promotion, or an escape from an intolerable colleague. Once
over thirty-five or forty, the prospect is faced—grim for some and
pleasant for others—of permanent residence until retirement. And
personal exposure to the "activists" of the discipline becomes limited
to an occasional appearance at a convention where one stands in awe
or ridicule of the inscrutable antics of the full-fledged participants.

Be it a major university or a minor college, however, the work week
of academics at each has at least one thing very much in common: it
is dotted and sometimes dominated by committee meetings. Everyone
supposedly despises committee work, but somehow there is always
need, real or imagined, for yet another committee. Should the military-
industrial complex fail to undermine liberal arts education, the related
process of bureaucratization seems prepared to carry on the battle.
Course offerings and requirements are continually devised and revised,
professors meet with students in "faculty-student relations" committees, graduate students require three to five mentors to lead them
through the Ph.D. maze, and departmental members meet weekly to
discuss at length vitally important administrative matters. Is it possible to effectively shift mental gears from a trite debate one hour
over whether or not majors must take English III to a probing comparative analysis the next hour of Marx and Marcuse? Either administrative and intellectual work are not wholly antithetical or academics are masters of compartmentalization, for the shift back and
forth between the two is being made with increasing frequency in the
work day of academics. (For an early and insightful discussion of the
bureaucratization of higher education and the patterns of adjustment to
this process by academic personnel, see Page, 1951.)

Work as Leisure

To his nonacademic friends, relatives, and neighbors, the college
teacher appears to have a superabundance of leisure time. Supposedly,
he has the entire summer off, plus several free weeks during the academic year, and, of course, the weekends. Moreover, he seems to be
home during the day when everybody else is hard at work. A six to
twelve hour teaching load tends to be equated with a six to twelve
hour work week by the envious observer.

But ask the academic about his leisure. Summers, vacations, and weekends often are time to "catch up" with a heavy backlog of administrative, research, reading, and writing responsibilities. He is several issues behind in the half dozen journals he tries to read. His book shelf is overflowing with new copyright which he probably will never have the time to get to. And if he is teaching graduate students, there may be a half dozen theses in his file waiting to be critically read, and another half dozen in the mill. A research proposal must be written. Two book reviews have been promised, but the books have yet to be read. A manuscript to be evaluated for a journal has suffocated under a pile of circulars for a couple of months, and most depressing of all, there is, perhaps, that unfinished manuscript. Needless to say, the majority of academics never feel caught up with their work. When a professor has truly caught up with his work, he is intellectually dead; his curiosity is no longer functioning. He becomes a clerical automaton punching a time clock on a seven-hour day, five-day week basis.

Do professors complain about their 50 to 60 hour weeks? Only when drudgery is involved. Grading blue books and sitting through enervating conferences is clearly work; reading an unusually lively term paper or directing a heated seminar discussion is not strictly play but is surely a most enjoyable kind of work. An evening spent sitting in the concert hall or a winter afternoon spent riding chairlifts and hurtling down a mountainside with a colleague must certainly be leisure. Or is it? Is a medieval historian's trip to Florence work or leisure? How does a geologist or anthropologist define his summer in Colorado or New Mexico? A marine biologist spends four months at Woods Hole: work or leisure? What is reading *The New York Times* for a sociologist or a political scientist? Or reading novels for a professor of literature? A consuming interest in one's subject matter and the generalization of that subject matter to other spheres of life often obscures the meaning of work and leisure. There is simply time, and usually never quite enough of it to go around. Events shade off into one another, and there are few sharp breaks on clock or calendar.

The scientist, however, typically views work and leisure as separate spheres. But this does not mean that he is alienated from his work. More often than not, in fact, the scientist is very much absorbed in his work. Stationary equipment and precision instruments consign the scientist to long hours in the laboratory, and occasional prods by his family are needed to convince him to take time off. Unless he has the endurance to work at being a scientific humanist (and there are such creatures—more than persons in the arts and letters realize), he does not consider reading *The Nation* or traveling as part of his academic responsibilities. On the other hand, scientists are able to mix work and leisure by shop-talking in the course of casual visiting with colleagues.

In their strictly off-the-job leisure time, what level of taste do academics display: elite or mass, craftsman or consumer? Academic intellectuals are perhaps the most numerous of the gatekeepers of social criticism and creative culture, but the profession is large and contains enormous variation in leisure style. Data presented by Gerstl (see Chapter 9) and Anderson and Murray (see Chapter 10) suggest that a large segment of the academic profession uses considerable discretion in culture consumption and attempts to focus on serious media.

Exactly how academics differ from their white-collar and professional neighbors in overall family orientation is unclear. That academics have rather weak extended family ties has some documentation (see Chapters 9 and 12; and Murray, 1969). However, comparative occupational research investigating academics' family size, child-rearing practices (except for those studies of religious socialization noted below), marital adjustment, and home-centeredness is lacking. We suspect that the average academic family is slightly smaller than those of other professionals and that child-rearing practices emphasize early independence, achievement, impulse gratification, and psychological punishment. Though the academic may not be involved in family-centered activities more or less often than anyone else, it is highly likely that he is around his family more. As we mentioned previously, a comment sometimes heard in the neighborhood concerns the undue amount of "time-off" the college teacher has to spend at home.

Work as Alienation

What are the psychological consequences for an individual who commits himself to an examination of ideas for their own sake? What are the social consequences for a person who for five, fifteen, or twenty-five years has devoted his time to reading and writing articles and books? Can his ways be understood by others who may not have grappled seriously with an idea since they gave up trying to crack the enigma of the Divinity as teenagers? And can he understand them?

In many instances, the gulf between the academic intellectual and the surrounding society appears to be unbridgeable, and neither side makes much of an attempt to cross it. The academic may dismiss the rest of the populace as culturally illiterate robots, while the populace often views the academic with suspicion and disdain. Coser (1965: x) has remarked that "Intellectuals . . . are not only puzzling but upsetting to the run of ordinary citizens." It is somewhat of a paradox, then, that academics feel that they have fairly high status in the general society—and they tend to be correct in their perceptions (see, for example, Laumann, 1966; Hodge, et al., 1966; and Gerstl, 1961).

Yet anti-intellectualism, if not always overt and strident, does run deep in the American grain (see Hofstadter, 1963), and demagogues periodically have been at least moderately successful in evoking an active anti-intellectual reponse from within the population. Not all academics, of course, have served as targets. No one has yet succeeded in arousing popular sentiment against, for example, either the "new mandarins" working on defense projects or the science wizards masterminding labor-saving gadgets. Some academics are useful and serve a purpose; others are social parasites. Some academics help put a pie on your table; others are after pie in the sky. Some teach young men and women practical, hardheaded bureaucratic or technical skills; others raise disturbing philosophical and social questions in the minds of youth and subvert sacrosanct traditions. (That students have as much and often more of a liberalizing influence on one another than do their professors is generally not considered by parents prepared to slice the university budget.)

Regardless of who is responsible for the split that exists between many academics and the general populace, the cleavage is there, and it seems to be widening as academics increase in number and fashion a self-sustaining community of their own. This breach is not rooted in simply different political or religious views, though these are sometimes involved. Rather, it is a result of a basic difference in life styles and world views. In the extreme case, academics and nonacademics inhabit almost completely different worlds of sensibility. The universe of discourse and levels of consciousness may find only the most superficial common ground. The academic is comfortable in his intellectual cocoon, while his white-collar acquaintances are equally at ease in their bureaucratic and pecuniary shells (academics are, of course, far from immune to the latter). When one momentarily crosses over into the other's subculture, communication is often brief, innocuous, and strained—whether the setting is a congressional hearing or a class reunion.

The academics who feel most marginal to the social mainstream are the intellectual craftsmen, that is, persons who see their work as a type of play and take their play seriously (on the notion of craftsmanship, see Mills, 1953: 220-224). There is much in the nature of the academic intellectual's role in addition to its ideational content that alienates him from the society in which he lives. The intellectual takes a critical stance toward the world. It is his responsibility to subject social practices and beliefs to scrutiny, challenge cherished traditions, and pose new alternatives. Such activity is unlikely to win many popularity awards. Just as the individual would often like to rid himself of his own conscience, so many people wish to rid society of its intellectuals. But if intellectuals were to be completely pre-empted by technicians, contends Coser, "modern culture would likely perish through ossification" (1965:x).

Seeman's (see Chapter 11) observation that the social science and humanities professors he interviewed displayed in their responses a language typical of minority groups attests to the feelings of separation from the social mainstream often experienced by academics. In a similar vein, Lazarsfeld and Thielens (1958:14) reported that "Professors, at least social scientists, seem to consider themselves an occupational minority toward which significant sectors of the community hold contemptuous attitudes." Professors in the natural sciences report less alienation from the larger society than do non-scientists, perhaps because of both the psychological distance of their studies from social and cultural phenomena and their greater acceptance by a technologically-minded populace (see Hajda, 1961; and Chapter 12).

Work as Community

Though to varying degrees alienated from mainstream society, the academic is not a social isolate. In addition to fostering certain alienating qualities, the demands of academic work also require that its practitioners be in communication with one another. Ideas cannot be born, nurtured, refined, and discredited within the confines of a single mind. Ideas must be stirred into being and tested against reality through interpersonal relationships, dialogue, and conversation. The seminar is the ideal typical institutional manifestation of verbal exchange. No less important, however, is the primary group—the arena of highly personalized, face-to-face social relationships. Social interaction within the primary group has the quality of mutual trust, loyalty, and intimacy; few topics of concern are too personal to be considered. Because of its informal nature, the primary group serves as an ideal setting for the gestation and evaluation of concepts and ideas.

Theoretically, the primary group is part of the "non-work" side of academic life. But just as work and leisure is a meaningless dichotomy to many academics, so the primary group is an integral part of the formal academic environment. Indeed, the work setting is the chief locus for the formation of primary groups which subsequently flourish off-campus. Only where vocation tends to be an avocation and work commitment is high do members of occupational groups form social communities off the job. Only when work carries over inexorably into leisure and leisure intrudes indiscriminately upon work, do occupational categories become social groups.

Evidence shows that academics constitute a relatively cohesive and committed occupational community (see Lazarsfeld and Thielens, 1958; Gerstl, 1961; Wilensky and Ladinsky, 1967; and the papers in Section VI). The majority of academics' closest friends tend to be colleagues, either located at their present job or scattered across mountain, plain, and sea. Academics are restless animals and friendships often cover great distances. As Caplow and McGee noted, professors are on the job market, at least passively, most of the time. Cliques crystallize in graduate school or on the job, most typically around a departmental nucleus, but overlapping into other departments through a variety of intermediaries and sifting and sorting mechanisms. A geographical move rarely severs group ties; old friendships are renewed under any possible pretext. New ties with colleagues are solidified in time within a new setting. It often appears that academics are obsessed with contacts, for reasons ranging from self-aggrandizement to pure sociability and a chance to talk shop. This social cohesiveness is strongest among professors in the humanities and social sciences, for it is precisely in these disciplines where preoccupation with ideas most thoroughly pervades all spheres of life and commitment to broad intellectual concerns tends to be most intense. But occupational community is relatively strong in the sciences as well. Often, however, and not surprisingly, an age cleavage fractures the cohesiveness of academic communities, with younger and older faculty members separated off from each other socially. (We shall comment later on the influence of the age factor upon the political attitudes of professors.)

More intriguing than the pattern of social cohesiveness which binds together academics is Gordon's (see Chapter 13) suggestion that the social networks of academics and intellectuals are relatively free of ethnic divisions.[2] In contrast to the larger society, the academic community

2. Whether we choose to call much of the academic community a component of an intellectual subsociety, as Gordon has, or, rather, a complex kaleidoscope of interlocking nation-wide cliques, is a matter of terminology and level of conceptualization.

tends to resist the forces of ethnic parochialism and prejudice. The primary groups of academics tend to be ethnically mixed to a far greater extent than the social circles of mainstream society (see the papers in Section VI; Friedman, 1969; and Anderson, 1968). Nowhere has the melting pot ideal been more closely approximated than in the academic community. Protestant, Catholic, Jew, and others mingle informally with relative comfort and ease.

Professors themselves sense that ethnicity is far less influential within the academic world than elsewhere. In interviews conducted by one of the editors (Anderson, 1966: 73-74), a Protestant professor remarked, "In the academic world there tends to be an ignoring of the religious question as a functional matter. This situation is much different from the background in which I grew up." A second commented, "I've spent considerable time in the business world and the academic world, and in a comparison of the two, I see far more religious considerations entering the business world." And, "The academic world is not a utopia, but it's much more liberal than the general population." Similarly, a Jewish professor observed that "There is much mobility and freedom of movement and mixing of religious backgrounds. Assimilation is in process here and in other areas where preoccupations center on other than background variables." Another reflected, "Some academics would not invite Jews to their homes, but very few. New York Jews of the middle classes encounter prejudice, but few academics and intellectuals do." A third commented, "I know what it is to be identified as a Jew before I am identified as an individual. But the university setting seems to neutralize much of this and produce a common frame of reference."

The actual degree of interethnic contact and assimilation among academics varies, of course, by individual, department, college, and region. Catholic academics teaching at Catholic colleges, for example, experience greater religious community—more than can be attributed simply to the Catholic college teaching situation—than other academics. Furthermore, Catholics at nonsectarian schools may be more involved in religious groups than are their non-Catholic colleagues (see Chapters 15 and 17). And in one case, Protestant scientists were found to be as committed to the religious community as were Protestant nonacademics in the same city (see Anderson, 1968). Generally, liberal arts professors see their academic division as being more open, in a socioreligious sense, than other divisions on the campus. But as a Protestant academic in a predominantly Jewish psychology department commented to one of the editors, "Jews have an unmistakeable affinity toward one another . . . things that the outsider is not aware of." And this Protestant may have been correct, for a Jewish colleague in the same department declared, "One cannot deny the role played by general cultural background in easing the creation of friendships. If I meet a Jew from New York, we have a cultural image of things in common and these act as some of the building blocks to friendship. Other things being equal, I might out of tribal loyalty first invite Jews to the house" (Anderson, 1966: 75). Furthermore, older academics have been found to be less likely than younger teachers to cross ethnic lines, a fact associated with the preponderance in the academic community of Protestants among those professors over 45 years of age.[3] And academics teaching at a school with a distinctly professional as opposed to intellectual orientation, though the school itself was not the determining factor, were found to experience stronger ethnic ties (see Chapter 16; and Mazur, 1969).

Thus, we are not dealing with a seamless ethnic web that stretches uniformly across the academic community. Ethnic cleavages do exist. But, as the high rates of interreligious marriage in the academic community confirm, ethnicity, overall, does not play a significant role in the lives of academics.

How might we account for this advanced stage of assimilation in the academic community? Gordon's argument that ethnic parochialism is overridden by a situation of people with deep and shared interests in ideas coming together was confirmed by the responses from academics in samples which we studied. Assimilation among academics is explained not so much by weak religious socialization (academics as a group have received only slightly weaker religious upbringing than nonacademics) as by universalizing experiences within the academic environment. Even when religious socialization is held constant, academics are found to display weaker ethnic ties and engage in greater interethnic contact than nonacademics (see Chapter 16; and Anderson, 1968). On the other hand, the importance of religious socialization in the assimilation process is not to be discounted. Academics with weak religious upbringing are the most likely to be involved in mixed marriages (see Chapter 16). And academics involved in mixed marriages, in turn, cross ethnic lines in group life with the greatest

3. For example, the proportion of Protestants among a random sample of sociologists receiving their doctorate before 1948 was almost three-fourths, compared to about one-half for those completing their doctorate between 1958-1967 (Glenn and Weiner, 1969: 297). The percentage of Jews rose from 14 to 24 percent and Catholics from 7 to 10 percent during the same period.

frequency and show little concern for the ethnic affiliation of their children (see Anderson, 1966: 120-122). Such people compose the veritably ethnic-less center of the academic community.

Does the religious factor exert an influence on academics' lives in areas other than primary relationships? On the whole, professors are an irreligious group. Formal religious affiliation and participation is less than half that of the general population (see Thalheimer, 1965). However, academics on the average have as much religious exposure in early youth as do nonacademics (see Chapters 15 and 16; Thalheimer, 1965; and Anderson, 1966: 111). Indeed, the majority remains roughly abreast of nonacademics in religious participation through the high school years. Rates of religious involvement among academics, particularly Protestants and Jews, begin to drop sharply in the undergraduate years, but so does religious participation among future nonacademics as well. In comparison with their former classmates, however, academics much less often return to active church or synagogue roles once settled in work and family. By the time most academics have entered graduate school, with the exception of Catholics (see Chapter 15; Hajda, 1961; Stark, 1963; and Greeley, 1965), religious observance is relatively infrequent.

Do irreligious people self-select themselves, consciously or unconsciously, into academic careers? Or is the academic environment itself a depressant on religiosity? The question is similar to the "chicken or egg" dilemma. Actually, the large majority of academics experience conventional religious upbringings. But why, after the customary decline in religious interest in late adolescence (perhaps better put as an increase of personal choice in the matter of attendance), do future professors continue to decline in overall religiosity instead of taking up roles in church and synagogue beside nonacademics.

An important part of the answer may be found in the context of the previous discussion of assimilation. Religious beliefs and norms require social support as much as any other ideological and normative system. The academic community, with its extensive socio-religious mix and primary group variety, serves as a poor stimulant to religious activity. If Protestant, Catholic, and Jewish professors are close friends, they meet in the house rather than the church, parish house, or synagogue. In so doing, religious preconceptions are not reinforced as they would be in the more typical homogeneous gathering, but, rather, are set still further apart from the flow of ideas, argument, anecdote, and confession.

Moreover, it is precisely among academics who are most involved in the process of assimilation that religiosity is weakest: humanities and social science faculty, Protestants and Jews, and younger teachers. Catholics at both Catholic and nonsectarian colleges tend to remain more active in organized religion than do Protestants or Jews, and Catholic professors more often show a personal concern with theological currents within their faith. Thus, academic "theologians" are more likely to be Catholic than not; they are also more likely to be liberal Catholics (see Chapter 17).

A strong correlation also exists between religiosity and the extent to which an academic's subject matter appears compatible or incompatible with religious orthodoxy (see Lehman and Shriver, 1968; Stark, 1963). Professors in the humanities and social sciences who study religious phenomena as part of their discipline and hence endeavor to understand and explain religious systems in purely anthropological terms, estrange themselves from religious orthodoxy more than do scientists, engineers, and administrators.

Although both religious socialization and the affinity of an academic discipline with religious phenomena must be considered as relevant in understanding academic irreligiosity, nonetheless, the major depressant on religious activity among professors seems to be extensive religious assimilation and, thus, lack of colleague support. The academic who perceives little support of religion among his colleagues is likely himself to be weak in religious practice and belief.

Work as Political Responsibility

The role of the academic in the political arena is very much in question today, both within and without the profession. Should professors, as disinterested scholars and scientists, jeopardize their objectivity by playing active political roles? Do they have a moral responsibility, as men of knowledge, to strive politically for the humane use of social and scientific information? Before exploring these issues concerned with the public responsibilities of professors, the more basic question of the extent to which academics are actually politically involved has to be examined.

In the popular imagination the college professor is very much politically engaged. Whether it concerns the environmental crisis or the peace movement, government "braintrusts" (one hears less of this today) or campus "revolutions," the press conveys the image of the college professor as an actively involved political animal—and a rather radical one, at that. But exactly how valid is this conception?

Certainly there are more than a few academics who have heard the call of Professor George Wald and have become concerned about, and active in, the current campaign to save the environment. Though vital, such activity is hardly controversial, for who today would oppose it? On the other hand, the peace movement which surfaced during the sixties has been a decidedly controversial issue in America. How widespread and radical has been the involvement of academics here? Contrary to popular impression, academics have not been a single-minded group on the Vietnam War issue. In 1967, for example, only a minority of the faculty at the University of Michigan could be considered "doves," and these were mainly younger men. Since that time, many more professors, at Michigan and elsewhere, undoubtedly have climbed aboard the bandwagon for withdrawal and have become increasingly vocal in their opposition to official Indochina policy, which, of course, makes the professors not unlike the population at large. And even the response of many college faculties to the American invasion of Cambodia and the events of May 1970 fails to place professors in the forefront of political action. For the college "strikes" and community canvassing overwhelmingly were student-inspired and student-led. With few exceptions, where faculties voted to suspend examinations, traditional grading procedures, or normal classroom activities, they were essentially responding to what the students made inevitable. Moreover, faculty support for these "radical" actions was far from unanimous; at many colleges proposals which would disrupt the normal academic routine passed by slim majorities, and, at times not at all.[4]

All of this does not mean that faculty members are apolitical or that college faculties are without their radicals. There are, for example, the 45 professors, including three full professors, at the State University of New York at Buffalo who were arrested and charged with criminal trespassing following their expression of displeasure over police activities on campus in the Spring of 1970. There are sociologists and political scientists who serve as sources of discontent for university administrators and local police departments. And there are others. But contrary to the current popular imagination, professorial provocateurs do

4. At Harvard, for example, the faculty, by a vote of over three to one, defeated a proposal to reshuffle vacation periods to allow students two weeks off to work for candidates in the Fall, 1970 political campaign, an action passed by the faculties of other major universities such as Princeton, Columbia, Cornell, and Rutgers. See: *The Boston Globe*, June 9, 1970, p. 3.

not dominate faculties. In fact, with regard to current campus unrest, professors are decidedly conservative. In one recent survey of 60,447 college and university faculty members, over 80 percent of the teachers felt that demonstrations by student activists threaten academic freedom and over three-fourths favored expelling or suspending students who disrupt the functioning of academic institutions.[5] As Horowitz has said of the politically liberal professors who dominate the American academic world today, "When students were politically quiescent, the professoriate condemned them for being a 'silent generation'; now that the student population has become politically alert and demanding, the professoriate condemns them either on tactical grounds or for lacking the requisite calm and judiciousness needed in public affairs" (see Chapter 21).

Overall, the politics of most college professors probably differs little from the profile drawn by Lazarsfeld and Thielens (1958: 148-152) of academics as an example of a minority group in support of liberal ideas and the Democratic party—a posture that could hardly be termed radical. As in the 1950's, so also today it is the younger professors teaching in the humanities and social sciences at large schools who are the most liberal grouping among academics. Whether this liberalism is rooted in minority identification and sympathies, or in tradition-weakening objective scholarship, or in family political background, or in the interaction of these variables, the professors in the humanities and social sciences today consitute one of the most, if not the most, politically liberal occupational groups in the nation—at least rhetorically. But, as C. Wright Mills has argued, to be liberal today means nothing for social change.

Nowhere is the non-radical posture (and ultimate political impotence) of American academics more evident than in the activities of those who serve in government "braintrusts," ostensibly involved in significant federal policy formation. The Moynihans and McBundys, the Kissengers and Schlesingers have received substantial attention from the press. Nonetheless, the question remains: Are academics taken seriously as decision-makers in foreign or domestic policy formation? Few are, for the role of most academics in government has been that of ideological apologist or technical expert. Unless they have been thoroughly purged of utopian or communitarian tendencies, academics are unlikely ever to be called upon for serious advice; if by mistake a

5. See *The Chronicle of Higher Education* 4 (April 6, 1970), pp. 1, 4-5.

visionary is hired, he is not likely to be around long enough to provide a test of whether intellectuals can survive qua intellectuals in a bureaucracy. Top officials want practical information from academics, information which will facilitate the achievement of pre-defined goals. As Nieburg (1966: 125) said, ". . . the real centers of power . . . pick and choose those scientists [or scholars] who will proffer the advice they want; the chosen scientists provide a rationale and a justification for policies arrived at by other means." Or in Mills' (1959: 193) words, academics' relations to the powerful "are more likely to be only such relations as they [the powerful] find useful, which is to say that we become technicians accepting their problems and aims, or ideologists promoting their prestige and authority." If the academic does cooperate in this manner, he becomes a technician in the field of corporate capitalism. For as Merton (1957: 218) argues, "The bureaucratic intellectual who must permit the policy-maker to define the scope of his research problem [and this is the typical case] is implicitly lending his skills and knowledge to the preservation of a particular institutional arrangement."

And what of the rare academic who does become engaged in policy-formation and decision-making? Because all human decisions are ultimately political, that is, they involve explicit value-judgments and personal preferences rather than simply disinterested objectivity and scientific confirmation, an academic intellectual who does in fact attain a high policy-making position, or the ear of a top policy-maker, no longer acts strictly as an independent intellectual or scientist. Indeed, his value premises may become, though not inevitably, as narrow as those of many politicians and bureaucrats. Chomsky (see Chapter 19) has argued of those academics who have been actively involved in the governmental bureaucracy, they have contributed their share to the sorry mess of foreign policy, propounding erroneous history and engaging in unabashed deceit.

But few academics do directly participate in governmental policy-formation, and most of those who are involved in the federal bureaucracy, as we have said, function as technical experts rather than decision-makers. Conceivably, this explains why ". . . the largest single intellectual-interest group in our society—the learned professors—has opted out of politics" (Roszak, 1967: 38): they recognize their relative powerlessness and see no hope of loosening the corporate stranglehold on American government and society. Others, judging that participation in partisan controversy transforms intellectuals into opportunistic politicians and ritualistic bureaucrats, argue that the responsibility of academics is simply to raise important questions while remaining aloof from concrete policy-formation and implementation.

As men of knowledge, what is the public responsibility of professors? Should they remain apart from political engagement, thus avoiding the possible contamination of their objectivity with political passion? Does the basic demand of the academic life, disinterested inquiry, reduce the professor ". . . to being either a hench-man of the military-industrial complex or a recluse in an apolitical ivory tower" (Roszak, 1967: 21)?

The operating political and economic ideology of American elites is, of course, that of corporate capitalism. The academic on a government- or business-payroll is in clear danger of selling out to already powerful and vested interests, particularly in the United States where government is usually dominated by narrow business interests. Although it may be couched in liberal rhetoric as change-oriented (and all change is clearly not progressive), the probability is great that his research is merely adjustment-oriented or obfuscatory. (For an historian's account of the debasement of social science by American business interests, see Baritz, 1960.)

Academics, then, and particularly those in the natural and social sciences, should fully evaluate the possible political implications of their work; simply because the money comes from Health, Education, and Welfare rather than the Defense Department or General Motors is no guarantee that a research project will be in the public interest (HEW continues to discriminate against a number of outstanding scholars because of their political views). And regardless of the source of funding, since much social scientific knowledge may be used for manipulating people, social scientists have an added responsibility to communicate this possibility to the public.[6]

Occasionally, an academic dissident turns the tables and *critically* studies the ruling government and business elites and the social and economic system that they run, with the help of academic technical experts, so efficiently (see Mills, 1956; Kolko, 1962, 1969; Nieburg, 1966; Domhoff, 1967). But there are few funds for such critical research (Mills

6. Huxley (1965: 28) wisely reminds us that extensive training in the social sciences does little if anything in the way of preparing one for the democratic use of power: "There seems to be a toughening belief among certain Ph.D.'s in sociology that Ph.D.'s in sociology will never be corrupted by power. Like Sir Galahad's, their strength is as the strength of ten because their heart is pure—and their heart is pure because they are scientists and have taken six thousand hours of social studies."

was denied foundation grants after he published *The Power Elite*) and few people willing and able to conduct it. Certainly, academics study violence, poverty, unemployment, deviance, race, automation, and other social problems. But on whose behalf and for whose interests? The information, often solicited and funded by the heads of powerful bureaucracies, has traditionally been used on behalf of stability and the status quo rather than much needed ferment and change (see Sjoberg, 1968).

In the words of an economist, "The view that a scholar may in good conscience grind a political or ideological ax is anathema to most American intellectuals" (Rosen, 1967: 72). But the value-free stance of American academics has often by default resulted in the grinding of the ideological axes of status quo interests. Under the guise of the end of ideology, academic and academically-trained researchers have pursued technical solutions to allegedly purely technical problems: how to avert social disorders, contain revolutions, devise weapons systems, condition social behavior, and control mental processes. For some, the claim of objectivity has served well as an excuse for irresponsibility and unaccountability.

In his essay on the university, Lippman (see Chapter 22) attributes enormous responsibility to the academic intellectual, nothing less than filling the void of meaning left by the erosion of traditional forms of authority and guidance. This responsibility, Lippman asserts, can best be fulfilled by searching for truth and defining reality without thought of secondary consequence or application. But such knowledge should not be sold to the highest bidder or allowed to be indiscriminately used by whoever is politicized enough to act, for knowledge is neutral and may be used for either insidious or humane purposes. Therefore, academics must be involved in the task of transforming knowledge into means for meeting human need and human hope. The just and the wise use of knowledge for the benefit of all rather than the aggrandizement of a few requires that academics revolt in mass against all forms of intellectual prostitution, whoever might be the client. The professors who believe in the liberal intellectual tradition of fraternity and equality, as most profess to do, have a responsibility to actively pursue these goals while combating national arrogance, class privilege, and powerlessness. But such a commitment, we believe, requires the shedding of the mantle of ideological neutrality and the advocating of radical changes in the distribution and use of social, political, and economic resources. There are, of course, other interpretations of the academic intellectual's role, but those who oppose these changes should at least acknowledge the possibility that they may be accessories to the demeaning of the powerless.

More than ever, academics today need to answer Robert Lynd's "Knowledge for What?" (1939) with an affirmation of "the human community." The academic has a universal responsibility, one that should not be narrowed through promise of political and material reward. "This is a time," Mills (see Chapter 18) contends, "when the power of the intellectual has become potentially very great indeed." A society deserves more from its men of knowledge than to have this potential remain largely untapped while academic intellectuals either busy themselves with vested interests or rest in apolitical impotence.

References

Anderson, Charles H. 1966. "The Intellectual Subsociety Hypothesis: An Empirical Test." Doctoral Dissertation, University of Massachusetts.
—— 1968. "Religious Communality Among Academics." Journal for the Scientific Study of Religion 7 (Spring): 87-96.
Baritz, Loren. 1960. The Servants of Power. Middletown, Conn.: Wesleyan University Press.
Barzun, Jacques. 1968. The American University, New York: Harper & Row, Publishers.
Caplow, Theodore and Reece J. McGee. 1958. The Academic Marketplace. New York: Doubleday and Company.
Coser, Lewis. 1965. Men of Ideas. Glencoe: The Free Press.
Domhoff, G. William. 1967. Who Rules America? Englewood Cliffs: Prentice-Hall, Inc.
Friedman, Norman L. 1969. "The Problem of the 'Runaway Jewish Intellectuals': Social Definition and Sociological Perspective." Jewish Social Studies 31 (January): 3-19.
Gerstl, Joel E. 1961. "Determinants of Occupational Community in High Status Occupations." Sociological Quarterly 2 (January): 37-48.
Glenn, Norval and David Weiner. 1969. "Some Trends in the Social Origins of American Sociologists." The American Sociologist 4 (November): 291-302.
Greeley, Andrew. 1963. "The Religious Behavior of Graduate Students." Journal for the Scientific Study of Religion 5 (Fall): 34-40.
Hajda, Jan. 1961. "Alienation and Integration of Student Intellectuals." American Sociological Review 26 (October): 758-777.
Hodge, Robert W., Paul M. Siegel, and Peter H. Rossi. 1966. "Occupational Prestige in the United States: 1925-1963." in Reinhard Bendix and Seymour M. Lipset (eds.), Class, Status, and Power (Second Edition). New York: The Free Press.

Hofstadter, Richard. 1963. Anti-Intellectualism in American Life. New York: Alfred A. Knopf.

Huxley, Aldous. 1955. Brave New World. New York: Bantam Books.

—— 1965. Brave New World Revisited. New York: Harper & Row.

Jencks, Christopher and David Riesman. 1969. Anchor Books edition. The Academic Revolution. New York: Doubleday.

Klaw, Spencer. 1969. The New Brahmins: Scientific Life in America. New York: William Morrow Company, Inc.

Kolko, Gabriel. 1962. Wealth and Power in America. New York: Praeger.

—— 1969. The Roots of American Foreign Policy. Boston: Beacon Press.

Laumann, Edward O. 1966. Prestige and Association in the Urban Community. Indianapolis: Bobbs-Merrill.

Lazarsfeld, Paul F. and Wagner Thielens, Jr. 1958. The Academic Mind, Glencoe: The Free Press.

Lehman, Edward C., Jr. and Donald W. Shriver. 1968. "Academic Discipline as Predictive of Religiosity." Social Forces 47 (December): 171-182.

Lippmann, Walter. 1966. "The University." The New Republic 154 (May 28): 17-20.

Lynd, Robert. 1939. Knowledge for What? Princeton: Princeton University Press.

Mazur, Allan C. 1969. "Resocialized Ethnicity: A Study of Jewish Social Scientists." Doctoral Dissertation. Johns Hopkins University.

Merton, Robert. 1957. Social Theory and Social Structure. Glencoe: The Free Press.

Mills, C. Wright. 1953. White Collar. New York: Oxford University Press.

—— 1956. The Power Elite. New York: Oxford University Press.

—— 1959. The Sociological Imagination. New York: Oxford University Press.

Murray, John. D. 1969. "The American Catholic Intellectual: An Empirical Test of the Intellectual Subsociety Hypothesis." Doctoral Dissertation. University of Massachusetts.

Nieburg, H. L. 1966. In the Name of Science. Chicago: Quadrangle Books.

Page, Charles H. 1951. "Bureaucracy and Higher Education." Journal of General Education 5 (January): 91-100.

Ridgeway, James. 1968. The Closed Corporation. New York: Random House.

Roszak, Theodore (ed.). 1967. The Dissenting Academy. New York: Pantheon.

Rosen, Sumner M. 1967. "Keynes Without Gadflies." from The Dissenting Academy. T. Roszak, (ed.). New York: Pantheon.

Seeman, Melvin. 1958. "The Intellectual and the Language of the Minorities." American Journal of Sociology 64 (July): 25-35.

Shuman, Howard and Edward O. Laumann. 1967. "Do Most Professors Support the War?" Trans-action 5 (November): 32-35.

Sjoberg, Gideon (ed.). 1968. Ethics, Politics, and Social Research. Cambridge: Schenkman.

Stark, Rodney. 1963. "On the Incompatibility of Religion and Science." Journal for Scientific Study of Religion 3 (Fall): 3-20.

Thalheimer, Fred. 1965. "Continuity and Change in Religiosity: A Study of Academicians." Pacific Sociological Review 8 (Fall): 101-108.

Veblen, Thorstein. 1957. The Higher Learning in America. New York: Sagamore Press.

Wilensky, Harold and Jack Ladinsky. 1967. "From Religious Community to Occupational Group: Structural Assimilation Among Professors, Lawyers, and Engineers." American Sociological Review 32 (August), 541-561.

Wilson, Logan. 1942. Academic Man. New York: Oxford University Press.

Znaniecki, Florian. 1940. The Social Role of the Man of Knowledge. New York: Columbia University Press.

II

WORK AS INCOME: ON THE JOB

Veblen's idea of the appropriate function of a college professor is congruent with the role being demanded of the academic by today's radical critics of the higher learning: the stimulation and pursuit of the instinct of curiosity. This desire to know the how and especially the why about man, his creations, and nature must not be corrupted by business interests and concern with monetary matters, as Veblen stressed repeatedly. But what Veblen witnessed in his time was a comparatively innocuous contamination of higher education by American business interests. Today the adulteration of disinterested academic work by capitalist interests has proceeded so far and on such a gigantic scale that vital and healthy curiosity is seriously threatened on many campuses.

The impoverished colleges which in Veblen's day favored professors who, with their own resources, could put on an impressive display of expensive taste and pecuniary refinement for wealthy business donors now seek professors who are skilled in writing expensive research proposals for business and government interests, resulting, at times, in single university budgets larger than those of the governments of some developing nations. Other of Veblen's criticisms, "the danger of becoming too scholarly or scientific and ignoring polite conventions," "university men going to seed in routine work and extra-scholastic duties," and faculty-student relations degenerating into the grade-conscious schoolmaster-pupil type, sound most familiar today. The monstrous, self-justifying bureaucracies of the contemporary multiversity would have sent Veblen back to his father's farm in utter scholarly frustration.

Bernard's portrayal of the "man of knowledge," or professor role, is obviously Veblen's ideal. The professor innovates, stimulates, and deals with abstract relationships; the teacher, by contrast, conserves and trasmits. The former allows curiosity and ideas to stand on their own; the latter employs grades as bludgeons and levers on students. Cultural preconceptions about the nature of sexual differences shunts academic women into subjects which tend to require the teaching role (for example, elementary literature and languages), while academic men predominate in the professor role. Bernard writes in Academic Women *that the proportion of women in the academic profession has declined in the past generation because of a decline in the pool of eligible female faculty and loss of eligible females to competing non-academic occupations.*

The acquisition of the skills possessed by the man of knowledge is the topic of concern for Jencks and Riesman in their essay "The Art of Teaching." A professor's intellectual skills cannot be systematically inculcated into the student as an electrician might train his apprentice. Learning how to become a professor proceeds mostly on a trial and error basis with the end product unable to directly articulate the sequence to others and even uncertain about his own effectiveness. Emphasis on research is probably not the culprit when teaching weaknesses are present; rather, Jencks and Riesman see research as a prerequisite to good teaching. They explore the possibility of a special teaching doctorate and, dismissing it, suggest the development of postdoctoral internships in staff courses and seminars.

All academics are not intellectuals, nor do they claim to be. Coser's discussion of academic intellectuals, professors preoccupied with critical examination of abstract ideas and broad fields of knowledge, considers the "anti-intellectual" forces at work in the modern university—influences such as specialization, nonacademic reference groups in business and government, administrative duties and time pressures, and research entrepreneurship. The university ideals of disinterested scholarship, intellectual breadth, and a community of equals, notes Coser, are threatened by contracted research, specialization, and fragmentation.

1. The Academic Personnel

THORSTEIN VEBLEN

The conservation and advancement of the higher learning involves two lines of work, distinct but closely bound together: (a) scientific and scholarly inquiry, and (b) the instruction of students.[1] The former of these is primary and indispensable. It is this work of intellectual enterprise that gives its character to the university and marks it off from the lower schools. The work of teaching properly belongs in the university only because and in so far as it incites and facilitates the university man's work of inquiry,—and the extent to which such teaching furthers the work of inquiry is scarcely to be appreciated without a somewhat extended experience. By and large, there are but few and inconsequential exceptions to the rule that teaching, as a concomitant of investigation, is distinctly advantageous to the investigator; particularly in so far as his work is of the nature of theoretical inquiry. The instruction necessarily involved in university work, therefore, is only such as can readily be combined with the work of inquiry, at the same time that it goes directly to further the higher learning in that it trains the incoming generation of scholars and scientists for the further pursuit of knowledge. Training for other purposes is necessarily of a different kind and is best done elsewhere; and it does not become university work by calling it so and imposing its burden on the men and equipment whose only concern should be the higher learning.

University teaching, having a particular and special purpose—the pursuit of knowledge—it has also a particular and special character, such as to differentiate it from other teaching and at the same time leave it relatively ineffective for other purposes. Its aim is to equip the student for the work of inquiry, not to give him facility in that

1. Cf. Geo. T. Ladd, *University Control*, p. 349.

conduct of affairs that turns such knowledge to "practical account." Hence the instruction that falls legitimately under the hand of the university man is necessarily subsidiary and incidental to the work of inquiry, and it can effectually be carried on only by such a teacher as is himself occupied with the scrutiny of what knowledge is already in hand and with pushing the inquiry to further gains. And it can be carried on by such a teacher only by drawing his students into his own work of inquiry. The student's relation to his teacher necessarily becomes that of an apprentice to his master, rather than that of a pupil to his schoolmaster.

A university is a body of mature scholars and scientists, the "faculty,"—with whatever plant and other equipment may incidentally serve as appliances for their work in any given case. The necessary material equipment may under modern conditions be very considerable, as may also the number of caretakers, assistants, etc.; but all that is not the university, but merely its equipment. And the university man's work is the pursuit of knowledge, together with whatever advisory surveillance and guidance he may consistently afford such students as are entering on the career of learning at a point where his outlook and methods of work may be of effect for them. No man whose energies are not habitually bent on increasing and proving up the domain of learning belongs legitimately on the university staff. The university man is, properly, a student, not a schoolmaster. Such is the unmistakable drift of sentiment and professed endeavour, in so far as it is guided by the cultural aspirations of civilized mankind rather than by the emulative strategy of individuals seeking their own preferment.[2]

All this, of course, implies no undervaluing of the work of those men who aim to prepare the youth for citizenship and a practical career. It is only a question of distinguishing between things that

2. Cf., e.g., J. McKeen Cattell, *University Control*, Part III, ch. V., "Concerning the American University." "The university is those who teach and those who learn and the work they do." "The university is its men and their work. But certain externals are necessary or at least usual—buildings and equipment, a president and trustees."

The papers by other writers associated with Mr. Cattell in this volume run to the same effect whenever they touch the same topic; and, indeed, it would be difficult to find a deliberate expression to the contrary among men entitled to speak in these premises.

It may be in place to add here that the volume referred to, on *University Control*, has been had in mind throughout the following analysis and has served as ground and material for much of the argument.

belong apart. The scientist and the scholar on the one hand, and the schoolmaster on the other hand, both belong within the later growth of civilization; but a differentiation of the two classes, and a division of their work, is indispensable if they are to do their work as it should be done, and as the modern community thoughtfully intends that it should be done. And while such a division of labour has hitherto not been carried through with any degree of consistency, it is at least under way, and there is nothing but the presumption of outworn usage that continues to hold the two lines of work together, to the detriment of both; backed, it is true, by ambitions of self-aggrandizement on the part of many schools and many of their directorates.

The schoolmaster and his work may be equally, or more, valuable to the community at large—presumably more rather than less—but in so far as his chief interest is of the pedagogical sort his place is not in the university. Exposition, instruction and drill belong in the secondary and professional schools. The consistent aim there is, and should be, to instruct, to inculcate a knowledge of results, and to give the pupil a working facility in applying it. On the university level such information and training is (should be) incidental to the work of research. The university man is almost unavoidably a teacher, by precept and example, but he can not without detriment to his work as scientist or scholar serve as a taskmaster or a vehicle of indoctrination. The student who comes up to the university for the pursuit of knowledge is expected to know what he wants and to want it, without compulsion. If he falls short of these respects, if he has not the requisite interest and initiative, it is his own misfortune, not the fault of his teacher. What he has a legitimate claim to is an opportunity for such personal contact and guidance as will give him familiarity with the ways and means of the higher learning,—any information imparted to him being incidental to this main work of habituation. He gets a chance to make himself a scholar, and what he will do with his opportunities in this way lies in his own discretion.

The difference between the modern university and the lower and professional schools is broad and simple; not so much a difference of degree as of kind. There is no difficulty about apprehending or appreciating this difference; the dispute turns not on the practicability of distinguishing between the two, but on the desirability of letting such a distinction go into effect. It is a controversy between those who wish to hold fast that which once was good and those who look to make use of the means in hand for new ends, and meet new exigencies.

The lower schools (including the professional schools) are, in the ideal scheme, designed to fit the incoming generation for civil life; they are therefore occupied with instilling such knowledge and habits as will make their pupils fit citizens of the world in whatever position in the fabric of workday life they may fall. The university on the other hand is specialized to fit men for a life of science and scholarship; and it is accordingly concerned with such discipline only as will give efficiency in the pursuit of knowledge and fit its students for the increase and diffusion of learning. It follows that while the lower schools necessarily take over the surveillance of their pupils' everyday life, and exercise a large measure of authority and responsible interference in that behalf, the university assumes (or should assume) no responsibility for its students' fortunes in the moral, religious, pecuniary, domestic, or hygienic respect.

Doubtless the larger and more serious responsibility in the educational system belongs not to the university but to the lower and professional schools. Citizenship is a larger and more substantial category than scholarship; and the furtherance of civilized life is a larger and more serious interest than the pursuit of knowledge for its own idle sake. But the proportions which the quest of knowledge is latterly assuming in the scheme of civilized life require that the establishments to which this interest is committed should not be charged with extraneous duties; particularly not with extraneous matters that are themselves of such grave consequence as this training for citizenship and practical affairs. These are too serious a range of duties to be taken care of as a side-issue, by a seminary of learning, the members of whose faculty, if they are fit for their own special work, are not men of affairs or adepts in worldly wisdom. . . .

A university is an endowed institution of culture, whether the endowment take the form of assigned income, as in the state establishments, or of funded wealth, as with most other universities. Such fraction of the income as is assigned to the salary roll, and which therefore comes in question here, is apportioned among the staff for work which has no determinate market value. It is not a matter of *quid pro quo*; since one member of the exchange, the stipend or salary, is measurable in pecuniary terms and the other is not. This work has no business value, in so far as it is work properly included among the duties of the academic men. Indeed, it is a fairly safe test; work that has a commercial value does not belong in the university. Such services of the academic staff as have a business value are those portions of their work that serve other ends than the higher learning; as, e.g., the prestige and pecuniary gain of the institution at large, the pecuniary advantage of a given clique or faction within the university, or the profit and renown of the directive head. Gains that accrue for services of this general character are not, properly speaking, salary or stipend payable toward "the increase and diffusion of knowledge among men," even if they are currently so designated, in the absence of suitable distinctions. Instances of such a diversion of corporate funds to private ends have in the past occurred in certain monastic and priestly orders, as well as in some modern political organizations. Organized malversation of this character has latterly been called "graft." The long-term common sense of the community would presently disavow any corporation of learning overtly pursuing such a course, as being faithless to its trust, and the conservation of learning would so pass into other hands. Indeed, there are facts current which broadly suggest that the keeping of the higher learning is beginning to pass into other, and presumptively more disinterested, hands.

The permeation of academic policy by business principles is a matter of more or less, not of absolute, dominance. It appears to be a question of how wide a deviation from scholarly singleness of purpose the long-term common sense of the community will tolerate. The cult of the idle curiosity sticks too deep in the instinctive endowment of the race, and it has in modern civilization been too thoroughly ground into the shape of a quest of matter-of-fact knowledge, to allow this pursuit to be definitively set aside or to fall into abeyance. It is by too much an integral constituent of the habits of thought induced by the discipline of workday life. The faith in and aspiration after matter-of-fact knowledge is too profoundly ingrained in the modern community, and too consonant with its workday habit of mind, to admit of its supersession by any objective end alien to it,—at least for the present and until some stronger force than the technological discipline of modern life shall take over the primacy among the factors of civilization, and so give us a culture of a different character from that which has brought on this modern science and placed it at the centre of things human.

The popular approval of business principles and businesslike thrift is profound, disinterested, alert and insistent; but it does not, at least not yet, go the length of unreservedly placing a businesslike exploitation of office above a faithful discharge of trust. The current popular animus may not, in this matter, approach that which animates the business community, specifically so-called, but it is sufficiently "practical" to approve practical sagacity and gainful traffic wherever it is found; yet the furtherance of knowledge is after all an ideal which engages the modern community's affections in a still more profound way, and, in the long run, with a still more unqualified insistence. For good or ill, in the apprehension of the civilized peoples, matter-of-fact knowledge is an end to be sought; while gainful enterprise is, after all, a means to an end. There is, therefore, always this massive hedge of slow but indefeasible popular sentiment that stands in the way of making the seats of learning over into something definitively foreign to the purpose which they are popularly believed to serve.[3]

Perhaps the most naïve way in which a predilection for men of substantial business value expresses itself in university.policy is the unobtrusive, and in part unformulated, preference shown for teachers with sound pecuniary connections, whether by inheritance or by marriage. With no such uniformity as to give evidence of an advised rule of precedence or a standardized schedule of correlation, but with sufficient consistency to merit, and indeed to claim, the thoughtful attention of the members of the craft, a scholar who is in a position to plead personal wealth or a wealthy connection has a perceptibly better chance of appointment on the academic staff, and on a more advantageous scale of remuneration, than men without pecuniary antecedents. Due preferment also appears to follow more as a matter of course where the candidate has or acquires a tangible standing of this nature.

This preference for well-to-do scholars need by no means be an altogether blind or impulsive predilection for commercial solvency on the part of the appointing power; though such a predilection is no doubt ordinarily present and operative in a degree. But there is substantial ground for a wise discrimination in this respect. As a measure of expediency, particularly the expediency of publicity, it is desirable that the incumbents of the higher stations on the staff should be able to live on such a scale of conspicuous expensiveness as to make a favourable impression on those men of pecuniary refinement and expensive tastes with whom they are designed to come in contact. The university should be worthily represented in its personnel, particularly in such of its personnel as occupy a conspicuous place in the academic hierarchy; that is to say, it should be represented with becoming expensiveness in all its social contact with those classes from whose munificence large donations may flow into the corporate funds. Large gifts of this

3. It was a very wise and adroit politician who found out that "You can not fool all the people all the time."

kind are creditable both to him that gives and him that takes, and it is the part of wise foresight so to arrange that those to whom it falls to respresent the university, as potential beneficiary, at this juncture should do so with propitiously creditable circumstance. To meet and convince the opulent patrons of learning, as well as the parents and guardians of possible opulent students, it is, by and large, necessary to meet them on their own ground, and to bring into view such evidence of culture and intelligence as will readily be appreciated by them. To this end a large and well appointed domestic establishment is more fortunate than a smaller one; abundant, well-chosen and well-served viands, beverages and narcotics will also felicitously touch the sensibilities of these men who are fortunate enough to have learned their virtue; the better, that is to say, on the whole, the more costly, achievements in dress and equipage will "carry farther" in these premises than a penurious economy. In short, it is well that those who may be called to stand spokesmen for the seat of learning in its contact with men and women of substantial means, should be accustomed to, and should be pecuniarily competent for, a scale of living somewhat above that which the ordinary remuneration for academic work will support. An independent income, therefore, is a meritorious quality in an official scholar.

The introduction of these delegates from the well-to-do among the academic personnel has a further, secondary effect that is worth noting. Their ability freely to meet any required pecuniary strain, coupled with that degree of social ambition that commonly comes with the ability to pay, will have a salutary effect in raising the standard of living among the rest of the staff,—salutary as seen from the point of view of the bureau of publicity. In the absence of outside resources, the livelihood of academic men is somewhat scant and precarious. This places them under an insidious temptation to a more parsimonious manner of life than the best (prestige) interests of the seat of learning would dictate. By undue saving out of their current wages they may easily give the academic establishment an untoward air of indigence, such as would be likely to depreciate its prestige in those well-to-do circles where such prestige might come to have a commercial value, in the way of donations, and it might at the same time deter possible customers of the same desirable class from sending their young men to the university as students.

The American university is not an eleemosynary institution; it does not plead indigence, except in that Pickwickian sense in which indigence may without shame be avowed in polite circles; nor does it put its trust in donations of that sparseness and modesty which the gifts of charity commonly have. Its recourse necessarily is that substantial and dignified class of gifts that are not given thriftily on compunction of charity, but out of the fulness of the purse. These dignified gifts commonly aim to promote the most reputable interests of humanity, rather than the sordid needs of creature comfort, at the same time that they serve to fortify the donor's good name in good company. Donations to university funds have something of the character of an investment in good fame; they are made by gentlemen and gentlewomen, to gentlemen, and the transactions begin and end within the circle of pecuniary respectability. An impeccable respectability, authentic in the pecuniary respect, therefore, affords the only ground on which such a seminary of learning can reasonably claim the sympathetic attention of the only class whose attentions are seriously worth engaging in these premises; and respectability is inseparable from an expensive scale of living, in any community whose scheme of life is conventionally regulated by pecuniary standards.

It is accordingly expedient, for its collective good repute, that the members of the academic staff should conspicuously consume all their current income in current expenses of living. Hence also the moral obligation incumbent on all members of the staff—and their households—to take hands and help in an endless chain of conspicuously expensive social amenities, where their social proficiency and their ostensible ability to pay may effectually be placed on view. An effectual furtherance to this desirable end is the active presence among the staff of an appreciable number who are ready to take the lead at a pace slightly above the competency of the common run of university men. Their presence insures that the general body will live up to their limit; for in this, as in other games of emulation, the pace-maker is invaluable.

Besides the incentive so given to polite expenditure by the presence of a highly solvent minority among the academic personnel, it has also been found expedient that the directorate take thought and institute something in the way of an authentic curriculum of academic festivities and exhibitions of social proficiency. A degree of expensive gentility is in this way propagated by authority, to be paid for in part out of the salaries of the faculty. . . .

To return to the academic personnel and their implication in these recurrent spectacles and amenities of university life. As was remarked above, apart from outside resources the livelihood that comes to a university man is, commonly, somewhat meagre. The tenure is uncertain and the salaries, at an average, are not large. Indeed, they are notably low in comparison with the high conventional standard of living which is by custom incumbent on university men. University men are conventionally required to live on a scale of expenditure comparable with that in vogue among the well-to-do businessmen, while their university incomes compare more nearly with the lower grades of clerks and salesmen. The rate of pay varies quite materially, as is well known. For the higher grades of the staff, whose scale of pay is likely to be publicly divulged, it is, perhaps, adequate to the average demands made on university incomes by polite usage; but the large majority of university men belong on the lower levels of grade and pay; and on these lower levels the pay is, perhaps, lower than any outsider appreciates.[4]

With men circumstanced as the common run of university men are, the temptation to parsimony is ever present, while on the other hand, as has already been noted, the prestige of the university—and of the academic head—demands of all its members a conspicuously expensive

4. In a certain large and enterprising university, e.g., the pay of the lowest, and numerous, rank regularly employed to do full work as teachers, is proportioned to that of the highest—much less numerous—rank about as one to twelve at the most, perhaps even as low as one to twenty. And it may not be out of place to enter the caution that the nominal rank of a given member of the staff is no secure index of his income, even where the salary "normally" attached to the given academic rank is known. Not unusually a "normal" scale of salaries is formally adopted by the governing board and spread upon their records, and such a scale will then be surreptitiously made public. But departures from the scale habitually occur, whereby the salaries actually paid come to fall short of the "normal" perhaps as frequently as they conform to it.

There is no trades-union among university teachers, and no collective bargaining. There appears to be a feeling prevalent among them that their salaries are not of the nature of wages, and that there would be a species of moral obliquity implied in overtly so dealing with the matter. And in the individual bargaining by which the rate of pay is determined the directorate may easily be tempted to seek an economical way out, by offering a low rate of pay coupled with a higher academic rank. The plea is always ready to hand that the university is in want of the necessary funds and is constrained to economize where it can. So an advance in nominal rank is made to serve in place of an advance in salary, the former being the less costly commodity for the time being. Indeed, so frequent are such departures from the normal scale as to have given rise to the (no doubt ill-advised) suggestion that this may be one of the chief uses of the adopted schedule of normal salaries. So an employee of the university may not infrequently find himself constrained to accept, as part payment, an expensive increment of dignity attaching to a higher rank than his salary account would indicate. Such an outcome of individual bargaining is all the more likely in the academic community, since there is no settled code of professional ethics governing the conduct of business enterprise in academic management, as contrasted with the traffic of ordinary competitive business.

manner of living. Both of these needs may, of course, be met in some poor measure by saving in the obscurer items of domestic expense, such as food, clothing, heating, lighting, floor-space, books, and the like; and making all available funds count toward the collective end of reputable publicity, by throwing the stress on such expenditures as come under the public eye, as dress and equipage, bric-a-brac, amusements, public entertainments, etc. It may seem that it should also be possible to cut down the proportion of obscure expenditures for creature comforts by limiting the number of births in the family, or by foregoing marriage. But, by and large, there is reason to believe that this expedient has been exhausted. As men have latterly been at pains to show, the current average of children in academic households is not high; whereas the percentage of celibates is. There appears, indeed, to be little room for additional economy on this head, or in the matter of household thrift, beyond what is embodied in the family budgets already in force in academic circles.

So also, the tenure of office is somewhat precarious; more so than the documents would seem to indicate. This applies with greater force to the lower grades than to the higher. Latterly, under the rule of business principles, since the prestige value of a conspicuous consumption has come to a greater currency in academic policy, a member of the staff may render his tenure more secure, and may perhaps assure his due preferment, by a sedulous attention to the academic social amenities, and to the more conspicuous items of his expense account; and he will then do well in the same connection also to turn his best attention in the day's work to administrative duties and schoolmasterly discipline, rather than to the increase of knowledge. Whereas he may make his chance of preferment less assured, and may even jeopardize his tenure, by a conspicuously parsimonious manner of life, or by too pronounced an addiction to scientific or scholarly pursuits, to the neglect of those polite exhibitions of decorum that conduce to the maintenance of the university's prestige in the eyes of the (pecuniarily) cultured laity.

A variety of other untoward circumstances, of a similarly extra-scholastic bearing, may affect the fortunes of academic men to a like effect; as, e.g., unearned newspaper notoriety that may be turned to account in ridicule; unconventional religious, or irreligious convictions —so far as they become known; an undesirable political affiliation; an impecunious marriage, or such domestic infelicities as might become subject of remark. None of these untoward circumstances need touch the serviceability of the incumbent for any of the avowed, or avowable, purposes of the seminary of learning; and where action has to be taken by the directorate on provocation of such circumstances it is commonly done with the (unofficial) admission that such action is taken not on the substantial merits of the case but on compulsion of appearances and the exigencies of advertising. That some such effect should be had follows from the nature of things, so far as business principles rule.

In the degree, then, in which these and the like motives of expediency are decisive, there results a husbanding of time, energy and means in the less conspicuous expenditures and duties, in order to a freer application to more conspicuous uses, and a meticulous cultivation of the bourgeois virtues. The workday duties of instruction, and more particularly of inquiry, are, in the nature of the case, less conspicuously in evidence than the duties of the drawing-room, the ceremonial procession, the formal dinner, or the grandstand on some red-letter day of intercollegiate athletics.[5] For the purposes of a reputable notoriety the everyday work of the classroom and laboratory is also not so effective as lectures to popular audiences outside; especially, perhaps, addresses before an audience of devout and well-to-do women. Indeed, all this is well approved by experience. In many and devious ways, therefore, a university man may be able to serve the collective enterprise of his university to better effect than by an exclusive attention to the scholastic work on which alone he is ostensibly engaged.

Among the consequences that follow is a constant temptation for the members of the staff to take on work outside of that for which the salary is nominally paid. Such work takes the public eye; but a further incentive to go into this outside and nonacademic work, as well as to take on supernumerary work within the academic schedule,

5. So, e.g., the well-known president of a well and favourably known university was at pains a few years ago to distinguish one of his faculty as being his "ideal of a university man"; the grounds of this invidious distinction being a lifelike imitation of a country gentleman and a fair degree of attention to committee work in connection with the academic administration; the incumbent had no distinguishing marks either as a teacher or as a scholar, and neither science nor letters will be found in his debt. It is perhaps needless to add that for reasons of individious distinction, no names can be mentioned in this connection. It should be added in illumination of the instance cited, that in the same university, by consistent selection and discipline of the personnel, it had come about that, in the apprehension of the staff as well as of the executive, the accepted test of efficiency was the work done on the administrative committees rather than that of the class rooms or laboratories.

lies in the fact that such outside or supernumerary work is specially paid, and so may help to eke out a sensibly scant livelihood. So far as touches the more scantily paid grades of university men, and so far as no alien considerations come in to trouble the working-out of business principles, the outcome may be schematized somewhat as follows. These men have, at the outset, gone into the university presumably from an inclination to scholarly or scientific pursuits; it is not probable that they have been led into this calling by the pecuniary inducements, which are slight as compared with the ruling rates of pay in the open market for other work that demands an equally arduous preparation and an equally close application. They have been apportioned rather more work as instructors than they can take care of in the most efficient manner, at a rate of pay which is sensibly scant for the standard of (conspicuous) living conventionally imposed on them. They are, by authority, expected to expend time and means in such polite observances, spectacles and quasi-learned exhibitions as are presumed to enhance the prestige of the university. They are so induced to divert their time and energy to spreading abroad the university's good repute by creditable exhibitions of a quasi-scholarly character, which have not substantial bearing on a university man's legitimate interests; as well as in seeking supplementary work outside of their mandatory schedule, from which to derive an adequate livelihood and to fill up the complement of politely wasteful expenditures expected of them. The academic instruction necessarily suffers by this diversion of forces to extra-scholastic objects; and the work of inquiry, which may have primarily engaged their interest and which is indispensable to their continued efficiency as teachers, is, in the common run of cases, crowded to one side and presently drops out of mind. Like other workmen, under pressure of competition the members of the academic staff will endeavour to keep up their necessary income by cheapening their product and increasing their marketable output. And by consequence of this pressure of bread-winning and genteel expenditure, these university men are so barred out from the serious pursuit of those scientific and scholarly inquiries which alone can, academically speaking, justify their retention on the university faculty, and for the sake of which, in great part at least, they have chosen this vocation. No infirmity more commonly besets university men than this going to seed in routine work and extra-scholastic duties. They have entered on the academic career to find time, place, facilities and congenial environment for the pursuit of knowledge, and under pressure they presently settle down to a round of perfunctory labour by means of which to simulate the life of gentlemen.[6]

Before leaving the topic it should further be remarked that the dissipation incident to these polite amenities, that so are incumbent on the academic personnel, apparently also has something of a deteriorative effect on their working capacity, whether for scholarly or for worldly uses. *Prima facie* evidence to this effect might be adduced, but it is not easy to say how far the evidence would bear closer scrutiny. There is an appreciable amount of dissipation, in its several sorts, carried forward in university circles in an inconspicuous manner, and not designed for publicity. How far this is induced by a loss of interest in scholarly work, due to the habitual diversion of the scholars' energies to other and more exacting duties, would be hard to say; as also how far it may be due to the lead given by men-of-the-world retained on the faculties for other than scholarly reasons. At the same time there is the difficulty that many of those men who bear a large part in the ceremonial dissipation incident to the enterprise in publicity are retained, apparently, for their proficiency in this line as much as for their scholarly attainments, or at least so one might infer; and these men must be accepted with the defects of their qualities.

As bearing on this whole matter of pomp and circumstance, social amenities and ritual dissipation, quasi-learned demonstrations and meretricious publicity, in academic life, it is difficult beyond hope of a final answer to determine how much of it is due directly to the masterful initiative of the strong man who directs the enterprise, and how much is to be set down to an innate proclivity for all that sort of thing on the part of the academic personnel. A near view of these phenomena leaves the impression that there is, on the whole, less ob-

6. Within the past few years an academic executive of great note has been heard repeatedly to express himself in facetious doubt of this penchant for scholarly inquiry on the part of university men, whether as "reseárch" or as "résearch"; and there is doubtless ground for scepticism as to its permeating the academic body with that sting of ubiquity that is implied in many expressions on this head. And it should also be said, perhaps in extenuation of the expression cited above, that the president was addressing delegations of his own faculty, and presumably directing his remarks to their special benefit; and that while he professed (no doubt in ingenuously) a profound zeal for the cause of science at large, it had come about, selectively, through a long course of sedulous attention on his own part to all other qualifications than the main fact, that his faculty at the time of speaking was in the main an aggregation of slack-twisted schoolmasters and men about town. Such a characterization, however, does not carry any gravely invidious discrimination, nor will it presumably serve in any degree to identify the seat of learning to which it refers.

jection felt than expressed among the academic men with regard to this routine of demonstration; that the reluctance with which they pass under the ceremonial yoke is not altogether ingenuous; all of which would perhaps hold true even more decidedly as applied to the faculty households.[7] But for all that, it also remains true that without the initiative and countenance of the executive head these boyish movements of sentimental spectacularity on the part of the personnel would come to little, by comparison with what actually takes place. It is after all a matter for executive discretion, and, from whatever motives, this diversion of effort to extra-scholastic ends has the executive sanction;[8] with the result that an intimate familiarity with current academic life is calculated to raise the question whether make-believe does not, after all, occupy a larger and more urgent place in the life of these thoughtful adult male citizens than in the life of their children.

7. The share and value of the "faculty wives" in all this routine of resolute conviviality is a large topic, an intelligent and veracious account of which could only be a work of naïve brutality.

> "But the grim, grim Ladies, Oh my brothers!
> They are ladling bitterly.
> They are ladling in the work-time of the others,
> In the country of the free."

(Mrs. Elizabret Harte Browning, in *The Cry of the Heathen Chinee*.)

8. What takes place without executive sanction need trouble no one.

2. Teachers and Professors: Subject-Matter Areas

JESSIE BERNARD

Academic Institutions as the Natural Habitat of Learning

Institutions of higher education perform many varied services in our society. They conserve accumulated knowledge and transmit it to succeeding generations, they create new knowledge, and they interpret, criticize, and honor knowledge. They serve as the natural habitat of learning. They create a certain kind of ambience which is important just by the fact of its existence. They serve, that is, merely by being places where people can sit and think,[1] where ideas are valued for themselves.[2]

It takes a great many people in many roles to insure that all these services are performed. Of all the functional positions required . . . two are of special relevance for our discussion here: the key or core professions subsumed under the rubrics "faculty for resident instruction in degree-credit courses" and "professional staff for organized research." Women . . . constituted 19.4 percent of the first and 11.4 percent of the second category in 1959-60.[3] What, exactly, were they doing, and how well were they doing it?

---

1. It is becoming difficult for all these services to be performed by the same institutions. Students get in the way. There is beginning to develop a new kind of institution, such as the institutes at Princeton and at Stanford, in which scholars and scientists can think without distraction.

2. From the point of view of the student, in addition to offering teaching and training, universities and colleges confer the status symbol required for success, the academic degree; they serve as channels of upward social mobility and allocate talent to the several areas of learning by offering a wide choice of alternative careers. Much as some might deplore the fact, the modern academic institution serves also as a mating agency.

3. Office of Education, *Summary Report on Faculty and Other Professional Staff in Institutions of Higher Education, 1959-60* (Washington: GPO, 1961), table 3.

Teaching and Professing

A college or university, then, is much more than a place where generations of students are processed for later life. It is a place where, even if there were no students, ideas would flourish. Face-to-face teaching may be important, although it has long been pointed out that since the invention of printing the strictly information-conveying function of teaching has become anachronistic. Motivated people can learn by reading materials themselves. The so-called teaching boxes, in fact, can do the job of this kind of teaching faster and better than the human teacher.

Much more than teaching, however, is involved in the atmosphere of a good college or university. There must be people around who are enthralled by their subjects. Students must learn that there are people vitally interested in ideas, people to whom ideas are important. There have to be people who "profess," debate, argue, stand for something, live their subject. It is worthwhile for the student to know that there are such people in the world, not that he will necessarily take them as models—students in most universities won't. In later years, however, the student as board member, executive or voter will know that there are people desperately attached to certain values and that these values are good and must be protected. The man who has never been exposed to men-of-knowledge will be cavalier about voting support for a community "culture"—in the narrow sense—center. The man who has been exposed to a great Shakespeare scholar—who may have been a poor teacher or lecturer—may live a no more "cultured" life for the exposure, but he will be aware of "culture" and the public that loves it.

Teaching Role and Man-of-Knowledge Role

In order to understand the contribution which women have made to the academic enterprise in the United States a distinction between the roles of "teacher" and "professor" or "man-of-knowledge" is useful. This distinction is not identical with one commonly made between "discipline loyalty" and "institutional loyalty," though it may be related, nor is it identical with the ancient "teaching" and "research" polarity, though, again, it may be related. The professor or man-of-knowledge may or may not also be a researcher.

It is a distinction more like Franz Adler's between means and ends. If we view both professors and teachers as performers (as well as models), the following statement shows how their roles differ:

The performer may be defined as a middle man between the author and the publics. Performance may be divided into two classes; those that are more or less ends in themselves and those that are means for facilitating the presentation of a work. The first kind is produced by a "charismatic mediator," the latter by a performer who may be called a "tool." The charismatic mediator deserves to be considered as an author in his own right. His authorship comes into play after rather than before that of the official author. In this it differs from most kinds of true authorship. The performance of the charismatic mediator tends to carry high prestige and is rightly regarded as a sign of creative ability. The performance of the tool is less likely to carry a high prestige, and whatever prestige it does carry derives from technical perfection rather than from creativity.[4]

The role of the teacher, in brief, is to serve as an instrument of communication; the role of the man-of-knowledge is to serve as a collaborator with the original author.

We are speaking of roles; the same people may perform both roles at different times. Generally, however, as the following discussion indicates, the tendency has been for women to perform primarily in the teaching role. The professor or man-of-knowledge role has been performed primarily by men.

A second distinction between the teacher and the professor or man-of-knowledge roles has to do with the nature of the materials dealt with. The teacher often deals with the established, hence usually elementary, aspects of his discipline. He is conserving, not innovating. Again Adler:

Where orthodoxy or exact performance is emphasized, the teacher will be under specifically heavy scrutiny by members of the general public, his colleagues and, if such exists, the hierarchy of performers. And woe indeed to him who becomes a heretic while instructing. . . . This is easily understandable if the tremendous potential influence of the teacher is considered. The teacher is believed because he is a teacher. It is assumed by his audience that what he is going to tell them is true, that is, orthodox. If he is found out, then, to teach opinions of his own and not those shared by his colleagues or his superiors he will find himself rapidly discredited except where he is able to assume the role of a new author and is recognized in it. It will take a special public for such a recognition. . . . The performer in general and the teacher in particular are factors for the maintenance of existing forms and contents and serious obstacles to innovation. As they transmit orthodoxy to future authors and performers they are instrumental in shaping future works and their presentations. As they transmit orthodoxy to members of publics

4. Franz Adler, "Toward a Sociology of Creative Behavior," p. 6.

they shape their expectations and their readiness to accept or reject new works and new performances.[5]

The professor or man-of-knowledge deals with controversial, hence usually with advanced, aspects of his discipline. He stands for a point of view in the field, a fact which leads students to say "I would like to study with Professor Blank at Kanwisota University."[6] He does not take orthodoxy for granted. He modifies, performs exegesis, tells his listeners that this author is clearly wrong, that one mistaken. Although he may never do much writing of his own, the performance of his role as a man-of-knowledge requires a kind of effort quite as rigorous as that of research. As systematizer he has to make sense out of the vast torrent of findings that pour from the laboratories and libraries. He puts findings in their place, in perspective. He has to see implications, relationships, total structures, and gestalts as well as small details. He must know less about more rather than more about less. He is, in brief, a generalist. The professor or man-of-knowledge role calls for a heavy load of intellectual baggage. It requires that the

5. *Ibid.*, p. 10. It would take us too far afield to relate in detail the comparative success of women as scholars in the Middle Ages and Renaissance to the above analysis. Reference is only made to the idea that where the major function of the man-of-knowledge is primarily one of conserving and transmitting knowledge, as in the case of sacred knowledge, women can perform well if they wish to. There is no problem of innovation, no problem of convincing reluctant colleagues, no problem of application. Such a conserving and transmitting function, characteristic of the monasteries and convents of the Middle Ages, does not preclude women. This might help explain why, according to historical account, they did so well. During the Renaissance, although the contents of learning changed from sacred to secular, again the function of the man-of-knowledge was a conserving and transmitting one. Again, this was something women could do well. Classics and rhetoric, it will be noted, were the subjects taught by the academic women in the Renaissance. When, with the beginning of the modern era, knowledge became more technological and scientific, however, other functions had to be performed by the man-of-knowledge, including the far more aggressive one of creating knowledge and fighting for its acceptance. This new function was less consonant with traditional feminine roles. It was one thing to be knowledgeable about religious tradition and the classics, a passive role; it was something else again to create new ideas and new knowledge, an active, even aggressive, role. This attempt to relate the nature of knowledge with women's contribution to it, based on Florian Znaniecki's analysis, is meant only to be suggestive, certainly not definitive. Too many other factors and forces were also at work to produce the situations described by the historians to make any one wholly adequate. Not until the sociology of the role of the woman-of-knowledge is written will all the elements become clear.

6. Caplow and McGee report that in the physical sciences professors disclaim the existence of "schools" of thought. That professors of science in different universities emphasize different aspects and approaches to their subjects is, however, clear from the work that issues from their laboratories.

performer keep his eyes open for trends in a wide variety of areas. The performer of this role is the one who makes use of the researcher's findings, often conferring more value on them in this way than the researcher does. It is in this sense that, as Adler pointed out, the man-of-knowledge becomes a collaborator with the original author.

Naive people do not understand the difference between the function of the man-of-knowledge role and the teacher role. Thus, for example, members of the American Legion or the Veterans of Foreign Wars or other conservative organizations feel called upon to scrutinize what is being taught. If what they find is contrary to the accepted patterns of thought in the community, they raise a hue and cry. This is not what they pay teachers to do. It is the academic person performing the man-of-knowledge function who is most likely to have problems with academic freedom. Indeed, it is the institutionalization of academic freedom which alone makes possible the performance of the man-of-knowledge role at all. Without it, the man-of-knowledge role would be assimilated by the teacher role.

The fact that women are more likely to be in the teacher role than in the man-of-knowledge role and hence less likely—even in the social sciences—to be dealing with controversial materials may help to explain why they were found to be less apprehensive than men in the McCarthy era, as reported by Budner and Meyer.

A third difference between the roles of teacher and professor of man-of-knowledge has to do with the complementary role of student. The teacher is often performing his role in a required course, one in which the interest of the student cannot be taken for granted. The relationship between teacher and student is influenced by this fact; it is peculiar in that the teacher is, so to speak, at the mercy of his students to the extent that their achievement is a test of his competence. The importance of student achievement often gives a kind of stark urgency to the relationship from the teacher's point of view. Because the student can use refusal to learn as a strategic weapon against the teacher, the teacher is usually surrounded with powerful weapons of deterrence or defense—an apparatus of grades and attendance requirements which serve as potential threats. The teacher pushes; the student often resists. The score is evened up by the weight of the institutional support back of the teacher.

There is less likely to be this kind of conflict between the student and the professor or man-of-knowledge. He invites the student to share his enthusiasm for the subject matter. There exists, theoretically, a joint enterprise in which motivation is assumed on the part of the student. To the extent that he performs as a professor rather than as a teacher, the academic person does not need the institutional apparatus of grades and compulsory attendance for support. Znaniecki has described the professor-student relationship as follows:

What binds this group of professors and students together is knowledge as such—the scholarly type of theoretic, systematically ordered, absolutely true knowledge. Its cultivation and perpetuation is the primary task of the group and the chief reason of its existence; if it ceased to perform this task, it would also cease to be a center of higher intellectual education. No matter what psychological motives induce particular individuals to seek admission to the group, so long as they are its members they are bound to accept its appreciation of knowledge as the highest common value.[7]

A final difference between the two roles is a corollary of the third one. Both the teacher and the man-of-knowledge must be as well as do, that is, they must serve as models for the young. But they do so in quiet [sic] different ways. One author has distinguished at least five model-related demands which students may legitimately make of teachers: (1) that they be cultural and aesthetic examples; (2) that they exhibit serious scholarship; (3) that they have social sophistication, that is, poise and self-assurance; (4) that they show professional responsibility, that is, a serious attitude toward their jobs, their colleagues, and their environment; and, finally, (5) that they serve as ethical and moral arbiters, willing to make known their commitments rather than hide behind a facade of objectivity or neutrality.[8] The great teacher, according to these specifications, has to be a certain kind of person as well as do certain things:

Every genuine teacher is concerned with assisting his students to develop and to educate themselves. And beneath all the trappings of pedagogy and erudition one of the most significant means of doing this is by his own example, whether he wishes it or not. The old saw, "What you do speaks so loudly I cannot hear what you say," applies with painful accuracy to the student-teacher relationship. To be a teacher means the acceptance of that responsibility, no matter how embarrassing, enervating, or humbling the prospect may be. While we lament, as we so often must, that students just don't listen to us, we must also remember that they do note with frightening accuracy what we stand for. When we become discouraged about their seem-

7. Florian Znaniecki, *The Social Role of the Man of Knowledge* (New York: Columbia Univ. Press, 1940), pp. 154-155.

8. Emerson Shuck, "Teacher's Role Book," *AAUP Bulletin*, 46 (Sept. 1960), p. 269.

ing resistance to much we try to tell them, we must remember that very fleeting impressions may have far more effect in the long run than hours of very laborious exposition in some good cause.[9]

As the transmitting function imposes hazards on student-teacher relationships, so also does the model-serving or socializing function. At more elementary levels the community often demands that its school-teachers behave much better than other citizens. Until fairly recently they were not permitted to smoke, and their recreational life was strictly policed. They are required to be conservers of the mores as well as of knowledge. At the college and university level the model is less circumscribed—[10] except, perhaps, at conservative church-affiliated schools—but there still remains a barrier. Indeed, the resulting *persona* often becomes so fixed that some college teachers can be spotted as such in a crowd.

The kind of socialization for which the man-of-knowledge is responsible is of a quite different kind: He must socialize the student into his intellectual, not his citizenship, role:

A secular university is an association of mature persons in which professors have positions of authority. Although, like every other social group, it exercises some control over the conduct of its members, yet it does not try to educate them physically or morally, to guide their personal evolution so as to make them fit for social participation, since it presumes that this has already been done during their childhood and early youth. . . .

The school of higher learning performs the specifically social function of an educational institution only because its main activities are not social but scientific,[11] do not aim to contribute to the maintenance of the social order but to the maintenance of knowledge as a supersocial domain of culture supremely valuable in itself. Therefore, the chief personal duty of every member is to share in the activities by which knowledge is maintained, even if only by faithfully assimilating that relatively small portion of knowledge which is transmitted to him during the period when he is a mere student.

9. *Ibid.*

10. About 35 percent of the women in a sample of college teachers in Minnesota had come to their present positions from a job in a lower school and hence, presumably, they were more inured to the exigencies of serving as a moral model for the young (Ruth E. Eckert and John E. Stecklein, *Job Motivations and Satisfactions of College Teachers: A Study of Faculty Members in Minnesota Colleges* [Washington: GPO, 1961], p. 59).

11. Znaniecki here uses the terms science and scientific in their broadest sense, referring to any systematic body of learning.

Academic Women as Teachers

These functional distinctions between the roles of teacher and man-of-knowledge help to explain why women, by and large, have made their most important contributions to the academic enterprise as teachers, both at the bottom of the academic hierarchy and at the professional school level, and to a greater extent in some subjects than in others.

The earliest catalogs of both Vassar and Smith College showed only two ranks, professors and teachers. The professors were, for the most part, men and the teachers, women.[12] The distinction by sex at Smith did not, however, last very long:

Among the men and women on the Faculty no discrimination in rank or tenure of office was made on account of sex. The title "professor" was not at first given to the women, because most of them preferred not to receive what seemed an absurd and pretentious appellation, which had been retained, apparently, for men only by force of an ancient tradition. In the earliest official circulars, the women were designated simply as teachers, but it proved a needless and vain attempt to emphasize feminine distinctions and was not long continued.[13]

On the basis of a survey of college catalogs over a century and of more recent studies in several different kinds of institutions, it may be said that women have carried a disproportionate share of the heavy, "back-breaking"—anyone who has ever sat grading examination papers will recognize the literalness of this adjective—load of introductory instruction. At Vassar—and the situation was essentially the same in other colleges—women constituted almost the entire "teaching" or "instructor" faculty until well into the twentieth century (Table 1). No doubt much of this introductory work has been, and is, done by women in the status of fringe benefits, but some of it is doubtless done by professionals, at least by women with Ph.D. degrees. . . . It is suggested here that there may be a functional reason for the distribution of academic women by rank, that they are likely to be found at the lower ranks in part, at least, because they teach the less controversial, more standard, aspects of their subjects.

12. At Vassar, only one of the nine professors was a woman; all but one of the twenty-two teachers were women, and the one exception was an instructor. The proportion of professors who were women remained low until the 1920's and 1930's, reaching a high point in the 1930's and declining thereafter.

13. L. Clark Seelye, *The Early History of Smith College, 1871-1910* (Boston: Houghton Mifflin, 1923), p. 54.

Table 1.

Proportion of Professorial and Instructor Ranks Who were Women in Four Subject Areas, Vassar College, 1865-1956

Year	Science and Mathematics		Language and Literature		Social Science and History		Art and Music	
	Professorial	Instructor	Professorial	Instructor	Professorial	Instructor	Professorial	Instructor
1865	25	100		90				100
1874–75	50	100		100				100
1884–85	50	100		100				100
1894–95	43	100	25	100	50	100		100
1904–1905	29	100	40	100	50	100		50
1914–15	17	100	57	100	40	100		60
1924–25	63	92	91*	90	57	100	20	71
1934–35	87*	85	77	100	56	57	22	60
1944–45	58	86	78	82	71*	100	29	63
1955–56	67	67	71	68	55	60	17	77

* High point.

The Elementary Level of Instruction

A glance at Table 2 shows that the proportion of, for example, mathematics teachers who were women (1954-55) was much greater than the proportion of women receiving the doctorate in mathematics (1955-56). (The difference in date must, of course, be taken into account in interpreting these figures, for the teachers with Ph.D.'s in 1954-55 reflect doctorates of previous years, but the difference is not great enough to nullify the point being made here.) In brief, a great many college and university mathematics teachers were women without doctorates and hence, presumably, were not teaching advanced courses. A similar comment might be made with respect to the physical sciences, to the health professions, to businesss and commerce, to education, to English, journalism, and foreign languages, to fine and applied arts, to home economics, and to library science. That women without doctorates were probably teaching elementary courses does not mean that those with doctorates were necessarily teaching the advanced courses. The relatively low rank even of those with doctorates . . . suggests that they were not.

Table 2.

*Doctors in Specified Fields, 1955-56, Who Were Women and
Teachers in 673 Institutions Who Were Women, 1954-55**

Field	Percent Doctors Who Were Women	Percent Teachers Who Were Women
All Fields	9.9	22.0
Agricultural and Biological Sciences	9.0	10.3
Mathematics	4.3	14.2
Physical Sciences	4.1	6.0
Psychology	13.6	13.4
Geography and Anthropology	6.4	15.5
Health Professions	4.9	46.9
Business and Commerce	0.0	20.2
Education	17.8	36.9
English, Journalism, Foreign Languages	17.0	27.5
Fine Arts	13.2	27.3
Social Sciences	10.0	10.6
Library Science	6.6	71.5
Home Economics	84.8	96.4

* Data on doctorates adapted from Office of Education, *Statistics of Higher Education: 1955-56* (Washington: GPO, 1958), pp. 96 ff. Data on teachers, National Science Foundation, *Women in Scientific Careers* (Washington: GPO, 1961), p. 9.

Women as Teachers in the Professional Schools[14]

Further evidence that academic women tend to be teachers of the more stable subjects and the more elementary levels may be adduced from the situation in professional schools. The teacher-professor distinction helps to explain the anomalous fact that women entered the faculties of the great universities at the level of the professional schools. At Harvard in the 1920's and 1930's women came as instructors in child hygiene, in nutrition, and in vital statistics.[15] At the University of Michigan there was a woman professor of public health nursing in the 1920's, the only woman among 209 professors, but with the obvious role of teacher.[16]

14. See Appendix A.
15. Mainly they came in interstitial positions such as associates in research or research fellows.
16. Three women out of 108 held the rank of associate professor: one in library science, one in anatomy, and one in personnel management and economics. There were eight with the rank of assistant professor out of 231, one of whom was a research associate, one an assistant custodian in a specialized library, two in piano,

The acceptance of women in professional, especially medical, schools, which are of graduate level standing, more readily than in Ph.D.-granting faculties reflects a difference in the nature of the training for the several doctoral degrees and in the faculties which confer them. The M.D., for example, is not a research degree and does not call for the same kind of relationship between faculty and student. The M.D. calls for the absorption of a certain amount of scientific knowledge, the acquisition of technical skills, and socialization into a certain occupational culture. The faculties of such schools reflect a division of labor with respect to these functions. Those who convey the theoretical knowledge are primarily teachers of science; those who serve as clinical teachers are practice-oriented.[17] The teachers of the sciences are likely to be Ph.D.'s,[18] the clinicians, M.D.'s.

Among the Ph.D.'s on the faculties of professional schools, some perform the teacher role primarily, others the professorial or man-of-knowledge role. In relation to medical school faculties, the following account is illuminating:

There is undoubtedly a relationship, although not a necessary one, between style of teaching in these courses and advances in science. Gross anatomy is a morphological study, and the morphology of the body has been known for many years. Teachers of the subject are somewhat in the position of Latin teachers in high school. There is an old discipline with many teaching traditions. . . . Physiology and microanatomy are rapidly advancing fields; outmoded knowledge must be constantly replaced by the results of research and new knowledge integrated with old. . . .[19]

Both teachers and professors are required, the first for the settled areas

---

one in library science, one in pharmacology, and two in psychology. Of the 360 instructors, 30 were women, including one in economics and two in sociology.

17. The long struggle between the theoretical and the practical approaches to learning has been reviewed by Znaniecki: "practical people for the last seven or eight centuries have been continuously complaining about all that useless knowledge which candidates for professional roles had to acquire in academic schools before they were allowed to participate in active life. No doubt, practical people are right in a way; for the systematic organization of knowledge as taught in learned schools is radically different from that which a man must acquire to be occupationally efficient. But if practical people had their way, professional instruction would have remained in the stage of medieval apprenticeship" (Social Role of the Man of Knowledge, p. 163).

18. Scientists on the faculties of professional schools have lower status in their professions than those on faculties granting the Ph.D. degree, according to one group of informants.

19. Howard S. Becker and others, Boys in White (Chicago: Univ. of Chicago Press, 1961), pp. 132-133.

of science, like anatomy, and the second for the evolving areas, like physiology. Women have been successful in performing the teacher role, even at this advanced level, especially in the field of anatomy.

In a study of the proportion of women on the faculties of twenty leading universities in 1960, for example, anatomy stood out as especially hospitable to women. Disregarding for the moment such subjects as home economics, library science, and education, we find that it leads all other subjects, with 15.6 percent of those teaching anatomy being women, almost twice as many, proportionately, as those teaching physiology (8.4 percent). They achieved top rank in this subject more often than in any other, 9.4 percent of the professors of anatomy being women. The next subject below anatomy in proportion of women professors was music (5.9 percent). There were no women professors of physiology.[20]

Without pressing the suggestion too far, it does seem that the character of the subject matter taught is a relevant variable in explaining the contribution which academic women have made. They seem to have done most in the stable areas of learning. For all subjects, this would be at the introductory level; for some subjects, it would also be at the professional level.

There are, to be sure, anomalies. Alice Hamilton became a member of the Harvard University medical faculty in 1918; she came as an assistant professor and retained this rank until she became emerita in 1939. Hers was certainly a growing field—indeed one to which she was herself a major contributor—and should, therefore, according to the suggestion offered above, have been preempted by a man. It so happened, however, that she knew more than anyone else in the world about industrial medicine. It was a choice between filling the post with her or leaving it unfilled. But her rank conformed to her sex; it remained low to the end.[21]

20. John B. Parrish, "Women in Top Level Teaching and Research," *Jour. Amer. Assn. Univ. Women*, 55 (Jan. 1962), p. 102.

21. In her autobiography Alice Hamilton recounts an interesting example of status inconsistency: "Nor did I embarrass the faculty by marching in the Commencement procession and sitting on the platform, though each year I received a printed invitation to do so. At the bottom of the page would be the warning that 'under no circumstances may a woman sit on the platform,' which seemed a bit tactless, but I was sure it was not intentional" (*Exploring the Dangerous Trades* [Boston: Little, Brown, 1943], p. 253).

The Social Sciences[22]

The distinction between the roles of teacher and professor helps to explain also the areas in which women have made their most important contributions, as well as the levels at which they have done so. It is, to be sure, only one factor. The subjects women teach are related to market demand and to their interests. The under-representation of women in the physical sciences, for example, can be plausibly explained by the lack of interest of women in this field. No matter how great the market demand and no matter how stable the introductory aspects, women are not attracted to it.

Women are also under-represented in the social sciences. Next after the physical sciences, the social sciences are the most "masculine" subjects. As shown in Table 2 . . . , the proportion of women teaching in these subjects is low.

A possible interpretation of the relative under-representation of women in the social sciences, especially in the great universities, may be sought not in lack of interest on the part of women[23] but in the nature of the subjects themselves. Except for statistics, the social sciences are less standardized than, for example, grammar, rhetoric, mathematics, or the physical and biological sciences. In these areas the teacher is conveying relatively fixed and standardized knowledge. The teacher can usually rely on the authority of fixed principles, little subject to controversy. Grammar is grammar, atoms are atoms, cells are cells, at the elementary level, however controversial they may be at advanced levels. The same is less true in the social sciences, where there are more likely to be many schools of thought[24] and more room for interpretation and controversy. Even elementary textbooks reveal many different points of view as reflected in the selection of materials and the relative emphasis given to them. The teacher is therefore often on controversial ground,[25] dealing, furthermore, with issues

22. See Appendix A for further discussion of this topic.

23. Since 1951, the number of women getting Ph.D. degrees in the social sciences has consistently exceeded the number getting degrees in arts and humanities; since the middle of the 1950's the number in the social sciences has approximated that in the physical and biological sciences.

24. Caplow & McGee, *The Academic Marketplace* (New York: Basic Books, 1958), pp. 87-89.

25. This is especially true in economics and political science, and it is precisely in these fields where women are most likely to be under-represented. In 1960, only 4.8 percent of those in economics were women; 2.8 percent of those in political science.

on which the opinions of women often do not carry much weight. In many matters in the social sciences the experience of women is not always judged to be relevant.[26] The teacher is also often on the opposite side of the fence from his students politically.[27]

Another aspect of this situation has to do with the function of the social sciences in the university as sources of social criticism. At the elementary levels of the social science disciplines a bland picture of the functioning of our society is presented according to theory, but at the higher levels the defects as it actually operates are, of necessity, also presented. The great social critics, from Veblen, Beard, Ross, Commons, and Hart, to Galbraith, Riesman, and Mills have been academic men. This is an integral part of the role of the academic man as man-of-knowledge. The one area in which women have traditionally served as social critics has been that of the place of women in our society, and even here their contribution has often been one of waspish special pleading rather than serious, responsible social criticism. The great reformers among academic women . . . were just that, reformers primarily rather than social critics.[28] Conscience, not science, was their forte.

It has been in languages and literature—English composition, French grammar, German grammar, Spanish grammar, and the like (sometimes euphemistically classified with the humanities)—and the elementary levels of the several physical and biological sciences, and mathematics that women have traditionally made their major contribution.[29]

26. The important relationships in modern societies tend to be those centering about power, and the observations and reports of women do not seem to have as much cogency and immediacy as those of men in this area. By way of contrast, the observations and reports on preliterate societies made by women are accepted; the kinds of phenomena—family, kinship—which are basic in the organization of such societies are the kinds which women may even have an advantage in interpreting. Women are therefore listened to more readily in anthropology.

27. Faculties, by and large, tend to have the traditionally-defined "liberal" orientation; students often come from conservative backgrounds. Faculties tend to be Democratic; students in many colleges are predominantly Republican. Logan Wilson, Paul Lazarsfeld, and Seymour Lipset have all commented on these points.

28. Lucy Salmon's treatise on domestic service was, in a way, a social critique.

29. At one time, for example, nine out of ten of both professors and instructors in language and literature at Vassar were women. The highest proportion of women professors and instructors in the social sciences and history—in the 1940's—was only 71 percent. . . . The same contrast characterized the situation at Smith where women have equalled if not excelled men in language and literature, but have been sparsely represented in history and the social sciences. Swarthmore presents a similar picture, despite the fact that Maria Sanford taught the social sciences there

In the areas and at the levels where women have made their major contributions as teachers, then, they have had behind them the weight of definitive bodies of knowledge about which relatively little controversy or few differences in interpretation exist. They did not have to defend themselves, being primarily agents or "tools" of transmission. Sex as such is apparently no handicap in this kind of role, but in less defined and stabilized and established areas the problem of competence becomes more difficult even to conceptualize; the professor or man-of-knowledge role seems to be demanded. In addition, the function of social criticism, which is part of the man-of-knowledge function of the social scientist, has not been one customarily assigned to women, except in limited areas.

Among the consequences of the differences between academic men and academic women in areas of interest is one of special relevance. Academicians in different fields have different positions in the market. Some, because of great demand, are in better bargaining positions than others and hence can demand better rewards. Others do not have good bargaining positions. In general, these differences in bargaining power tend to operate against women, since they are more likely than men to be in the areas with poorer bargaining power, namely the humanities.

That the major contribution of women to the academic enterprise should have been as teachers is related also, presumably, to the fact that the role of teacher is consonant with that of other roles assigned to women in our society. As mothers, women have been traditionally conservators and transmitters of non-controversial knowledge.

Academic women, then, have performed some of the hardest work that has to be done by academic institutions, the grinding drudgery of

---

in the earliest years. Of the land-grant colleges, Kansas State showed little difference between the sexes at the instructor level, but the usual difference at the higher levels. The contribution of women in the fields of the sciences and mathematics seems to have varied from school to school. In the early years at Vassar about half of the professors in these fields were women. At Smith the contribution of women in science and mathematics was second only to that in language and literature. With the exception of one woman in science and mathematics at Swarthmore in the nineteenth century, however, there have been none in that field there. The land-grant colleges have not used women extensively in this field either, except at the lower levels. At Harvard there were two astronomers in the 1930's. At the University of Michigan women were instructing in anatomy, geology, roentgenology, physiological chemistry, astronomy, botany, and the like. At the lowest levels, as assistants, they were contributing in pediatrics and bacteriology at Harvard and very considerably at the University of Michigan in the medical and dental schools and laboratories.

unchallenging introductory courses, and have thus released academic men for the more rewarding assignments, graduate courses in new and more exciting areas, of the professor of man-of-knowledge role.

3. The Art of Teaching

CHRISTOPHER JENCKS and DAVID RIESMAN

We have already suggested that teaching is not a profession in the way that research is. There is no guild within which successful teaching leads to greater prestige and influence than mediocre teaching, nor any professional training program that develops pedagogic skills in a systematic way. Indeed, there is very little knowledge about which teaching strategies work with which students. Under these circumstances it is hardly surprising that a great deal of teaching at both the graduate and undergraduate level is dull and ineffective. No form of success that depends on luck and individual initiative is ever widespread. No doubt most professors prefer it when their courses are popular, their lectures applauded, and their former students appreciative. But since such successes are of no help in getting a salary increase, moving to a more prestigious campus, or winning their colleagues' admiration, they are unlikely to struggle as hard to create them as to do other things. Indeed, good teaching can be a positive handicap in attempting to meet other payrolls, especially in a place where most teaching is mediocre, for the able teacher finds students beating a path to his door and leaving him little time or anything else. If he is really committed to research he may well find that the only way to make free time is to remain aloof.

Most professors become good teachers only if it comes fairly easily and naturally. Those who do not have much natural flair seldom know how to begin remedying their failings even if they have the impulse. They certainly get little help from their colleagues. The reasons for this are not hard to discover. It seems easier to judge individuals on the basis of papers they turn out than to judge them on the basis of their interaction with other people. A graduate student's performance in comprehensive examinations is said to provide hard evidence of his competence, while visits to his classes provide only soft evidence. A professor's book can be evaluated in "objective" terms, whereas his course syllabi, lectures, and examination questions can be valued only "subjectively." The adjectives re-enforce the prejudices of the profession even though they throw little light on the actual criteria for judgment. These prejudices are not simply a matter of valuing research over teaching. A tenure committee member, for example, who argues for a particular man because of his catalytic qualities in helping his colleagues do better research also finds himself up against an ideology that insists men be judged entirely in terms of their own paper output rather than in terms of their effect on others.

In discussing these matters many critics talk about research versus teaching. We have found no evidence, however, that the two are antagonistic. Teachers cannot remain stimulating unless they also continue to learn, and while this learning may not focus on small, manageable "research problems," it is research by any reasonable definition. When a teacher stops doing it, he begins to repeat himself and eventually loses touch with both the young and the world around him. Research in this general sense does not, of course, necessarily lead to publication, but that is its most common result. Publication is the only way a man can communicate with a significant number of colleagues or other adults. Those who do not publish usually feel they have not learned anything worth communicating to adults. This means they have not learned much worth communicating to the young either. There are, of course, exceptions: men who keep learning but cannot bring themselves to write. Some have unrealistically high standards regarding what deserves publication. Some know no journal which is interested in the kinds of problems that interest them. Some are simply afraid of exposing themselves to their colleagues' criticism, even though their ideas could in fact withstand such scrutiny. Some of these men *are* constantly learning, and some of them are brilliant talkers and teachers. Still, these are the exceptions.

While we do not think there are many brilliant teachers who never publish, we do think many potentially competent teachers do a conspicuously bad job in the classroom because they know that bad teaching is not penalized in any formal way. They have only a limited amount of time and energy, and they know that in terms of professional standing and personal advancement it makes more sense to throw this into research than teaching. Yet even under these circumstances much can be done. Both good and bad teaching have many varieties. Some bad teaching is the result of inadequate preparation, but some is the result of inadequate perception. Most teachers find it hard to realize how they affect students, and critical supervision can be invaluable here. The sarcastic teacher, for example, may be too insecure to let up even when he considers his effect on his students, but that is not always true; at least he should be forced to think about it. The same is true of other pedagogic styles.

Another danger in judging men by their output is that it puts a premium on a particular kind of research for which there is relatively little need. The feverish competition for talent in the contemporary academic market place puts an enormous premium on judging men young and giving them tenure early. This, in turn, creates a climate in which men feel they must produce early, so that their tenure committee will have something to judge and they will not be left behind. The results, at least in the social sciences and humanities, tend to resemble finger exercises for the piano. Such exercises may be useful preparation for something better, and they may even allow a skilled judge to predict whether the man in question will mature into a star performer. The difficulty is that, having gotten tenure on this basis, many never outgrow this stage. Indeed, many do not even see it as a stage, but assume that such work is intrinsically worth while. As a result, a large proportion of the research published in the disciplines we know best exhibits no genuine concern with answering real questions or solving important problems; it is simply a display of professional narcissism. Instead of recording a struggle with methodological and substantive issues that actually matter to either teachers or students, it is simply a roller coaster ride along a well-worn track.

A man who does research of this kind may at times perform a useful service to his colleagues simply because he collects data somebody else can put to use. But such a man is a menace in the classroom, for he re-enforces the anti-academic prejudices of his students. The problem is especially serious among the best students at the best universities. These are not mostly students who demand flashy lectures by professional showmen or easy answers to recalcitrant questions. But they do insist that there be a visible relationship between knowledge and action, between the questions asked in the classroom and the lives they live outside it. Confronted with pedantry and alienated erudition, they are completely turned off. All too often the job of turning them back on goes by default to critics of higher education who encourage the students to believe that all systematic and disciplined intellectual effort is a waste of time and that moral assurance will suffice not only to establish their superiority over their elders but to solve the problems their elders have so obviously botched.

The "research-teaching" dilemma is, then, a false one. The real problem is to marry the two enterprises. But contrary to a good deal that is written by defenders of the status quo this is precisely what the present system fails to do. Teaching is often adjusted to the exigencies of research, but research is almost never shaped by the experience of teaching. We have almost never encountered a professor, for example, who said he was working on a particular research problem because year after year his undergraduate students showed an interest in it. Involved here is not only the understandable fear of one's own showmanship or of sycophancy toward the young, but actual ignorance of what even the most sensitive undergraduates are interested in. Professors do listen to the questions their already socialized graduate students and postdoctoral fellows raise, but most undergraduate courses are so constructed as to provide almost no feedback directly to the professor. Even if they did, it would seldom occur to a professor that the questions raised by bright yet only half-socialized students might be important enough so that, if the answers were not known, an effort should be made to discover them.

The relationship between graduate and undergraduate teaching is equally unsatisfactory. Many undergraduate courses at large universities are taught by one or two senior faculty and a group of graduate assistants. The issues raised in these courses are—or should be—of fundamental importance to graduate students as well as undergraduates. Yet we know no university where the staff of such courses habitually meets together, discusses the intellectual questions being raised, and initiates research in areas where it would be helpful. (Chicago is the closest approximation.) A serious effort along these lines would probably require constituting the staff of big undergraduate courses as a graduate seminar, having the participants meet weekly to discuss the books they were reading with undergraduates, asking them to prepare seminar papers that would also be delivered as course lectures, and discussing individual lectures given in the course in both substantive and pedagogic terms.

This scheme also suggests a possible device for avoiding incompetent amateurism in teaching and developing pedagogic colleagueship. Staff-taught courses that held regular meetings to discuss the intellectual substance of a course could also discuss and evaluate its effect on the students. A staff is by definition a potential colleague group with common problems, common experience, and perhaps even a common objective. If professors are suffciently secure so that they can elicit and encourage criticism of their performance, and if the graduate students are open enough and interested enough to visit one another's classes, the beginnings of a clinical training program are in hand. These possibilities have been explored on a number of campuses, notably Chicago, and the second author teaches a course at Harvard that tries to achieve this sort of critical perspective on itself. Although there is no quantitative evidence that the staff members of this course are better teachers at the end than the beginning, most of them believe they are.

For one thing, they are encouraged to become more aware of the variety of students they face even in a highly selective college, and this itself is apt to make their teaching more interesting as well as more taxing. Then too, some of the most conscientious come to realize that their tacet hope of reaching every student is an unwarranted demand on both themselves and the students, not all of whom are capable of learning from any particular teacher at a particular moment in their lives. At the same time, staff members seem to become more aware of the often cruel effect they can quite unintentionally have on the more vulnerable students. Since most still think of themselves as inoffensive neophytes, struggling to cope with their own senior professors, the idea that they have power often comes as a shock.

Innovations of this kind are extremely time-consuming and tiring. A course of the sort we have just described, which combined a graduate seminar with an undergraduate course composed partly of lectures and partly of small-group meetings, and in which the staff also made an effort to supervise one another's pedagogic efforts and discuss the effectiveness of books, lectures, and the like, would be virtually a full-time job for all concerned. This does not mean it is impractical: the cost of such a system need be no greater than the present system, and the yield per dollar might be considerably better. But such an effort can be sustained only if the faculty as a whole believes in its importance and has a real conviction that the present less taxing system is failing so badly that it cannot be allowed to continue. Only a minority has had such feelings for the past two generations.

But suppose a cadre of committed faculty and graduate students could be assembled and an effective clinical training program for undergraduate teachers worked out. How should such a program relate to the traditional doctoral program of lectures, seminars, reading courses, comprehensive examinations, and dissertations? Many critics of doctoral programs have argued over the years that, while these programs do an adequate job of research training, a different program is needed to train college teachers, perhaps giving a new degree. Such proposals must grapple with two issues: who would enroll and what would they be taught. On the first score the answer is clear: very few able students would enroll. Only about half of those now taking Ph.D.s take academic jobs. Perhaps half of those who take academic jobs are at universities where research and graduate teaching take as much time as undergraduate work. A program aimed strictly at training undergraduate teachers could thus hope for no more than a quarter of the present doctoral market, plus an indeterminate number of would-be teachers who now drop out of doctoral programs because these do not fit their needs or interests. But even this is optimistic. A teaching doctorate would have less status and attract less talented students than one aimed at training scholars. Its graduates would have difficulty getting good jobs, even in colleges that claim not to be concerned with whether their faculty do research. This would scare away able students interested in teaching, simply because they would not want to settle for a degree that kept many academic doors closed to them. (There is, however, much to be said for awarding a degree to all students who have taken the courses and passed the general examinations for a Ph.D. Such a degree—a Ph.D. without a dissertation—would not be "second-rate," but simply "preliminary." Anyone who held it would be entitled to submit a thesis and receive a Ph.D. if the thesis was acceptable. Those who did not submit a thesis would have evidence of competence that they could use in seeking teaching jobs in community colleges and perhaps elsewhere.)

Even if prospective college teachers could be siphoned out of traditional doctoral programs into special teacher-training alternatives, this would probably be a mistake on intellectual grounds. As already indicated, we think the divorce of teaching and research is bad for both parties. Teachers need at least as much expertise and technical competence as researchers, and almost anything that has a defensible place in a doctoral program for scholars can also be defended in one for teachers. Everyone, for example, bewails the standard doctoral dissertation, constructed with scissors, paste, five or ten pounds of 3×5 cards, a few hundred obliquely relevant citations, and (in some fields) a few hundred tests of statistical significance. This sort of exercise is usually attacked as irrelevant for future teachers and defended as appropriate for future scholars. In most cases, however, it is irrelevant for anyone, no matter what his plans. In the natural sciences, indeed, where the proportion of future researchers is highest and the proportion of future teachers lowest, book-length dissertations are increasingly rare and have been gradually supplanted by shorter journal articles. The same trend ought to be encouraged in the social sciences and the humanities—not on the ground that dissertations are irrelevant for teachers but that make-work is bad for anyone, be he a future Labor Department economist or a future Antioch professor.

The whole spirit of proposals for a separate teaching degree is, indeed, probably self-defeating. No real progress will ever be made as long as teaching is seen as a soft option for those who cannot make it in research. It is, in truth, a hard option for those who find a research career insufficiently challenging or excessively routinized. A teacher needs to know as much as his research colleagues know, and more. He needs the scholarly competence Ph.D. programs claim to develop, but he also needs expertise in working with late adolescents, both in the classroom and outside it. In this context the present pattern of preparing college teachers, far from looking too extended or too rigorous, looks both too hasty and relatively undemanding.

It is often argued, for example, that since men typically earn their Ph.D.s anywhere from six years (in the natural sciences) to ten years (in the humanities) after their B.A., doctoral programs are too long and should be shortened. The typical Ph.D. does not, however, spend anything like this long actually pursuing his degree. To begin with, only half of all doctoral candidates move directly from undergraduate work to doctoral study. The others take jobs, join the army, or begin graduate work in another field before starting a Ph.D. program. The elapsed time between actually starting a Ph.D. and finishing it ranges from 4.5 years in the natural sciences to 6 years in the humanities. But even this is misleading, for doctoral candidates seldom work full time at their studies for this long. They take part-time jobs teaching or doing research, drop out for a year or two to work, and so on. This is especially true of those writing dissertations. When this is taken into account it turns out that the typical doctoral candidate spends the equivalent of between three and four full-time years working on his degree. This is true in all fields except education, where the average is less than three.[1] This is a little more than law, a little less than medicine, and

1. These calculations are taken from Berelson, pp. 156 ff.

hardly seems excessive. To be sure, some doctoral candidates are kept around too long out of compassion or favoritism or indifference to their fate. Other cases of prolongation reflect the decision of individual students, for financial, personal, or intellectual reasons, to mix their doctoral work with other things—though when they delay too long, they often make demands on themselves for a super-dissertation, thus entering a vicious circle.

Under these circumstances it seems to us that the basic problem is not that too much is demanded of Ph.D.s on the scholarly front, but that having met their academic requirements, those who plan to teach get no specific training for this. The need is for an internship and residency program somewhat comparable to those in medicine, which would come *after* the completion of the doctorate. The newly anointed Ph.D. could be inducted into teaching through staff courses and seminars of the kind already described. He would teach undergraduates either at the university where he had just taken his Ph.D. or at another university that offered more attractive conditions. He would be paid a salary comparable to those now offered new Ph.D.s. Such internships would be the pedagogic counterpart of a postdoctoral fellowship for a researcher. If they actually enhanced a man's competence in the classroom, the more student-oriented colleges and universities might eventually begin to make the completion of such an internship a prerequisite to permanent employment as a teacher. The beginnings of such developments can be seen in the Danforth Foundation's Teaching Internships and in the efforts of a few colleges like Monteith [at Wayne State University] to induct novices into interdisciplinary teaching and then send them out as missionaries to other campuses. But here as elsewhere, real progress depends on an institutional commitment from a few leading universities, and this does not seem imminent.

This sort of internship can perhaps best be viewed not as an extension of graduate training but as a modification of the working conditions for assistant professors at leading universities. A number of private universities already hire assistant professors for relatively short periods, with the understanding that many will not get tenure. Even those denied tenure, however, get more visibility than they would at a less prominent institution, and usually find attractive jobs at other places. Under the arrangement we are suggesting, the university would merely assume explicit responsibility for putting these novice teachers through a systematic training program, and would certify their competence (or incompetence) to others when this was done. No university we know now does this, for none collects information on either its graduate assistants or its assistant professors that enables it to make intelligent judgments of their classroom strengths and weaknesses. Nor does any university we know make a systematic effort to supervise beginning teachers or give them help in doing a better job.

A program of this kind would have other virtues. For one thing, the staff courses in which young Ph.D.s became involved would in most instances be for freshmen and sophomores, simply because these are the big courses in which a team approach can be justified economically. These are also the courses most likely to deal with issues of interest to laymen, and therefore most likely to provide a useful counterpoint to the emphasis on professional problems characteristic of doctoral training. Involving a new Ph.D. in faculty-level discussion of these issues, forcing him to prepare papers on them and to accept his colleagues' criticisms, and giving him a sense that other men cared enough to listen to him would encourage young scholars to take such matters seriously.

It could be argued that internships of this sort, however valuable, should not be postponed until men have earned their Ph.D., since by then they may have become irreparably committed to a research career. Instead, an attempt might be made to provide more supervision for teaching assistants still working on their doctorate.[2] Yet if the men involved in a staff course all have their Ph.D.s, it may be easier to create an atmosphere of colleagueship and equality than when one man is a tenured professor and the others are "his" graduate students. If interns have completed their Ph.D.s this also gives them added status in the eyes of undergraduates, many of whom refuse to take graduate assistants seriously and therefore cannot learn anything from even the most competent and dedicated. Perhaps most important of all, the fact that these men have Ph.D.s would make it impossible to exploit them economically, for they would be in a much stronger bargaining position vis-à-vis the universities than most graduate students now are.[3]

2. The most conspicuous efforts to improve doctoral programs in this way have been the Ford Foundation's recent grants to a dozen leading universities for five-year doctoral programs. At least one of these years is to be devoted exclusively to teaching, and the apprentice is supposed to get supervision from senior men. Already established Harvard programs of this sort have, however, done little to develop either faculty or student interest in the technical problems and possibilities of teaching, and have only rarely led to the kind of collaborative teaching we are urging.

3. Any program which involves a large training component is likely to be underpaid relative to the value of the services being rendered, simply because those who are being trained will accept less than the open market value of their services in

Not only would internships of this kind help focus faculty attention on pedagogic problems, but they might even help redirect research energy in somewhat more fruitful directions. The relatively rigid separation between theoretical inquiry and practical experience as ways of learning is considerably harder to maintain in a setting where students and their problems are taken seriously, for close acquaintance with students makes it perfectly clear that they learn in many ways at once. Conversely, if inability to get through to undergraduates were defined as a serious professional problem, the faculty would almost certainly show more interest in the possible pedagogic value of non-academic experience.

---

order to get the training they want. Internships and residencies in leading hospitals, for example, have traditionally paid less than those in mediocre hospitals because doctors knew interning at, say, Johns Hopkins or the Massachusetts General Hospital would bring them more professional prestige and more income later. Something similar can also happen even when no training is actually offered. Harvard's Faculty of Arts and Sciences offers its young Ph.D.s lower salaries than many less prestigious institutions, but it still gets most of the men it wants. To some extent this reflects the young Ph.D.'s feeling that he will learn more and be happier as an assistant professor at Harvard than at, say, CCNY. But it also reflects the fact that his having been an assistant professor at Harvard will open the door to more lucrative and prestigious jobs later. The man is paying, in other words, for certification more than for training. Nonetheless, there is a limit to the amount of income men will forego for such reasons, as leading teaching hospitals have recently begun to discover. Harvard can pay less, but not *much* less. Since research organizations are also bidding for young Ph.D.s, teaching internships could not offer much less than the market rate for such men's services.

4. Academic Intellectuals

LEWIS COSER

The modern university is a huge, sprawling, and multifaceted institution. It is devoted to teaching as well as to research, and it includes academic departments as well as professional schools. Some departments within it may live up to the traditional aim of the scholar, the disinterested pursuit of truth, while others may be only vocational schools in disguise.

Given these many aspects of the modern university, it stands to reason that its personnel is also varied. Most professors hold Ph.D. degrees, but there are obvious differences between a man who teaches Sanskrit and one engaged in research on soil conservation. Not all those holding Ph.D. degrees or all those teaching within a university can be considered intellectuals—not only because the activities and professional involvements of many readily suggest that they have narrow intellectual horizons, but also because they do not define themselves as intellectuals. One study of the self-images of academicians in a variety of fields excluding the natural sciences, engineering, and applied fields, concludes: "Indeed, one of the real surprises, during the course of these interviews, was the rarity of real acceptance of intellectual status. This non-acceptance is revealed in several ways. First, there is the frequency with which this freely offered remark appears: 'Intellectuals, I hate the word!' Second, there are the direct denials to the question, 'Do you consider yourself an intellectual?' . . . A third denial of membership is shown in the efforts that are made to avoid having one's affiliation publicly known".[1] Even people who may be publicly defined as intellectuals may not have corresponding self-definitions. An excellent example is provided by the poet and novelist Randall Jarrell, who says of one of his academic characters, "He had never been what intellectuals consider an intellectual, but other people

1. Melvin Seeman, "The Intellectual and the Language of Minorities," *American Journal of Sociology*, LXIV (July, 1958), No. 1, 25-35.

had thought him one, and he had had to suffer the consequences of their mistake."[2]

In order to account for the heterogeneity in the staff of the modern university, we must first consider the heterogeneity in its structure.

The historical development of the American academy can give us some clues to its present condition. The contemporary university grew from at least two different historical roots, the early college and the modern professional and graduate school. Until roughly the middle of the last century, the American college was mainly a school for training clergymen, lawyers, and gentlemen. It was dominated by theologians, legal scholars, and classicists, united, in most cases, in a common contempt for science and technology, in fact, for anything that might be considered even remotely practical and useful. The men who set the tone in these colleges were considered, and considered themselves, an intellectual elite. Their training was often narrow, and it was circumscribed by often rigid standards of gentility. This narrowness led to estrangement from the social and economic realities of the country at large. But within these confines, the colleges harbored professors who displayed concern with the major values of the society, endeavored to preserve and extend its cultural heritage, and strove to define standards of moral excellence appropriate for gentlemen.

After the Civil War, when industrialization began to make major strides in America, a new type of university emerged. Instruction and research in scientific and technological subjects were required by growing industry, and they began to achieve ascendancy over the traditional academic disciplines. "So," to quote Veblen, "the university of that era unavoidably came to be organized as a more or less comprehensive federation of professional schools or faculties devoted to such branches of practical knowledge as the ruling utilitarian interests of the time demanded."[3] After Johns Hopkins University and the University of Chicago had taken the lead, the major colleges were gradually turned into universities and graduate schools in emulation of the great German universities. They conducted research and offered instruction in many subjects, ranging from the nonutilitarian and scholarly to the near vocational. In the process, the university lost its character as a relatively homogeneous community of like-minded scholars and became a federation of faculties

2. Quoted in *ibid.*, p. 27, from Jarrell's *Pictures from an Institution*, p. 110.
3. Thorstein Veblen, *The Higher Learning in America* (New ed.; New York: Sagamore Press, Inc., 1957), p. 26.

and professional schools staffed by professors of heterogeneous training, background, and cultivation.

Its twin historical roots in a community of genteel scholars and loosely grouped purveyors of professional training help to explain the present diversity within the American academy. Yet historical antecedents cannot fully account for present operation. It is to the present functions of universities that we must now turn.

The University Today

The contemporary American university is a multifunctional organization. First, it provides undergraduate and graduate instruction for rising numbers of students. Between 1939 and 1961, the number of students enrolled in colleges and universities and earning credits toward degrees rose from about 1.3 million to more than 3.9 million. In 1939, college and university enrollments composed about 14% of the population between eighteen and twenty-one years old, while by 1961 that figure was about 38%. The majority of these students are enrolled in undergraduate colleges, but graduate students numbered about 280,000.[4] These enormous numbers of students are offered instruction of great variety in quality as well as in content. For most of them, college education is closely geared to occupational aspirations and achievements. Since the beginning of the century, new units designed to fit students for specific occupations have appeared and have become respectable: schools of journalism, business, librarianship, social work, education, dentistry, nursing, forestry, diplomacy, pharmacy, veterinary surgery, and public administration.[5] The college of liberal arts, on the other hand, attracts those undergraduates who seek education less directly geared to future occupational roles. These colleges allow their students a period before occupational placement, in which more generalized cultural concerns can be cultivated alongside preparation for later professional careers. Most of these colleges, however, tend to be partly high school, partly university, partly general, partly special in character.[6] Finally, advanced instruction is offered in such traditional professional schools as law and medicine, in the newer professional schools, and in the graduate departments

4. *Cf.* Martin Trow, "The Democratization of Higher Education in America," *Archives européennes de sociologie*, III (1962), No. 2, 213-62.

5. Robert M. Hutchins, *The Higher Learning in America* (New Haven: Yale University Press, 1936), pp. 33-4.

6. *Ibid.*, p. 2.

offering M.A. and Ph.D. degrees. Given this variety, it stands to reason that standards and expectations differ widely among the branches of a single university and among similar departments or schools in different universities. Only the foolhardy would venture to assess the general level of instruction in America; in dealing with such widely different types, no useful comparisons can be made. It is, of course, possible to rank American universities in terms of some particular criterion, the number of Ph.D. degrees given, for example, and such rankings have in fact often been attempted.[7] What emerges in such comparisons is the enormous gap between the head and the tail of the academic procession, to use David Riesman's vivid image.[8] To sum up, the American university is at present geared to serve the education of very diverse students. It is therefore highly differentiated functionally, split into a number of segments usually only loosely connected, offering specialized types of instruction that may or may not be geared toward occupational or professional preparation and that differ considerably in quality.

Education, however, is only one of the functions a modern university performs. In addition, the university is the major locale for research. Such research, however, like teaching, differs widely in the various segments of the university. In some, research may be neatly articulated with the requirements of particular occupational or professional fields. In others, the emphasis may be on more general cultural or theoretical pursuits. In some, the pursuit of knowledge for its own sake predominates. To quote Veblen again, "from the first this quest of ideal learning has sought shelter in the universities as the only establishment in which it could find a domicile, even on sufferance, and so could achieve that footing of consecutive intellectual enterprise running through successive generations of scholars which is above all else indispensable to the advancement of knowledge."[9] In other areas, the research carried out has none of the qualities suggested by Veblen. There may be instead concern with the useful arts, from agriculture and forestry to "police science" or dental surgery. The general term "research" covers so many disparate activities that we must conclude, as we did about the educational aspect of the uni-

7. Bernard Berelson, *Graduate Education in the United States* (New York: McGraw-Hill Book Co., Inc., 1960), pp. 124ff.

8. David Riesman, *Constraint and Variety in American Education* (Anchor ed.; Doubleday & Company, Inc., 1958).

9. Veblen, *op. cit.*, p. 27.

versity, that it is vain to venture generalizations. University research today is carried on by many professionals and specialists who seem to have little in common beyond the fact that they all operate within the confines of particular universities.

When an organization is divided into a great number of differentiated parts, a need for co-ordination develops. This need explains the rise of academic bureaucracy. As long as universities were relatively small communities of scholars, they could run their affairs with a minimum of formal structure and needed few specialized administrators. They were institutions in which administrative functions, beyond those vested in the office of the president, were mainly performed by professors on a part-time and rotating basis—a pattern that partly survives in the various colleges of Oxbridge. Modern American universities, however, have reached a size, both in student enrollment and research operation, that precludes the possibility of self-administration by professors. Hence the rise of a huge academic bureaucracy made up of deans, registrars, bursars, research administrators, and the like. All these men are not directly involved in the main activities of the university, teaching and research, yet these activities could not be pursued if nobody were in charge of the administrative problems that large-scale organization naturally brings in its wake.

The power that administrators have attained in the modern university by the simple fact of their indispensability has naturally led to tensions between them and the faculty. Much of the history of modern academic institutions could be written in terms of such tensions. In particular, administrators are naturally intent on reducing the sprawling diversity of the university by imposing a minimum of patterned uniformity on the whole enterprise. They attempt to introduce tables of organization and well defined channels of authority and communication to combat what may seem to them at times the chaotic laissez-faire of the academician. The faculty, on the other hand, may feel that routinization and bureaucratization reduce its scholarly prerogatives and academic license. Thorstein Veblen's The Higher Learning in America, though written a half-century ago, remains the classic statement of the scholar's case against the "captains of erudition": "In order to their best efficiency, and indeed in the degree in which efficiency in this field of activity is to be attained at all, the executive officers of the university must stand in the relation of assistants serving the needs and catering to the idiosyncrasies of the body of scholars and scientists that make up the university; in the degree in which the converse relation is allowed to take effect, the unavoidable consequence is wasteful defeat. A free hand is the first and abiding requisite of scholarly and scientific work."[10]

The University as a Setting for Intellectuals

In the earlier type of college, intellectuals had pre-eminence and constituted the major body of teachers and scholars. But in the modern academy they do not. Today intellectuals may play a role within the university, they may benefit from affiliation with it, but they can no longer *be* the university.

Although the modern university has assumed a variety of tasks that call for unintellectual personnel, it remains, despite certain countertrends about which more will be said later, the most favorable institutional setting for American intellectuals today, for several reasons:

1. It provides a *milieu* in which men sharing a common concern with the untrammeled pursuit of knowledge can communicate with one another and thus sharpen their minds in continuous interchange.

2. It affords its professors regular remuneration, which, although far below that prevalent in a number of nonacademic professions, allows them a middle-class life style.

3. It provides security of tenure for senior academicians. This point and the last one together account for the fact that the academician is institutionally protected from the vagaries of the market place so that he can devote himself to his work without being distracted by economic pressures.

4. It has institutionalized the time allocation of academicians in such a way that they can devote a major part of their working time to independent thought and autonomous research.

5. Finally, and most important, it grants academic freedom to its members.

The freedom of speech, opinion, and publication claimed by the university professor is no different in principle from that claimed by other men in liberal society. The issue of academic freedom arises mainly from the fact that the academician is also a salaried employee who claims the license to disagree in his teaching and writing with the views of those who provide or administer the funds from which he

10. *Ibid.*, p. 63.

is paid. Arthur O. Lovejoy put it neatly: "The principle of academic freedom asserts . . . that those who buy a certain service may not (in the most important particular) prescribe the nature of the service to be rendered."[11] Claims of this sort depart widely from the mores of a society based on the ethos of business. It is therefore hardly surprising that the American university, after it had successfully freed itself from clerical domination, found it difficult to impress on trustees, regents, and other representatives of fund-granting institutions, that he who paid the piper was not expected to call the tune. That the major American universities—though by no means all the minor or "middling" colleges and universities—have succeeded in imposing this principle is the foremost reason why they continue to be strongholds of intellectual activity. By and large, members of the academic professions have won freedom from outside control by successfully asserting the claim that their socially indispensable tasks cannot properly be carried out if their performance is dictated or controlled by those who pay for it.

Expectations concerning such matters as academic freedom, remuneration, tenure, teaching loads, and the like are not always met in all academic settings. But, more important, and quite independent from such departures from institutionalized expectations, there are a number of built-in countertrends within the very structure of the modern university that make it a somewhat less favorable environment for intellectual activity than its ideal image would lead one to expect. Such countertrends have not yet subverted other major forces operating within the academy, but they have often deflected them. It is to an examination of these countertrends that we must now turn.

Career Pressures and the Departmentalization of Knowledge

The career of the academician typically proceeds by a series of slow steps through the ranks up the academic ladder. This process may be an impediment to the achievement of intellectual excellence because the requirements for academic advancement and the optimal conditions for the advancement of knowledge do not necessarily coincide. It has been pointed out, for example, that Kant would probably not have achieved professorial rank in a modern university, for he published nothing of consequence until he was fifty-seven. There is a built-in pressure on the young academician to publish. In other words, uni-

11. Arthur O. Lovejoy, "Academic Freedom," *Encyclopedia of the Social Sciences*, I (New York: The Macmillan Company, 1942), 384-7.

versities have institutionalized a graded system of advancement for professors in which each successive promotion is forthcoming only after a satisfactory publication record is achieved. The aspiring academician may be deflected from planning a large-scale intellectual undertaking that may take years to mature, in order to publish narrower contributions that can be of more direct use in the advancement of his career. As Logan Wilson says, "Distinterested activity and the slow ripening of long-term projects become well-nigh impossible as situational pressures call for quick results."[12]

Pressures from the requirements of academic promotion are not the only ones that may detract the scholar from pursuing broad-gauged intellectual undertakings. The modern academy is divided into a number of departments corresponding to scholarly disciplines and professional training centers. As the fields represented in these departments develop and as the departments grow, departmental boundaries tend to become rigid and to discourage intellectual curiosity beyond the administratively defined departmental settings. Lip service may be paid to "cross-fertilization," but in actual fact young scholars are generally advised to stay within the boundaries of the "field." In addition, as a particular academic field becomes professionalized, those active within it are expected to take their colleagues in the profession, as well as their professional clients, as their main reference groups. This expectation contributes further to the weakening of ties to the academy as a whole and to a tendency to eschew those intellectual undertakings that might cross departmental boundaries and not fit into the framework of the profession.

Expectations of colleagues and superiors within his department exert pressure upon the junior incumbent to play by the rules of the academic game. These rules require, among other things, intellectual discipline, the observance of fixed standards of scholarship, attention to the contributions of senior men, and, above all, respect for the boundaries of the various specialized fields. Those who attempt to create *ab ovo* are likely to be considered "unreliable" "outsiders" to be mistrusted.[13] Such an emphasis discourages potential generalizers, and young scholars may well feel that safety lies in involvement with

12. Logan Wilson, The Academic Man (New York: Oxford University Press, Inc., 1942), p. 219. This volume, though somewhat dated, remains the major sociological study in this area.

13. Cf. my more detailed comments on this point in Lewis A. Coser, "Georg Simmel's Style of Work: A Contribution to the Sociology of the Sociologist," American Journal of Sociology, LXIII (May, 1958), No. 6, pp. 635-40.

narrow problems rather than with broad questions. What is at issue is not the necessary drift toward a measure of specialization that the rapid accumulation of knowledge in all fields has called forth but rather an additional source of professionalization that arises, not from the inherent development of knowledge, but from the specific organizational framework of the modern university.

Time Pressures

Ideally the university affords its professors an environment in which only a fraction of their time is directly committed; a maximum of it remains institutionally unallocated and at their free disposal. Yet this ideal state, which was perhaps approximated in the leisurely styles of the eighteenth-century college, hardly prevails today. Not only have the demands of mass education, combined with the peculiarly American form of instruction through lecturing, led to an obligation to teach many more hours than is customary in European universities, for example, but the typical American professor is also involved with various types of committee work that require considerable chunks of his time.

Precisely because the modern university is no longer a community of scholars but a huge and heterogeneous assemblage of different schools, it requires large-scale efforts of administrative adjustment and regulation. If academicians are unwilling to let themselves be entirely regulated by professional administrators, they are forced to relinquish large parts of their own "free" time for administrative tasks. We face here an interesting paradox: The very effort among academic men to prevent the academy from becoming too highly bureaucratized leads them to engage in activities that necessarily distract them from those scholarly tasks that the academy is supposed to foster and protect.

Sheer scarcity of time may be a very serious impediment to intellectual activities in the modern university. In addition, alleged scarcity of time may be a kind of defense mechanism available to those academicians who wish to hide lack of scholarly productivity behind a respectable cloak. Anyone familiar with modern academic life knows of the well-nigh universal complaint among academicians about lack of time. But a great deal of familiarity with the case at hand is required in order to know whether or not those who complain actually are pressed for time or whether or not they involve themselves in time-consuming administrative tasks in order to distract attention from their sterility. The academy provides mechanisms that can be used for an institutionalized evasion of the academic norms of scholarly productivity. More generally, to the extent that the academy permits an allocation of the scarce time resources of its members in ways unconducive to intellectual activity, it hinders the intellectual vocation within its confines.

Skill Versus Cultivation

In the nineteenth century, it was generally held that the university had functions other than those of inculcating specific skills. J. H. Newman may have provided a somewhat idealized picture in his *On the Scope and Nature of University Education:* "The culture of the intellect is a good in itself and its own end . . . As the body may be sacrificed to some manual or other toil . . . so may the intellect be devoted to some specific profession; and I do not call *this* the culture of the intellect . . ."[14] In actual fact, the nineteenth-century university did not fully live up to these high demands. But most cultivated opinion would at least have agreed with Newman's ideal. That is not true of contemporary America. In fact, an influential group of educators and academic decision-makers has now publicized the opinion that the university ought in fact to be nothing but a training ground for marketable skills and for the absorption of professional norms, beside being a locale for specialized research. Bernard Berelson, the author of a recent and influential study, *Graduate Education in the United States,* puts the matter with commendable frankness: "The graduate school should aim at training the skilled specialist—not . . . at producing the 'educated man,' the 'cultured man,' the 'wise man' (nor, for that matter, the 'mere technician,' either)."[15]

The reason for the shift in emphasis from cultivation to skill that Berelson represents, even while he aims to accentuate it, must be sought both inside the academy and outside. The increase in college and graduate-school enrollments has produced a student population qualitatively different from that of the nineteenth-century academy. An earlier student population may have gone to the university mainly in quest of genteel cultivation and the acquisition of gentlemanly graces, while a minority acquired broad skills in such professional fields as law, theology, and medicine. In contrast, the majority of

14. J. H. Newman, *On the Scope and Nature of University Education* (New York: E. P. Dutton & Co., Inc., 1915), p. 255.
15. Berelson, *op. cit.,* p. 222.

present-day students goes to colleges and universities in order to acquire much wider ranges of diversified skills. No longer does only a small elite of wealth or of intelligence go to college and even graduate school; as indicated earlier, nearly 40% of the population between eighteen and twenty-one years old is now enrolled. Under this mass demand for higher degrees, both college and graduate school have increased enormously, and they have moved further in the direction of the kinds of specialization their students require. The demand for specialized training on the part of the majority of the student audience has accentuated more general trends toward the specialization of knowledge.

The shaping of the university by the demands of its student population is only a part of the story. External demands have also had a major part in the type of instruction offered. Berelson[16] specifies this point for the graduate school: The largest market for graduate students will not longer be college teaching, as it has been in the past. Only 20% of successful recent Ph.D. candidates have gone into undergraduate teaching in liberal arts colleges. The demands of industry and the government for Ph.D. holders have been increasing very rapidly. These "users" of academic products, however, want skilled specialists rather than cultivated generalists, and they therefore exercise pressures toward greater specialization paralleling those coming from vocationally oriented students.

The academy, though it is partially shielded from its surrounding social and economic environment, can hardly escape its influence. Although it may resist or lag behind the demands of society at large, it cannot fail to respond in some measure. And as it does so, it inevitably moves further in the shift from cultivation to the inculcation of usable skills. And the services it provides inevitably contribute to a certain reshaping in the roles of academicians; many of them are bound to become retailers of useful knowledge rather than producers of ideas.

The Consultant Role of Academic Men

The increasing recognition granted to academic men by decisionmakers in business and government has had unanticipated consequences within the academy, consequences that may also decrease the chances for intellectuals within it. No longer do most professors lead

16. *Ibid.*

lives sheltered behind academic walls. Many are now consultants to industry and the government, and their advice is eagerly sought by powerful decision-makers. Of course, in many branches of study—literature, history, the classics—professors have been unable to assume such extra-academic roles, but these roles have become almost routine in the natural and social sciences. As a consequence, many academicians have been able to widen their horizons and to shed a certain academic parochialism that clung to scholars of an earlier age. But those academicians who now move among decision-makers in the world of affairs have also acquired a new public, which affects their previous self-image.

The traditional audience of the scholar was found in the community of scholars. The sense of identity of the traditional man of knowledge was largely shaped through the rewards that recognition and esteem among his peers would bring him. But once a scholar acquires a new extra-academic audience, he is subject to new influences that reshape his self-image. When recognition is bestowed by extra-academic men whose problems the academician has helped solve, a tendency may arise for the academician to seek recognition less from his peers than from decision-makers who are able to reward him. As academicians are in increasing demand for the solution of problems in both private and business bureaucracies, they tend to be deflected from the pursuit of more general or theoretical problems for which there is no demand outside the academy. The fact that academicians are now being sought by industry and government to a greater extent than ever before accounts, at least in part, for their rising prestige in the community at large. When the academy can furnish so many men who can give advice on practical matters, the negative stereotype of the "impractical professor" tends to decline. Yet this greater acceptance of "practical professors" should not be mistaken for a general decline in anti-intellectualism in America. It is mainly those men of knowledge who have become more like the managers for whom they provide services that are now welcome and accepted in the community at large; those scholars who have eschewed extra-academic roles have not profited, nor can they be expected to profit, from such reappraisal of their worth among the decision-makers and the public.

In later chapters, we shall return to this problem in the context of the natural sciences and of the general public roles of intellectuals. Here we need note only the fact that the involvement of modern academicians with decision-makers in public and private organizations, while often broadening in its impact, has also led to increasing concern with applied problems and has therefore prevented certain academicians from turning to larger intellectual tasks.

Research Entrepreneurship

In most academic fields outside the natural sciences, the dominant pattern of academic work in the past has been that of the researcher-writing-a-book-from-library-sources. But with the increasing complexity of research in the social sciences and even sometimes in the humanities, with the refinement of method and the attendant growth of necessary apparatus, researchers have found it more and more difficult to do their work without considerable outside aid. This necessity has led to the growth of research institutes within the academy and to the development of university research teams made up of professors, junior assistants, and auxiliary personnel.

The restriction of intellectual horizons and the fragmentation of research tasks that programed research entail will be discussed in detail in the next chapter. Here we need only note two additional impediments to intellectual growth that such programed research may bring in its wake. Insofar as senior members serving as research entrepreneurs are concerned, we may notice a significant diversion of their efforts from scholarly to administrative and fund-raising activities. Warren Bennis describes the problem: "[The new social scientist] cannot engage in successful research operations in the pristine isolation of his chambers . . . He has to interview subjects and 'establish rapport.' . . . Over thirty per cent of his day is spent in administrative tasks such as interviewing personnel; attending staff meetings and seminars; preparing speeches, consulting; meeting with important experts in his field . . . corresponding with colleagues, sponsors, and users of research. Much time is spent preparing research proposals for the Foundation. Here the research man has to balance budgets . . . choose personnel, and come up with a financial request."[17] A research entrepreneur so engaged will hardly be able to turn his full intellectual energies to the work at hand.

It might be objected that those who have chosen to play the new role of research entrepreneur are hardly predisposed to intellectual

17. Warren G. Bennis, "The Social Scientist as Research Entrepreneur: A Case Study," *Social Problems*, III, No. 1, 44-9. See also Bennis, "Some Barriers to Team Work in Social Research," *Social Problems*, III, No. 4, 223-35.

tasks in the first place. Yet anyone familiar with the current academic scene will not find it hard to name a number of instances in which men whose earlier contributions showed great intellectual promise failed to continue producing work of major importance once they became involved in directing research teams or institutes.

The possible negative effects of such research enterprises on the production of ideas of wider scope is perhaps more pronounced among junior academicians than among senior research leaders. The young scholar is unlikely to have much access to research funds of his own and is therefore generally forced to attach himself to a "collaborative" project headed by a senior member who has access to fund-granting institutions. As a result, he is likely, in the formative years of his career, to work on projects defined by others. That is, just at the stage of his career when a young scholar might be expected to "bubble over with ideas," he is constrained to fetter his creativity in order to fit into someone else's project. (By the time the young man has grown to head a project himself, the likelihood is great that he will be so absorbed in administrative tasks that he cannot fully devote himself to creative intellectual work.)

One of the traditional virtues of academic employment has been, as we have seen, the security it affords. But matters are different in research institutes. Here all but the top personnel, who hold full university appointments, suffer from chronic uncertainty, for each project is dependent on foundation or other support that may or may not be forthcoming next year. Bennis describes this uncertainty vividly: "The Development project was threatened by the yearly scrutiny of the Foundation, and consequently, an annual bout with uncertainty. For the past two years the Foundation has not announced the grant until the end of May . . . the Development personnel see the Foundation as a towering overshadowing Moloch. Each year, during the past two years, with growing intensity from January to May, the payoff question raised by the Development personnel has been, 'will the funds come through?' "[18] One cannot help but feel that little work of intellectual stature on either senior or junior level is likely to be produced under the shadow of Moloch.

Not all research groups and institutions work in the extreme conditions of insecurity described by Bennis. But, in general, as the academician becomes a man with a staff and overhead, he faces pres-

18. *Ibid.*

sures that, at least in many cases, stultify his own intellectual capacities, as well as those of his staff.[19] The dilemma seems inescapable: Much scholarly work nowadays requires sustained support from outside foundations and organization within bureaucratic settings, yet the very means of research may so affect the results and the practitioners that significant intellectual work is frustrated rather than sustained. A variant of Parkinson's Law seems to operate here: Research paraphernalia, routines, and overhead expand to use the funds available for the completion of the research. But too often, the more research there is, the less intellectual product.

Bureaucratic Impediments

A few years ago, Jacques Barzun, the Provost of Columbia University, asked, "Why has the American college and university so little connection with intellect?"[20] His question was no doubt meant as rhetorical overstatement, but is nevertheless relevant. I have already identified some potentials for anti-intellectualism in academic career requirements: time allocation, academic specialization, and the demand of the "users" of academic products for men with specialized skills rather than generalized cultivation. Still another source of pressure is located in academic bureaucratization itself. The vast internal bureaucratic apparatus of deans, directors, registrars, of administrators of the most variegated kind, today exercises a type of control over faculties that is quite different from that wielded by trustees and those "captains of erudition" with whom Veblen was familiar. They are not intent, in the vast majority of cases, upon restricting the expression of unpopular opinion within the university. But committed to a bureaucratic outlook on life, an outlook in which primary emphasis is given to smooth operation and in which the minimization of organizational friction is seen as a main task, academic administrators quite naturally distrust "trouble makers" who might upset the routines. It is not that they love academic freedom less than their colleagues on the faculty; it is that they love efficient operation more.

The internal operation of the academic bureaucracy is not the only issue to be considered here. Academic administrators are now part of

19. *Cf.* C. Wright Mills, *White Collar* (New York: Oxford University Press, Inc., 1951), pp. 131-6.
20. Jacques Barzun, "Foreword," Theodore Caplow and Reece J. McGee, *The Academic Marketplace* (New York: Basic Books, Inc., 1958). This fine volume on the career patterns and working conditions of academic men has been valuable to me, although I have not dealt directly with these topics here.

a much wider web of power and influence that links them with their fellows in fund-granting institutions, whether public or private. In our days, no university has an independent budget sufficient to provide the necessary money. Institutional funds must be supplemented from the outside. And the administrators of foundation and government grants are likely to have criteria for the choice of recipients to match those of their colleagues within the academy. They too are likely to distrust not unconventionality *per se*—in fact they have been known even to seek out an occasional "odd ball"—but those unconventional men who cannot be fitted into organizational plans of research teams or who do not stay within neatly circumscribed academic niches. We may therefore witness within the academy a selective process operating by means, as it were, of a series of close-meshed sieves through which the faculty is passed. Gradually the usable particles are separated from the coarser ones—and the latter are generally shunted to the sidelines.

Sixty years ago William James could proudly say at a Harvard Commencement Dinner, "Our undisciplinables are our proudest product."[21] It is no longer so—not because modern administrators possess vices from which earlier administrators were exempt but rather because the older pattern in a few elite universities could permit "undisciplinables" a freedom that has been much more difficult to grant in a highly bureaucraticized organization. In the modern, intricately organized university, men not fitted into tables of organization might create long-range administrative havoc far beyond their immediate and direct impact.

To be sure, modern universities have their share of "undisciplinable" intellectuals. Yet many observers have pointed out that, over the years, the denizens of faculty clubs, even in major universities, have tended to look more and more like the men one encounters in the executive cafeterias of major corporations. Kenneth Burke's memorable maxim—"People may be unfitted by being fit in an unfit fitness"[22]—seems to apply to the case at hand. The selection criteria typically applied by administrators and other bureaucratic officials contribute to the predominance of an academic type that, while admirably fitted into departmental tables of organization, may not be

21. William James, "The True Harvard," *Memories and Studies* (New York: Longmans, Green & Co., Ltd., 1911), p. 355.
22. Kenneth Burke, *Permanence and Change* (New York: The New Republic, 1936), p. 18.

so fitted for creative scholarly tasks. The means of academic administration may be in danger of subverting the ends of the academy.

An unusually reflective participant-observer of the academic scene, Charles H. Cooley, once made an observation on the "genius on the faculty" that sums up much of what I have been trying to say, even though it was written in the Twenties when many of these developments were only beginning to appear. "It is strange that we have so few men of genius on our faculties; we are always trying to get them. Of course they must have undergone the regular academic training (say ten years in graduate study and subordinate positions) and be gentlemanly, dependable, pleasant to live with, and not apt to make trouble by urging eccentric ideas. Institutions and genius are in the nature of things antithetical, and if a man of genius is found in a university it is peculiarly creditable to both."[23] Not all intellectuals are geniuses, of course, yet what Cooley said applies to them too, to some extent. Although the university is theoretically the ideal environment for the intellectual, its institutionalized practices too often operate in such a way that the intellectual vocation within the academy is fraught with perils.

Prospects

The picture of the academy that has gradually emerged from this review of trends and countertrends within it departs markedly from the picture that exclusive preoccupation with widely held ideals and generalized expectations about universities would suggest. "Academic organization is ideally expressed in the free association of equals, yet everywhere there is a hierarchical arrangement, in which independence is limited by the delegation of functions."[24] Ideally, the university is a community of equals but in fact it may be only a loosely federated group of scholars, vocationally oriented teachers, and men concerned with practical arts. Ideally, it said [sic] to cultivate broadness, but practically it often cultivates narrow specialization. Ideally, it is devoted to disinterested scholarship, but practically it may often succumb to a variety of interests. Even its academic freedom, its greatest achievement, may degenerate through disuse into the mere freedom to be academic, to use Paul Goodman's phrase.[25] Despite all these flaws, the

23. Charles H. Cooley, *Life and the Student* (New York: Alfred A. Knopf, Inc., 1927), p. 184.
24. Wilson, *op. cit.*, p. 218.
25. Paul Goodman, "The Freedom To Be Academic," *Growing Up Absurd* (Vintage ed.; New York: Random House, Inc., 1962), pp. 256-79.

university remains today and is likely to remain in the future the major locale for intellect. There are two main reasons why: recognition of academic freedom by the society at large and the institutionalized removal of the academic man from the pressures of the market place.

The academician enjoys an unusual degree of freedom because, unlike most men, he receives a guaranteed salary that is not tied to the offering of particular products on the market. Or, to put the matter somewhat differently, the salary for his teaching furnishes the economic foundation for his free research and general scholarship.[26] Similarly, academic men are assured, in principle, freedom to pursue their scholarly tasks without regard for the opinions and desires of those who provide their funds. These twin rights, even though they may often be infringed in practice, make the academy a privileged locale for intellectuals. No doubt, in the future as in the past, many creative intellectuals will continue to make their contributions outside the academy. Comte, Marx, Darwin, Nietzsche, Kierkegaard, Freud—those giants who shaped the modern mind—were not academic men, and upon occasion they would all pour scorn upon the academy and make fun of academic men. Yet their own achievements would hardly have been feasible had they not been able to stand on the shoulders of many others who did find in the academy the environment in which their talents could be sheltered and fostered. Genius may upon occasion transcend the limitations and do without the protection of institutional orders, but ordinary intellectuals, like ordinary men, need sustaining institutions. The academy is likely to continue as such an institution in the future. As long as free universities exist, the chances for intellect remain open.

26. *Cf.* Theodor Geiger, *Aufgaben und Stellung der Intelligenz in der Gesellschaft* (Stuttgart: Enke Verlag, 1949), p. 109.

III

WORK AS INCOME:
GETTING AND HOLDING THE JOB

Educational background, previous employment record, and publications serve to sift and sort prospective candidates for faculty positions into jobs of commensurate income and prestige. Faculty recruitment, as Caplow and McGee noted in The Academic Marketplace *(1958), in theory is open, but in practice it tends to be closed. The criteria for employment are most often personal repute and publication, with the former largely derived from the latter. (However, educational background, that is, prestige of doctorate, has been shown to be more important than publication record for hiring at the "top twenty" academic institutions.[1]) Not only is the hiring department interested in the candidate's own potential contribution per se, but often in his prestige potential for attracting future candidates. In the essay included here, Barzun describes several aspects of academic training, recruitment, and mobility in the late sixties, noting shifts in emphasis from earlier years.*

Once hired, an important component of the total "life insurance" policy for many, perhaps most, academics is tenure. However, Nisbet argues that tenure should not be considered as the privilege of, or reward for, an individual. Rather, it should be evaluated in the light of its contribution to the university. Although tenure may once have been a defensible system of privilege because of the occupational limitations of academics, the university need no longer guarantee its faithful employees lifetime job security. Overall, the academic has as many job alternatives as anyone else in the labor force, and probably more than most workers. Moreover, Nisbet contends, tenure has

1. Diana Crane, "The Academic Marketplace Revisited: A Study of Faculty Mobility Using The Cartter Ratings." *American Journal of Sociology* 75 (May, 1970), pp. 953-964.

*doubtful relevance for academic freedom; indeed, tenure provides a
disservice to the university by interfering with a retention system
based on merit alone.*

*But how is merit to be judged? Hexter explores the various criteria
of academic performance. After a quarter century of experience, Hexter
himself is uncertain of his own teaching ability. Clearly, certain professors are effective in particular situations and not in others. Different
students desire different qualities in their teachers. But teaching ability
as a criterion of academic performance, Hexter concludes, seems impossible to operationalize. In contrast, publication has evaluational
merits that are fairly reliable and objective. Publishing, argues Hexter,
is teaching and on a much greater scale than simply classroom contact, because an increasing proportion of formal education, and nearly
all informal education, comes from reading books and articles. Furthermore, Hexter surmises (as did Jencks and Riesman in the previous
section), the best teachers probably do research and write in the first
place, and there is no proof that those who do not write are spending
their time preparing lectures. The challenge Hexter thus extends is
that large universities can benefit by dismissing faculty who have not
taught by publishing and who promise nothing. Hexter's comments,
however, have limited application to professors at many smaller colleges, where heavy teaching loads and committee assignments often
preclude any possibility of engaging in publishable scholarship.*

*Hexter argues that publication is necessary in order to avoid aca-
demic stagnation; Wolfe suggests that stagnancy increasingly can be
expected of college faculties, but for reasons other than professorial
nonpublication. Because an expanding number of Ph.D's is emerging from the graduate schools concurrent with a national economy
drive affecting higher education, there now exists an academic labor
surplus in most disciplines. The consequences of this surplus for colleges and universities may prove disastrous, for, Wolfe writes, faculty
and prospective faculty must now be careful to appear "safe," specifically in their general behavior, political attitudes, and teaching methods,
thus eliminating a source of potentially creative tension. Others besides the real or imagined faculty radicals are affected by this surplus;
the job security of even the most conventional junior faculty members and, in particular, of women, traditional targets of discrimination in the academic world, is being eroded.[2] With the well-educated*

2. The declining status of professional women, including college teachers, is
documented in Cynthia F. Epstein, "Encountering The Male Establishment: Sex-Status

joining the ranks of America's unemployed, more than simply the colleges and universities, Wolfe suggests, are likely to feel the effects of the academic surplus. Clearly, Wolfe's judgments do not agree with those of Nisbet concerning job alternatives for unemployable teachers.

Limits on Women's Careers in the Professions. *"American Journal of Sociology* 75 (May, 1970), pp. 965-982.

5. Scholars in Orbit

JACQUES BARZUN

The Faculty: Its Provenance and Promotion

After an imaginary tour of the new university and a reading of the daily papers, there is no mystery in what professors do and where they go; but where do they come from? Who are these people? How does one get to be full professor at Harvard, Princeton, Columbia, so as to qualify for Washington, Karachi, and the front page of the *New York Times*? The simplest answer is to describe appointment procedures. They tell us what merit consists of, merit once defined influences the direction that talent and young ambition take, and the outcome exemplifies the modern idea of the university.

Professors are made from graduate students—graduates in arts and science or in the several professions that are taught in university schools. Graduate students come out of colleges, where the later professions and specialities are anticipated by appropriate courses, early "research," and a more or less elaborate system of student advising. The new university is of course strong on professional training, but the main theater of its recent upheaval has been to so-called nonprofessional sector, the forty to sixty departments of instruction covering the arts and sciences—English, Chemistry, History, Mathematics, and the like.

In these departments the road to a professorship opens with a student's indicating that he "intends to go into teaching." This is the standard phrase and it may be true. On learning of this purpose, one of the young man's instructors may appoint him his research assistant—to fetch books from the library and verify footnotes. Or, without this preliminary, the beginner may be given a section of an elementary course to teach. At Columbia, no such teaching appointment is allowed until the candidate has passed his oral examinations in subject matter, halfway to the Ph.D.[1] Elsewhere, first-year graduate

---

1. But laboratory assistants in the sciences are first- or second-year graduate students.

students are sometimes relied upon for all "section work" in freshman courses. But the choice among candidates is based largely on the capacity to do research. The presumption holds that anyone who possesses certified knowledge and is not a deaf-mute can teach. No formal attempt is made to impart to the novice any notions of lecturing, examining, grading, or conducting a discussion group.[2]

College and university teaching is thus the only profession (except the proverbially oldest in the world) for which no training is given or required. It is supposed to be "picked up." But it is only fair to add that many who start are eliminated by the end of their first year. Though teaching is hard to test, their inadequacy somehow gets to be known: their student victims or their young colleagues talk. For those who survive a trial appointment, the next step is to "get on with the dissertation"—an easy resolve hard to act on: teaching three courses each term makes writing a book a heavy task.[3] Yet it must be done and an examination passed upon it within a specified time, usually seven years from the beginning of graduate work; that is, some three or four years after the end of course-taking and preparing the subject orals.

Fortunately, the old monumental, life-sentence, eiderdown-quilt dissertation, which I described and deplored in *Teacher in America*, is receding into the past. Most departments approve only manageable topics and set limits to the number of pages that may be catapulted at a sponsor. The change has come partly in response to repeated urgings by graduate deans[4] and partly in self-defense: the sponsor is swamped; he needs a pitchfork to turn over the papers on his desk, and he therefore views with a lackluster eye the student who has chosen to tell all in twelve hundred typed pages.

The dissertation over, the graduate-student-instructor turns over-

2. In some universities, such as Harvard, an elective course in teaching problems and methods is offered to graduate students who are intending teachers. When that Harvard course recently attained a registration of 100, there was much rejoicing over the triumph. That peak number amounted to 1 in 18 graduate students. At most other universities such a course would be considered superfluous. Accordingly, some graduate professors take occasion to give their students, in passing, a few tips about teaching.

3. Hence the introduction at Columbia of the grade of preceptor, charged with a two-thirds load and supposedly overseen by an older colleague who encourages the production of the thesis. Not all departments like preceptors: they want whole men, for administrative convenience. But then they are also surprised and sorry when the full-time instructor "doesn't get on with his book."

4. See Appendix D, Nos. 39, 44, 55, 57, 68, and 69.

night into an assistant professor, with an increase in salary of possibly $1,000 or $1,500. The great change from as recently as ten years ago is that the beginning grade of instructor hardly counts; it is regularly by-passed. The shortage of able men is acute, and anyone completing the Ph.D. at one university and invited by another now goes there as an assistant professor from the outset, instead of ripening several years as instructor.[5]

Seeking the Rare Bird

The next hurdle in the path is the ad hoc committee that determines tenure, ordinarily linked with the rank of associate professor. The procedure varies at different universities, but all the self-respecting ones go through a fixed series of steps. When a vacancy, natural or contrived, occurs in the tenure ranks of a department, the chairman names a search committee, which is charged with surveying the cosmos for the best possible candidate. That committee reports its findings to the executive committee of the department (i.e., the tenure members), which names a first choice, followed by one or more alternatives. The list may include the assistant professors already in the institution. The chairman then goes to the dean for reassurance that the empty salary line will be kept in the next year's budget or augmented to meet rising rates.

If the departmental choice is the man on home ground, the promotion ordinarily lifts him to the lower level of the scale set for associate professors. If the choice is for an outside man, or if the home product is being bid for by another university (or government or industry), the dean is asked not for a fixed salary but for a bargaining range. Bargaining goes on not only about salary but also about teaching load, fringe benefits, and possibly special perquisites, such as extra leaves, research assistance, laboratory space and equipment, or an allocation to the university library for the purchase of books at the incumbent's pleasure. With outsiders the dickering is often viva voce, each party desiring to take a good look at the other. When the hunted man is an undoubted catch in this matrimonial market, the passionate offer may be made by the chairman in person at the pursued's own university. Or, again, the president of the suitor institution may invite the man and his wife for a few days' visit, preferably at the presidential house.

---

5. "Instructor" is both a rank and a generic term designating anyone who teaches in the university. "My instructor" may well mean "my professor." Similarly, "officer of instruction" applies to anyone entrusted with teaching duties, regardless of rank.

The headiest form of flattery so far devised is to receive as the opening bow-and-scrape a letter from the president *handwritten*. It implies: "We love you! We mean it!"

This courtship must be kept in mind if one is to understand the workings of the ad hoc committee which is the gateway to tenure professorships, as has been said. Not all candidacies, of course, call forth the full deployment of lures and bribes. The more common ones take the form of an inquiry from the chairman to find out whether the scholar would move from his present post. This starts a conversation that may take most of an academic year. When the original plan is not realizable on any customary terms, it is because the brilliant scholar has just done something spectacular and is being bid for by two, three, or even five great universities simultaneously. The etiquette then gets complicated and the terms flamboyant. Feelings get hurt if reponses are not candid or prompt, but no one is shocked if the scholar asks for the moon.

A very usual demand is to have the wooing university also offer positions to one or two of the man's protégés. They then move in a team—a "package deal." The justification is that they are jointly engaged in some important research, or else that the senior man, a great specialist, "needs somebody to talk to." An algebraic topologist, for example, would expect to wither if he were alone of his kind in a mathematics department. The modern university needs—or at any rate the modern scholar wants—clusters of talent. Genius itself no longer wants to be *sui generis*.

Equally common is a type of offer which seems to imply exactly the opposite principle, and which has caused much criticism within the university and outside. I mean the offer of a professorship without teaching or other duties.[6] "Come to us and grace our campus." In practice this usually means "grace our catalogue," for the only reason why anybody should accept such an offer is to give all his time to research, and specialized research can hardly invigorate an institution or a department. The eminent but solitary scholar goes abroad or hides

6. To cite a pair of examples: "We will pay you $10,000 more than your present salary. You need not teach. You will have $12,000 for research assistants and books. You may be away from the campus every third term. If you do want to teach, you will receive additional compensation at the rate of $1,000 for each semester course."

Or again: "Your salary will be $32,000 (an increase of $11,000). You can order the library to buy all the materials you want, for we are building it up from scratch. Your own research account can in addition be drawn on up to $30,000 a year. We should like you to teach, but that is at your discretion."

in the library or directs his own laboratory, with few or no other contacts. Yet when foundation gifts or state university budgets provide the money for such professorships it is usually in the hope that a great man will start or strengthen "new centers of excellence." What has generally resulted is the demoralization of those already in the department at salaries half the "distinguished" salary—the rabble who not only teach but do the dirty work. Nor has it always been good for the star to end his career as a remote luminary, barely perceptible to his resentful colleagues, and badgered not by students but by a bevy of research assistants asking for something to do.

We now approach the consummation of the bargain. If the terms do include special privileges and allow the new recruit to maintain a golden silence, it is likely that the chairman has been assisted in the negotiations by the graduate dean, the dean of faculties or provost, the academic vice-president, or even the president. It is—has been—major business. Any deal that shatters the salary norm must also have been approved by the budget committee, of which more later. When all is cleared, the dean of faculties (or vice-president) appoints an ad hoc committee to review the candidate's qualifications. Details of its working may differ, but the principle is uniform, namely, that a group of tenure faculty members, other than those in the department involved, shall give their assent to promotions and tenure appointments.[7] The effect is that instead of putting the choice of new professors in the hands of the candidate's future colleagues, backed by the administration, the choice is ratified by five additional judges having the power to seek opinions wherever they like.

Trial By One's Peers

The procedure for ad hoc committees is elaborate and therefore described in the *Faculty Handbook*. The chairman of the department that asks for the new man procures copies of his works in print, or a representative sampling. This material is read by the members of the committee, together with letters from scholars outside the university detailing the candidate's good points. (Adverse remarks in writing are rare.) On the day, the chairman appears before the com-

7. At Columbia, the system was instituted in 1954, after a university committee had decided that departmental decisions by themselves were not a sufficient guarantee of excellence. In some of the professional schools, notably Law, Architecture, Medicine, and Social Work, such a guarantee is obtained by requiring the entire tenure faculty to vote on tenure posts.

mittee and makes a case for the appointment or promotion. The dean of faculties (or graduate dean) is present, but as a referee only. He does not vote or express opinions. The chairman answers the committee's questions, then withdraws, and discussion begins. The candidate's biography and writings, and his character as it emerges from the letters or the direct knowledge of members of the committee, are scrutinized.[8]

The hoped-for-end is a unanimous vote for or against, and it is generally obtained. A division of 3 to 2 often means that the department has put up one of its younger men prematurely. In the view of some "he hasn't published enough," as when an ingenious young scholar produced nine long articles, in three languages, which turned out to be three articles slightly altered at head and tail to fit the needs of foreign journals: $3 \times 3 = 9$.

Again, a man from outside may be deemed a poor choice, because too far along in his career. Faculty members tend to want incompatible merits—great fame and the intellectual vigor of youth. Hence the differences of opinion in certain ad hoc cases: "He's not likely to do much more at his age"; or "He sounds good but hasn't produced much yet."

Everybody honestly wants to "strengthen the department"—in scholarly eyes departments and faculties are always anemic—but does strength consist in productivity or in prestige? There is a touching faith that scholarly reputation, which naturally betokens past achievements, will attract good students. In some close-knit of highly specialized fields, such as mathematical statistics or molecular biology, this is no doubt true. But over the whole range, students go here or there for other considerations, often more practical than intellectual. Even when they know a "great name" from his books or public acts, they maintain a wise skepticism about his ability to teach or the likelihood of his being in residence when they appear.

When the ad hoc committee has decided, it reports its findings, often in great deatil, to the dean of faculties, who is supposed to verify the procedure and forward his recommendation to the president. Since

8. In a valuable work, *The Academic Marketplace*, now somewhat out of date, the sociologists Caplow and McGee produced evidence that the practice of ad hoc committees does not always conform to the theory, especially in the matter of reading the candidate's scholarly works. But such variations are only to be expected in an environment where impatience with "administration" and a dislike of taking oneself solemnly sometimes tempt men of integrity to neglect their obligations.

the dean has gauged the candidate's merit, in person and through reading, well before naming the ad hoc group, what happens is that a unanimous approval by the committee is simply recorded as a final judgment, which the president is notified of in due course. If the committee is split 3 to 2 and the reasons given are such as to suggest a poor
choice (or a possible source of faculty dissension), the dean declares
the majority inadequate to pass the candidate. If the dean is doubtful
all on his own, he naturally advises the president. From beginning to
end the administration plays the role of midwife only. No unanimous decision by the committee, whether positive or negative, would
nowadays be flouted by a president or his academic second. In a word,
the faculty recruits itself.[9]

And that is how Ph.D.'s wind up sitting in chairs.

Seven Types of Assiduity

The climb upward is naturally hedged about by many unwritten
rules, and there are professorships and professorships. A four-year liberal arts college wants good teachers as well as respectable scholars;
whereas a great university, while it may sincerely want good teachers, will compromise and take the great inaudible expert whom it
would be cruelty to both sides to put in front of a class. The related
issue popularly known as "Publish or Perish" is almost always confused, because the disputants see different aspects of an improbable
goal—the multiple perfection that all desire in other men. The "grand
teacher" whom students idolize seems to his departmental colleagues
an indifferent asset—he publishes mediocre articles or too few or none
at all. "He has tenure, we're stuck with him—one of our mistakes."
It is part of the settled order of Nature that every department of every
university has at least one such member.

Another academic type is that of the man who has a public reputation for writings that his fellows deem "not scholarship"—"He's a
critic or worse, a journalist." Sometimes—as was true of Veblen—the
discredited works turn out to be epoch-making. Next come the men of
action, who may once have been excellent scholars but who have discovered the knack of reassuring statesmen and comforting indus-
trialists, who devise projects smiled on by foundations, who foment

9. In England, as Mr. Bruce Truscot (pseud.) reminded us some years ago in his
excellent book *Red-brick University* (London, 1943-1945), an election to a professorship may entail the approval of several thousand people, most of them, of course,
giving only a formal "aye" in a routine agenda.

conferences and lead an airborne existence. Universities seeking "visibility" have a penchant for such men and sometimes look for them among ex-ambassadors, deposed heads of foreign states, international bankers with government experience, or artists of renown, all of them supposedly image-enhancing.

Whatever the new university may wish to be, its administration has a duty to maintain a balance among types of talent. And first of all it must ensure the continuity of teaching: a nonteaching university is a contradiction in terms. Still, contradiction has never stopped corporate bodies from forgetting their purpose. At Columbia, the ad hoc procedure states in black and white that promotion to tenure may properly be given to a scholar who does not publish much (or at all) if evidence shows that he is indeed a scholar. A teacher who lives on old notes and earns popularity by being always accessible for a chat may add to the warmth of college halls, but in the long run he causes more harm than good. A scholar-teacher (as the hopeful phrase goes) is a man who loves teaching, does it well, and continues to study his subject.[10]

It usually takes a stubborn tradition to make room for such men in the vicious rivalry of the new university. Just because the bidding is feverish, choosing the right headliners takes experience; it is easy to be deceived by glitter and vogue and to pay a ruinous price for them. This is true equally when the man sought is a public-affairs extrovert and when he is a touted authority on an abstruse new field. In this last situation the chances are that faddishness reigns and genius is proclaimed on slender grounds. Use mathematical symbols to discuss French irregular verbs and your fortune may be made—for a while. But it does not take divination to recognize the profound scholar in an established field. The question for the university then is what it wants him for. Is it to impart knowledge? Is it to give him sanctuary for his remaining years? Is it to show him off?

These aims are not incompatible, but if one clearly predominates it should be acknowledged, particularly if the university is tying up one of the fattest stipends in the department for eight or ten or twenty years. One thing is plain: the man's glory will not be transferred from

10. A notable example at Columbia College was the late Professor Andrew Chiappe, who never published between his Ph.D. dissertation and some essays on Shakespearian romance, which are to appear posthumously. But for twenty years his several courses on Shakespeare were fruits of deep scholarship and performances of high originality.

the institution where he did his great work to that which has bought him. The risk then is: will he retire on salary? It is the duty of a dean of faculties, at the cost of his own popularity, to make vivid these possibilities and repeatedly put Benjamin Franklin's question—do you want to give all your money for that whistle?

The question is particularly cogent when the candidate is from a foreign university. The other side of the Atlantic is always greener; the very names of foreign universities suggest scholarship incrusted; and it seems like a coup to detach a man from Leyden or Munich or Paris or Oxford, even for a visiting professorship. All the same, recruits from the Continent must be closely scanned. Can they speak English? And, even more important, will they accept American ways of higher education—frequent lectures, accessibility to students, a heavy schedule of examinations, departmental and university committee work—a hundred things that the free-floating foreign professor knows nothing of and may well resent as infringing his independence.[11]

That independence extends to the course offering, and American chairmen, in their eagerness to land the foreign catch, are inclined while negotiating to slur over the department's expectations. The great scholar may do "just what he wants." Yet if, as once happened, the visiting professor offers American students courses ostensibly on the history of medieval trade but actually on the condition of the roads in Flanders during the twelfth century, the students will attend a few times, then withdraw until the return from leave of the wider-ranging American historian. Meanwhile, the deserted foreigner enjoys an unintended sabbatical of his own. The department rationalizes the event by saying that the great man's presence, at lunch and in the corridors, was "extremely stimulating."

The upshot of such mistakes and misunderstandings is that conscientious deans, who are themselves academic men but who see more cases of disillusionment, draw up guidelines for both appointments and course offerings. With luck and cunning these documents get adopted, become part of the lore. They set forth not only the conditions under which replacements for those on leave are allowable but also the traps surrounding the recruiting of foreigners—the dangers of overripe fame, the treacherousness of narrow fields and vague under-

11. One such scholar, reared and trained in Germany, was found after a few semesters to have ingeniously excluded all women students from his classes.

standings by letter; together with warnings about visa regulations, the cost of moving household goods, and the need to announce new courses.

The Sport of Buccaneers: Raiding

The reverse face of recruiting is raiding. When university A is attempting to recruit Mr. X, his university, B, is being raided. The act flatters both the man and his institution, but he enjoys it more. For he is now in a position to bargain with his chairman, dean, and president, and they must ask themselves: what is he worth to us? Of late years—say, the past ten—raiding at (or against) the best universities has been continuous. No institution is so high on Olympus as to be immune from aggression. As the government, the foundations, and other patrons have spread the wealth to spread the talent more evenly across the country, the tenders of salary and privilege have overcome the former feelings of devotion to one place, to say nothing of inertia and the pleasure of linking one's name permanently with that of an ancient seat of learning.

The rejoinder to a raid is a counteroffer, which comes after asking the incumbent what would make him happy where he is. Some increase in rank or salary is inevitable and taken for granted; one "matches" the opposition. But there has grown up since 1950 a vast menu of fringe benefits that cover almost all the needs of man, from parking and children's schooling to travel and moving allowances, major medical insurance, faculty apartments, corner offices, summer grants, and reduced teaching load.[12]

We saw above some examples of municifent offers designed to alienate the affections of the most loyal. Those bids were made to senior men of wide repute. But there is also raiding in the lower ranks, for at the present time the greatest shortage of talent occurs in the generation of men between 28 and 38. The assistant professor is at a premium and is correspondingly coddled.

This cherishing usually takes the form of a one-year leave, early in his holding of the rank, to enable him to write his "first real book."[13] The dissertation, so important twenty months before, is now

12. An admirable critical survey of their kinds and forms has been compiled by Professor Mark H. Ingraham: *The Outer Fringe: Faculty Benefits Other Than Annuities and Insurance,* University of Wisconsin Press, 1965.
13. With this end in view Columbia College established for its younger faculty members the Lawrence H. Chamberlain Fellowships, which combine honor and stipend.

dismissed as prentice work, and he is expected to produce something earth-shaking enough to justify his prompt promotion to tenure. He can only remain an assistant professor five years, and it takes a full year to go through the promotion procedure. Add to this the one-year advance notice required if there is no intention to promote, and it follows that judgment on him must begin in his third year.[14]

What creates these stringent conditions is not solely the competition for young men, which has greatly lowered the age at which tenure is allotted. It is also, and mainly, the pressure put on colleges and universities by the American Association of University Professors, which has decreed that anyone teaching full time for seven years at any rank in a given institution obtains automatic tenure.[15]

In addition to the paid year's leave, the young scholar is at many institutions eligible for a summer research grant of about $1,500, which permits him to turn down the summer teaching post he would otherwise seek. He submits a project to a faculty committee on research and, unless he is grossly careless or badly advised, he gets his grant. For everybody understands like the Psalmist that "promotion cometh neither from the east nor from the west nor from the south," but research is the test.[16]

It is obvious that all this fueling of research works in one respect against the university. For when the young scholar brings out his monograph, he becomes "visible" to other institutions and begins to be wooed. He is "one of four in the country that everybody wants." It is prestige-cashing time and he develops a severe itch of the overnight bag. Tagged as brilliant on the strength of perhaps one long article, he assumes rather independent airs, is handled with kid gloves by his chairman and warmly nodded to by his dean, whom the chair-

14. In order to lengthen the chance to do scholarly work and have it fairly judged, the faculties at Columbia decided in 1965 to permit assistant professors to hold the rank for seven years, provided their first appointment at the university was at that rank.

15. The only latitude afforded by the Association is that the strict observance of an eight-year rule (ten years in medical schools) is accepted as evidence of good faith. Since no administration likes to tangle with the AAUP and incur well-publicized odium on the charge of "exploiting young men," the rule of up-or-out in eight years is observed at all reputable schools.

See the report "Academic Freedom and Tenure: Statements of Principle Endorsed by the Association of American Colleges and the American Association of University Professors." (Reprinted from the *Bulletin* of the latter association, vol. 39, no. 1, Spring 1953.)

16. At Yale the subsidy of summer research for assistant and associate professors is automatic—part of the bill of rights.

man has alerted. Either the home university must pay the competitive price to retain its own man or must let him go elsewhere and start developing his successor out of the raw material at hand. Whatever one may think of the effect of early eminence on young scholars, the effect on the university is to diminish greatly the sense of hierarchy and to increase in like amounts preoccupation with staffing and administrative paper work.

This description is of course one-sided. The university is glad to further a career, develop a talent, and through his research possibly add to the sum of human knowledge. But the one-sided view has point in relation to the material welfare of the best universities, for it is clear that in the sequence just described they are using their resources, as often as not, for the benefit of four-year colleges and the lesser universities. The balance of trade has so far been in favor of these institutions. There can be no objection to this natural flow of the current since the nation as a whole benefits, but when we come to the question of costs we shall remember that here is a large unpaid claim.

6. The Permanent Professors:
A Modest Proposal

ROBERT A. NISBET

1

Although tenure is widely regarded as essential to the idea of the university, I would like to suggest it is far from certain that such is the case. Tenure differs sharply from academic freedom in this respect. A university worthy of the name is simply unimaginable apart from a broad and fully protected policy of freedom for each faculty member (tenure and non-tenure alike) to teach, write, and advise without interference from within or outside the university in all matters germane to his academic competence. Whatever qualifications of this right may exist, they are established by the corporate faculty itself, not by the administration or the public. More, it is, today at least, the very essence of academic freedom that a faculty member's views on matters outside his stated professional competence—however shocking these views may be, however suggestive *prima facie* of want of ordinary intelligence or moral responsibility— shall not be held against him when he is being considered for retention or promotion.

Academic freedom, so conceived, justifies itself not by what it grants the individual but by what it does for the university. We have learned that it is absolutely necessary to the search for, and the communication of, knowledge. It is an essential attribute of the university; not a special privilege of the individual.

Can the same be said for academic tenure? If the university is to be regarded as a center within which the governing criteria are those of intellect, given visible sign by continuing creativeness in study or classroom, should there be any limitation on these criteria, even those provided by a man's age, rank, or length of service?

The case for tenure, if there is one, must be made to rest upon what it does for the university, not upon a claim of special privilege for a class of individuals who form today but one part of the larger corps of the creative and intellectually productive in society. Tenure must be divorced from mere gratitude for prior services rendered. Such gratitude can be expressed in other ways—by honorary degrees, plaques, professorships named after the meritorious, even money payments. Tenure must also be divorced from need by the individual and his family for financial security, for this is a universal need in society, not one confined to professors. It could be met precisely as it is met in other areas of the economy—by unemployment insurance, by severance pay, by more liberal pension provisions, and by the varied modes of job security which exist in law offices, newspapers, the theatre, industry, and other parts of our diverse and creative society.

It is surely possible to reward the professor, to honor him, and to reinforce his security without, however, committing the university to his permanent tenure, thereby crippling departmental teaching and research programs, and stupefying generations of students, which is what happens all too often today. If academic tenure is to be justified, it must be done in terms that relate to some unique role occupied by academic man in society; a role demonstrably different from the roles held by all the non-academic professionals and intellectuals who also serve the cause of knowledge and culture but are denied anything resembling tenure. Once, such justification would have been easy. Today, frankly, it is not.

2

Few outside the academy are likely to appreciate what is fully involved today in academic tenure as it exists in practice. They may suppose it is simply the academic equivalent of the type of job security that exists in, say, General Motors, the Bureau of the Budget, or the Los Angeles Dodgers. (I deliberately select three organizations that the contemporary university, in one or other of its phases, comes more and more to resemble. The first two require no explanation, but the last-named may. I am referring to the now common quest in professional sports and the university for stars and superstars whose names and salaries are the source of as much pride and publicity to faculties as to trustees and club owners.) In each of these a man is guaranteed his job so long as he competently fulfills its specification, whether this be installing carburetors, performing an audit, or playing second base, and he is not likely to be dismissed or demoted on grounds extraneous to his competence except possibly for commission of felony or flagrant insubordination.

Any supposition that this describes academic tenure is, however, pure illusion. Tenure as we find it in the university today is as nearly impregnable a form of differential privilege as the mind of man has ever devised. Once attained by an individual, it is, on the evidence, proof against virtually any degree of moral obliquity, mental deterioration, or academic torpor. Tenure in the academy is more than economic security. It cannot even be understood in economic terms. One would have to go to the realm of religion for its exact counterpart in its blend of mystique and the sacred.

Most of us on university faculties rationalize the guilt that occasionally assails our consciences—as we look at our friends who do not possess tenure but who also contribute to scholarship, culture, and creative imagination—by our imagining of the dread spectacle of Administration ever ready to fire amiable, elderly scholars, each cast in the role of Mr. Chips, deeply devoted to, and loved by, his students, unworldly in manner, probably a utopian socialist in politics, unfitted for any other type of occupation, long sworn to the scholar's role and poverty, and therefore utterly helpless, were he to be dismissed.

This individual, as I shall emphasize later, hasn't existed on a major university campus for at least two decades, but he is, so to speak, our Folk Hero. It is his abiding reality in our minds that gives us the strength to insist upon tenure for ourselves when our friends in the theater, in journalism, in the foundations, and in industrial or government laboratories do not have it. I will come back to this lovely ghost later. For the moment, I want only to emphasize that did our Folk Hero in fact exist on the campus today, administrators and trustees would surround him in near rapture—socialist convictions and all—for he makes *them* no trouble and he would represent the embodiment or fulfillment of an old image of teaching and scholarship that they like to discuss nostalgically in their offices and clubs. Moreover he would be immobile; hence not a replacement problem. The real enemies that this departed Hero would face, were he to be resurrected, would be not administrators but colleagues. The Grand Inquisitor would be, not a dean or president, but a faculty associate, ferociously productive and unable to suffer amiable age and socialist dreams gladly—not when their presence threatens to cut off a million dollar grant from the National Institute of Mental Health.

But let us return to the reality of tenure. What is it? To begin with, it is granted to an academic person when he reaches a certain rank (usually associate professor, irrespective of age) or has served a certain number of years in the institution (ranging across the country from three to eight). Far from fearing a man's acquisition of tenure, administrations and faculties today grant it every more freely as bait for appointment or retention. What a tenure code or tradition says (on the evidence, *unwritten* tenure systems are stouter than those written—for here, as elsewhere in life, words can be hostages) is innocuous enough. Once granted, tenure shall not be abrogated except on good cause and after equitable and duly prescribed hearing by the man's colleagues. There is surely nothing wrong with this. One's only thought, viewing it abstractly, is: why not the same for *all* members of the faculty? On what basis other than "good cause" and with the assent of those faculty qualified to judge, would even a first-year instructor be dismissed?

"Good cause" is today more and more often left undefined, and this, it must be emphasized, is at the behest of faculties themselves. Historically it meant—and in some places is still specified as—"moral turpitude," "gross insubordination" and "mental or academic incompetence." The first two have a quaint sound today and their decreasing appearance in published statements is testimony to the increasing embarrassment most of us feel in trying to imagine, much less define, them in a degree that would today warrant dismissal of even *non*-tenure faculty.

Some years ago an able faculty member, who held tenure rank, was dismissed by his university when he confessed to, and was found guilty by the Superior Court of, a felony—repeated thefts over a period of years of substantial amounts of property from nearby wealthy homes. His dismissal produced no outcry from the faculty. From the Court he received a ten year suspended sentence—which could easily have been synchronized to the demands of his professorship. Today we would ask: why, therefore, was he dismissed? He had been found guilty of no *academic* wrong. He was a fine teacher, good scholar, and impeccable in moral behavior on the campus. I venture the guess that, in many institutions today, given the same circumstances, the outcry from students and faculty would be immediate, and that under the charge of "double jeopardy" the institution would be hard put to dismiss a man on whom neither the label of intellectual incompetence nor insubordination or *academic* moral turpitude could be accurately placed. And I am inclined to think such a position would be, today, defensible.

Once, many years ago, the university stood *in loco parentis* (whatever that really meant) to its students, and moral probity could therefore be made a binding requirement of continuing faculty appointment. But today, by common assent of students, faculty, and, more slowly but surely, parents, it does not stand in this role, and it may therefore be properly asked: what does a man's status before the law or his extra-mural morality have to do with his eligibility to teach? Homosexuality is the commonest basis today of dismissal on the ground of moral turpitude, but even here (and especially in light of the ever-rising status that modern literature has given the homosexual) it is hard to suppose that, except in circumstances of extreme repugnance to academic sensibility—involving, I should guess, chronic forays on unwilling students—an otherwise acceptable faculty member (*with* or *without tenure*) would be dismissed on this count. Not, certainly, without strong opposition of the faculty. For, again, the question could be asked: what, precisely, in an institution devoted strictly to the discovery and teaching of *ideas*, does a man's "moral turpitude" have to do with his appointment?

If moral turpitude has become a virtually extinct ground of dismissal in the university, what about that other hoary ground, "insubordination?" It is hard to know what this word means in practice. The university, as President Robert Gordon Sproul of the University of California used to say, differs from all other corporate institutions in that no one, not even the president, ever actually gives orders. For the university does not have a very clear-cut chain of command. Sound academic tradition, with large grants of autonomy to faculty committees, insures this. It is impossible for me to imagine any act of "insubordination" by an individual at the present time, against *either* faculty or administration, where dismissal would not predictably be followed by powerful dissent. Admittedly, ways can be, and usually are, found, most often by professors themselves, whereby, through processes of harassment, ostracism, repeated recommendations against salary increases, extra-microscopic scrutiny of academic record, etc., life for the insubordinate or fractious faculty member can be made so unattractive that he tends to leave—with warm recommendations, naturally, from his colleagues—for another job. The point is, however, that "insubordination" like "moral turpitude" is a vanishing concept in tenure codes. For quite apart from the antique flavor of each, nothing is said that is not today equally relevant to the status of the non-tenured. There is, after all, no more legitimacy to a dismissal of the non-tenured on these grounds than there is of the tenured. Or, putting it in reverse, if we are justified in dismissing the instructor or assistant professor for these offenses, then we are equally justified in dismissing the full professor.

Today the only ground of dismissal of the tenured that has ready and instantaneous acquiescence from the faculty is that of mental or academic incompetence. Never, in a quarter of a century of university teaching, have I ever heard dissent from a faculty member from this proposition: no man's job, however securely rooted in past achievement or glory, or in whatever number of years of service, should be proof against manifest intellectual incompetence. *But neither, in the same quarter of a century, involving association with literally thousands of faculty members, have I ever seen a single case in which a tenure faculty member was in fact dismissed or demoted on grounds of academic incompetence or mental deterioration.* The nearest to an instance in my own experience is that of a physical scientist in a distinguished department some twenty years ago, whose academic incompetence and mental frivolity had become so appallingly evident, so embarrassing and crippling to colleagues and students, that the trustees bought up the ten-year remainder of the man's tenure (involving a very substantial sum of money, for he was a fairly high-salaried full professor), thus permitting him, with his own signed concurrence, to resign.

Perhaps this was indeed the best way. As I said earlier, the least important aspect of the consequence of tenure is financial. Its crime is not what it costs in dollars but in creativeness. How often does not one hear anguished reports from friends in adjacent departments, or in other colleges or universities, of the intellectual blight caused by a single man, year after year, in his association with students and faculty? But only the naive or non-academic would ask the obvious question.

3

Although the rise of tenure is to be seen, historically, as a part of the wider movement of worker security that began in the United States in the early part of the century, its justification, both then and since, has been largely built around the claimed uniqueness of the academic function. So unique is the university, the argument goes, that the person who makes it his career—who deliberately consecrates himself to it in preference to other, better paid and more prestigious opportunities for self and family—is stuck with it. His commitment—like that of the clergyman—has made him immobile. Once, there was a great deal of truth in this statement.

Down until about the end of the Second World War, the university had two central functions: teaching and scholarship. A gulf existed between the university and the rest of society that was seldom crossed, occupationally, by academic man. He had, as it were, a trained incapacity for performing any of society's other jobs, whether in industry or government.

Scholarship and teaching were the professor's functions and in each lay a fragility that required special protection. A work of scholarship, typically, required years of preparation, resulting from the need for bibliographic research, thoroughness, and specialized depth of inquiry. The product did not often become visible through publication. "Productivity" indeed, as a word, was still confined to the assembly lines of factories. It was not brilliance that was sought after in scholarship, but thoroughness, soundness, and mastery. I do not wish to glorify. A great deal of this scholarship was dull, unimaginative, and, in the long run, useless even to scholars. The case might even be made that it sank eventually from its own leaden weight. There is much reason to suppose that in the humanities influences outside the academy—of such men as T. S. Eliot, Edmund Wilson, R. P. Blackmur—were required to revitalize what had threatened to become stifled. None of this, however, is to the point. What is to the point is that, good or bad, scholarship was academic man's unique mode of expressing himself in print; it was not something that non-scholars could, or were expected to, appreciate; it required years of preparation and, by any assessment, demanded the security of tenure for the man willing to undertake it. The wall then between what professors wrote and what non-academic intellectuals wrote was very nearly an impenetrable one.

Equally fragile was the teaching role, which, even in the great universities was regarded, down until a decade or two ago, as more fundamental, more truly identifying of academic man than even scholarship. Teaching was fragile for a number of reasons. First, there was the deep-seated conviction in this country, largely as the result of the American system of lay boards of trustees, that the professor was an employee, literally a hireling, and hence as subject to the wishes of his "employers" as anyone who worked for a railroad or department store. It is not easy today to summon up an accurate vision of how powerful trustees, individually and severally, once were in the minute decisions of colleges and universities—or how fundamentally indifferent they were to those values of teaching and scholarship that had come to this country at the end of the nineteenth century from Europe.

In addition, there was the fragility of academic role that came from a professor's commitment to *campus*. The academic world was composed exclusively of "locals" in contrast to "cosmopolitans." Characteristically, a man's status and his advancement depended far more upon what he was in the eyes of those immediately around him— colleagues, administration, and students—than upon whatever reputation he may have acquired in national or professional terms. Transfers were, to be sure, not unknown, but even through the nineteen thirties, so vivid was a professor's "local" identity in contrast to his "professional," that such transfers, once a man became established, occasioned surprise. There may have been some virtue in this localism, but it contained also the insecurity that is always the price of immobility.

Even less was the likelihood of a professor shifting to a non-academic occupation, even temporarily. To suppose that an academic man—whether scientist, social scientist, or humanist—might be able to shift from academy to corporation, government, or agriculture, as he so plainly does today, would have been to suppose the impossible. Did anyone imagine that practical men of business or government could conceivably profit from academic advice? Consulting, even for the physical scientists, was negligible as a source of income and altogether absent in the other disciplines.

Finally, the very image of academic man in the public mind contributed to his immobility and his utter dependence upon the academic institution. This image was for the most part that of an unworldly, impractical, idealistic individual, lost when it came to the responsibilities of administration, budgets, and management of affairs outside classroom or study. Contributing to the uniqueness of the image was the fact that, although the professor's income was small, his social status was vaguely that of the gentleman of leisure. To conceive of him as a man of affairs, as consultant and advisor to corporations, professional associations, and departments of government was fanciful. It is nearly as easy to imagine, today, a clergyman taking appointment in State or Defense, in General Electric or the Auto Workers Union, as it once was to imagine an academic man shifting regularly to these and many other non-academic pursuits. And with the possible exception of the clergyman—with whom on so many counts the professor was once comparable—no social type was so immobile and hence occupationally dependent as was academic man until a couple of decades ago in this country.

4

But this picture has changed substantially. There is no longer uniqueness, only moderate and diminishing differentness, in the role of the academic man. Through vast changes in the nature of the university and in what the academic man typically and actually does today— paralleled by the immense changes that have taken place in the non-academic culture of the United States, witnessed (for our purposes) by the extraordinary proliferation or research, consultative, and intellectually and artistically creative jobs in all parts of the economy— academic man has become ever more like, at the one extreme, businessmen and administrators and, at the other, the non-academic intellectuals.

Consider the latter. Nothing is more striking than the narrowing of the gulf that once existed between writers, artists, and journalists outside the academy and those today working within it. I think it would be difficult at the present time, in looking through *Commentary, Partisan Review*, the *New York Review of Books, The Hudson Review*, and other prestige-journals to decide, simply on the basis of subject and style, which were the academic and which the non-academic writers. The decision would once have been simple. In such journals, had they existed at the beginning of the century, there would have been few, if any, academic contributors. In the first place academic thought and style would not often have passed muster (one recalls here the experiences of editors like Albert Jay Nock and H. L. Mencken with academics in the twenties). The few who could have passed muster would then have had the frightful experience of justifying their devigations to shocked department chairmen and colleagues.

Admittedly, non-academic literary intellectuals today are still less likely to author substantial, deeply researched volumes on minor poets or major influences; they require the income and nourishment of prestige that more frequent publication insures. But the difference is offset, I should say, by the fact that fewer academics are writing those either; for academic intellectuals also increasingly require the reinforcement to ego and competitive position that frequent publication insures, and, beyond this, academic humanists draw a larger measure of prestige from publishing in, say, *Partisan Review* than in *PMLA*.

There is the further fact that the context of the humanities in the universities is rapidly changing. It is becoming more like the sciences. Within the past ten years it, too, has become institute-infested, center-grown, and the not very secret dream of most humanists of becoming the director of a Center for Renaissance Studies is nearly as widespread as its counterpart in other areas. Once a Federal foundation for the humanities appears—and it is as certain as anything I can think of, if only to allay restlessness in this final fastness of academic individualism—the conversion will have become as complete as in the sciences. Institutes and centers, to receive huge Federal grants, will mushroom.

Consider now today's every more typical scientist. He is engaged in large-scale research, working on an around-the-calendar basis, housed in special institute or center, equipped with staffs of secretaries formidable enough to frighten away all but foundation executives, with budgets to prepare constantly, grants to apply for, payroll sheets to fill out. Is it not easier to conceive of him as corporate executive or civil servant rather than professor? Add to this his governmental, professional, and industrial consultantships, his membership on national and international committees, his almost ceaseless travel to meetings and conferences, and the traditional image of academic man seems almost as archaic as that of guildsman or cavalryman.

Once the distinction of type between the academic scientist and his industrial or governmental counterpart was striking. Today, changes in all three areas have reduced this to near nullity. For just as business and government have, on the whole, come to grant a larger measure of individual autonomy to scientists working in their laboratories, so academic scientists have voluntarily committed themselves to forms of contract research that sometimes threaten to bring them closer to the norm of their professional colleagues in General Electric or the Department of Agriculture.

What is so evident in the humanities and natural sciences is equally evident in the social sciences. Scholarship, in the old sense of this word, is fast disappearing from what is today known as "the behavioral sciences," leaving in the wake of this disappearance, at one extreme, minds primarily interested in impressionistic analysis or criticism of the social order and, at the other, those engaged in the preparation of reports and surveys in closely-administered centers and institutes or in professional consultantship. At each extreme it becomes ever more difficult to distinguish the academic from the non-academic. Today a Distinguished Service Research Professor in Political Science at a major university can, in subject as well as style, compete (and month after month does compete) with a Walter Lippmann or even a Joseph Alsop or James Reston. And at the other extreme one finds it ever harder to distinguish between what comes out of non-academic centers for the analysis of public opinion, attitudes, purchasing habits, religion, education, government, and what comes from the universities. At social science association meetings, the papers presented by academic and non-academic technicians have become the same—a fact which says as much for the rise in level of the latter as for what has happened to the former.

Why, we are thus led to ask again, should one part of the intellectual corps in modern society be granted the privilege of absolute tenure when, by no stretch of vision or imagination, can it be found in the other, the non-academic, part? Except in the rarest instance, we can no longer claim the kind of precariousness of status that once lay in our uniqueness of type, and the evidence shows we are hardly blind to the near infinity of jobs that today have opened up in all sectors of the economy for the intellectual-technician, whether he be chemist or economist, biologist or sociologist, or even historian or philologist. Non-academic intellectuals and professionals live by fee, royalty, salary, and wage, and I assume that there are varying degrees of security attached to income, once a name for excellence has been acquired. But they do not live by tenure.

5

Despite the gradual disappearance of academic man and the conversion of universities into institutions more and more like corporations or government bureaus, there are two possible defenses of tenure, either of which, if valid, would justify continuation of the system.

First, it is said—though not as often as it once was—that tenure has been responsible for the gradual rise in salary levels for university professors over the past half century. This is historically dubious. What is certain is that tenure could be abolished tomorrow, and, given the critical shortage of academic talent—a *persisting* shortage —and the ever greater dependence of society upon the skills and

knowledge of our academic technicians and professionals, there would
be not the slightest effect registered upon salary scale.

The second, and much more common, assertion has to do with the
relation between tenure and academic freedom.

Tenure, we read in countless declarations, is the steel frame of freedom of teaching in the classroom, the solid base of the scholar's exemption from erosive fears of status and livelihood that would otherwise
attend his teaching and publication of truths distasteful to dean or
president, government or public. "If I didn't have tenure," one hears
in familiar refrain, "I wouldn't be free to teach as I want to teach."
If this is true, it alone offers all the justification necessary. But is it
true? Let us pass over the tens of thousands of public school teachers
—at elementary and secondary levels—who assuredly have tenure but
who equally assuredly do not have freedom in the classroom. Let us
confine ourselves to the university. Several points suggest themselves.

Academic freedom—the freedom of the teacher to teach, the scholar
to write—is supported today by a number of forces that did not exist
a generation ago. First, and most important, it is supported by the
mobility that the competent teacher-scholar has, given the huge increase in job opportunities, academic and non-academic. Second, there
is the enhanced respect in which university professors are today held
by business and government and, providing the solid base of this
respect, the indispensable position that the modern university holds
with respect to industrial, military, and national welfare. Indeed, the forces that have made a privileged aristocracy of the pro-
fessoriat have made for a degree of autonomy, boldness, aggressiveness and occasional arrogance and bad manners that have ever been
attributes of recognized aristocracies. Once a Northwestern University
trustee could say: "As to what should be taught in political science
and social science, they [the professors] should promptly and gracefully
submit to the determination of the trustees when the latter find it necessary to act. . . . If the trustees err it is for the patrons and proprietors,
not for the employees, to change either the policy or the personnel
of the board." Such a statement made today would embarrass fellow
trustees and shock editors, civic officials, and the industrial elite. But it
would not shock or shame academics; it would merely break them up
in hilarity. It is a mark of where we are at the present time that such a
statement would not even be dignified by a student revolt!

The rise in real academic freedom—defined in the terms with which
I began this article—has been among the more notable aspects of the

history of American culture during the past fifty years. It has been part of, and has drawn its essential support from, external currents of rising tolerance and sophistication that flow from an ever more educated citizenry. However, I will not press that point too hard. It may well be that the threats to academic freedom are today as great as they ever were in this country. Even if they are not, I am inclined to think that, for tactical purposes, it is always well to assume that they are and, accordingly, remain vigilant. The central point here pertains, in any event, to the role of tenure. Is it indeed a bastion of academic freedom?

I see little evidence that it is, or that it should be so regarded, *for the proper sway of academic freedom is faculty-wide, not merely for those holding tenure.* In point of fact, where academic freedom has been abrogated in recent years, as it was at the time the University of California imposed its loyalty oath, the tenure of nearly half the non-signers was no safeguard. And when, after court action, the non-signing faculty members were restored to appointment, those without tenure were restored along with their tenure colleagues. And during an earlier period, when American Legion squads were committing their nuisances upon universities, I recall no instance in my own university—which suffered its due share of the nuisances—in which there was discrimination between tenured and non-tenured in what the University was willing to do to protect its faculty. In one outburst, the American Legion called for the dismissal at Berkeley of an eminent tenured scholar in law and, at the same time, a teaching assistant in economics. Each, I recall, received the same assurance of protection from President Sproul.

Quite apart from the university's changed relation to state and society in these matters, there has been a substantial expansion of academic freedom by faculty members themselves. A half a century ago, the beginning instructor or assistant professor generally had no more freedom than tenure—measured by contemporary standards. Freedom —of teaching, research, and extra-mural utterance—was a state to which he could only aspire; one that would come with seniority. The situation is dramatically different today. We divide a faculty between the tenured and the non-tenured, but we certainly do not divide it— not in any first-rate university—between the academically free and unfree. The chemist, sociologist, or philosopher has as much academic freedom, both in principle and in practice, at the beginning of his career as at its zenith. He may, as a tyro, be given more chores and fewer plums, larger teaching loads, scanter office space, smaller research funds, etc., but his academic freedom could hardly be greater than when he takes appointment. Despite a popular supposition that the assistant professor is more likely to be timorous or discreet than his tenured brethren, little that I have seen in a quarter of a century within the University of California, or witnessed from afar in the academic world, suggests that this is the case. Indeed if sheer volubility and intensity of attack upon "the Establishment" be taken as the true measure of academic freedom prevailing in an institution, one could make out a stronger case for the non-tenured—who are younger, and have given fewer hostages to fortune—than the tenured.

6

We have gradually banished from the academic world, over a period of many years, the criteria of ethnicity, political membership, and religious belief, each of which once held all-too-substantial a place in the appointment and retention of faculty members in American universities. On what logical ground, then, do we claim exemption for age and rank, in certain respects the most feudal of all feudal qualities? We pride ourselves, as professors, upon inhabiting a shining fastness of meritocracy in a society that still bears too many elements of traditional privilege. How, then, do we legitimately rationalize a system of privilege which can, and frequently does today, exempt a person of thirty or thirty-five years of age (the lowest age at which I have seen life tenure granted is twenty-seven, to a mathematician) for the rest of his life from the competitive pressures and insecurities to which the rest of the intellectual world is subject?

It is hardly conceivable that the senior university professor would be jobless if let out by his university for reason of loss of the brilliance that had led to his initial appointment. To begin with, there are hundreds of administrative jobs open in the university world. To say that these men are for the most part unsuited to administration, by reason of temperamental disinclination, belies everything I have seen over a period of twenty-five years in teaching and administration. "Scratch a faculty member and you find an administrator" is an aphorism the truth of which has, with only the rarest of exceptions, been made steadily more emphatic in my experience. Administration is (or at least is commonly regarded as being) power; and there is nothing the intellectual, academic or nonacademic, craves more.

Administrative jobs in the universities are, however, only the beginning. There is, as I have before suggested, the whole burgeoning area of industry and government, in each of which there is almost child-like pride today in taking onto its public roster university faculty members. In government, one need but think of the voracious needs in the years immediately ahead of the Department of Health, Education, and Welfare. In the multitude and layers of command posts that this single Federal department represents, there must be opportunity for all of the academics who would be dismissed, were tenure to be denied them as further support. And we have said nothing about the other departments and divisions of government—local, state, and federal. Of how many professors might it not be said that, by leaving their university and joining the government, they raised the intellectual level of each?

But to return to the matter of tenure: how, it will be asked, can equitable and accurate decision be made as to the relatively small number of senior members of the academic meritocracy who are to be let out annually in favor of those more brilliant, more productive, non-tenured faculty members who are ever ready to move into the places of their seniors?

Andrew Dickson White, notable early president of Cornell, once proposed, we are told, annual scrutiny of each faculty member by the trustees, with dismissal to follow upon a certain number of negative ballots. Balloting by trustees on a matter in which they could not possibly have informed judgment is certainly a grotesque and repugnant thought. But what about balloting by a man's colleagues? I do not mean balloting in any literal sense, of course, but simply in that of continuing scrutiny by those of his peers who are plainly qualified to judge—those within his institution and those in other institutions who might be engaged as confidential consultants. We do this now for those under consideration for promotion to a tenure position or for initial appointment at highest rank in an institution. And we do this, even with those who possess tenure, when it comes to such matters as promotion from associate to full professor, salary increase, nomination of a colleague to an endowed chair, or to academic-administrative positions such as chairman or dean. Why not also for decisions as to continuation?

We are in part victims of the system of academic promotion that prevails almost universally in this country. When a faculty committee and dean consider the promotion of a man from one rank to another, the question that is now asked is: has this man *earned* it? This is unfortunate, for experience shows that the advance set of mind of both committee and administration tends to be favorable. After all, what person has not done *something* that cannot be said to qualify him for promotion? How much better it would be if we asked the altogether different question: Is there at this time, available in the profession, someone who is superior to the individual under review and who may therefore be appointed to the position for which this individual, through promotion, is being considered? If there is, we appoint; if not, we promote. In a genuine intellectual meritocracy, this would be the criterion in promotion, and it could be equally the criterion of *retention* of faculty—of all faculty.

A distinguished colleague of mine, who will himself never need the support of tenure and who shares many of my convictions about the evil of the matter, proposes a fundamental modification of the present system. Let us, he says, reaffirm tenure but reverse its application. Grant beginning instructors (who, of all faculty, plainly most need it) tenure of perhaps fifteen years. When, however, they receive promotion to assistant professor, tenure will be reduced to ten years; with advancement to the associate professorship, it will drop to five years. But with the full professorship all tenure ceases, for, by very proof of his right to this exalted rank, he has proved also his capacity, through teaching and scholarship, for retaining it on merit.

There is much to recommend this, but I think the tensions under it would be horrifying. For the stablest element in the academic community—that is, in terms of guarantees of position—would be the instructors and assistant professors. The ferocity with which they now view their elders would be intensified by the feel of power. Possessing tenure, they might well wish to do what tenure faculty now do; decide the fate of the non-tenured. No, it is far better to abolish tenure outright.

The abolition of tenure, it goes without saying, will not be initiated by trustees or administration in this country. The mere prospect would shrivel these bodies, leaving them in helpless panic at the thought of the consequences that would be visited upon them. Nor can it be done by government action, which is normally the liberal and progressive way of attacking privilege in our country. The academic community has become much too powerful for even the Federal government to risk its alienation.

From the faculty alone can action properly come, and it is in this light that I propose leadership by the American Association of University Professors. This is the proper body; it is national, it has a distinguished history, and, in past decades, has been the chief lobby *for* tenure. Such leadership could give new vitality to the Association itself and free it for its central function, that of acting as watchdog of academic freedom. I think it would be impossible to exaggerate the tonic effect that such action, coming from the united faculty itself, would have upon the morale of the rest of the intellectual community in the United States, and upon the vitality and effectiveness of the university.

Need I also say that I think it impossible to exaggerate the un-likelihood of the A.A.U.P. doing any such thing?

7. Publish or Perish—A Defense

J. H. HEXTER

To academics, or at least to this particular academic, one of the most fresh and fascinating aspects of the student revolt is the extent to which it is directed against Academia itself. A generation ago, student revolt rarely took that odd turning—perhaps because students did not really give enough of a damn about Academia to bother. For me, the most interesting episode occurred a few years back, not among the large and rackety academic demimonde on the shores of San Francisco Bay, but rather in the ordinarily tranquil environs of New Haven. That at Yale University—Yale, of all places, with its broad, well-padded bottom, its ancient reputation for unassailable complacency, its undergraduate body about one half out of plush private schools —should witness a continuous seventy-two hour vigil of protest against a refusal to grant a permanent position on the faculty to a thirty-two-year-old associate professor, and that such a demonstration should elicit the support of a considerable fraction of the undergraduates— this was revolutionary indeed. It was evidence of a concern about education in general, and their own education in particular, rare among the sons of Eli in the good old days of the Whiffenpoof rampant.

That particular revolt failed. Despite a bit of static in the administrative circuit through which the case passed, Yale's message came through loud and clear: however talented a man might be as a classroom teacher, the Yale faculty would not grant him a permanent position unless in its view he had already published work of considerable distinction and unless prospects were favorable that he would continue to do so. The message was immediately translated into a slogan long current in the academic world but never before so widely publicized outside it: Publish or Perish.

In view of the subsequent fortunes of the victim, the wording of the slogan seems a little melodramatic. He is said to have received thirty-four job offers at other institutions, and he now holds the posi-

tion of chairman of a department and a full professorship—with tenure
—in one of the very best colleges in the United States. Yet Publish or
Perish was indeed the message. Lest any doubt it, the Yale faculty reiterated its stand quite firmly and unambiguously less than a year after
the initial eruption. As a sequel to that affair, a faculty committee—
the majority of whose members did not have permanent appointments
—investigated the whole area of appointment and promotion policy.
They solicited and considered advice and suggestions from anyone at
Yale who cared to offer them. They worked hard and conscientiously
and deliberated with care through a long summer. Their report was
singularly free of that smog of academese and ambiguity with which
so many university committees manage to conceal from the consumer
not only their conclusions but their premises. The report was unani-
mously endorsed by the Academic Establishment—the Boards of Permanent Officers of Yale College and the Graduate Faculty of Arts and
Sciences—those favored beings who are surrounded by the mystic
aura called Tenure. On the issue which generated the committee's investigation the report was unequivocal: "As a university, Yale's future
will be determined by the extent to which she is able . . . to keep and
to attract distinguished scholars. An insistence on excellent undergraduate teaching as a condition for tenure, without a rigorous adherence to scholarly criteria, could lead to a deterioration in Yale's
scholarly contribution and hence its national and international stature
as a university." Of the one concrete suggestion that ran counter to this
position, the committee made short work. "The Committee received a
number of suggestions for the establishment of Teaching Professorships. It rejected these because it is convinced that original scholarly
work is the surest proof of intellectual distinction and the surest guarantee that intellectual activity will not cease."

So, after the tumult, the Academic Establishment flatly reiterated
the position it took in the first place—Publish or Perish. "Perish," as
has been pointed out, is a somewhat hyperbolic description of the
actual situation. As an eminent official of the university has put it:
"Yale does not say 'Publish or Perish,' it only says, 'Meet Yale's current standard of productive scholarship as reflected in the printed
word or go elsewhere; take a position in an academic institution that
does not demand such evidence of scholarship.' In the long run you
may well be happier in such an institution." Even the most inveterate
faculty Blue at Yale is faintly aware of the existence of other institutions, purportedly academic, at which other men somehow stumble
through their allotted span of years.

Still that is not quite the point. The point is the twenty to forty great universities that maintain the "hard line" on publication. For a variety of reasons they are the most desirable places at which to teach. They have prestige and confer status. They also tend to provide the lushest fringe benefits—retirement plans, medical insurance, summer grants, leaves with pay. Moreover, they offer the less heavy teaching schedules—six to nine hours rather than nine to fifteen. They invariably get the best students and usually pay the best salaries. These great universities are the pace-setters; where they lead, the rest of Academia follow, especially on the rare occasions when, in a solid phalanx, they all move in the same direction. And in the matter of Publish or Perish they so move.

This is especially alarming for the man who may love to teach but does not care to write. For at almost any university or college to which he retreats, a starry-eyed young dean or president may show up with the dream that he can exalt old Somnolent U. into the Big Twenty or Forty. This troublesome character pays exhorbitant salaries to a few young "hot shots" brought in from outside, who publish at the drop of a hat; and he suggests that those who would enjoy a like shower of gold do likewise. The unfortunate classroom teacher, who is not interested in publishing and had no reason to think his university cared either, finds himself shafted again. Thus in higher education in America the classroom teacher, however excellent, who refuses to present the appropriate offerings before the brazen idol of publication set up by the great universities, finds fewer and fewer places to hide, and those places more and more dingy and repellent.

The Students' Case

On the academic front, therefore, it is against the formidable and serried array of the great universities that the student revolt has chosen to give battle, and the students have well identified one true issue in their conflict with the Academic Establishment. The university, they say, is a teaching institution, and they have come to the university to be taught. But, they go on to observe, those who teach them well know that, if they devote themselves wholly to teaching and neglect to write for scholarly publication, they will shortly face a door marked, "This Way Out." Consequently instead of giving the students the full attention which is their due and his duty, the typical member of the university faculty directs far too much of his energy to research and writing.

As infuriating to the students as this system is, the Establishment's refusal to adopt the straightforward measures which would reform the system is more so. All that the universities need do, the students claim, is reward teaching on a parity with publication of research— and not only by retaining nonpublishers, but by advancing them at the same rate as their publishing colleagues. Then, knowing that entire and sole devotion to teaching is not merely the way to academic suicide, young academics will summon up the courage to refuse complicity in the publication racket, and the balance, now absurdly out of kilter between devotion to teaching and devotion to research-with-a-view-to-publication, will be redressed.

The Problem of Evaluation

It is at this point that the Academic Establishment has a chance to edge in with a mild observation. "Teaching rewarded in proportion to its merit? Ah, yes, of course! And now, tell us, how do we go about evaluating merit in teaching?" And then the Academic Establishment smiles gently, and the smile is the smile on the face of the tiger. By long experience the Establishment knows that, while the proponents of a system of equivalent rewards wrangle over the right way or ways to evaluate teaching, it will be able to go on enforcing its own pet rule of Publish or Perish. It knows that it can go on enforcing that rule forever, because the wrangle will never end.

The problem of evaluation cannot be shuffled aside; it is at the very heart of the matter. It is not enough to say that teaching ought to be rewarded; it is not even enough to separate the good teachers from the bad, supposing even that operation to be feasible; it is necessary to *rank* teachers according to their merit. This is unavoidable, because there is no way to reward differential merit in teaching until the operation of differentiation is performed. With respect to scholarship evidenced in publication, that operation is performed in the academic marketplace by methods too intricate to describe here. Despite an occasional notorious aberration, scholars would agree that the mechanism through which the pecking order gets set in the various fields of learning is on the whole reasonably satisfactory; it distributes differential rewards in reasonable—although surely not perfect—correlation to differential merit in published scholarship. Until the proponents of rewards for meritorious teaching can come up with a method of scaling those rewards approximately as accurate as the current method for establishing the pecking order in published research and scholarship, they will have to put up with the obduracy of the Academic Establishment.

What is Good Teaching?

The problem is complex. Many variables go into the process of teaching as currently conceived, and there is no agreement as to the relative values to be assigned to the variables. To be sure, out of debate, discussion, letters to the editor, picketing, sign-carrying, and so on, that has accompanied the Student Revolt against Academia, it is possible to derive a reasonably concise definition of what *the students* (and many of the professoriate) think of as "teaching." As currently conceived, teaching only takes place at the point of direct confrontation between teacher and student; the only common element among the various forms of activity that are designated as "teaching" is that they occasionally bring face-to-face a person designated as a teacher with persons designated as students. If we give a somewhat extended definition to the term classroom, teaching then becomes "classroom performance." This definition itself, however, creates some difficulties in evaluating teaching.

The most familiar form of classroom performance takes place in the lecture. There the teacher addresses a group of students numbering somewhere between one (1) and 2,000 for approximately 50 minutes on a subject concerning which he is presumed to know more than they. A second form of teaching is carried on by discussion. There are two major subtypes of teaching by discussion. In the first, a large lecture class is broken down into smaller groups, usually somewhere between 10 and 20. Having heard a number of lectures, members of these smaller groups—sometimes called quiz sections—meet with a teacher to discuss their substance along with such reading as has been assigned. In the second kind of discussion group there is no formal lecturing. The whole course is conducted on the basis of discussions between the instructor and the students.

A third form of face-to-face performance occurs in the research seminar. A small group of students work under the supervision of a single instructor, ordinarily meeting once a week for a couple of hours. The student works more or less independently, on a topic of more or less his own choice; he reports his progress to the rest of the seminar; and the final product of his effort, his seminar paper, is subjected to rigorous criticism both by his fellow students and by the seminar instructor. Another form of face-to-face instruction is the supervised, individual, independent research that the graduate student does in fulfillment of his final requirement for a doctorate, the doctoral dissertation. Finally in some fields there are postdoctoral groups or teams working together to solve related sets of problems under the direction of a man who heads up the project.

Suppose that there were an accurate way to rate excellence of teaching within each of these categories. How are the judges to weigh the relative claims to rewards of A and B under the following circumstances? A rates excellent as a lecturer in a class in which he teaches 2,000 students, poor in a quiz section with 10 students, and poor in a seminar with 8 students. He is so terrible at direction of dissertations that he has no students in that category. B rates poor in a lecture in which he teaches 80 students, excellent in a quiz section with 10 students, excellent in a seminar with 11 students, and excellent in the direction of the four students preparing dissertations for him. Is A or B the better teacher? Clearly it depends on the multiplier one chooses. On a 20 (excellent), 10 (good), 0 (poor) scale, if we make the number of courses the multipliers, B scores 60; he is three times as good a teacher as A, who scores 20. If we make students the multiplier, A is 80 times as good as B. On the first basis of calculation, B averages Excellent-Minus; on the second Poor-Plus; on the first A averages Poor-Plus, on the second Excellent. Which, then, is the right multiplier?

Surely, it may be argued, the man who year-in, year-out, teaches 2000 students excellently must be given the edge over the one who teaches 25 excellently. But why? If we simply apply to teaching the applausometer standard, this is so; and it seems undemocratic to do otherwise. The trouble is:

1) The applicability of that standard is precisely what is in question. To build it into the system assumes what is to be proven, a procedure known unfavorably as question-begging.

2) We are trying to decide, not what is democratic, but what is just; and the two can be made identical only by fiat.

Consider an extreme example. Suppose C is a superb biochemist, but so shy that, face-to-face with more than one person at a time, he becomes incoherent. He has directed 50 doctoral dissertations in 25 years, and that is all the "teaching" he has done. During the same span, in large lectures A has taught 50,000 students excellently, while C was teaching only 50. Our applausometer calculus of happy customers registers a 100,000 per cent superiority of A over C. But it turns out that eight of C's students win Nobel prizes in the sciences, and all eight ascribe their achievement in some measure to C's teaching. This dramatic evidence of C's pedagogic proficiency becomes available only after he has been teaching for years, perhaps only after his retirement or his death. Is A the better teacher?

Who Should Judge? How?

So far we have assumed that at least it is possible within each category accurately to rate teachers on a scale from excellent to poor. But just how do we go about doing this? *Who* decides whether a teacher is good, bad, or indifferent? The students, that is the customers, perhaps; but *which* customers—D, or C, or B, or A? D is a fine fellow; a future good citizen; respectful, unassuming, conscientious, and quite, quite stupid. He can be taught only by some pedagogic equivalent of the Chinese drip torture. C—gentleman C, he is called—is ingratiating, bright enough to do excellent work, and lazy enough not to try; in order to satisfy the requirements of the university and to continue to receive regular drafts from father (while avoiding one from Uncle Sam), he absorbs enough to get by. In his view, an excellent teacher is one who provides entertainment not markedly inferior to that purveyed in the neighboring movie palace or discotheque. B is competent; he works hard and steadily; he is 100 per cent reliable; his feet are on the ground, his mind not far above it. He likes a good steady-going teaching performance; but erratic flashes of brilliant light from the lecture platform upset him. He wants to be instructed, not to be disturbed or perplexed. Finally there is A, mercurial, arrogant as Lucifer, bright as a button, slightly unbalanced, with a mind like a razor and the manners of a hog. With fine impartiality, he is contemptuous of all who imagine they might have anything to teach him. How do we judge whether a man has taught excellently a mixed class of D's and C's and B's and A's? By answers to a questionnaire? Such answers might indicate whether D and C and B and A got the kind of teaching they *wanted*. But in three out of four of those cases—D is the exception—the best teaching for them would have been a kind that they did *not* want, and that they probably would have given a low rating in a questionnaire.

If this seems unpromising, we might consider an alternate procedure—a canvass of the opinion of the A students. Because it is largely composed of former A students, surely the professoriate will accept their evaluation? Unfortunately there are problems here too. Who are the A students? How many A's make an A student—all A's? three quarters A's?, half A's? And is an A in Home Economics equivalent to an A in Boolian algebra? To anyone familiar with the proceedings of academic bodies, the potentialities for a proliferation of hair-splitting latent in these questions conjure up a vision of committee meetings stretching from here to eternity.

And of course this is only the beginning. *Which* teachers is our A student to judge? Is he to judge only those splendid fellows who exhibit their attunement to real merit by awarding him an A, or is he also to judge the egregious louts who manifest their ineptitude by giving him a C? And *when* is he to judge them? By moderately high standards, I was an A student as an undergraduate. In my sophomore year I had a brilliant teacher who really made the past come alive to me. Francis of Assisi, Martin Luther, Queen Elizabeth, Thomas Hobbes, Oliver Cromwell—either they were really ordinary fellows, or a bit crooked, or a little queer in the head, just like folks. Naturally, of course, their opinions were funny and out-of-date because they lived in the benighted ages before science and democracy and toleration and liberalism. It was refreshing to be told, by someone who really knew how to debunk, what those fellows were like, and at the end of the year I would surely have given that teacher an enthusiastic A. As it happened, I took another course from him the following year. By that time the glamor had faded. The jokes were the same jokes, and the second time around they were not very funny. That second time around, I would have rated this teacher B rather than A—not bad, but not good enough to deserve a special reward for meritorious teaching. Today, after forty years of fairly ardent pursuit of historical understanding, my judgment may be presumed to be better than it was when I was nineteen. I now think that this teacher deserved neither an A nor a B but an F. He was a traitor to his vocation; he unscrupulously disfigured the past. He did nothing to enable us to understand and respect the great dead who were so much superior to what we ever would be, thus by an inch or so enhancing our own stature. Instead he transfigured giants into pygmies and afforded us adolescents the gratifying illusion of looking down on them. Given the inordinate self-righteousness of bright adolescents, it is hard to imagine a pedagogic device better calculated to appeal to them. It is also hard to imagine a pedagogic device better calculated to firm up their hold on immaturity.

In this case, the C and D students might have rated my teacher more justly. His wit, though not very lofty, still sailed right over their heads. They resented his jibes at ancient superstitions and pieties, which they were loath to reconsider or renounce. And, anyhow, he made fun of them. So for peculiar reasons the C and D students would have arrived at an evaluation of his teaching that corresponds with my current one, while forty years ago as an A student I made the opposite evaluation.

The Professors' Interest

In any case, the vociferous demand of some leaders of the Student Revolt for a student role in the deciding on academic advancement of their teachers is not about to get anywhere. It runs contrary to the vested interest of the professoriate. And for obfuscation, foot-dragging, and sabotage when its vested interests are at stake, the professoriate has incomparable gifts. It could allow the students a role in the apportionment of academic rewards only at its own expense. And while some professors are momentarily foolish enough to court popularity by uttering sweet nothings about taking council with students on the merits of faculty members, the corporate professoriate is not going to surrender lightly such power as it has.

To allege that the professoriate is protecting a vested interest may seem invidious. It is not so intended. Few institutions or human arrangments survive or remain stable unless some men have a vested interest in their survival and stability. Granted the faculty's vested interest, is their control of the distribution of academic rewards more or less desirable than any likely alternative? To the extent that undergraduates take over the choice of *who* should educate them, they also choose *how* they shall be educated. And, contrary to the opinion of the students, it is not the duty of the faculty simply to provide the kind of education students want. Indeed, few young people between the ages of 17 and 21 know what kind of education they want. That a considerable number of such young people are pretty sure they do not want the kind of education they are getting is only mildly disturbing. It has ever been thus. Whatever students think they want, the professoriate has to give some consideration to what the larger community needs. About their capacity wisely to judge the current and future needs of the community, they are—and should be—fairly humble. Still, they see no group better equipped to do the job—not students, not state legislatures, not boards of trustees, not federal bureaucrats, not philanthropic foundations, not university administrators.

Dilemmas of Classroom Evaluation

Suppose, then, that student evaluation of differential merit in teaching is useless and that the Academic Establishment's opposition to it will in any case frustrate its effects. Still, it is absurd to deny the importance of teaching in institutions putatively dedicated to the dissemination of the higher learning. Nor can the Establishment readily deny that teachers should receive rewards at least roughly proportional to their aptitude in performing this important function. So somehow effectiveness in teaching *should* be one of the determinants of the way the academic salary-and-status pie is divided. It is all very well to reject student claims to a hand on the knife that cuts the pie; but someone has to cut it, and who then is left to do the job?

The most obvious answer is the faculty itself. But I must now report that I have no confidence whatever in my own competence to evaluate the teaching of my colleagues, let alone the competence of my colleagues to evaluate my teaching. With more than a quarter of a century of teaching experience under my belt, I do not feel any great assurance that I know whether or when my own performance as a classroom teacher is good, bad, or indifferent. There are times when I have a finger-tip sense that I am doing pretty well and others when I feel I am doing very poorly; but I am not at all sure that my finger-tip sense is accurate. It may all be a matter of classroom geography—whether the most conspicuous occupant of the front row is a sour-looking youth with a facial set indicative of supreme boredom or a starry-eyed young female who has managed to train her face to express rapt interest while her mind is occupied elsewhere. The fact that some students voluntarily come back for more after having had one course with me provides me with no assurance, because I have as little confidence in the judgment of such students as I have in my own. If, after twenty-five years, I am so doubtful about the measure of my own ability, just how sure can I be about the ability of my colleagues?

And how do I find out about my colleagues' teaching? Do I prod students with questions about it? Leaving aside the moral problem of the propriety of encouraging students to gossip to me about their academic betters and my colleagues (although I do not see how one can actually leave aside such a problem), to what end do I prod them, since I do not trust the accuracy of their appraisal? Do I go around to the classes of my colleagues and observe them? The imagination boggles. In a large department the time required for systematic classroom visitation would be enormous. And unless I much mistake the character of my colleagues, they would take kindly neither to visiting nor being visited. They would feel, with reason, that direct faculty evaluation in order to provide rewards for teaching would provide splendid opportunities for a reversion to the jungle in matters of academic politics, in those institutions and departments where such a reversion has not yet taken place. So this is one the faculty had best duck.

But if not the faculty, why not the university administration? There is always some administrator heroically prepared to leap into the breach. If he does, one can envisage three alternative outcomes, all in varying degrees bad:

1. The administrator quickly discovers that he has undertaken a hopeless task. He then a) scuttles the job (happiest outcome, but a waste of his time), or b) maintains a small staff to pretend that he is doing the job (a waste of time and considerable money).

2. The administrator takes a long time to learn that he has undertaken a hopeless task. Meanwhile he spends an inordinate amount of time and money on experiments, consultations, statistical studies, etc., *ad nauseum.*

3. The administrator actually thinks he has solved the problem, in which case a) he presents it to the faculty for suggestions, approval, and implementation (a most unfortunate course, since the faculty simply hacks his brainchild to bits before his very eyes, and forever after distrusts his judgment), or b) he tries to effect his proposals for evaluation without faculty consent (sheer disaster that can only end in his resignation, or the permanent embitterment and departure of a considerable part of the faculty, or both).

So the administrators had better duck, too.

The Other Way of Teaching

Exploration of means to evaluate teaching seems to lead, by a circuitous and thorny path, into the Slough of Despond. But really there are no grounds at all for despair. While we have been pursuing the bluebird of evaluation-of-university-teaching, he has all along been at home and doing reasonably well. In the great universities, the work of evaluating faculty members as teachers *is* currently being performed, and being performed more accurately than it would be by any of the disastrous procedures hitherto canvassed. The standard for this evaluation is: Publish or Perish. In effect the faculty member is rewarded *as a teacher* on the basis of the scholarly community's evaluation of his published work.

The advantage of Publish or Perish is that it breaks through two parochial and absurd assumptions: 1) that all university teaching goes on in the classroom, and 2) that all the teaching that goes on there is a pure act of creation on the part of the classroom teacher. The second proposition was never correct. Even when Thomas Aquinas was bringing illumination to youthful minds by lecturing to students at the University of Paris in the thirteenth century, he owed a good bit of what he taught to Holy Writ, Aristotle, St. Augustine, and a number of lesser lights. The first proposition began to lose force at some time between the middle of the fifteenth century and the early decades of the sixteenth. During that period, pedagogues discovered that the process of printing had made books so cheap that students could buy them, and that if they bought them and used them under appropriate conditions, and with appropriate sanctions for failure to read and master their contents, *they learned things without actually having to be told them.*

The invention of printing is not so recent that I lay myself open to the charge of radicalism in attempting some cautious explanation of the educational effect of the existence and use of printed books. More recent, to be sure, is the Paperback Revolution; but even the effects of this phenomenon should by now be sufficiently obvious. As one watches hordes of young people moving from class to class laden with vast stacks of paperbacks, it is difficult to avoid the impression that the reading and study of printed books probably play a considerable part in education, and that the instructors whom they meet face-to-face in the classroom expect students to do much of their learning by reading books. And, of course, if students learn from reading books, then conversely books, or more precisely the authors of books, teach students. To omit from our evaluation of teaching all the teaching done by the living writers of books from which students learn is an oversight that we can no longer permit ourselves. We must take into account the impact of printing on the pedagogic process.

Not only do students read books at the behest of those who instruct them in the classroom; the classroom teachers themselves read and have read a far greater number of books. The classroom teacher acts mainly as a mediator between the writers he has read and the students in the classroom whom those teachers teach through his mediation. If he performs this act of mediation very badly, then he may block or impede the communication between the writers he has read and the students whom they instruct with his assistance. Only rarely will his classroom teaching be superior in quality to what is in the books from which he has learned. I can never hope to teach my students anything about Renaissance diplomacy half as good, or wise, or sound as what I read in Professor Garrett Mattingly's book on the subject. At best what I say in class will be a boiled-down version of what I learned from that book.

A little hard data is in order here. I have been a classroom teacher since 1936. In that time, on a fair estimate I have taught about 5000 students face-to-face. In the past three years I edited one book, contributed a large section to another, and wrote a third. All are for the use of college students. The combined sales of the three are already more than 100,000 copies and the end is not yet in sight. Therefore, in the past three years I taught 2000 per cent more students by publishing than I have taught face-to-face in thirty-three; and I will be teaching many more. Whether I taught better I do not know, nor can I think of any way to find out. Teachers who have graded the examinations of students they have taught are unlikely to be sanguine about the pedagogic effectiveness of either publication *or* confrontation, although the two exhaust the options.

Besides the three publications directly aimed at college students and personal profit, I have over the years published several books and articles aimed at neither. They are all the sort of thing that the students, educationists, and muddy-minded reporters of educational news contemptuously refer to as mere scholarship or mere research. Through these publications I am sure I have taught better than I have in the classroom. They represent the most intense and precise effort I am capable of in that pursuit of the truth about the past, which is my calling. Unlike the publications aimed directly at undergraduates, which only gathered together knowledge retrieved by other historians, they explored areas not hitherto investigated or cleared up confusions left by earlier explorers. To some degree these works of scholarship improved and increased the available knowledge of the past. College teachers read such works and other scholars incorporate their findings in their own studies. Thus, scholarly efforts of this kind teach a host of students who will never have heard the names of the men who wrote them. It is mainly works of this kind that academics are required to publish, or perish; and it is in the publication of such works that those who publish well do their best and most important teaching. In his "mere research and scholarship" a man provides the most reliable measure of his worth as a teacher.

Writers of books, then, teach students through the books they write and students read, and through the books they write and classroom teachers read. Once we add to our problem of evaluation of teaching the ingredient of book learning, once we accommodate our minds to the novel idea that, in most of higher education, books do most of the teaching and the best teaching, the whole problem changes in character. Teaching by publication emerges as qualitatively superior to almost all face-to-face teaching of undergraduates; in substance the former can be strikingly original, in substance the latter is bound to be in the main derivative.

There is also another sense in which the scholar who teaches by publishing is likely to do a better job qualitatively than the one who teaches face-to-face in the classroom—better especially than the academics who achieve the widest reputation as great classroom teachers through their proficiency in lecturing. The great publishing teacher does a more important job than the great lecturing teacher because he leads students along the path where their future chances of further learning lie, while the latter is likely to divert them from that path. From the time that the student enters primary school to the time he leaves college, he acquires the kind of knowledge that schools purvey decreasingly from the spoken word and increasingly from the printed word. After he leaves the academic community, the college graduate will usually acquire most of his further increments of knowledge from the printed word. His whole school education is a long process of weaning to prepare him to continue to feed himself at the table of knowledge rather than to rely on some mother figure in trousers to nurse and nourish him with a flow of spoken words. Unless this process has been brought to completion by the time he graduates from the academy, prospects for his future education are dim, for they will depend mainly on what is called self-education, which is actually education by independent reading of books. Some of the most beloved and dedicated lecturers have actually impeded the educational process by developing in their admirers a resistance to this traumatic but essentially indispensable process of weaning.

Some Familiar Fallacies

It may not have escaped notice that my discussion of teaching-by-publishing has a large built-in bias. What is involved is the assumption that the published works of scholarly research are near the level of Garrett Mattingly's, that they are usually intellectually nourishing to both teacher and student. In fact, such examples of teaching-by-publishing are hardly typical or characteristic or normal or random samples—would to God they were! Below them on the scale of teaching-by-publishing descend the rest of the species, down to the hideous, enormous, trivial mass near the bottom. To teach less or worse in the classroom, except by standing mute, than by publication of this sort is impossible, since it virtually teaches nobody anything. And yet in sheer volume the so-called scholarly work clustered near the lower end of the scale of teaching effectiveness massively outweighs the scholarly work at the upper end. In this matter, the criticism of those who do not publish is fervently and powerfully supported by those who teach most and best by publishing. It is the most conscientious among the latter group who suffer most from the masses of printed nonthink that the enforcement of the publish-or-perish principle pours into channels of learned communication. It is such men who futilely and carefully sift through the darksome sludge in time-consuming (usually time-wasting) quest for the precious nugget of learning that is so rarely there.

If the principle of publish-or-perish drives men who might profitably spend their time in preparing to teach their classes into the unrestrained effluxion of pseudoscholarly glop, would it not be better to relax that pressure so that they would devote their efforts to classroom teaching? As posed, the question encases a fallacy familiar in economics: that of the perfect transferability of resources. It assumes that all resources invested in one particular enterprise can and will fully and freely be transferred to an alternate and better enterprise—for example that if the chromium on cars were banned, all the capital invested in it could be transferred to the production of Shakespearean plays or bourbon whiskey. This is not so. Those who devote themselves to the production of scholarly nonthink lest they perish would not necessarily divert all or even any of the energy so deployed to improving their classroom teaching. They could find other ways of wastefully disposing of their time—and they do, as any citizen of Academe knows.

Even less plausible is the belief that academics who publish necessarily neglect their classroom teaching, and face-to-face with students teach worse than those who do not publish at all. Of this there is not a scintilla of credible evidence. Indeed the notion bears marks of *prima facie* improbability. It suggests that those who, by publishing, give some overt evidence of continuing engagement with the discipline to which they are presumed to have dedicated their lives are less concerned with how they teach it in the classroom than those who have provided no such evidence.

The University's Responsibility

Suppose that somehow it were possible to demonstrate that a particular academic in a great university, one who gave no credible indication that he ever would publish, was a classroom teacher superior to a colleague who was teaching by publishing. Should the responsible colleagues of those two men choose the latter over the former? Ought they, indeed, be faced with such a choice at all? Ought they not to feel free to keep both men as valuable members of the academic community of which they are a part, each with his important contribution to make? In inverse order the answers to these questions are 3) they ought not to feel free to keep both men; 2) they ought to be faced with the choice; 1) they ought to choose the man who publishes over the man who teaches well in the classroom. To give these answers is not to banish the nonpublishing teacher from plying his trade; at the probable rate of expansion of what passes for higher education, there will be a place for him somewhere; *but that place is not in a great university.* To think that it is, is gravely to misunderstand the prime function and prime obligation of a great university in the United States in the latter half of the twentieth century. It is indeed to think of those institutions in a framework appropriate perhaps to American higher education in the 1880's, but increasingly anachronistic now for almost a century.

Through most of the nineteenth century, the United States was almost wholly parasitic on Europe for the advancement of learning. Insofar as American higher education depended on knowledge and understanding generated in that century, it was massively the importer of such knowledge and understanding, while it produced very little of it for export or even for domestic consumption. Slowly at first, more conspicuously after World War I, and at a helter-skelter pace since World War II, the terms of trade have shifted. Over the whole frontier of knowledge, the current contributions of the United States to its advance varies from the impressive to the overwhelming. The whole world depends heavily on knowledge that is generated in the United States. And here the vital centers of the advancement of learning are the great universities. More and better than any other institutions, they provide the indispensable resources and conditions for that advancement—the laboratories, the libraries, the leisure to write, so that the scientist and the scholar can teach by publishing what they have discovered.

In a land of over 200,000,000 inhabitants, there are places on the faculties of the great universities for less than .01 per cent of the population. A considerable number of those places are necessarily occupied by young people in the process of acquiring the skills which sooner or later will enable them to teach by publishing. A much smaller number are occupied by rather old men no longer likely, for the rest of their professional lives, to do much more teaching of that kind. The academic places occupied in a great university by men who publish nothing might otherwise be occupied by men who do teach by publishing, men who with full access to the resources of a great university would teach more and better by publishing. With few exceptions, a great university could replace every faculty member who has taught nothing by publishing, and promises to teach nothing that way, with a new appointment who has taught by publishing already or who shows some promise of doing so in the future. Actually, great universities sometimes do rather more than this. After a scrutiny of the evidence, they replace those who *have* taught by publishing with men who, they believe, have so taught better and more, or who show promise of doing so. For them to do other and less than this would be a gross abdication of responsibility at once fiscally imprudent, economically wasteful, and morally delinquent. It would be particularly reprehensible for them to do what many of the young people involved in the student revolt demand. A great university cannot rightly offer a man a position that provides him with a life-long claim on both its financial assets and its scholarly resources without consideration of the alternative possible investment of those assets. It certainly cannot do so just because undergraduates proclaimed him to be a popular, a great, or a charismatic classroom teacher.

Classroom Teachings

Here it may be well to bury, with hopes that he may rest in peace, an old and rather seedy bogey man, the fear that the emphasis on scholarly production is such that soon all the best scholars will entirely cease to teach in the classrooms, preferring to spend all their time on research which receives more generous rewards. This supposes that given the option, many teachers-by-publishing would choose to do no classroom teaching. I know of no reason to believe that this is so.

There are indeed a few such teachers. If the value of their teaching by writing is high enough, they should probably not be inflicted on students in a classroom or have students inflicted on them; some alternative provision that would not diminish their value should probably be made for them, not because they have "earned" it, but because there is no gain in punishing them or the students by a forced and fruitless contact. There may also be a very small number of academics so obsessed with one-up-manship that temporarily at least they would find some assuagement to the anguish of their crumpled egos in the "privilege" of not teaching students face-to-face. Few scholars, however, would find such a privilege a privilege at all. The very ancient combination of scholarship and face-to-face teaching has about it an element of economic necessity, but this is not the whole of it. For most scholars their teaching-by-writing and their classroom teaching stand in symbiotic relation: each profits and grows in excellence from the practice of the other. From their classroom teaching the vast majority derive varied satisfactions: the excitement of present human response, an opportunity to try out their ideas, a chance to ham it a bit, an immediate direct sense of achievement and accomplishment, a change of pace, a relaxation of the total responsibility for their every word and statement that the printed page imposes, contact with the young and eager, and so on. To me the notion that a large number of the better teachers-by-writing are engaged in mass flight from classrooom teaching seems improbable. If I were in quest of men who would relish the nonprivilege of not teaching, I should seek not among the luminaries but among the dimmer bulbs of Academia.

The Built-in Check

There remains one small point to settle. The publish-or-perish standard admittedly generates an inordinate amount of trivial printed busywork. Can nothing be done, should nothing be done to reduce this muddy flow of words?

The answer, I think, is that not too much should be done. It is very easy for lucky, gifted men to condescend to the best efforts of others less gifted than they. But much that they have achieved, many of the able works they have published, would have been impossible or of less worth without the prior published efforts of men no less serious, no less dedicated, but simply less richly endowed than they. Published work that is less than first rate is not necessarily worthless.

Still, a considerable amount of such work is as near worthless as makes no difference. What is worse, young scholars, sensing the pressure to publish, choose busywork with a quick sure yield of publication rather than tackle something more important, more daring, but more risky. At least so it is said: and if it is true, it is not well. But the testimony of scholars who say they have to do less well than they can, in order to speed their way up the greasy pole, is a little suspect; it indicates an unbecoming obsession with poleclimbing; while allegations on such matters by those who have published nothing are even more than a little suspect.

In fact, current academic practice does incorporate some sanctions against the worst consequences of publish-or-perish. There are depths to which even the worst scholarly journals will not sink, so that the most disastrous scholarly efforts are in fact never published. Moreover, there is a hierarchy in scholarly publications, from the rock-bottom journals to the best in every field, from the vanity publishing houses to the "good addresses," and within the several disciplines the pecking order of standards is known. Finally, opinion to the contrary notwithstanding, the gerontocrats who uphold the publish-or-perish standard can and do read. At the point where they are about to pass on the grant of tenure to a colleague, and thus possibly saddle themselves with him for life, they read with considerable care. If, as is sometimes the case, the professoriate in a large department feels unable accurately to evaluate the published work of a junior colleague at a crux of his career, they seek the council of extramural experts; and in some universities resort to such counsel is a matter of course, a regular required step in the procedure of appointment or promotion to the higher academic ranks. A widespread illusion among the ill-informed to the contrary notwithstanding, what is published is not merely weighed and the number of pages counted. It is read and to the best of their ability judged by the professoriate. To require such judges to read a very large amount of fatuous prose devoted to trivialities on matters that are of no intrinsic interest to them is not a sure way to win their approbation and support. The belief that mere quantity of publication is the sole criterion for the distribution of rewards in academia would not long survive attendance of the meetings at which such distributions are decided. At such gatherings I have never heard it said, "Promote A. He has published 43,263 words more than B." What I have heard is:

1. "He could have got that whole damn book into two articles."
2. "What is left after you take the padding out?"

3. "He published that same piece twice as articles and in two different books. Plenty of mileage."
4. "I'd feel easier about recommending him if he hadn't published that last book."
5. "A young man in too big a hurry."

It is not always that way, nor are the judgments so expressed always the last word in wisdom or even justice. Still such remarks suggest that an immediate indulgence in publication is not necessarily the most prudent ploy for ambitious young academics. If they but knew it, there already exists a rule that might restrain their zeal for bursting into print for print's sake, a counterpoise to Publish or Perish. It is Publish *and* Perish.

8. Hard Times on Campus

ALAN WOLFE

Exactly how the American economy works has cutomarily been something that faculty members in other departments allowed the economists to wonder about. The academic year 1969-70 changed that. People in fields like English, history and physics discovered something basic about economics—they found out that there were more people looking for teaching jobs than there were jobs available. This labor surplus in academia—if not the first in history, certainly the first in almost anyone's memory—is certain to have very broad consequences.

The situation has been developing for some time. One aspect of the problem is that doctoral output has been increasing more rapidly than faculty positions. Between 1940 and 1964 the number of faculty positions rose enormously—from 146,929 to 494,514, an increase of 337 per cent. But in the same period, the number of doctoral graduates increased 441 per cent, from 3,290 a year to 14,490. Roughly four new Ph.D.s were granted for every three new positions available.

A closer look at doctoral output by field in recent years indicates that the surplus did not really become explosive until just recently. In most fields, the number of doctorates remained roughly the same from about 1955 to 1960. Since then, the number has doubled, and in some cases, more than doubled.

While the figures after 1967 are not yet published, preliminary reports indicate that in the past few years the rate of increase has continued to rise.

If this increase had occurred at a time when other segments of the university economy remained normal, its effect would have been severe, but not overwhelming. After all, one could have argued, it never hurts a society to have a few too many educated people. But two other developments have combined with the increase in doctorates to produce a situation much more serious than most forecasters expected.

These are the slowing down of the undergraduate boom and university budget cutting as part of a national economy drive.

Not long ago, it seemed that college enrollment would accelerate indefinitely, each year at a higher rate. Between 1946 and 1952, the number of students enrolled in American institutions of higher education remained fairly steady, increasing from 2,078,095 to 2,134,242. Then the rush began. Enrollments passed 3 million by 1957, 4 million by 1961, and 5 million by 1965. In the last few years, they have been going up by about half a million a year. A national drive was therefore undertaken to educate teachers who could teach all these students, but now there are signs that the student boom may have reached its peak. New projections by the U.S. Office of Education show that, while enrollments doubled in the ten-year period from 1957 to 1966, they will increase by only 50 per cent in the next ten years. As a reflection of the slackening pace, construction of new colleges is slowing down.

At the same time that enrollment increases taper off, "economy" has become the economic catchword. Higher education is a major victim, not only because some state officials find it easy to scare constituents with nightmares of student disruption but also because education expenditures do not result in immediately visible benefits. Some schools have instituted a policy of hiring no additional people; they recruit only to fill vacancies. Thus as the number of people coming out of graduate school increases, the number of positions into which they can step remains constant, or at best rises at a much slower rate. The human meaning of this cross-pressure is illustrated by some events that took place in the last six months of 1969:

626 people applied for jobs in the English Department of Penn State.

The contracts of eight sociologists at City College of New York were not renewed. The department had a total of twenty-seven.

Field	1957	1958	1959	1960	1961	1962	1963	1964	1965	1966	1967
English	350	333	382	397	400	486	516	556	689	714	848
History	314	297	324	342	371	343	378	507	576	599	655
Sociology	134	150	157	161	184	173	208	198	230	244	327
Psychology	550	572	635	641	703	781	844	939	847	1046	1231
Home Econ.	46	23	26	40	36	41	45	41	58	54	66
Accounting	14	17	18	15	15	27	23	21	32	34	43

At the American Historical Association meetings in December, 2,000 people were reported to be competing for 200 jobs.

At the Modern Language Association meetings, less than half of the departments that recruited in 1968 were looking for staff in 1969.

A job-seekers' caucus, created at the MLA, asked for unemployment compensation for those unable to get positions.

Brooklyn College's History Department let go seven junior members.

Early in the decade, a young person who entered graduate school was convinced that he would have a pick of jobs when he had earned his doctorate. He could not know that so many people had the same idea that the odds were about to turn against him. The shift is symbolized by changes in Selective Service regulations, the draft being the clearest indication, by its own confession, of what types of manpower are to be channeled where. In the early 1960s, graduate school was an attractive alternative to the Army, and the government agreed that an academic career was sufficiently in the national interest to warrant deferment. As the surplus developed, the regulations changed, and graduate study no longer earned deferment.

The problem is made worse because there is very little elasticity in the academic system, and what exists is threatened by the drive for economy. It is impossible, for example, for university employers to decrease wages, for the bulk of them are set by state regulations, and private universities generally must meet those standards. The wage scale slowly increases, preventing any department that operates on a more or less fixed budget from making new appointments in significant numbers. In fact, the reverse situation obtains. Most universities are now recalling senior professors from their leaves, so that all the courses can be taught. Since new labor cannot be purchased, old labor, which had been taking it easy, must speed up. It would be an understatement to say that there is resistance to this recall.

At the same time that wages steadily increase, the tenure system produces peculiarities in the distribution of faculty appointments within a department. Tenure, originally designed to protect the academic freedom of senior professors, now merely protects their job security. It guarantees that the least productive (in the sense of teaching load) members of a department will continue to be paid at higher wages than the more productive members. Meanwhile, the security of the more productive junior faculty becomes more shaky. One way that a department can gain some flexibility is by manipulating the junior faculty positions. Given the surplus, it is fairly easy to limit all junior appointments to three- or six-year terms. Then, instead of being promoted to associate professor status and salary, they are let go and a whole new group of junior faculty is brought in at the minimum rates. In large departments, such action might even release enough money to hire one extra junior faculty member. Many junior faculty now find themselves with less job security than their students, who are fairly sure to be around for four years. Actions like this also mean that the surplus affects junior faculty much more than it does any other group, with consequences that are potentially explosive.

Besides rotating junior faculty, the other ways a department can cut costs without tampering with the inefficient low teaching load of the senior professors is by exploiting part-time faculty and eliminating introductory courses. If a full-time, renowned professor is paid $25,000 for a six-hour teaching load, a part-time person can easily be obtained for a salary of $600 to $1,000 per three-unit course. Faced with a choice of $1,000 per course or $12,500 per course, the department sees an obvious way to make considerable savings. The part-time people—generally those with advanced degrees or close to getting them, but who have not found full-time work—are grateful for crumbs.

The large introductory courses were generally taught by teaching assistants, also grateful to receive derisory wages. Eliminating such courses means that the teaching assistants who remain (many of them have been active in campus political activities, and that is another reason for reducing their number) are free to teach higher level courses, thereby retaining for senior faculty their six-hour, two-graduate course teaching load. It will probably be a long time before the labor surplus changes that inequitable distribution, although it disrupts the entire system.

The forecasts of the appetite that new colleges would display for graduate students have proved sadly exaggerated. California leads the country in the building of new state colleges. Since 1960, seven of them have either opened or expanded enormously: Dominquez Hills, Fullerton, Hayward, San Bernardino, Sonoma, Stanislaus and Bakersfield (still unopened). Job-hunting graduate students are always told to check the California system; they find out how few posts there are. The seven new colleges had together an enrollment in the fall of 1969 of 28,273 (Michigan State alone has a student body of 45,950); it is not enough to absorb the excess doctorates of even one year, let alone year after year. A well-financed state university liberal arts college will usually employ one full-time English teacher for every 200 students. This means that the total enrollment of the six new colleges could hire 141 teachers of English. Since 900 to 1,000 doctorates in English will be produced in 1969-70, California will not be able to help much. And all the other state college systems are expanding at rates slower than California's. The State University of New York system plans only three new state colleges: one is open with 200 students; another will focus on the arts and therefore be small and specialized; and a third, planned for the Utica area, will cover only the third and fourth year, thereby having a proportionately smaller faculty (fewer introductory courses).

Much new college construction is at the community college and junior college level, and these institutions are the ones that might be expected to benefit most from the faculty surplus. But that is not quite true, for two reasons. One is that many community and junior colleges have small offerings in the liberal arts and physical sciences where the surplus is worst. Their needs are in applied areas, like home economics and accounting, where although doctorates have also increased since 1960 (see chart), there is still a shortage. Second, even though community colleges will be able to hire better qualified people in English and history, people trained in those fields were taught to concentrate on research, not teaching, and that community colleges are poor places to work. So, though community colleges may be able to hire them, they will try to get out as fast as possible.

There are also distributive problems with respect to the creation of new programs within existing universities. The demands for open admissions, colleges of urban studies, ethnic studies institutes and experimental colleges will add very little new faculty, and those that are hired will be in specialized areas relevant to those demands. Right now there is a shortage of nonwhite faculty. This may mean that a number of nonwhite students will go to graduate school in the hope of obtaining a faculty appointment when they leave ("Being black, you can name your own price"). This implies that the surplus will reach that area a little later (all deliberate speed, so to speak). Meanwhile, the scarcity of black teachers does little to alleviate the surplus in other areas. If anything, it adds to it, for more universities, when faced with the choice of hiring someone in Afro-American history or in intellectual history, will now decide on the former.

One final rigidity in the academic market place that doesn't show up in the hypothetical supply-and-demand market place of classical economics is the inability of the job seekers to move elsewhere in the economic system when the universities are closed to them. After World War II, large numbers of lower-middle-class upwardly mobile children went into academia rather than into their fathers' shops and stores. Thoroughly alienated from their parents' world, they have no place to go if not into teaching. High school teaching might be an alternative, but the surplus is heavy there also. The system has been cruel to the young scholars, holding out an empty promise. They will probably have no choice but to dawdle on their theses, in the hope that there will be a break in the cycle. They will be, to use Marx's term, the first reserve army of the unemployed with Ph.D.s. More important, they will also be a modified form of "scab" labor. Let there be unrest at a university, and department chairmen will know where to find replacements for the troublemakers.

What makes a labor surplus in any economic area interesting is not that fewer people work but that the nature of institutions changes. For example, a labor surplus among middle-class housewives who wanted to work but who were untrained was closely related to the rise of discount department stores. Such stores could hire at very low rates of pay, thereby cutting prices in competition with the older department stores. The surplus changed the institution of department-store shopping.

Similar consequences seem to exist for the university. The great shame of the faculty surplus and the economy moves is not only that trained people will be unable to put their skills to work but that those who do find jobs will be extra careful to keep them. It would be foolish to expect university employers not to take advantage of the labor surplus to promote the values that academic departments hold dear. A study of confidential letters of recommendations in sociology showed that the major virtue the writers emphasized was the ability of the prospective staff member to be harmonious and nondisruptive. We can therefore expect that the labor surplus will encourage departments to promote internal harmony by keeping potential troublemakers out and making sure that potential troublemakers within the department remain quiet.

The two groups most likely to be seen as not belonging in academia are women and radicals, and caucuses within professional associations representing both groups have already noted the effects of the surplus. It is not that women are biologically more likely than men to cause trouble. It is that the men who do the hiring think of women as supportive creatures, not faculty colleagues. Speaking at a

University of California Medical Center symposium a few years ago, Prof. David Krech, a famous psychologist, flatly asserted that "Women shouldn't have seats in postgraduate schools," and his opinion cannot be dismissed as the rantings of just one uptight male. A study asked respondents (all male) to rank essays for their suitability for publication in a journal. When a woman's name was placed as author of a paper, more responses like "unscholarly" or "emotional" came in than when a man's name appeared on the same paper. The respondents presumably agree with Bruno Bettleheim: "We must start with the realization that, as much as women want to be good scientists or engineers, they want first and foremost to be womanly companions of men and to be mothers."

Such perceptions of women must be widespread among men who hire for departments or who admit to graduate schools. How else explain that the percentage of women on faculties of American universities was lower in 1960 than it was in 1949, 1930 and even 1920? Such discrimination has always existed, but the surplus will intensify it. Women in 1952 received 31.4 per cent of all masters degrees and 9.3 per cent of all doctorates. By 1959, they had risen to 32 per cent and 10 per cent; in 1966, the figures were 34 per cent and 12 per cent. That trend means that the surplus will be even worse for women than for men.

Radicals face much the same problem. Again there is no proof of a correlation between radical politics and departmental disruption. With women, however, the surplus has the effect of reversing a slight trend in their favor; with radicals, it will intensify what was already a major repressive campaign.

It is impossible to document the number of radicals who have been fired from academic departments in recent years. Not only is information on political views a private matter (sometimes) but few departments will admit that an individual has been fired for his politics. Various forms of "conduct unbecoming a professor," like "turning on" with students, dressing casually, studying trustee backgrounds or using experimental classroom techniques, are more easily substituted. Nonetheless, conversations with many who are involved indicate that subtle forms of "black listing" are more prevalent than ever. Confidential letters of recommendation, combined with a general move against activists as a national trend, guarantee that the reputation of someone defined as a "radical" will follow him all the days of his life.

The surplus, however, will render black lists irrelevant. During a labor shortage, employers need some place to turn for ready information on the undesirable. Now they will simply pick the "safest" candidates from the enormous numbers available. The surplus will also mean that all faculty and prospective faculty will feel enormous pressure to appear "safe." The conformity, not only political but also in terms of teaching methods and general behavior that will stem from the surplus, could have an appallingly stagnating effect on higher education in America. Because of the surplus, in short, the universities in the near future will not provide much alternative to the quality of life to be found elsewhere in the society.

The only positive benefits of the surplus will be felt outside the United States. The much talked about "brain drain," in which American universities skimmed off the best minds from all over the world, or at least the non-Communist world, for use in American science, should be stemmed. The best result would be that many non-American students would take their skills and knowledge home, but that will not happen automatically. This country may continue to exploit non-American academics (and their countries) because it is cheaper to do so. That, of course, would make the situation still worse for American graduates, but in this area there is at least a chance that something relatively good will come from the surplus.

How accurate these predictions turn out to be depends, really, on whether the surplus is temporary or permanent, and that prediction is the most difficult. Yet is seems clear that the faculty surplus is not an event isolated from the rest of American society. For example, both the surplus and the national economy drive must be seen as parts of a current crisis in the American economy. Two aspects of that crisis which affect the universities are the anarchic way in which economic decisions are made in the United States and the influence of automation and its resulting unemployment.

A totally unplanned economy has always been something that smart capitalists knew they should avoid, but in this respect universities have never been smart. Decisions in academic life are still made by small units without coordination or long-range planning. Each unit operates according to its own immediate interest, and the entire system pays for the consequences. It is extraordinary that a surplus should occur in the labor market at the very moment when the employers begin an economy drive, yet it follows from the way universities do business.

Anarchy is not all. The automating American economy has begun to develop a vested interest in keeping people off the labor market as long as possible. Like the invention of adolescence, graduate schools contribute to that delay. An increasing number of people have not sought full-time work until they were into their late twenties. Now it seems that they may not find full-time work until much later.

This is a potentially incendiary situation. Because of the chaos created by lack of administrative planning, junior faculty and people just out of graduate school are once again paying for the follies of their elders. And they know it. Already a number of overeducated people without jobs are working full time for revolution in this country. Some are even sent to jail, which is one way of keeping them off the labor force. The numbers of such people will increase. Is that a positive or negative development? I think it positive, but the point on which we can all agree is that the faculty surplus and the economy drive may change, not only the American university but also the entire society.

IV

WORK AS LEISURE

Leisure, for most men, is the free and unoccupied time in which one rests from work. But for the intellectual craftsman, work and leisure are fused; one imperceptibly shades over into the other with no clear break in between.

A comparison by Gerstl of the leisure activity of academics with that of dentists and admen reveals some major differences between the groups. Unlike the admen and dentists, the professors were often unable to differentiate between work and leisure. In terms of distinctly "non-work" activities, professors more often than admen and dentists preferred to devote their time to reading and the performing arts, especially music. Television viewing was eschewed by professors, while informal visiting and conversation around dinner tended to be a norm. Social life through clubs and organizations was found to be minimal among academics.

A very similar image of leisure time activity among academics appears in the paper by Anderson and Murray. The fusion of job-related interests with media exposure and free time was marked. The influence of the disciplined and critical nature of the respondents' work environment was evident in their relatively selective orientation in regard to the offerings of American culture. Self-defined intellectuals reported more overlap between work and leisure and evinced greater discrimination in culture consumption. Clearly, the academic community remains an important bulwark against the debasement of the mind by peddlers of instant thrills through superficial entertainment and technological gimmickry, even though academics themselves have often sold their skills to the creation of counterfeit culture.

9. Leisure, Taste and Occupational Milieu

JOEL E. GERSTL

"Leisure—even for those who do not work—is at bottom a function of work, flows from work, and changes as the nature of work changes."[1]

While the question of the fusion and/or polarity of work and leisure has frequently been considered, the referent has usually been a generic one. Most often, the focus has been upon the situation of the industrial worker, or upon contrasts between the masses and the classes, or between society-wide status levels.[2] Certainly, in considering leisure as a social problem—for example, in projecting the differential changes in the workweek to a future in which the bulk of the population will work shorter hours while managerial and professional strata will continue to carry work home evenings and weekends—analysis must remain concerned with wide societal categories. However, to contrast manual workers' patterns of leisure with those of professional people is not to explain the differences. It may well be that much of the explanation of social class differences in the uses of leisure is spurious to the extent that such research obfuscates contrasts *within* a stratum. Whether spurious or not, this type of analysis fails to reveal the crucial link between structure and behavior.

Revised version of a paper read at the meetings of the Society for the Study of Social Problems, New York, August, 1960.

1. Glement Greenberg, "Work and Leisure Under Industrialism," in *Mass Leisure*, Eric Larrabee and Rolf Meyersohn, eds., Glencoe: The Free Press, 1958, p. 38.
2. The most immediate reference is David Riesman and Warner Bloomberg, Jr., "Work and Leisure: Fusion and Polarity?" in *Research in Industrial Human Relations*, Conrad M. Arensberg, *et. al.*, eds., New York: Harper and Brothers, 1957, and David Riesman, "Leisure and Work in Post-Industrial Society," in *Mass Leisure, op. cit.* Similar general referents are used in most of the literature in both the study of leisure and stratification; for example, Alfred C. Clarke, "The Use of Leisure and its Relations to Levels of Occupational Prestige," *American Sociological Review*, 21 (June, 1956), pp. 301-07; Leonard Riesman, "Social Class, Leisure and Social Participation," *American Sociological Review*, 19 (February, 1954), pp. 76-84; R. Clyde White, "Social Class Differences in the Use of Leisure," *American Journal of Sociology*, LXI (September, 1955), pp. 145-50.

It is not merely *because* a person is high in the prestige hierarchy of his society that he takes work home or belongs to a chamber music society (although he may well do both in order to maintain or reinforce his high status). While prestigeful leisure behavior is of course related to social class position, its explanation must be linked to intervening variables.

It is the argument of this paper that incumbency in a particular occupational milieu is one of the most crucial of these intervening variables. For, while the existence of occupational milieus is a seemingly patent feature of life, and while the descriptive literature of occupational sociology is voluminous, the importance of occupation upon style of life in studies of stratification has been minimized by using occupation merely as an index (or part of an index) of social placement.

In order to examine the effect of membership in a particular occupation upon non-occupational behavior while holding social class constant, it is obviously necessary to contrast occupations at approximately the same prestige level whose work situation differs considerably. Three upper-middle class occupational situations have been chosen for this purpose: the independent professional practitioner, the organization man of the corporate world, and the salaried intellectual. The occupations representing these three types are: the dentist (one of the few professionals still predominantly in solo practice and strangely enough almost missing from the growing sociological literature on professions), the adman (an intriguing villain of contemporary social criticism and archetype of the organizational world), and the college professor (an anomaly in the social order with high prestige and an incommensurate income).

The present study is based upon interviews, using both structured and open-ended items, with 75 respondents, one-third in each of the occupational groups, all conducted by the writer. The dentists and admen were from a large mid-western city in the United States; the college professors were on the faculty of a small residential college, which will be referred to as Sauk College, located some distance from an urban center. As a result of pre-determined controls for occupational stability and stage in life cycle, all respondents were around the age of 40.[3]

The aim of this paper is exploratory: to examine the links between

3. For a detailed discussion of sample selection and sample characteristics, see Joel E. Gerstl, *Career Commitment and Style of Life in Three Middle Class Occupations*, unpublished doctoral dissertation, University of Minnesota, 1959, pp. 27-50.

occupational milieu—including the nature of the work performed, the setting of the work situation, and the norms derived from occupational reference groups—and non-occupational behavior, the realm of leisure. The examination of leisure is undertaken in terms of its range—from the narrow circle of family, outward to the larger community.[4]

Home Life

There is probably no major activity under the broad heading of leisure which is more difficult to accurately account for than is time which is spent "at home." Without having attempted a detailed time-budget, the following account is restricted to the most salient categories revealed in response to open-ended questions concerning the ways evenings and week-ends were spent. These categories were: time with children, household chores, television viewing, reading, work-connected activities and specific recreational interests.

A major occupational contrast is the extent to which working time permeates the rest of life. This is clearly the basic effect of the structure of the work situation and of the possibilities stemming from the nature of particular types of work. The professors' 56-60 hour work-week necessarily includes evening and week-end work, usually done at home. The admen's working schedule averages 45 hours a week; although crises and deadlines seem ever-present, few do night work more than a dozen times a month. It comes as no great surprise that the dentists do not take their work home; their 40 hours a week rarely spill-over beyond office time.[5]

Interestingly, the nature of occupational milieu explains not only the actual distribution of working time, but also orientation to hypothetical time. The striking differences between occupations are shown in Table 1. In considering what they might do with two extra hours in the day, professors expressed no desire to relax and are most inclined to work more. The dentists wanted above all to spend time with their hobbies and recreational activities; almost an equal number gave first priority to relaxation, as they are tired after a long day of standing on their feet. Admen are equally desirous of recreational time, with fam-

4. This model is similar to that employed in the Kansas City Study of Adult Life. See Robert J. Havighurst, "The Leisure Activities of the Middle-Aged," *American Journal of Sociology*, LXIII (September, 1957), pp. 152-62, and Robert J. Havighurst and Kenneth Feigenbarm, "Leisure and Life Style," *American Journal of Sociology*, LXIV (January, 1959), pp. 396-404.

5. Working hours were ascertained by asking for a detailed account of the respondent's daily routine, with probes for evening and week-end work.

Table 1.

Hypothetical Use of Two Extra Hours By Occupation

Activity	Admen	Dentists	Professors
Relaxation	12.1%	29.4%	0.0%
Family-home	24.3	14.7	9.4
Recreational reading	12.1	14.7	28.1
Hobby or recreation	33.3	32.4	12.5
Work or work-connected reading	18.2	8.8	50.0
Total	100%	100%	100%
Number of responses*	(33)	(34)	(32)

* Multiple responses were given.

ily and home activity their second alternative. These contrasting wishes suggest that it is not merely high occupational prestige which makes for the convergence of work and leisure as previous research has indicated.[6]

While the amount of time spent with one's children is difficult to estimate accurately, respondents' statements can be readily rated as great, moderate or minimal. (Minimal time would, in the extreme, involve being with children only at meals.) The admen and dentists do not differ greatly in the amount of time spent with their children; 40 per cent of the former and 30 per cent of the latter spend a minimal amount of time in this activity, in sharp contrast, two-thirds of the professors do.[7]

The modal estimate of time devoted to household chores is between three and seven hours for each of the three groups. But, one-third of the professors, one-fifth of the admen and only a single dentist do *no* household work. This almost universal activity in household tasks among dentists is likely to be an indication of work upon leisure—in his facility in tinkering and the use of his hands.

6. Alfred C. Clarke, *op. cit.*, used the identical question of a hypothetical two hours. He finds the desire to work, read, or study to increase as one goes up in prestige level; those lowest on his prestige scale want, above all, to relax, loaf, and sleep. Curiously, he reports no category of hobbies or recreation.

7. The use of the hypothetical two hours (Table 1) is relevant here. It suggests that the admen *want* most to spend more time with their children, feeling that they do not spend sufficient time at present, and that they probably *do* spend less time than do the dentists. The professors appear content with the amount of time they spend with their families.

Both dentists and admen watch television for a modal five to ten hours, with one-third in each group watching 11 to 20 hours. Their viewing habits are considerably below the national average of 18 hours a week,[8] albeit interviewing was done in the Spring, when a man's fancy turns from the tube. The situation among the professors is quite different, for extended TV viewing is strongly against the norms of Sauk. Indeed, over half of the professors do not own a television set, and are proud of it. Two-thirds of the owners claim to watch less than four hours a week, and all but one of the rest watch less than ten hours. The one exception was quite conscious of his deviancy from Sauk TV norms.

The home life of the Sauk professor is distinct from that of the other groups largely due to the pervasiveness of his work-connected activities. Much of the time that the adman and the dentist spends with his children or watching TV is, for the professor, spent in his work. Probably this allows him to get away with doing less around the house.[9] The adman spends somewhat less time in household chores and with his children than does the dentist. The working hours and schedules of each as well as alternative recreational interests and amounts of time devoted to reading (which will be considered subsequently) help to account for these contrasting patterns.

Recreation & Vacation

Most obvious from the information conveyed in Table 2 is the sedentary way of life of the Sauk professors—not only in their work, but in their leisure as well.[10] Forty per cent took part in no sports activity of any kind; for all but three of the others, the extent of participation was low. While admen and dentists are represented in approximately an equal number of sports, the admen are more active. For example, the number of admen and dentists playing golf is almost identical, but while most of the dentists play but once a week, the admen play twice a week or more. Partially this is a result of the respective work schedules—the adman has more of a chance to sneak in nine holes or more during a "working" day. More important for the adman is the

8. Rolf B. Meyersohn, "Social Research in Television," in *Mass Culture*, Bernard Rosenberg and David M. White, eds., Glencoe: The Free Press, 1957, p. 345.

9. David Riesman, in commenting upon this finding, has suggested the importance of the differential cultural approval of work: there being little ambivalence concerning academic work, the wives and children must put up with it.

10. Cf. Herbert Collins, "The Sedentary Society," in *Mass Leisure, op. cit.,* pp. 19-30.

Table 2.

*Index of Sports Activity By Occupation**

Activity	Admen	Dentists	Professors
Golf	32	27	0
Hunting	7	18	1
Fishing	17	28	5
Bowling	8	4	0
Swimming	29	13	10
Boating-Sailing	8	2	2
Hiking-Walking	13	1	10
Skiing	10	0	3
Tennis	9	6	6
Other activities	18	19	10
Total recreational score	151	118	47

*The index consists of a combination of the number of respondents mentioning an activity (in response to the question: Do you take part in any recreational activities?) times the frequency of participation score. Infrequent = 1, Moderate = 2, Heavy = 3.

fairly common conduct of business on the green or in the club. Indeed, some indicated that they must play golf for business reasons, even though they do not like the game.

Another function of physical recreation frequently volunteered by the admen is for the release of strain and tension, which they admit to be considerable. While the dentist also feels great strains in his work—many are surprisingly sensitive about their sadistic functional role—the nature of work strains are quite different in the two cases. Both view physical recreation as escape, but for one it is to "blow off steam," for the other it is mainly to relax. While the adman finds his satisfactions in frequent and active sports, the dentist indulges more in routinized golf and seasonal hunting and fishing.

Items mentioned by respondents as hobbies include activities pursued frequently and with great zeal as well as sporadic or habitual time fillers. In spite of this ambiguity, there are occupational contrasts.

The most frequent hobby, mentioned by more than half of the dentists, consists of some variety of "do-it-yourself"—ranging from home repairs to wood-working to gardening. Only in one case was there a more immediate and direct vocational link to avocational interests, represented by metallurgical research.

Vocational influences are stronger among the admen. Reading and painting received almost as many mentions as did the do-it-yourself category. Half of those who paint in their leisure had in mind the non-commercial counterpart of their vocation; for the others, the day-to-day interaction with artists is probably a motivating factor. Similarly, references to writing were also frequent, involving the transfer of verbal facility from the writing of copy to the writing of "the great American novel" (or short stories for *Playboy*).

The professors care least for do-it-yourself. Music is the most frequent recreational activity at Sauk. Two-thirds of the professors mentioned it as a major leisure interest, and half of these are active participants in instrumental and vocal groups. In addition to general reading, many professors expressed interest in disciplines related to their own fields. In some cases this was thought of as the inseparable nature of literature, music, and art. In others, it was more a matter of the desire for intellectual awareness as such—the humanist might even read *The Organization Man* before blasting the sociologist.

Differences in vacation patterns clearly reveal occupational structuring. The adman's modal two or three weeks is a function of corporation policy. Less than a third of the professors take the full academic summer, but the potential is there—subject, above all, to financial possibility. Curiously, dentists have the most clearly defined vacation norm—three weeks—even though theirs is the most autonomous decision.

The fusion of work into leisure is again greatest among the professors. Even those who take the entire academic vacation claim not to forsake their calling, whether in European travel or a summer cottage in Maine. The majority of the professors, however, do not remain unemployed for the entire summer. Since Sauk has no summer school, they either teach elsewhere, take part in research projects, or hold positions in industry.

Almost half of the Sauk professors also take trips away from campus during Christmas vacation or between semesters; these are frequently a combination of attendance at professional meetings and other purposes. Most of the dentists, on the other hand, do not attend professional meetings outside the state. Business trips are quite frequent for the admen, one-fifth spending a week or more each month in travel. Of course not all of this time is spent entirely in work.

Visiting and Viewing

Although the admen are slightly more gregarious than the other two occupational groups, differences are minor. Four-fifths of the admen and three-fourths of the dentists and professors visit with friends at least once a week; more admen than either of the other groups visit more than once a week. The dentists have a larger number of close friends than do the admen or professors—the median number for them is six, while it is five for the latter two occupations.[11]

The content and purpose of social relations with friends varies among the three groups. Perhaps the major distinction centers upon patterns of conversation-drinking by admen, card-playing by dentists, and conversation-eating by the Sauk professors. The frequent exchange of dinners in the last mentioned group reflects the social life of a small community. Although the card-playing evenings of the dentists are sometimes accompanied by dinners, commensalism is less frequent for them than it is among the professors and is least frequent among admen. The emphasis upon conversation on the part of the admen and professors, as contrasted with the card-playing dentists, might well be a reflection of occupationally based verbal facility. Obviously, this is not to suggest that the dentists do not talk to their friends, but it would appear that while small talk during card playing is not thought of as a social *activity*, conversation—whether about people, ideas or business (not about teeth)—is more likely to be considered an end in itself.

While all three occupational groups visit with friends more frequently than is usual for an urban cross-section, admen and dentists visit with relatives at a rate roughly comparable to the population as a whole.[12] The majority of admen and dentists see their relatives (and/ or in-laws), at least once a week, one-fifth of each group see them twice a month, and the rest only several times a year or less. The Sauk professors, on the other hand, typically live far away from relatives and tend to see them but annually.

Apart from family life, recreational activity, and visiting, a consideration of uses of leisure time must also include spectator activities

11. While most of the professors and two-thirds of the admen have a high proportion of colleagues among their best friends, only 20 per cent of the dentists do. See Joel E. Gerstl, "Determinants of Occupational Community in High Status Occupations," *The Sociological Quarterly*, II (January, 1961), pp. 37-48.

12. Morris Axelrod, "Urban Structure and Social Participation," *American Sociological Review*, 21 (February, 1956) p. 16. In the Detroit area, association with relatives is reported as: 49 per cent at least once a week, 13 per cent a few times a month, 12 per cent about once a month, 22 per cent less often. For association with friends, the figures are: 28 per cent at least once a week, 19 per cent a few times a month, 18 per cent about once a month, and 31 per cent less often. Part of the difference between these figures on friends and ours is due to Axelrod's data not including neighbors as friends. More importantly, there is no reason to expect our three high status occupational groups to resemble an urban cross-section.

(supplementary to the previously discussed television viewing). Most relevant are attendance at movies and sports events.[13]

The Sauk professors attend movies more frequently than do either of the other two groups. Three-fourths attend at least once a month, and half at least twice a month. Certainly this is connected with their limited exposure to television. By sharp contrast, 44 per cent of the admen and only 28 per cent of the dentists attend once a month or more. One-fourth of the admen and almost half of the dentists hardly ever go to the movies; this is true of only three of the professors. While the contrast between admen and dentists is not great, the latter attend movies less frequently.

There are only minor occupational differences in attendance at sports events. One-fourth of the admen, over one-third of the dentists, and one-fifth of the professors never attend.[14] In each case, the modal pattern is to attend between five and ten games in the course of the year. The enthusiasts, those who attend eleven games or more, do not include more than a fifth of any of the groups.

Voluntary Associations

While membership in occupational associations is to a large extent dictated by particular occupational roles, the amount of participation represents an area of activity which falls between the spheres of work and leisure. The dentists are most active in their professional societies, while the Sauk professors are significantly less active than either of the other two groups. The consideration of participation in organizations which are not directly connected with the work role of the respondents again reveals the academic group to be least active.

Almost half of the Sauk professors denied even nominal membership in any non-professional organization. Negative responses included references to the "absurd waste of time that such nonsense often results in," and the virtue of a small town that does not necessitate such activity. One-fifth mentioned membership in a church or with a church-connected group as their only organizational affiliation. One-fourth were involved in college activities—including athletic, musical and social groups. In addition there were scattered references to membership in PTA, and activity with scout groups. There were but two major

13. Theater and concert attendance will be considered subsequently.
14. It should be noted that attendance at sports events is a different matter for the professors since all their attendance, with one or two exceptions, refers to Sauk sports. The professors in attending these events are not necessarily displaying their enthusiasm for sports, but rather for the glory of Sauk.

deviations from the norm of low participation and minimal activity in the non-college community.

The dentists belong to a larger number of groups than the admen, but participate less in each. Hence in an index which combines the number of organizations with a measure of the extent of participation, admen and dentists are quire similar. The high association between participation in occupational and other types of voluntary organizations for all three groups is shown in Table 3. This relationship—indicating that participation in professional societies is part of the syndrome of "joiner"—is strongest for the admen and the professors. Admen tend to be active in both professional and non-professional groups, professors in neither. The majority of dentists are active in their professional associations, whether or not they are active in other groups.

Unlike the Sauk professors, most admen and dentists are at least moderately active in various associations. While one-third of the professors hold no formal organizational memberships—outside of their professional societies—only one dentist and two admen are in a similar position.

The type of organization in which membership is held, as indicated in Table 4, is even more revealing of occupational differences than is the designation of the extent of participation. The most striking contrast is the concentration of dentists in fraternal organizations and that of admen in civic activity.

While it is not necessary to posit the furthering of one's contacts for

Table 3.

Extent of Participation in Voluntary Associations By Extent of Participation in Occupational Associations

Voluntary Associations	Professional Associations	
	Low	High
Low	77%	35%
High	23	65
Total	100%	100%
Number of cases	(35)	(40)

Chi square = 13.8, p<.001.

Table 4.

Types of Organizational Membership for Admen and Dentists

Type of Organization	Admen	Dentists
Church committees and clubs	4	12
Fraternal	3	24
Youth service	10	9
Civic	24	9
Recreational	19	12
Total number of organizational memberships	60*	66*

* Includes multiple memberships.

"business" reasons as the sole justification for membership in fraternal organizations, and while there probably is a segregation of work interests and leisure fellowship for some, business reasons are probably an important determinant of the large number of memberships by dentists in these groups. Similar reasons might also be relevant to their other memberships.

The dentists are not only the most active in church organizations, but are also most regular—or most compulsive—in attendance. All but two of the Protestant[15] dentists attend church at least three times a month, half claiming regular weekly attendance. By contrast, one-third of the Protestant admen and almost half of the professors attend church but several times a year, or not at all. One-fourth of the professors and a slightly larger proportion of the admen attend weekly. The extremes represented by the dentists and the professors are highlighted in that in the course of answering questions concerning religious attendance, the dentists apologized for not attending more, the professors for attending as much as they did.

Whatever the specific motivations for the differential membership and participation patterns, these patterns are indicators of life style. For the dentists, the concentration is in fraternal and church groups. This range of participation would in part explain the social image which they hold of themselves. For, although they consider their oc-

15. All the Catholic respondents claimed weekly church attendance, while the two Jewish ones attended only several times a year. This makes the appropriate occupational contrast one between Protestant respondents.

cupational prestige to be high they insist that their social position is not more than middle-class.[16]

In light of the positions held by many of the admen in large agencies, it would be less likely that membership in any voluntary association would be of direct assistance to them in terms of business contacts. Their occupational role does, however, explain the heavy concentration in civic work. About half of the admen have done work with voluntary health organizations and/or the Community Chest. Frequently this activity is part of their occupational role, utilizing vocational skills—for example, they may be the representative of their firm for a particular drive, or do the art work in a campaign. Often the activity may begin as part of their work task and then continue beyond it—in terms of both time and involvement. A more direct vocational link exists when a client is interested in a voluntary organization. But the range of civic activities is considerably wider than that which is represented by policy dictates of firms and clients.[17]

Just as the profession as a whole attempts to raise its societal image by concerted public service efforts through the Advertising Council of America, so local occupational associations and particular companies attempt to foster this type of activity. The larger companies all heartily support the time and effort their employees put into public service campaigns. Indeed, they advertise this activity. The occupation's attempt at raising its image has a counterpart on the level of the individuals

16. Over two-thirds of the dentists rated themselves as one of the top three occupations from a list of eleven consisting of: physician, business executive, lawyer, scientist, minister, architect, journalist, foreign service diplomat, dentist, adman, college professor. None of the admen or professors placed the dentists in the top three. See Joel E. Gerstl, *op. cit.* An open-ended social class question produced the following results:

Social Class	Admen	Dentists	Professors
Lower-middle, Middle, Common, or "Not Society"	32%	84%	72%
Upper-middle, Lower-upper	60	12	8
Don't know, Are no classes	8	4	20

17. Civic commitments include: the Citizens League, a hospital board, the Citizen's Committee for Education, the National Council of Christians and Jews, the NAACP Board, a township citizen's council, a Republican precinct chairmanship, the Chamber of Commerce, and several other businessmen's groups. In addition, memberships in youth service groups tend to be at the executive levels of such organizations as the YMCA or Big Brothers. (Dentists active in youth service were mainly referring to PTA and local scouting groups).

involved. In spite of the admen's enthusiastic statements of devotion to his work, he is bothered by the low status of his calling. He hopes that by doing good works he can help to alleviate the nasty image which, in spite of his protests, clings in the mind of the public. Certainly the striving for higher occupational prestige would be a major factor in determining the type of activity to which time and effort is devoted. While the adman recognizes the low status of his work he accords himself a high standing in his community.[18] His activity in civic associations helps to fill this gap.

The spread of various types of leisure time activities throughout the societal strata of the contemporary United States does not make it possible to ascribe prestige to *types* of recreational clubs. However, on the basis of an intuitive ranking of the prestige of the *particular* clubs in which respondents hold membership, it would appear that the admen more than the dentists belong to groups of a higher prestige level.

Consideration of the participation patterns of the respondents' wives in voluntary associations affords further indication of the contrasts in the life styles of the three groups. Each manifests a unique pattern as Table 5 indicates.

Table 5.

Wives' Organizational Participation By Occupation of Husband

Range of Participation	Admen	Dentists	Professors
None	42%	33%	23%
Church groups only	8	21	4
Local groups*	17	46	55
Civic, charity and professional	33	0	18
Total	100%	100%	100%
Number of wives	(24)	(24)	(22)

* The category designated as local groups consists of neighborhood women's clubs, youth service groups such as Boy Scouts, and the Parent-Teacher's association. Women's auxiliary groups of their husband's occupations have also been included in this middle category.

18. See the social class distribution in footnote 16. While the admen do not rate their occupational prestige as low as they are rated by professors and dentists, in conformity with the pervasive tendency to overestimate the status of one's own occupation, they accord themselves a fairly low status and are very conscious of their even lower status in the eyes of outsiders.

The correspondence of prestige levels of the organizational participation of husbands and wives is striking. Dentists reveal a life style consonant with a middle-class image, with fraternal lodges for the husbands and church clubs for the wives. The upper-middle class admen and their wives are, on the other hand, involved in a wider and more prestigeful range of organization—in the wider community.[19] Opportunities for organizational participation for the wives of the college professors are circumscribed. Indeed, the limitations of the community in this (as well as other) respects was a great source of discontent among faculty wives. Nevertheless, the academic wives, more than the wives of admen and dentists, do participate in at least some voluntary associations.

Taste

Apart from the general notion of range and of prestige levels, the foregoing analysis has been essentially quantitative: who does how much of what. A basic adjunct is in the realm of taste: who indulges in the "higher" things of life?

While the members of the three occupational groups are all more or less middlebrow (with a few possible shadings into high and low brow) in Lynes' use of the term,[20] the contrast between the extremes *within* the middlebrow category is most revealing. Accordingly, the present attempt is simply to make the gross distinction between "upper" and "lower" brow. Six items constitute the measure and operational definition of taste: attendance at theaters and concerts, musical taste, hours spent reading, number of books read, and types of magazines read.[21] The findings are summarized in Table 6.

19. The social background of wives is no doubt relevant in this context. (The respondents in the 3 occupations had similar backgrounds.) There is a decided tendency for dentists to have married "less well" than either of the other two groups. Whereas three-fourths of both admen and professors married the daughters of managers-proprietors or professionals, none of the dentists were married to professionals' daughters and only one-fourth of their wives had managerial-proprietor fathers; forty-five per cent had blue-collar fathers. Similarly, most of the dentists' wives did not attend college, while wives of admen and professors did.

20. Russell Lynes, *The Tastemakers*, New York: Harper and Brothers, 1955.

21. Obviously this brow measure is a crude one. It might be argued that to attend theater is not upper brow if the show is a banal musical comedy. Even more serious would be the charge that the brow of the book-reader could only be ascertained according to the nature of the book read. Certainly I would want to make such distinctions if the present "instrument" were to be elaborated. In the present context, however, I would argue that to read books—regardless of contents—is higher brow than not to read books at all. Similarly, even bad theater involves exposure to a range of

Table 6.

Percentage of Upperbrow Responses By Occupation

Brow Measures	Admen	Dentists	Professors
Theater attendance	68	32	64 (96)*
Concert attendance	44	28	64 (100)*
Musical taste	16	· 24	96
Hours reading	52	20	60**
Number of books	56	16	80**
Magazine type	0	0	68
Total score	236	120	432 (500)
Mean score	40	20	72 (83)

* The figures in parentheses include those who attended concerts and theaters only at Sauk.

** These figures refer to reading which it not concerned with work, a distinction many found difficult to make.

The first two measures, of theater and concert going, indicate those who attended at least one performance in the past year. Although the Sauk professor must travel a considerable distance to attend non-college performances, he attended the theater twice as much as did the adman (the frequent business trips of the latter to Chicago and New York notwithstanding). The professors also attended the largest number of concert performances.

Upper-brow musical taste indicates a preference for classical music. The majority of dentists and admen favored "pops" or "quiet dance music." Two respondents, both dentists, prefer "top-ten" tunes. One-fourth of the admen like "good jazz" in addition, or instead of, their diet of "pops." None of the dentists shared this taste. Most of the professors were more specific than "classical music" and several liked jazz in addition to the classics. Only one professor admitted preferring "light music" to classical. The pervasiveness of norms of musical taste at Sauk is corroborated by the high rate of attendance at Sauk concerts and in the amount of participation in musical groups by the faculty.

---

experience different from even the best of TV. For some insightful comments concerning brows (if not their measurement) see, Edward Shils, "Mass Society and Its Culture," and Ernest Van den Haag, "A Dissent from the Consensual Society," *Daedalus* 89 (Spring, 1960), pp. 288-324.

Comparison of taste and concert attendance reveals an interesting discrepancy. While only 16 per cent of the admen admit to enjoying classical music, 44 per cent have attended concerts in the past year. The implication is that 28 per cent of the admen doze through the concerts to which their wives drag them. The dentists are less concerned with this symbol of display—the discrepancy between likes and attendance consists of but a single person.

The dichotomy of high and low recreational reading was made on the basis of less than five hours and five or more. Although it is undoubtedly difficult to estimate the amount of time one has spent reading, less than five hours a week cannot involve very much more than the daily newspaper and glancing at some magazines.

Number of books read separates those who read at least one (non-work connected) book in the last month and those who read less than ten in the last year. Detailed contrasts are sharper than the dichotomy reveals. Fifty-six per cent of the dentists had read *no* books in the last year, while one-fourth of the admen and three professors made similar admissions. At the other extreme, 44 per cent of the professors, one-fourth of the admen, and two dentists claimed to have read three or more books in the month preceding the interview.

The final measure distinguishes between higher and lower brow magazines. Lowerbrow subsumes most of the mass periodicals: *House and Garden, Life, Saturday Evening Post, Reader's Digest, Argosy,* and downward. The upperbrow category includes: *Harper's, The New Yorker, Saturday Review, Encounter,* and up through the little magazines.[22] The list of magazines read by each respondent was categorized according to direction of emphasis. Interestingly, there was almost no contamination—the reader of some higher brow magazines reads many, and vice-versa. [sic]

While it is no doubt rather disconcerting to find almost a third of the professors limiting themselves to lowerbrow magazines, the zeros in Table 6 are no less than astounding. Apart from the crossbrow *Time* or *Newsweek,* the highest that the magazine brows of the dentists extend is to include a *New Yorker* and an *Esquire* thrown into a lowerbrow diet. And the admen, the professional purveyors of the mass media, have brows extending no higher than an isolated reference to *Holiday* and *The American Heritage.*

22. Some magazines would have to be omitted due to their cross-brow nature, *Time* and *Newsweek* being prime examples.

Conclusion

While the effect of occupational role upon the rest of life is frequently proclaimed in the context of occupational sociology, it has seldom
been examined in a comparative structural context. The foregoing comparison of admen, dentists and professors has attempted to reveal some
of the links between occupational milieu and non-occupational behavior. The contrasts between occupations all in a similar social stratum
indicate that the crucial explanatory factor is that of the occupational
milieu—consisting of the setting of the work situation, the nature of
the work performed, and the norms derived from occupational reference
groups—which allows, dictates or is conducive to particular patterns of
behavior.

The consequences of the structure of the work situation are seen
most directly in the extent to which hours of work provide the framework for other activities. For example, the professor's long hours of
academic involvement necessitate less time for his leisure and his home
life. Alternatively, the fluidity of the adman's business routine may
allow for recreational activity during the working day, a luxury in
which the dentist is most unlikely to indulge himself. Certainly contrasting vacation patterns are a function of working routine.

The nature of the work task has a variety of effects, the most immediate of which is dramatically illustrated in considering the possibility of the fusion of work with leisure. It is physically most difficult for the dentist to "take his work home" (although he could take
X-rays home for study or return to his office to do laboratory work).
But, even if the dentist does work overtime, this task is readily defined
as *work*. The professor, by contrast, is likely to find it difficult to say
whether reading in or around his field is working or not. Similarly, it
is absurd even to think of the dentist bringing his work on his vacation; such a fusion is more likely for the adman, and becomes probable for the professor. The nature of these occupations involve different types of cultural demarcation and evaluation, one indication of
which is seen in the responses of the three groups to the question of a
hypothetical two hours (Table 1). Again, the professors are most likely
to say they would do more work, the dentists least likely, and the
admen to have an intermediary position on the subject.

Intrinsic in the nature of work is a specialization of skills. The extent to which such skills spill over into the realm of leisure is seen in
contrasting hobby interests: use of their hands for the dentists, painting and writing for the admen, and intellectual pursuits for the profes-

sors. On the other hand, the nature of work in the context of particular work situations results in different types of strains, whether physical or emotional. These too are reflected in patterns of leisure, in "blowing off steam" for the admen and "taking things easy" for the dentists.

Participation in voluntary organizations may begin as a work task for the admen. But its justification (by either the admen or their organizations) is not only a function of their occupational skill, but also a rationalization and compensation for the marginal social status of their work. The types of organizational memberships in which the dentists are found also show both a direct occupational function—building a clientele—and a consequent status repercussion (Tables 4 and 5).

The influence of occupational reference groups appears to be most pervasive among the professors, as indicated by such norms as those against extended TV viewing or their similarities in musical taste, musical interest, and their high rates of attendance at theaters and concerts. Reference group influences are operative in the other groups also. Thus, it is not only the adman on the art side of the firm who paints for a hobby, but it is likely to be his influence which interests the account executive in a similar pursuit. Likewise, conviviality as a way of life, as evidenced by the admen's frequent cocktail parties, represents an occupational norm sanctioned by the reference group.

Although the account presented in this paper has emphasized the explanatory links between occupational factors and other types of behavior, one must be cautious of the tendency toward occupational determinism. Certainly such factors as national fads and fashions are most important in the analysis of leisure.[23] But even if do-it-yourself or painting seem to be sweeping the country at one particular period of time, the concentration of involvement with such activity in particular portions of the population still needs to be explained. The considera-

23. An additional problem which has not been considered is that of occupational selection. It is not merely occupational milieu that explains behavior, but occupational choice that selects personality and skills. The man who lacks manual dexterity is unlikely to manage to graduate from dental school. Avenues of vocational training are also important through the development of trained incapacities or compensations for various types of shortcomings. David Riesman, in a private communication, suggested that the dentists in order to get through their long training may have become somewhat cut off from people and therefore more oriented to family and do-it-yourself. Similarly, the professors might have turned to academic work as a retreat from their inabilities in sports as early as high school. But for the purposes of the present analysis, incumbency in the occupational role is taken as given.

tion of occupational milieu is crucial for this purpose, for it involves an individual's major connection with the larger social structure of which he is a part through the division of labor.

10. Kitsch and the Academic

CHARLES H. ANDERSON and JOHN D. MURRAY

While many of the middle-class Americans are bemused by *kitsch* (reading material, art, music, radio and television broadcasts, etc., of a more or less popular and entertaining nature), what are the middle-class counterparts who teach at the colleges and universities doing with their leisure hours? Are the professors as amenable as much of the rest of America to the enticements of mass culture?

Of all the professions which have traditionally been devoted to ferreting out the good, the true, and the beautiful, the academic profession is today by far the largest and most important. Higher education has enrolled in its service the bulk of American intellectuals. When one looks to the academic world, then, one would expect to find the hallmarks of higher culture displayed in leisure along with only limited doses of mass culture. To be sure, to escape the fallout of kitsch with only light or even moderate exposure would require conscious and concerted effort, and to remain completely uncontaminated would be a surpassing feat. If, however, the academic world is proving to be an altogether ineffective shield against mass culture, then the vitality of intellectual life in America is being threatened—the quest of the good, the true, and the beautiful jeopardized.

At least one researcher feels that the floodgates have been opened: "For both intellectuals and the general population . . . the cultural atmosphere is permeated by the mass media. There is little doubt . . . that educated strata—even the products of graduate and professional schools—are becoming full participants in mass culture. . . ."[1] However, a second study revealed consistent and significant differences in several areas of cultural behavior between college teachers and the members of two upper white-collar occupations.[2] Our paper reports on

1. Harold L. Wilensky, "Mass Society and Mass Culture," *American Sociological Review*, 29 (April, 1964), 190.

2. Joel E. Gerstl, "Leisure, Taste, and Occupational Milieu," *Social Problems*, 9 (Summer, 1961), 56-68.

the findings of another study of college and university teachers, drawing mainly from questions dealing with media behavior, in an effort to shed further empirical light on the question of the quality of academic non-work life.[3]

Sample Characteristics

The academics reported on here represent the arts and science faculties of a state university, three nonsectarian liberal arts colleges, a Catholic liberal arts college, and a Catholic university, all located in New England.[4] In all, 36 professors with Protestant origins, 25 Jews, and 60 Catholics are included in the analysis. The Catholic academics were evenly distributed between the Catholic and nonsectarian schools.

Other background characteristics of the respondents were as follows: all except one were white and all but eight were native-born; half of the Protestants and Catholics and all of the Jews were raised in cities of more than 100,000 population; all but 4 Protestants, 3 Jews, and 13 Catholics came from white-collar family origins (Protestants and Jews were decidedly higher than Catholics in occupational and educational family background); and half of both the Protestants and the Catholic sectarians (Catholic professors at Catholic colleges) were under 46 years of age compared to over four-fifths of the Jews and the Catholic nonsectarians (Catholic professors at the nonsectarian colleges).

Findings

Let us turn first to the role of television in the leisure life of our sample, the medium which Wilensky has dubbed "the chief culprit" in the cultural leveling of the intellectual professions. That television is standard diet among the educated is by now an unquestionable fact of American life. One recent survey estimated that the average college graduate logs about three hours a day in front of the TV.[5] To what extent does it penetrate the ranks of the Ph.D.'s?

Table 1 sums up the television viewing time of our respondents. Sixty-seven per cent of the Protestants, 84 per cent of the Jews, 56 per

3. As discussed in the conclusion of this paper, the majority of respondents could not clearly make a work-leisure dichotomy.

4. For a discussion of sampling procedures, see Charles H. Anderson, "The Intellectual Subsociety Hypothesis: An Empirical Test," doctoral dissertation, University of Massachusetts, 1966; and John D. Murray, "The American Catholic Intellectual: An Empirical Test of the Intellectual Subsociety Hypothesis," doctoral dissertation, University of Massachusetts, 1969.

5. Gary A. Steiner, *The People Look at Television* (New York: Alfred A. Knopf, 1963), p. 75.

Table 1.

*Distribution of Academics by Hours
Per Week of Television Viewing: Per Cent*

Hours per week	Protestants	Jews	Catholic Sectarians	Catholic Nonsectarians
None	17	16	13	33
Less than six	50	68	43	30
Six to ten	22	8	17	20
Over ten	11	8	27	17
Total N	36	25	30	30

cent of the Catholic sectarians, and 63 per cent of the Catholic nonsectarians reported no or less than six hours viewing per week. Among self-identifying intellectuals[6] the figures for those viewing no or less than six hours rose to 81 and 94 per cent for Protestants and Jews, respectively, while Catholics displayed no differences on this basis. Furthermore, the viewing that did occur was largely restricted to news reports and special shows on educational television. Late movies and professional football were the most frequent exceptions. Television, in other words, occupied a very inconspicuous position in the daily round of activities of a large majority of professors studied here.

In the realm of newspapers, few respondents admitted that they did not read at least the Sunday edition of a nationally prominent newspaper.[7] Among self-defined intellectuals, over three-fourths of all religious sub-groups read the daily or Sunday edition of the *New York Times.* The most popular sections among sample members were national and international news, book review, and theater; and the least popular, financial. A number of respondents also read local and regional newspapers. By way of comparison, only one per cent of the "middle mass" in Wilensky's study reported quality newspaper exposure.[8]

6. Each respondent was asked the question, "Do you think of yourself as an intellectual?" Twenty-one Protestants (58 per cent), 18 Jews (72 per cent), and 40 Catholics (67 per cent) affirmed an intellectual self-concept; these are the figures upon which the percentages which refer to self-identifying intellectuals are based.

7. The *New York Times* and *New York Herald Tribune, Washington Post, Christian Science Monitor,* and *Wall Street Journal* were the nationally prominent newspapers mentioned. However, the *New York Times* accounted for most respondents. Boston, Hartford, and Springfield papers were considered as regional.

8. Wilensky, *op. cit.* The same newspapers were considered as quality papers in both Wilensky's study and ours.

Turning next to periodicals (excluding professional journals), we observed that multiple and regular exposure to the mass circulation magazines was limited to a relatively small portion of the total sample. Table II summarizes the findings on periodicals. Only among Protestant and Catholic nonsectarian respondents who eschewed intellectual self-identification did the popular type and mass news magazines make important inroads: the Protestants averaged 2.34 of these types or 76 per cent of the total periodicals read; the Catholic sectarians, 1.92 or 77 per cent. On the other hand, the average self-defined Jewish intellectual read regularly 3.11 critical periodicals (which accounted for 66 per

Table 2.

Distribution of Kinds of Periodicals Read by
Academics, by Intellectual Identification

| | Protestants Intellectual Identification | | | | Jews Intellectual Identification | | | |
| | Yes | | No | | Yes | | No | |
Periodical type	Per cent	Mean	Per cent	Mean	Per cent	Mean	Per cent	Mean
Criticism*	42	1.33	9	.27	66	3.11	50	1.14
Special Interest†	33	1.05	15	.47	15	.72	19	.43
News‡	19	.57	35	1.07	11	.50	19	.43
Popular§	6	.19	41	1.27	8	.39	12	.29
	100		100		100		100	

| | Catholic Sectarians Intellectual Identification | | | | Catholic Nonsectarians Intellectual Identification | | | |
| | Yes | | No | | Yes | | No | |
Periodical type	Per cent	Mean	Per cent	Mean	Per cent	Mean	Per cent	Mean
Criticism*	54	1.86	45	1.56	54	1.89	13	.33
Special Interest†	15	.52	3	.11	21	.72	10	.25
News‡	17	.57	26	.89	9	.33	20	.50
Popular§	14	.48	26	.89	16	.56	57	1.42
	100		100		100		100	

* For example, *The Reporter, The New Republic, Commentary, Harper's*
† For example, *Films in Review; Hi-Fidelity, Art News*
‡ For example, *Time, Newsweek*
§ For example, *Life, Saturday Evening Post, Holiday, Reader's Digest*

cent of the total read), and his Protestant counterpart read 1.33 critical periodicals (accounting for 42 per cent of the total read). The self-defined Catholic intellectuals at both the sectarian and the nonsectarian colleges regularly read, respectively, 1.86 and 1.89 critical publications (accounting, in both groups, for 54 per cent of the total read). And even the Catholic sectarian self-defined nonintellectuals averaged 1.56 critical periodicals, or 45 percent of the total read. In contrast, Gerstle has noted that in a sample which included fifty upper-white-collar respondents only two upper-brow magazines were mentioned.[9]

A fourth cultural medium covered was that of books. Many respondents were unable to distinguish between work and non-work literature. The question was narrowed to call for an estimate of the number and type of books read the previous year outside the respondent's particular area of professional specialization. Forty-four per cent of the Protestants, 68 per cent of the Jews, 47 per cent of the Catholic sectarians, and 53 per cent of the Catholic nonsectarians declared that they had read more than twelve nonspecialization volumes the year before (Table III). The corresponding figures for self-identifying intellectuals were 62 and 83 per cent for Protestants and Jews, respectively ("over twelve" ranged into the "hundreds"), but again, Catholics revealed no internal differences by intellectual identification. What do the numbers represent—pulp or quality? By and large, the figures

Table 3.

Distribution of Academics by Number of Non-Specialization Books Read During the Previous Year: Per Cent

Number of books	Protestants	Jews	Catholic Sectarians	Catholic Nonsectarians
Over twelve	44	68	47	53
Seven to twelve	22	20	13	10
One to six	28	12	23	23
None	6	0	17	13
	36	25	30	30

9. Gerstl, *op. cit.*, p. 160.

stand for quality literature: novels, biography, contemporary history, and social analysis were the most frequently mentioned categories of reading for the sample as a whole. Once again, it was mainly the Protestant and Catholic self-defined nonintellectuals who expressed a greater preference for lower-brow reading and reported more of the standard fare of light fiction and detective mystery. As one respondent observed, "I read stacks of good detective stories during the summer, sometimes up to three a day."

In all religious subgroups, about two-thirds stated that reading, be it newspapers, magazines, or books, was their favorite leisure-time pursuit. This fact stands in marked contrast to the findings of Kramer and Leventman, for example, in their study of "North City" Jews where reading ranked behind gardening, do-it-yourself projects, golf and bowling, and cards.[10]

Movies were seen with considerable regularity by many respondents, particularly so among Protestants and Jews who affirmed an intellectual self-concept. Overall, 53 per cent of the Protestants, 64 per cent of the Jews, 27 per cent of Catholic sectarians, and 43 per cent of Catholic nonsectarians counted at least seven films viewed during the previous year. Among the self-defined Protestant and Jewish intellectuals these figures increased to 71 and 78 per cent, respectively. As with books, it was the number *and type* of exposure that we were interested in. Had there been indiscriminate or selective consumption? The standard flow of Hollywood footage tended to be by-passed by a large majority of respondents. Foreign films (many shown as series on the campuses) accounted for more than half of the total, while much of the remainder was attributable to Hollywood productions which had already passed the critical eye of reviewers or movie-wise friends. Yet, there were enough "spectaculars" and "escape" films on the list to attest to some, albeit modest, incursions of popular movie culture into the leisure style of our respondents.

Radio listening was largely confined to newscasts, news analysis, and classical music (preferably Baroque or Classical periods) on FM, the latter often acting as a tranquilizer to work in the home. Half of the group noted that they were serious classical music listeners and listened to hi-fidelity classical or jazz on a daily basis.

A final area of cultural exposure over which the respondents were

10. Judith R. Kramer and Seymour Leventman, *Children of the Gilded Ghetto* (New Haven: Yale University Press, 1961).

queried concerned the frequency of attendance at musical and theatrical performances and visits to museums and art exhibits. In general, the professors supported the arts on a regular basis; this was especially true of the self-defined intellectuals (Table IV). Forty-two per cent of the Protestants, 48 per cent of the Jews, and 23 per cent of the Catholics attended, in some combination, over twelve concerts, plays, operas, ballets, museums, or exhibits the year prior to the interview. Among self-defined intellectuals, percentages rose to 62, 50, and 61 for Protestants, Jews, and Catholics, respectively.

What do academics do with their much publicized and envied vacations? Much more often than not they work. As one professor remarked in response to a question on vacation use, "I don't know if you could call it a vacation. My family spends a couple of weeks at the beach, but I bring along manuscripts, work, and books, and end up ruining it for everyone." A sizeable number of respondents spent what vacations they did take in traveling. Here again, however, work enters the picture. In the words of one academic, "Every three years I take the summer off and travel to Europe or the West Coast, but the trips are usually in conjunction with some research I'm working on."

Conclusions

That leisure styles are not uniform throughout the academic world and mass culture has had differential success in penetrating its milieu is fairly obvious. On the whole, a person cannot deny that the popular arts have made important forays into various segments of the academic profession. Our data suggest, however, that major incursions may have

Table 4.

Distribution of Academics by Frequency of Attendance at Various Performing Arts the Previous Year: Per Cent

Performances attended	Protestants	Jews	Catholic Sectarians	Catholic Nonsectarians
Over twelve	42	48	23	23
Seven to twelve	22	36	20	30
One to six	25	12	14	40
None	11	4	13	7
	36	25	30	30

thus far been largely restricted to a minority of the occupation while a majority exercises a conscious and judged selectivity with respect to the various media of communication and leisure activities in general.

Specifically, we found that a favorable balance of our sample severely limited their television viewing time, read newspapers of national repute, subscribed to the little magazines while largely eschewing the popular periodicals, read quality nonwork books, attended the better films, and regularly patronized the concert hall, stage, or museum. In short, a majority remained on the perimeters of mass culture.

As a group, the Jewish academics evinced a greater highbrow media orientation than did those of Protestant origin and Protestants slightly more than the Catholics. However, self-defined Protestant and Jewish intellectuals displayed a nearly equally effective defense against mass culture and a taste for highbrow consumption, measurably diverging from their Catholic counterparts in certain instances.

To be sure, there were enough respondents who sufficiently approximated the typical consumer of mass culture to frighten a literary intellectual of the Dwight MacDonald stripe. But unless this is a burgeoning minority (it would seem unlikely that it is inasmuch as both kitsch and an enlarged academic profession have been in existence long enough to determine that if the former were going to overwhelm the latter this minority would by now have been a comfortable majority) and unless this is a very unrepresentative sample of American college and university professors, then we would argue that the academic world is in large maintaining its cultural integrity in a surrounding atmosphere which is directly inimical to its ideals.

Both our interviews and casual observations of academic life suggest that a fairly large number of academics fit what C. Wright Mills termed the "craftsman pattern" in styles of life. As Mills describes it, "In the craftsman pattern there is no split of work and culture. If play is supposed to be an activity, exercised for its own sake, having no aim other than gratifying the actor, then work is supposed to be an activity performed to create economic value or for some other ulterior result. Play is something you do to be happily occupied, but if work occupies you happily, it is also play, although it is also serious, just as play is to the child." Mills then goes on to say, "The craftsman's work is the mainspring of the only life he knows; he does not flee from work into a separate sphere of leisure; he brings to his non-working hours the values and qualities developed and employed in his working time. His idle conversation is shop talk; his friends follow the same lines of work as he, and share a kinship of feeling and thought."[11] As a related set of papers clearly documents, the latter characterization applies to many of our respondents.[12] Indeed, fully 90 per cent of self-identifying intellectuals in each religious subgroup declared that they experienced nearly complete overlap between what others call work and leisure.

Thus, the primary defense against mass culture is the pursuit of the ideal of craftsmanship in which the qualities of scholarly work are transferred to consumption and non-institutional settings. As a philosopher respondent with minimal kitsch exposure phrased it, "The dichotomization of work and leisure is meaningless—my life is an organic whole."

11.   C. Wright Mills, *White Collar* (New York: Oxford University Press, 1951), pp. 222-223.

12.   See Section VI.

V

WORK AS ALIENATION

Academics work with ideas, concepts, abstract relationships, and theories about people and things, more than they do with people and things. This distinction makes academics "different," "eggheads," or "intellectuals." Furthermore, the critical nature of much academic work imposes an additional type of alienation on its practitioners. Criticism evokes defensiveness—even hostility—more than it does gratitude. Thus, in terms of both an abstract observer-practical worker relationship and a critic-subject relationship, "we" are different from "them." From these types of relationships arise a number of social and cultural differences which tend to create psychological distance between many academics and nonacademics.

The extent of the social psychological separation of many academics from the larger society, Seeman observes, is manifest in their use of minority-like responses (those used by minority persons who have not come to terms with minority status) to questions about themselves. These minority-like responses of intellectuals include an acceptance of negative stereotypes of the intellectual, a concern over "abnormal" behavior by intellectuals, an approval of conforming behavior by intellectuals, a personal denial of intellectual status, and a fear of organized activity by intellectuals. Interestingly, Seeman discovered that professors who had successfully adjusted to their marginal position, that is, had rejected these negative minority-style attitudes and accepted themselves as members of a positive minority group, tended to be the more creative workers in their respective disciplines.

In the years that have elapsed since Seeman's mid-fifties study, academics do appear much less prone to think negatively of their minority status, in the sense Seeman described. On the contrary, positive intellectual self-image, diverse life style (a beard almost fired a professor in Lazarsfeld and Thielen's study in the fifties!) and affirmation of intellectual group membership and group action are common (see the papers in Section VI).

Anderson's essay suggests that academics today occupy somewhat of an ambiguous status vis-a-vis the general population. In terms of prestige and material reward, professors enjoy rather high status, both from their own and others' viewpoints. Yet, the majority of academics sustain few close friendships with nonacademics, perceive serious anti-intellectualism, feel they hold minority views on controversial issues, and are not especially optimistic over their power and influence. But in contrast to their marginal social position in the larger society, academics tend to be participants in a relatively cohesive occupational community (again, see Section VI).

11. The Intellectual and the Language of Minorities

MELVIN SEEMAN

1.

The signs of deep concern about the contemporary position of the intellectual in America are not hard to find. To be sure, as Merle Curti has stressed in his presidential address to the American Historical Society, anti-intellectualism—in one form or another—has a long history in American life.[1] But in recent years the situation of the intellectual has not resembled the mere continuation of a somewhat consistent and historically routine negativism. The current sense of urgency regarding the definition of the intellectual's role has found expression in a wide variety of places: from *Time* magazine's alarm about the "wide and unhealthy gap" between the American intellectuals and the people to a series of symposiums which have appeared in the *Journal of Social Issues*, in the book edited by Daniel Bell entitled *The New American Right*, and in the thoughtful British journal, *Encounter*.[2]

Yet, in spite of this volume of words, and the talent of those involved, it is still possible to agree with Milton Gordon's remark that "the man of ideas and the arts has rarely been studied seriously as a social type by professional students of society."[3] Whether, as some have argued, this retreat from self-analysis reflects a basic disorder in the scientific study of man is debatable enough; but the fact is clear that the research techniques which have been applied to nearly everybody

---

1. "Intellectuals and Other People," *American Historical Review*, LX (1955), 259-82.
2. Cf. S. S. Sargent and T. Brameld (eds.), "Anti-intellectualism in the United States," *Journal of Social Issues*, Vol. II, No. 3 (1955); D. Bell (ed.), *The New American Right* (New York: Criterion Books, 1955); and *Encounter*, Vols. IV and V (1955).
3. "Social Class and American Intellectuals," *A.A.U.P. Bulletin*, XL (1955), 517.

else—from the hobo to the business elite—have rarely been applied to ourselves.[4]

This paper is a report on one such study of ourselves, its aim being to determine how intellectuals in the current social climate deal with their identity as intellectuals and, beyond that, to suggest what difference it may make if this identity is handled in different ways.

The empirical base for this report was obtained through relatively unstructured interviews (on the average about one hour in length) with all the assistant professors teaching in the humanities and social science departments of a midwestern university.[5] These interviews were, not content-analyzed in any statistical sense but were simply examined (as the illustrations in the next section will show) for patterns of response.

The total number of persons interviewed was forty. They came, in the number indicated, from the following departments: Economics (7), English (6), German (2), History (4), Law (1), Mathematics (3), Philosophy (4), Political Science (2), Psychology (4), Romance Languages (3), and Sociology-Anthropology (4). The sample included no one from the physical or biological sciences, from the engineering and applied fields, or from the creative arts; and when an appropriate level in the staff hierarchy had been selected, there was no further sampling problem. Co-operation was good: of a total of forty-five persons listed in the university directory at the assistant-professor level, only one refused to be interviewed (and four were unavailable because of assignments out of the city).

The procedure in the interviews was consistent though not standardized. There was no attempt to get answers to preformed questions. We

4. The roster of those who have recently written, more or less directly, on the problem of the intellectual would comprise a list of the contemporary great and near-great in a variety of humanistic and social science fields (not to mention the physical sciences): e.g., Schlesinger and Hofstadter in history; Parsons and Riesman in sociology; Tolman and Fromm in psychology. Two well-known older works that embody the spirit of self-study are those by Znaniecki (*The Social Role of the Man of Knowledge*) and Logan Wilson (*The Academic Man*). There have, of course, been many commentaries on the intellectual, especially in the more or less Marxist journals; but I am referring here to the more formally analytic mode of investigation.

5. It seemed wiser, with a limited sample, to hold staff level constant rather than sample all levels of permanent staff. The assistant-professor group was chosen for two reasons: (1) it was large enough to provide suitable frequencies, yet small enough to be manageable without taxing time and finances, and (2) it is, in the institution studied, basically a tenure group like the higher ranks but presumably less involved in official committee work and graduate work and therefore more likely to give the time required for interviewing.

engaged, rather, in a conversation regarding a letter which outlined a plan for exploring the situation of the intellectual today. The letter was not mailed; it was read by the respondent at the start of the interview and served in this way as a common stimulus object. The body of the letter, which carried my signature, follows:

There is considerable evidence (though debatable evidence, to be sure) that the role of the intellectual has become increasingly problematic in American life. Such evidence includes: (1) the widespread expression of anti-intellectual attitudes; (2) the increasing pressure for conformity in intellectual work; and (3) the typical isolation of the intellectual in community life. These current trends are presumably matters of considerable moment to university people who are uniquely concerned with the social conditions under which intellectual activity is carried forward.

It seems to me that some effort to assess the problem among ourselves is in order; and that such an effort might proceed initially by calling together small, informal groups of faculty members to clarify issues and get an exchange of viewpoints. This letter comes as an invitation to you to participate in one of these discussions on the current situation of the intellectual. The discussion would include four or five other persons from the humanities and social sciences, and would take roughly one hour of your time. Since several discussions are planned, I would consider it part of my responsibility to provide you with some type of analytical summary of the sessions held—in effect, a research report.

Let me emphasize that the purpose of these discussions is not to canvass possible lines of action, but to achieve a clarification of issues on matters which are clearly controversial.

Would you indicate whether you wish to be included in the list of discussants by returning this letter to me with the appropriate notation?[6]

After the respondent had read the letter, he was encouraged to comment freely on any aspect of it; then each of the three points listed in

6. The italicized portion of this letter was underlined in the original; but in one-half of the cases a more action-oriented statement was substituted for the underlined portion given here. The two types of letters were randomly alternated in the interviewing program. In the second version, the underlined sentence read: "*Let me emphasize that the purpose of these discussions is not only to achieve a clarification of issues on matters which are clearly controversial; but also to canvass suitable lines of action.*" In all cases, at the end of the interview, the respondent was asked to comment on what his reaction to the letter would have been if the alternative not presented to him had been used. The variation in letter style is mentioned here for the sake of completeness; it is not directly relevant to the treatment of the interviews reported here. The proposed discussions never took place, owing to both the press of time and a certain lack of enthusiasm—a lack which the remainder of this paper may make more understandable.

the first paragraph of the letter was discussed; and, finally, I raised the question, "Do you classify yourself as an intellectual?"

The latter question raises for us, no less than for the respondents, the matter of definition. As a first approximation, I defined the intellectuals as a group for whom the analysis of ideas in their own right (i.e., for no pragmatic end) is a central occupation. The group I chose to interview was taken as a sample of intellectuals, in spite of the fact that some would surely not qualify on more stringent criteria (e.g., their degree of dedication to the life of the mind or the quality of their intellectual work). The sample is defensible, however, on the ground that by social definition—whether he or his colleagues prefer it or not —the university professor teaching in the humanities or social sciences is probably the prime case of intellectual endeavor (i.e., of non-pragmatic and ideological pursuits). Thus, we are concerned with the self-portrait of those who, by social definition at least, are intellectuals.[7]

2.

In a certain sense the chief finding of this study consisted of a "surprise": the unanticipated discovery of the extent to which these intellectuals use the language and mechanisms of minority status to de-

7. This assertion, obviously, is an assumption, since the public definition of an intellectual is not a matter of empirical record, so far as I know. One could hold, further, that, if they are not so designated, they should be—that, in the ideal university, the group I have described would be identifiable as intellectuals in the sense of my stated definition. That definition has its difficulties, to be sure. For example, one might ask why an intellectual cannot believe that (or behave as if) ideas are of more than simply aesthetic interest, that ideas have consequences, and that the analysis of them serves a "pragmatic" end. A host of names come to mind of persons who would appear to have indorsed this view and whom we would presumably not wish to dismiss as intellectuals—e.g., Marx, Lenin, Jefferson, among others. The best provisional answer to this, I should think, would be that being an intellectual is not the designation for a person but for a role and that many who play the intellectual role, and play it well, are also deeply involved with the course of societal and individual development. One does not need to say, therefore, that Marx was not an intellectual because he was also a revolutionary.

In any event, though this definition does not thoroughly solve matters, it does suggest a line of approach and clarifies, perhaps, the senses in which our sample may or may not be considered as members of the class. To my mind it is much less important to determine whether they are, so to speak, "in" or "out" of the category than it is to recognize that they are candidates in several senses: (1) in public definitions of them; (2) in their personal self-definitions; and (3) in the definition of a university ideal. The issue is nicely captured in Randall Jarrell's fictional *Pictures from an Institution*, where he says of an academic man: "He had never been what intellectuals consider an intellectual, but other people had thought him one, and he had had to suffer the consequences of their mistake" (p. 110).

scribe themselves and their situation. It may be suggested that this should have been no surprise—that arguments quite consistent with this have been advanced in many places. And to some degree that is true.

In a recent well-publicized paper in *Harper's*, for example, a French writer had this to say:

> It seems to me that the attitude of the American intellectual in comparison with his European counterpart is based on frustration and an inferiority complex. I am continually meeting people who tell me that the intellectual in Europe enjoys a position which, if not happier, is at least more dignified than that of the intellectual in America. . . . Whose fault is this? They go on to tell me that the fault rests with the American people, who have no appreciation for things of the intellect. I wonder whether it is not also in great measure the fault of the American intellectuals themselves.[8]

In a similar vein Riesman and Glazer have commented that "the opinion leaders among the educated classes—the intellectuals and those who take their cues from them—have been silenced more by their own feelings of inadequacy and failure than by direct intimidation."[9] And Marcus Cunliffe, describing the United States intellectual for *Encounter* magazine, concludes: "Altogether, there has been an unfortunate loss of self-respect. Some intellectuals have felt that, wrong about communism, they must be occupationally prone to be wrong about everything."[10]

But the point is that comments of this kind do not constitute evidence; and, indeed, it is possible, if one questions the evidence, to treat such comments themselves as reflections of a kind of minority-style indictment of one's own group (like the Jew who agrees that "we" are too clanish, the intellectual says that "we" are too weak in will). Furthermore, the comments we have cited do not provide a systematic view of the specific forms of minority language which intellectuals employ in discussing themselves. Our empirical task here is to indicate that such minority references are surprising, indeed, in their frequency and to make a start toward a categorization of the forms these references take.[11]

8. R. L. Bruckberger, "An Assignment for Intellectuals," *Harper's*, CCXII (1956), 69.

9. D. Riesman and N. Glazer, "Intellectuals and the Discontented Classes," *Partisan Review*, XXII (1955), 50.

10. "The Intellectuals: II. The United States," *Encounter*, XX (1955), 31.

11. A word is in order about the meaning of "minority" and the occasion for "surprise." On the latter I am aware of the fact that many occupational groups (and cer-

The clearest of these forms may be labeled *the direct acceptance of majority stereotypes*. Like the Negroes who have accepted the whites' definition of color and who choose "light" among themselves, our respondents appear eager to validate the outsider's negative view of them. One need only read these forty protocols to emerge with a collective self-portrait of the soft, snobbish, radical, and eccentric intellectual who is asocial, unreliable, hopelessly academic, and a bit stupid to boot. It is impossible to cite here the evidence for all this; but each of the stereotypes in the previous sentence has a parallel affirmation in the interview material. These affirmations are, to be sure, frequently hedged with restrictions and limitations—we are dealing, after all, with a group of highly trained qualifiers. But the significant thing is that the respondents take the opportunity to affirm the stereotype; and this affirmation is typically set in a context which makes it clear that the stereotype, rather than the qualification, has a competing chance to govern behavior. Let me give some examples:

If there is anti-intellectualism in our community, I feel frankly we are to blame. If we can't throw off our infernal need for preaching and dictating, they have a right to damn us, and we have no answer but our human fallibility [C-1].[12]

---

tainly "notorious" ones—e.g., policemen, farmers, or traveling salesmen) develop somewhat negative images of themselves. But two special conditions make this case, it seems to me, somewhat different. First, we are dealing with a high status group (note, for example, their generally high placement in the North-Hatt prestige scale); and, second, we are dealing with a group whose very function, in good part, is the objective analysis of society and its products. On these grounds, I would argue that it is not enough to dismiss the problem by saying that all occupations reflect negative self-images or that the problem approach in the stimulus letter occasioned the results obtained. The question is: What occupations have stereotypes about them, in what degree, and how are these stereotypes handled by the incumbents, with what consequences? This is the broader problem to which this paper is addressed.

With regard to "minority": I use it here to designate a group against which categorical discrimination is practiced. A minority, in this view, is determined not by size but by the behavior of being subjected to categorical discrimination. It should be clear, however, that I am not attempting to prove that intellectuals *are* a minority in this sense but that they use the typical language and forms of the classical minority groups in their self-descriptions.

12. The source of each quotation from the interviews is identified by an assigned case number so that the reader may note the spread of the illustrations. Departmental identifications are avoided, though these would be of some interest, to preserve anonymity. There is, I presume, every reason to believe that the frequency and subtlety of minority responses will vary among universities and departments—by region, eminence, and the like. But it also seems reasonable to believe that the bulk of American universities are not substantially different from the one involved here.

It's pretty difficult for the intellectual to mix with people. They feel ill at ease. Many intellectuals are not very approachable; perhaps his training is not complete enough. The intellectual may be more to blame for that than anyone else [C-2].

My general attitude is that some of the intellectuals are so concerned with academic freedom that it kind of tires me. And I think, this sometimes adds up to wanting more freedom than anybody else—the kind of freedom to be irresponsible. [And later, when asked whether the letter should include the action alternative, this subject said:] It shouldn't be in there, because basically I think that except in the most long-run sense there is not a thing you can do. Maybe we can breed a new line of professors [C-3].

We could go on here, if space permitted, about "the snobbishness we are all guilty of" and about the "queer birds" who "make a profession of being different" and "don't have sense enough to pour sand out of a boot" (these quotations coming from four different protocols). This direct acceptance by intellectuals of the negative stereotype regarding intellectuals follows the pattern of the minority "self-hate" which Lewin has described in the case of the anti-Semitic Jew[13] and which has been clearly expressed in Negro color attitudes.[14]

A second, and somewhat less extreme, variety of minority attitude may be labeled *the concern with in-group purification*. This label points to language and behavior which are guided by the idea that the minority's troubles are rooted in the misguided ways of a small fraction among them. The parallel with traditional minorities reads: for the Jews, it is the "bad" Jew—the one who is, indeed, aggressive and loud—who breeds anti-Semitism; and, for the intellectuals, it is the radical, asocial types who are responsible for the group's difficulty. Thus, on the radical issue, one respondent, speaking of his effort to establish a research contact downtown, said:

I realized we had one or two strikes against us because we were from the university. We had to have people vouch for us. We don't enjoy the best reputation down there; we're blamed for the actions of a few who make radical speeches and seem to overgeneralize [C-4].

Another respondent, speaking of an "extreme liberal" in his college, remarked:

13. K. Lewin, *Resolving Social Conflicts* (New York: Harper & Bros., 1948), pp. 186-200.

14. M. Seeman, "Skin Color Values in Three All-Negro School Classes," *American Sociological Review*, XI (1946), 315-21.

I've got nothing against it, but the average man might translate this [liberalism] over to our college. In this sense, he does a slight disservice to the college [C-5].

Similarly, on scores other than radicalism there are expressions of the view that the position of the intellectuals turns on the "impure" behavior of the intellectual himself. One respondent, discussing anti-intellectualism in general, remarked that we could lick the problem:

If we had people getting out and who really did mix, as speakers and members. . . . I've worried about this: would I be willing to be in an organization if I were only a member? We get to be president and vice-president all the time. It doesn't do any good to be in and be officers; in order to get over the thought of us as intellectual snobs, we have to be satisfied to be just members [C-6.]

This quotation highlights one interesting result of this concern with the "impure"—and a result which, again, has a clear minority flavor. The intellectual becomes involved in the need to prove that the impurity really is not there (or, at the very least, that the intellectual in question is not one of the "impure" few). We are familiar with the Jewish person who is inordinately careful to demonstrate in his own behavior that Jews as a group are not what the stereotype says; and Anatole Broyard has nicely described the various forms that Negro "inauthenticity" of the type may take (e.g., what he calls "role inversion" is a careful and extreme negation of precisely those qualities embodied in the Negro stereotype—"cool" music and passive behavior, for example, being a negation of the primitive, hot, carefree quality in the Negro stereotype).[15]

The interviews reveal a similar concern with disproving the stereotype. Thus, one respondent, discussing possible action alternatives, commented:

We could, of course, go out and make talks to various groups— show them that intellectuals really aren't bad guys [C-7].

Another, speaking about the isolation of the intellectual, said:

Well, in neighborhood isolation, there's a lot of it due to their initial reaction—when they find out you're a professor they slightly withdraw, but, if you continue to make connections, then they find out you're a human being [C-5].

Still another person commented:

15. "Portrait of the Inauthentic Negro," *Commentary*, X (1950), 56-64.

If we mixed more, and became known as people as well as college teachers, maybe it would be better. Frequently, the antipathy to college teachers melts when they meet you personally; though we do have a tendency to carry our classroom personality into other areas [C-8].

A third major category of minority-like response may be titled *the approval of conformity*. In a certain sense, of course, the pattern just described is a specialized form of conformity; for its main aim is to emphasize the conventional as against the divergent aspects of the intellectual's behavior. But the pressure for conformity goes beyond this. It involves the same kind of passive, conservative, and attention-avoiding behavior that Lewin has described as prototypical for minority leaders, his "leaders from the periphery."[16] And, in the long run, this pressure for conformity leads to assimilationism—to the very denial of any significant observable differences on which minority status may rest. As far as the more traditional minorities are concerned, the classic Adorno volume on prejudice and personality has put one part of the conformist case as follows:

Since acceptance of what is like oneself and rejection of what is different is one feature of the prejudiced outlook [i.e., of the authoritarian personality], it may be that members of minority groups can in limited situations and for some period of time protect themselves and gain certain advantages by conforming in outward appearance as best they can with the prevailing ways of the dominant group.[17]

As with these minorities, we find that there is considerable commitment to conformity among intellectuals and that this is expressed variously as a need to adjust, to avoid controversy, or to assimilate and deny differences entirely. Thus, one respondent, discussing the conformity question raised in the letter, said:

On that, I can't say I've experienced it. I'm in a pretty safe field. . . . [He then described a book of readings he had collected and said that there was a short passage from a well-known writer which had been taken out before publication.] There's no use stirring up trouble. I don't think it was a lack of courage on my part. We thought—that is, the editor and I—that it was too touchy. It's a very beautiful thing, but we took it out [C-9].

Another individual, discussing the community life of the intellectual, noted that they often do not take an active part and added:

16. *Op. cit.*, p. 196.
17. T. W. Adorno *et al.*, *The Authoritarian Personality* (New York: Harper & Bros., 1950), p. 974.

Part of that is good, in that they are lending the prestige of the university when they do take part, and shouldn't be doing that. I don't want to be written up in the paper as Professor X of university holding a certain opinion. I've deliberately refrained from expressing political opinion [C-5].

Still others appear to argue for conformity by denying that there is a difference to which the notion of "intellectual" points:

I don't feel any different from my electrician-neighbor [C-10].

I get a kind of inferiority complex if they call me "professor"; I know that my work with the intellect is on the same level in the eyes of the man in the street as, say, a chain-store manager [C-11].

Or else there is insistence that is is important for the intellectual to assimilate or disguise himself more successfully. Thus, one respondent, speaking of occasions when he makes public addresses, said:

When I go out and meet these people, I try to fit myself into their realm, into the climate of the various groups [C-12].

Another gave, as part of his recipe for the intellectual's behavior, the directive:

He should adjust his personality so he can mix in better with the person who isn't an intellectual [C-2].

And one I have quoted before, speaking of the intellectual's isolation in community life, said:

You must make concessions. I would find it pretty hard to have contacts, for example, in places like Wilder's *Our Town* or Anderson's small Ohio town, but I couldn't accuse the people in the town of being anti-intellectual; it's probably my fault. If you make a certain amount of concession, you will find a way [C-11].

There are other comments which are less clear in their conformist implications—for example, more than faintly guilty remarks to the effect that "my neighbors see me home in the early afternoon and wonder just what it is I do in my job" (C-13). On the whole, there is considerable evidence in these protocols that the typical minority response of conformity is found in a variety of forms among intellectuals.[18]

18. Two of the respondents themselves commented on this "trimming of sails" in the university setting. One, for example, after noting an increase in anti-intellectual pressures, said:
"If you work at the university, you want the outside to be as non-controversial as possible; to say, 'Look at me, I'm just like anybody else.' This is part of the general line

The fourth category of response represents the extreme of minority assimilation from the standpoint of the individual, namely, *the denial of group membership*. Like the name-changing Jew and the Negro who "passes," many intellectuals find means to hide or escape their unwelcome identity. An interviewee nicely described this pattern as follows:

One consequence of anti-intellectualism is for some intellectuals to deny that they are intellectuals. This is a behavioral denial; it's part of the psychological revolution, the adjustment trend. . . . The pressure to be well-adjusted is high, and so he becomes non-intellectual and begins to deny in some respects that he is an intellectual [C-15].

The evidence in the interviews indicates that the retreat from membership is a substantial one and takes many forms. Indeed, one of the real surprises, during the course of these interviews, was the rarity of real acceptance of intellectual status. This non-acceptance is revealed in several ways. First, there is the frequency with which this freely offered remark appears: "Intellectuals, I hate the word!" Second, there are the direct denials to the question, "Do you consider yourself an intellectual?" A complete listing of the protocol responses on this point would reveal a quite consistent, though subtly varied, pattern of maneuvering, all aimed at being counted out—the kind of "Who, me?" response one gets from the obviously guilty.[19] Thus, one respondent said:

That's a word that always does bother me. I don't think of myself so. It's a self-conscious word that sets us apart from the rest of the population. The only thing that sets us apart, in fact, is that we have gone to school longer than some, and there are doctors who have gone longer and we don't consider them intellectuals [C-10].

Another said:

I don't apply it to myself. I never use it myself. It's sort of snobbish [C-17].

And still another:

---

of not hurting the university by getting in the news in negative ways" (C-14).
Another person, in similar vein, remarked:
   "The intellectual is assuming more of the role of the non-intellectual and seeks to be a part of the gang—denies that he's different" (C-15).
   19.   Even where there is acceptance of the "intellectual" label, there is sometimes a suspicious belligerence about it. One respondent, who vigorously denied the validity of the view embodied in the stimulus letter and felt that anti-intellectualism was a fictitious problem, said: "You need to live your life as if you were proud of it—talk it up" (C-16).

I would [use the designation "intellectual"] in the professional sense only. . . . Professionally, I suppose we can't avoid it. Only in the very narrow professional sense, in the sense that we are trying to improve the intellect of students, I suppose it applies. I don't see how a university professor can escape the narrow meaning of the term [C-1].

And, finally, one respondent clearly recognized the social definition of himself yet reflected no eagerness in his personal definition:

I suppose I would [consider myself an intellectual]. . . . I don't know if I am twenty-four hours a day, but still I suppose my work would be classified or considered an intellectual [sic]. . . . I teach the best I can, and certainly I'm classified as an intellectual by the community, my neighbors, and my colleagues [C-9].

A third kind of denial of membership is shown in the efforts that are made to avoid having one's affiliation publicly known. Thus, one respondent said:

When I'm away from the university, I usually have plenty of dirt under my nails, or I'm getting a harvest. Some of us fool ourselves into believing that the stain of our profession doesn't follow us. I can work with a carpenter for several weeks, and he has no notion I'm a university professor. I take a foolish pride, I suppose, in this [C-1].

Another remarked:

By training we get so we show contempt for those who overgeneralize, as in the Rotary, and we don't want to be in arguments all the time so we stay away. And how often do we go out of the way to announce that we're college professors. I don't conceal it; but I don't volunteer it. It would change your relation to the group [C-4].

Thus, in one way or another, many of our respondents indicate that they do not cherish either their name or their identity as intellectuals; and they adopt a language of evasion and anonymity which is minority-like, indeed. Though one may argue that this rejection of the name is not, after all, so terribly important, it seems to me more reasonable, in this case, to see the "naming trouble" as an essential part of the status involved.[20]

20. On a similar point Everett Hughes has written in an essay titled "What's in a Name": "Words are weapons. As used by some people the word 'Hebrew,' for example, is a poisoned dart. When a word is so expressively used, we are face to face with no simple matter of social politics, but with part of the social process itself. This is, in part, what Durkheim had in mind in his long discussion of collective symbols and concepts. Words, he pointed out, are not merely something that happens along with the social process, but are its very essence. Naming is certainly part of the social pro-

The fifth, and last, category of minority-like response can be designated *the fear of group solidarity*. This label indicates behavior whose essential function is similar to the conformist response; namely, behavior calculated to keep the majority's attention off the minority as such. In our intellectuals this typically takes the form of strong resistance to any clearly identifiable group action on the group's problems; the answer lies, rather, in individual goodness. One respondent, in fact, while stating the case against group action, made the minority tie himself:

The notion of action involves the whole place of the intellectual in society. In addition, direct action puts us in the position of special pleading. It's like a Jew going out and talking about anti-Semitism [C-7].

Another said:

Individual action seems more feasible. One has to measure one's forces and deploy them properly. . . . If you try to organize a society for X, Y, or Z, and you have the right people on the letterhead, maybe you're O.K.; but otherwise you're considered radical. Many things can be carried out without anybody knowing there is an organization [C-18].

Still another remarked:

I'm frankly very much afraid of any action that has the label of the organized action of the intellectuals—not afraid of what they might do, but of public reaction. It ought to be unorganized [C-19].

Many of those interviewed seem committed to "having an effect the individual way" and are against "forming an organization that's militant." They wish, in a certain sense, to be (as one respondent [C-20] described himself) "the kind of social actionist who never appears to be one." I am interested here not in asserting that the strategy of organizational effort is a sounder strategy but in noting that the arguments against it frequently reflect a desire—common in other minorities—not to become too visible or too aggressive in one's own interest.

3.

Neither the quotations nor the categories given above exhaust the minority language in these protocols. Moreover, I have intentionally failed to analyze or report in any fulness the more "positive" remarks

cesses in inter-ethnic and racial relations" *(Where Peoples Meet* [Glencoe, Ill.: Free Press, 1952], p. 139).

on the intellectual's role in society or on the anti-intellectualism within university life itself (as one person put it [C-21]: "the destruction of the intellectual community within the university"). It was, in fact, only after the interviews were almost completed, and the variability in self-definition became ever more striking, that it was clear we might treat intellectual status directly, as one which presents a standard problem in minority adjustment.

I have argued elsewhere that marginalities of this kind provide the opportunity for the development of perspective and creativity—an opportunity whose realization depends upon the adjustment which is made to marginal status.[21] In this earlier study, using the Jews as a case in point, I found that favorable adjustment to marginality was, indeed, associated with what was called "intellectual perspective"; and it now seemed possible to apply the same general logic to this sample of intellectuals.

Certainly many have asserted that there is an inherent alienative potential—an inescapable degree of marginality—in the intellectual role; and the assertion usually follows that the individual's style of adjustment to this marginality affects his performance as an intellectual. The usual view, of course, is that those who are "frozen" by this marginality and who retreat into conformity are less creative as intellectuals. Cunliffe, almost incidentally, makes this tie between mode of adjustment and creativity in advancing his distinction between two types of American intellectuals, whom he calls the *"avant-garde"* and the *"clerisy"*:

> So, if there have been many alienated Western intellectuals since 1800, whom I will label the *avant-garde*, there have also been others, [the "clerisy"] of similar intellectual weight, though as a rule of less creative brilliance, who have remained more or less attached to their society.[22]

The discovery, in the interviews, of so many and so varied responses to this marginal aspect of the intellectual's position suggested the possibility of testing, in a small-scale empirical way, such common assertions about the consequences (or correlates) of the intellectual's adjustment to marginality. The hypothesis to be tested parallels that given in the earlier paper on the Jews as a minority; namely, that those intellectuals who have successfully adjusted to the marginal character of their role—those who, let us say, reveal a minimum of our five

21. M. Seeman, "Intellectual Perspective and Adjustment to Minority Status," *Social Problems*, III (1956), 142-53.
22. *Op. cit.*, p. 25.

minority-style attitudes toward themselves as intellectuals—will be, in turn, the more creative workers in their respective crafts.

For a provisional glimpse of such a test, and to illustrate at the same time one possible utility of the descriptive categories developed in the previous section, I attempted to score the forty protocols for evidence of commitment to, or rejection of, each of the five categories. At the same time, I asked a group of persons in the various departments (in all cases, men of higher academic rank than the individual in question) to judge the professional creativity of those interviewed. Creativity here refers to the ability to make the "given" problematic: the ability to challenge the routines and to provide alternatives to the standardized "right answers" in the respective fields.

Unfortunately, though expectedly, the free-response character of the interviews led to some serious limitations as far as the present more quantitative interest is concerned. For example, on two of the five minority categories (No. 2, "concern with in-group purification," and No. 5, "fear of in-group solidarity") more than one-third of the protocols received a score of 3, which indicated a lack of substantial evidence in the interview; and, in addition, among the remaining two-thirds of the cases, there was a very poor numerical split between "high" versus "low" adjustors on these two categories.

In view of these limitations, I shall not attempt to present what would amount to a complete, but premature, account of the adjustment ratings and creativity judgments.[23] But it is of illustrative interest to note what happened on the three remaining "minority response" categories where a more reasonable split between high versus low adjust-

23. I am indebted to Mrs. Frances Mischel, a graduate student in sociology and anthropology, for the two hundred "minority" ratings (five ratings on each of forty protocols). These ratings were "blind" as far as identification of individuals or specialty fields was concerned. They were done as independently as possible, as far as the five categories are concerned, to minimize "halo." A total of 120 creativity judgments by colleagues were secured; and the evidence suggests that there is substantial agreement among them. Both the adjustment and the creativity ratings were made on five-point scales. For minority adjustment, the scale read as follows: 1—very much evidence of this; 2—some evidence of this; 3—no evidence one way or the other; 4—some evidence of rejection of this mode of response; 5—clear evidence of rejection of this mode. The creativity scale ran simply from 1 ("low in creativity") to 5 ("high in creativity") and was accompanied by a full-page explanation of both the meaning of creativity in this context and the method to be used in making the ratings. It should be clear that the term "adjustment" does not refer to the standard psychological meaning of the term; it designates only whether the respondent reflects or does not reflect the five categories of response described here. Thus, "high adjustment" refers to those who scored either 4 or 5 on the given category; "low" refers to a score of 1 or 2 on the category.

ment was obtained. "High" adjustment refers to a tendency to reject the use of the indicated minority-like modes of response in self-description; "low" adjustment refers to a tendency to embody the indicated minority-type response. Table 1 reveals what was obtained when individuals who scored 3 (no evidence) on each category were eliminated and when the high and low adjustors were compared on their average creativity. The data in Table 1 are read as follows: For the twelve persons who scored either 4 or 5 on category 1 (i.e., whose responses were antithetical to the acceptance of majority stereotypes about the intellectual), the mean creativity score was 3.27, with a standard deviation of 0.65. For the thirteen persons who scored low in adjustment on this same category (i.e., who revealed a clear tendency to accept negative stereotypes), the mean creativity score was 2.54, with a standard deviation of 1.19.

The differences in creativity between adjustment groups are consistently in the direction of higher ratings for those who do not use the minority-style response to intellectual status. Though the N's are small, and the differences are not uniformly great, the trend is clear, and the difference between adjustment groups for Category 1 is statistically significant.[24]

Table 1.

Mean Creativity Scores and Standard Deviations for Individuals Scored High versus Low on Three Categories of Minority Response to Intellectual Status

Adjustment Group	Category 1—Acceptance of Stereotypes			Category 3—Approval of Conformity			Category 4—Denial of Membership		
	N	Mean	S.D.	N	Mean	S.D.	N	Mean	S.D.
High	12	3.27	0.65	16	2.74	0.84	13	2.48	1.02
Low	13	2.54	1.19	15	2.53	1.35	15	2.34	1.06

24. A test of the homogeneity of the two variances for the adjustment groups yielded an F ratio which approximated the 0.05 level of significance and raised doubt about the wisdom of pooling the variances for the two groups in computing the t test between the creativity means. The obtained t ratio for the test of Category 1 was 1.841, a figure which is significant at the 0.05 level using a one-tailed test. Neither of the two remaining categories yielded a significant t. The method used to test for homogeneity of variance and for the significance of the difference between means is given in A. Edwards, *Statistical Methods for the Behavioral Sciences* (New York: Rinehart & Co., 1954), pp. 271-74.

I do not take this as an unequivocal demonstration of the hypothesis in question. For one thing, there are other variables of considerable relevance (e.g., the age of the respondent) that cannot be controlled adequately in a sample of this size; and, in addition, questions remain open about the reliability of the adjustment ratings.[25] But for purposes of illustration the trend revealed in Table 1 is of considerable interest, for it suggests that the minority orientations I have attempted to specify here may be treated (provisionally, at least) not simply as categories of description but as relevant factors in the performance of the intellectual role as such.

It is customary, of course, to conclude by noting the need for further research—in this case, research on the forms and consequences of anti-intellectualism. But there is one crucial thing.—To find, as we have, that many intellectuals adopt, without serious efforts to build a reasoned self-portrait, an essentially negative, minority view of themselves and to find, in addition, some plausible ground for believing that this failure in self-conception is not independent of role performance—gives a special cast to the usual call for research. Thus it would seem essential to recognize that this research must include, if we may call it that, an "inward" as well as an "outward" orientation—that is, we must presumably conduct two related research operations: a study of the attitudes that others take toward intellectuals as well as a more intensive study of the intellectuals' attitudes toward themselves. A serious effort along those lines might yield considerably more than the usual research project; it can become an opportunity for self-discovery.

25. The question of reliability of rating may not be a serious problem. The same judge who did the ratings in this case was also used in the previously mentioned study of Jewish adjustment; and in that case the ratings of two independent judges, completing a task quite similar to the rating task involved here, were quite reliable (see the paper cited in n. 21 above). I have not deemed it essential for purposes of this illustration to compute another reliability figure for the judge in question.

12. Marginality and the Academic[*]

CHARLES H. ANDERSON

In his recent study of "men of ideas," Coser (1965:360) remarked that "A certain measure of alienation seems to be the perennial lot of the intellectual; he can never be 'like other men'. . . . he will always be *in* society without fully being *of* it." Several other writers (cf. Gordon, 1964; Hajda, 1961; Seeman, 1958; Lazarsfeld and Thielens, 1958) have theoretically or empirically drawn attention to what they consider to be a marginal social and psychological status for many academics and intellectuals. Collectively, these studies suggest that the intellectual has limited informal and formal social ties within the larger society, feels himself to be the object of anti-intellectual sentiments, to occupy minority status, and to be relatively powerless.

Although the evidence regarding the *experience* of marginality by academics and intellectuals has not been directly contradicted by research, it is far from definitive. To be sure, there has been extensive comment, both popular and academic, on the social *acceptance and salience* of the intellectual (cf. Kristol, 1966; Lippmann, 1966; *Time*, 1965; Lipset, 1960). The public's high regard for certain of the intellectual professions such as college professor and scientist has been documented by NORC surveys, although artist, author, and musician were comparatively low on the rankings (Hodge et al., 1966). And in his research on social distance in the stratification structure, Laumann (1966:42) discovered college professors to be the third most acceptable group out of seventeen different occupational groups. Thus, there obviously remains unresolved some ambiguities surrounding the social location of the intellectual.

Marginality is, of course, a variable and certain segments of the intellectual world may experience social separation quite keenly while others feel it more mildly or not at all. Also at issue in comparative

* I am grateful to Edward O. Laumann of the University of Michigan for critically reading an earlier draft of the paper and offering a number of very helpful suggestions.

terms is the feeling of social categories, particularly other upper-white-collar persons. How occupationally mixed are the primary groups of doctors, engineers, and businessmen? How many organizations do they participate in? Do they feel that they are the object of an anti-occupational animus, that they occupy minority status, and that they are powerless? Unfortunately, there is a dearth of hard data on most of these comparative questions; much of what is available in the literature will be introduced below in connection with the discussion of my own findings.

In this paper, I shall further pursue the question of marginality as it pertains to the academic, the academic representing only one albeit important locus of intellectual life.

Procedures

In order to gain further insight into the problem of alienation among academics and intellectuals in America, I propose to review results of interviews completed with sixty-one college and university professors during the fall of 1965. The respondents represented the arts and science faculties of three nonsectarian private liberal arts colleges and a state university located in the Connecticut River Valley of Massachusetts. Respondents were selected by way of a random sampling procedure which stratified them (disproportionately) on a religious background basis. In all, thirty-six persons with Protestant origins (fourteen held church memberships) and twenty-five with Jewish origins were retained for analysis. Catholics were excluded from this study, but were considered subsequently by Murray (1969)—data which shall be used comparatively in a few instances in this paper.

Other background characteristics of the sample were as follows: all were white and all but four were native-born; half of the Protestants and all of the Jews were raised in cities of more than 100,000 people; only four Protestants and three Jews came from blue-collar origins; half of the Protestants and four-fifths of the Jews were under forty-six years of age; and all but seven spouses held college degrees and twenty-three held advanced degrees. In short, the sample was largely native, urban, middle-class in background, disaffected white Protestant or Jewish in ethnicity, as well as comparatively young with highly educated spouses.

Both structured and open-ended questions were used to ascertain respondents' informal and formal group ties, perception of anti-intellectualism, self-status rating, perceived majority or minority position on important social issues, and assessment of intellectuals' power and influence. It should, of course, be kept in mind that aside from group ties it is the respondents' definition of the situation which has been tapped and not the situation itself.

Although it is likely that "Academic intellectuals ... are numerically and strategically the most important group among contemporary intellectuals" (Coser, 1965: 249), not all academics conceive of themselves as intellectuals. In this sample, twenty-one Protestants (58 percent) and eighteen Jews (72 percent) responded in the affirmative to the question "Do you think of yourself as an intellectual?"[1] Self-defined intellectuals tended to be younger and in the humanities and social sciences. The remainder, those who negated the intellectual self-concept, shall on occasion serve as a control group with which to draw limited comparisons. The comparisons of self-defined intellectuals and self-defined non-intellectuals are meant to be suggestive only.[2] Comparisons are also made between members of the social sciences-humanities and the natural sciences on several selected variables, though these were strongly influenced by intellectual self-identification.

Findings

Clique Ties. A question directed at the occupational composition of respondents' circle of close friends[3] revealed that the primary group life of the sample was shored up mostly by other academics, and in some cases with members of the non-academic intellectual professions such as artists, musicians, writers, and scientists. Only in a small minority of cases—mostly among self-defined non-intellectuals—were other white-collar occupations well-represented. Seventy-seven percent of the Protestants and 68 percent of the Jews declared that "all" or "most" of their close friends were academics. Comparable figures for Protestant self-defined intellectuals and non-intellectuals were 90 and

1. The term "intellectual" has been used to designate a variety of different types of persons by various authors. In this paper, it is being used primarily in the sense of "... a person who takes a wide range of abstract symbols and ideas seriously, and who does so in relation to a wide range of topics outside his immediate field of specialization." See Deutsch (1959). Intellectual self-identification was found to be strongly related to a six-item media behavior scale including newspaper, periodical, book, film, artistic, and television exposure (point-biserial r equals .66 for Protestants and .54 for Jews, both significant at the .01 level).

2. Statistical tests were based on 2×2 contingency tables using Yates correction factor.

3. The notion of "close friend" was defined to respondents as "people whom you see socially very often and are very comfortable with."

60 percent (p < .05). Fully three-fourths of the Jewish self-defined intellectuals and half of the Protestant could count *no* close associates outside one of the intellectual professions.

In answer to the question on close friends, one professor remarked, "Entirely academics. I'm interested in intellectual things and this requires getting together with people who are also interested in such things. For me, these people are academics." Another observed that "Insurance salesmen are the only conversational contacts at all outside of colleagues. You won't find a banker invited to a college teacher's house." And, "I don't want to appear snobbish, but we don't have many friends and the ones we do have are academics." A fourth declared, "I live a cloistered life among academics." Finally, "You will find very few intellectuals who have more than a small number of the general population in their circle of friends."

Several respondents pointed out that although they had close associates outside the academic world, these persons belong to a friendship pattern which stresses intellectual orientation: "Most of our friends are academics. The rest are people who are of an intellectual cast of mind, usually in a profession." And, "Ninety percent are academics. The remainder are intellectually oriented."

Some delineated reasons for their paucity of white-collar intimacies:

I wouldn't feel at home in most sections of the middle class. I would feel very much out of place in the typical middle-class crowd. My friends are men whose lives are devoted to ideas and books. If I go home to the old neighborhood, I run out of things to say and do with my old buddies; they talk about the stock market. The higher the educational level attained the more you are alienated from more and more people and the more you must rely on university colleagues for friends.

Several alluded to the fact that they "rubbed the wrong way with white-collar people." We might note here that the Catholic academics studied by Murray (1969: 27) also drew friends mainly from academic circles, but reported more social contact with white collar persons than did Protestants and Jews.

Whether occupational segregation in clique life reaches these proportions in the case of other individual occupations is unclear. There is some evidence to indicate that close friendships along individual occupational lines may have a tendency to develop among the more highly skilled occupations (see Bensman, 1967 on musicians; Lipset et al., 1963 on printers). However, Gerstl (1963) found that very few dentists in his sample had a high proportion of colleagues as best friends, and Wilensky and Ladinsky (1967) reported that professors in their sample were significantly more likely to find their three closest friends among members of their own professional group than were samples of lawyers and engineers.

Kinship. Another possible avenue of informal contact within the larger society is kinship. However, kin ties tended to be weak and social contact limited. Seventy-six percent of the Protestants and 72 percent of the Jews reported no more than two visits annually with family or relatives. Although excessive travel distances posed obstacles to kin interaction in some instances, most respondents stated that a majority of kin resided in neighboring states or only a short drive away. This suggests that the hiatus between the academics and their extended families was not entirely, or even chiefly, a function of geography, but was in good measure due to socio-cultural differences. As a Jewish professor explained with some candor:

I'm more comfortable with colleagues from the academic environment. When I visit my sister and brother-in-law there are antagonisms at the surface ready to break open at any time, especially if I'm in their presence for an entire evening. I have nothing in common with the New York middle-class strata—Jewish or non-Jewish.

Correspondence with kin was almost entirely restricted to parents.

Comparatively, several studies of social participation (cf. Tomeh, 1967; Adams and Butler, 1967; Laumann, 1966; and Axelrod, 1956) have demonstrated that relatives are important, if not the most important, source of friends among both white-collar and blue-collar people. Frequency of contact with kin apparently varies inversely (and usually weakly) with socioeconomic status, but even among upper-white-collar groups it does drop to the low level found among these academics.

Neighborhood. A question regarding the role of the neighborhood in social relationships disclosed that for respondents who lived in areas without an academic population, the social role of the neighborhood was negligible. Among twenty-eight such persons, only one could claim a close friend in the neighborhood, the rest only casual hellos. In contrast, of twenty-five professors who lived in areas inhabited by other academics, eleven counted neighbors among close friends. Several respondents were unable to describe the occupational stripe of their neighborhoods. Tomeh (1967), by contrast, found that neighbors were a more frequent source of friends than co-workers among college educated and white-collar people.

Organizations. Outside of church and synagogue (39 percent of the Protestants and 8 percent of the Jews belonged) and professional organizations, only 15 percent of the sample were even dues-paying members of more than one club or voluntary association. More than half belonged to no organizations. What membership cards were held were mainly in the form of financial support of civil rights, poverty, and peace groups, especially self-defined intellectuals.

Thus, rates of organizational participation more closely resembled those characteristic of working-class people than the more active associational life found among the academic's counterpart in the upper middle class (cf. Hagedorn and Labovitz, 1967; Scott, 1957). In sum, neither clique, kin, neighborhood, or club acted as a social bridge to surrounding society.

Anti-Intellectualism. In answer to the question, "Do you think that there is serious anti-intellectualism in America today?" 67 percent of the Protestants and 84 percent of the Jews responded in the affirmative (see Hofstadter, 1963 for a discussion of anti-intellectualism). Self-defined intellectuals in both groups were more likely ($p < .05$) to perceive anti-intellectual sentiments in society than were their colleagues: 81 and 94 percent of Protestants and Jews, respectively, compared to 47 and 57 percent of self-defined non-intellectuals. The proportion of Catholic academics who perceived serious anti-intellectualism in Murray's (1969) study was nearly identical to the Protestant response here. What is the nature of these anti-intellectual sentiments?

I get it from business people I meet. They refer to college teachers as fuzzy-liberals, or even communists. They think we don't do any work and are impractical.

Anti-intellectualism in American life is very strong. Those suspicious of the intellectuals' activity feel it the strongest. Many feel threatened politically and economically by the intellectual.

A certain antagonism and fear is usually running along political and economic lines. I get it constantly when working public social situations. Sometimes I wish I could engage in such things without being known as a professor.

This country is profoundly anti-intellectual. It is most evident in certain businessmen's groups and in various organizations that display a subtle right-wing orientation. (See Murray, 1969: 126)

It is noteworthy that 89 percent of respondents in the social sciences and humanities (N = 43) but only 33 percent of those in the natural sciences (N = 18) discerned salient anti-intellectualism ($p < .01$ for both Protestants and Jews). This finding is in accord with Hajda's (1961: 764) finding and remark that ". . . natural scientists feel less their separation from the non-academic world and in turn get greater support for their work from non-academicians than do social scientists and humanists."

Self-status Rating. Despite their perception of anti-intellectualism, 80 percent of the sample felt that the intellectual had "fairly high" status and another 7 percent felt that he had "high" status; 10 percent rated his status "medium" and 3 percent "low." Moreover, many felt the lot of the intellectual and academic to be markedly improving, to be gaining on medicine and coming abreast with law. However, a strain of inconsistency appeared at times. As a Catholic respondent in Murray's sample remarked, "American intellectuals occupy an ambivalent status. The society feels threatened by the intellectual, but somehow feels that he is necessary. I suspect, however, that we probably have a higher status than many of us think." As a group, Catholic academics rated themselves lower in status than did Protestants and Jews (Murray, 1969: 128), a fact possibly stemming from their lower origins in the occupational structure.

Minority Feelings. Respondents were asked, "Do you feel that your position on various social, political, and economic issues of importance to you frequently differs from what you perceive to be the majority position?" Although the question taps what might be for some a rather amorphous feeling, 64 percent of the Protestants and 84 percent of the Jews indicated that they frequently occupied a minority and opposition stance on important problems facing society. Again, self-defined intellectuals experienced separation more strongly ($p < .05$): 81 percent of the Protestants and 94 percent of the Jews versus 40 and 43 percent for self-defined Protestant and Jewish non-intellectuals, respectively. By academic division, 86 percent of those in the social sciences and humanities answered yes, to only 39 percent of the natural scientists (p. $< .05$ in both religious groups).

Power Assessment. In an essay on the intellectual, Lichtheim (1960: 295) contended that "So far from inflating its own importance, the intelligentsia, it might be said, pretends that it does not carry much weight . . . ." The sample at hand was divided on this point. In response to the question "Do you feel that the academic or intellectual has much social and political power and influence in this country?" 67 percent of the Protestants and 48 percent of the Jews were affirmative. Murray's (1969) Catholic academics were evenly divided on the question. Rather

unexpectedly, the self-defined intellectual group was more optimistic
($p < .05$ in both religious groups): 81 percent of the Protestants and
56 percent of the Jews were affirmative as opposed to only 47 and 14
percent of the Protestant and Jewish self-defined non-intellectuals.
Finally, those in the humanities and social sciences expressed somewhat more confidence in the intellectuals' power and influence than
their natural science counterparts: 65 versus 44 percent (difference not
significant).

The most frequently mentioned vehicle of power and influence was
that of advisor to government on problems demanding expertise in
economy, urbanism, emerging nations, etc. For example:

In an advisory capacity, nationally, the intellectual has some power. And
there is a degree of sensitivity shown by the administration to the ideals of the
faculty. I wouldn't exaggerate it, but contrary to some beliefs, the intellectual
has some power.

In the area of governmental programs, on both the social and technical levels,
there is a respect for the intellecuals' ideas.

Quite a bit of power, especially as economic advisors. Although they may not
always be listened to, they are more and more given the opportunity to speak
out on issues.

They have tremendous power, particularly as advisors on the Federal level.
In government circles today, no decision is made without consultation with
intellectuals. But this does not mean that their advice is always followed.
(Murray, 1969: 129).

Other views were more in accord with Coser's (1965: 321) aphorism
that "He (the intellectual) thinks that he will be on top, but he usually
is only a tap."

Some think we have more power than we actually do. It is often overestimated.
More often than not, academics are ignored.

The intellectual does not really play an important role in shaping the course
of events. He is not a maker and shaker. It's mostly window dressing about
brain trusts.

Intellectuals are not taken seriously by people in power. If I were running for
president, I would rather have the intellectuals against me. They are out to a
large extent.

Technicians, yes. Humanistic intellectuals, very little.

The techocrats exercise a great deal of power, but intellectuals do not have as
much power as they think they have. They talk mainly to one another and

after a while, because of their limited acquaintances, they really think they are on top. (Murray, 1969: 130)

However, some of the same respondents who expressed doubt about the intellectuals' direct impact on public affairs envisioned him working through other, more covert, channels to power:

The academic has power in a respect he himself often underestimates and has been timid in making use of: that of being in contact with minds of people in their learning stage. It is not measurable, but very great.

In a way not usually thought of, but very obvious. A teacher stands in front of a class of three hundred and, if effective, can influence their thought and actions.

Not so much political power as cultural power, which sooner or later translates into political power. If a scholar establishes a relationship with a Russian and explores some area of common interest with him and they uncork an argument on a subject, the fact of intellectual agreement itself stands as a repudiation of impregnable hostility. As long as cultural understanding of this sort is possible, it can become a sort of political fact in itself.

In brief, the majority of self defined intellectuals assigned *some form* of power and influence to the intellectual world. Interestingly, from the public perspective, Rose (1967) observed in his study of power in America that college professors were credited by several samples of Minnesota respondents with notable amounts of influence, particularly in regard to economic matters. Yet, political figures, labor, and business were generally considered *more influential* than academics.

Discussion

First the findings lend support to the view that academics function marginally to the main social structural framework of society, especially self-defined intellectuals. Protestant self-defined intellectuals and Catholic intellectuals in Murray's sample were equally as marginal as Jews, though more of the latter identified themselves as intellectuals. Respondents were not part and parcel of their community's group life, informal or formal. They bypassed the cliques, clubs, and organizations of the core society.

This does not mean that the academic or intellectual is socially adrift without group ties or anchorage. As Gordon (1964:224-232) has theorized, and as our findings on social participation and attitudes suggest, marginal intellectuals may coalesce around common interests to form a subsociety of marginals, as it were, an intellectual subsociety. Indeed, half of the Protestants and three-fourths of the Jews felt that they belonged to an intellectual community: "I have no difficulty in moving in and out of situations dominated by intellectuals. They are a group of people who I feel comfortable with and can talk with at some length, regardless of occupation." And, "I mesh better with people of this kind [intellectuals], but not so well with others. People in this layer think, talk, and act on a different level." An additional aspect of Gordon's intellectual subsociety concept is that it is trans-ethnic in nature, i.e., it reveals none of the typical racial or religious cleavages found in American society at large. Although the data presented here do not deal with the latter hypothesis, a set of related findings (Anderson, 1968a; Murray, 1969) did in fact offer evidence in its support (see Section VI). A more recent inquiry of mine (1968b) produced similar results.

Secondly, the academic seems to be separated in an attitudinal sense: a majority of respondents indicated perceiving a serious amount of anti-intellectualism and felt that they held minority views on salient issues. Yet, the academics did not appear to experience status and power deprivations which one might expect as a corollary of social and psychological marginality. A feeling of powerlessness was expressed by a minority of sample members, and a very small minority felt that the academic or intellectual has been consigned to low or even medium status by their society—an accurate piece of role-taking for those not familiar with occupational prestige studies.

In sum, on certain dimensions the social location of most of these academics seems to be one of separation: namely, the social structural and attitudinal, or social psychological. Underlying these dimensions is very likely a cultural-behavioral dimension (cf. Anderson, 1967; Gerstl, 1963) (See Section IV). On other variables—class, status, and power, or those basic to stratification—many of the professors found themselves in the swim. Evidently it is possible to enjoy prestige and objective reward contemporaneously with types of social psychological alienation.

In light of the significant differences between self-defined intellectuals and non-intellectuals, it would be highly plausible to argue that marginality and alienation are not endemic to academic life but rather to intellectual life. Academic responsibilities and routines do not seem intrinsically alienating to role incumbents. It is when the intellectual role of social criticism is combined with the academic role of instruction and learning that the academic person begins to more keenly experience marginality. As Coser has pointed out, a degree of estrangement and detached concern is a precondition to the intellectual role.

In the same vein, it seems possible to reconcile the apparent paradox of marginality together with prestige and acceptance. The academic intellectual sizes up his relationship to society vis-a-vis his role of intellectual, whereas society prefers to evaluate him in terms of his teaching, technical, and service roles. Should society choose to stress the critical activity of the academic rather than the need for his expertise, and many middle class "dissenters" are already questioning the beneficence of technology, his reservoir of acceptance, prestige, and objective reward may well suffer a sharp decline.

References

Adams, Bert N. and James E. Butler. 1967. "Occupational Status and Husband-Wife Social Participation." Social Forces 45 (June): 501-515.

Anderson, Charles H. 1967. "Kitsch and the Academic." Sociology and Social Research 51 (July): 445-452.

1968a "The Intellectual Subsociety Hypothesis: An Empirical Test." Sociological Quarterly 9 (Spring): 210-227.

1968b "Religious Communality Among Academics." Journal for the Scientific Study of Religion 7 (Spring): 87-96.

Axelrod, Morris. 1956. "Urban Structure and Social Participation." American Sociological Review 21 (February): 13-18.

Bensman, Joseph. 1967. "Classical Music and the Status Game." Trans-action 4 (September): 54-59.

Coser, Lewis A. 1965. Men of Ideas. Glencoe: The Free Press.

Deutsch, Karl W. 1959. "Comments on American Intellectuals." Daedalus 88 (Summer): 488-491.

Gerstl, Joel E. 1961. "Leisure, Taste, and Occupational Milieu." Social Problems 9 (Summer): 56-68.

Gordon, Milton M. 1964. Assimilation in American Life. New York: Oxford University Press.

Hagedorn, Robert and Sanford Labovitz. 1967. "An Analysis of Community and Professional Participation Among Occupations." Social Forces 45 (June): 483-491.

Hajda, Jan. 1961. "Alienation and Integration of Student Intellectuals." American Sociological Review 26 (October): 758-777.

Hodge, Robert W., Paul M. Siegel, and Peter H. Rossi. 1966. "Occupational Prestige in the United States: 1925-1963." In Reinhard Bendix and Seymour M. Lipset (eds.), Class, Status, and Power (Second Edition). New York: The Free Press.

Hofstadter, Richard. 1963. Anti-intellectualism in American Life. New York: Alfred A. Knopf.

Kristol, Irving. 1966. "The Troublesome Intellectuals." The Public Interest 2 (Winter): 3-6.

Laumann, Edward O. 1966. Prestige and Association in an Urban Community. Indianapolis: Bobbs-Merrill.

Lazarsfeld, Paul F. and Wagner Thielens, Jr. 1958. The Academic Mind. Glencoe: The Free Press.

Lichtheim, George. 1960. "The Role of the Intellectual." Commentary 36 (April): 295-307.

Lippmann, Walter. 1966. "The University." The New Republic 154 (May 28): 17-20.

Lipset, Seymour M. 1960. "American Intellectuals: Their Politics and Status." Political Man. New York: Doubleday.

Lipset, Seymour M., Martin A. Trow, and James S. Coleman. 1963. Union Democracy. New York: Doubleday.

Murray, John D. 1969. "The American Catholic Intellectual: An Empirical Test of the Intellectual Subsociety Hypothesis." Doctoral Dissertation. University of Massachusetts.

Rose, Arnold M. 1967. The Power Structure. New York: Oxford University Press.

Scott, John C. 1957. "Membership and Participation in Voluntary Association." American Sociological Review 22 (June): 315-326.

Seeman, Melvin. 1958. "The Intellectual and the Language of the Minorities." American Journal of Sociology 64 (July): 25-35.

Time Essay. 1965. "The Flourishing Intellectuals." Time 85 (May 21): 32-33.

Tomeh, Aida K. 1967. "Informal Participation in a Metropolitan Community." Sociological Quarterly 8 (Winter): 85-102.

Wilensky, Harold and Jack Ladinsky. 1967. "From Religious Community to Occupational Group: Structural Assimilation Among Professors, Lawyers, and Engineers." American Sociological Review 32 (August): 541-561.

VI

WORK AS COMMUNITY

The papers included in this section are keyed to Gordon's hypothesis of an intellectual subsociety. Gordon posits that American intellectuals, among whom academics are the most numerous group, form the outlines of a subsociety within which the divisiveness of ethnic backgrounds has been largely eliminated by a shared and overriding interest in ideas. Except for a certain amount of cultural and historical interest in one's ethnic background, the facors of religion, national origin, and even race (all of which are subsumed under the notion of ethnicity) tend to be functionally ignored within the academic community. But as Gordon points out, the academic or intellectual community does have its ethnic-oriented members, either actively involved in the promotion of ethnic group vitality or simply passive ethnic participants in the customary sense. The largest segment, however, is composed of marginal ethnics.

The shortage of supporting evidence that Gordon notes has been somewhat alleviated, and the data that now exist tend to substantiate the hypothesis, but not entirely. Anderson's study of Protestant and Jewish academics disclosed that the large majority of both groups confined their social participation to academics, were cognizant of an intellectual community, were ethnically marginal, and were engaged in close and frequent inter-ethnic contact. Murray's investigation of Catholic academics produced quite similar results in the case of a sample of teachers from non-Catholic colleges, but revealed the presence of considerable religious communality in a Catholic college sample. While the younger and intellectually oriented Catholic professors in the nonsectarian college sample were the most ethnically marginal, their counterparts at the sectarian colleges were the most communal. Significantly, in both samples, early socialization was a poor predictor of current ethnic orientation. Also, in both samples, Catholics reported more contact with non-academic white collar people than did Protestants and Jews. Furthermore, Catholics were much more likely than Protestants and Jews to note the existence of religious prejudice in the academic community.

Mazur's research on a sample of Jewish social scientists on the faculties of three universities in the Boston area (also the residence of Murray's Catholic sectarians), shows that while differences in ethnic identification and communal ties did exist among the respondents, these academics ethnically were considerably more marginal than the Greater Boston Jewry as a whole. As with the Jewish professors in Anderson's study, Mazur's academics identified with the traditional Jewish emphasis upon intellectual achievement, political liberalism, and Jewish social ethics. There was a rejection of identification, however, with the Jewish middle class. Although much of the difference in current ethnic communalism among the professors could be accounted for by non-academic influences, that is, by childhood socialization and, more importantly, by primary relationships in adult life, particularly intra-ethnic marriage, the influence of work and the academic environment was found to be basic to an explanation of the marked differences existing between these academics and Jewish non-academics.

Regardless of their earlier particular ethnic orientation, college professors, overall, in comparison with the general populace, are quite irreligious. Although a rather large minority of academics has no religious preference, only a very slight percentage of the larger society are so totally uninvolved religiously. But important exceptions to this generalization do exist. For example, in comparison with their respective non-academic populations, Catholic professors are more devout than Protestants or Jews. Murray's research suggests that this holds true for Catholics on the faculties of both non-sectarian and Catholic colleges, although Catholic professors at non-Catholic colleges appear weaker in overall religious interest than their Catholic college counterparts. Moreover, intellectually oriented Catholic academics in Murray's study often took an active interest in religious questions and controversies and were more liberal on religious issues than their non-intellectually oriented Catholic colleagues. Murray suggests that updated conceptions and more sophisticated measures of religiosity would reveal, at least in the case of Catholics, less incompatibility between religious and intellectual interests than is commonly believed.

13. The Intellectual Subsociety

MILTON M. GORDON

It is my hypothesis that intellectuals in the United States interact in such patterned ways as to form at least the elementary structure of a subsociety of their own, and that this subsociety is the only one in American life in which people of different ethnic backgrounds interact in primary group relations with considerable frequency and with relative comfort and ease. Research which would definitively prove or disprove this hypothesis does not exist. The intellectuals have discussed themselves and their role with abiding passion,[1] but empirical studies of intellectuals which would be related to the verification of our thesis are few and far between. Those that have been found will be mentioned briefly below. But first some remarks on a definition of the term "intellectuals" are in order.

Intellectuals are "people for whom ideas, concepts, literature, music, painting, the dance have intrinsic meaning—are a part of the social-psychological atmosphere which one breathes."[2] Occupationally, they are characteristically found in the professions, particularly college teaching, research, and the upper reaches of journalism (to a lesser degree, law and medicine), and in the arts, either as creators or performers. If they are engaged in business, they are likely to be in communications or publishing. Not all persons in each of these occupational categories are intellectuals, and intellectuals will at times be found in other occupations. The academic world of teaching and research, supplemented now by the world of the Foundation, which either carries out or commissions research, is the most salient concentration point of the intellectual life, and this becomes increasingly so as writers, artists, and musicians begin to take on the role of faculty members and "artists-

1. See George B. de Huszar (ed.). *The Intellectuals: A Controversial Portrait*, Glencoe, Ill., The Free Press, 1960.
2. Milton M. Gordon, "Social Class and American Intellectuals," *American Association of University Professors Bulletin*, Vol. 40, No. 4 (Winter, 1954-55), pp. 518-19.

in-residence," alongside professors of the humanities and the natural and social sciences.

As Lipset has noted, the number of intellectuals in the United States is now so great and this number is so dispersed over the vast geographical area of the country, that it is impossible for the American intellectual, in contrast to his counterpart in some European countries, to know personally more than a tiny fraction of his peers.[3] There are about 9000 college and university teachers in the Boston area alone, 14,000 or so in northern California centered on the San Francisco area, over 20,000 in and around New York City.[4] By the same token, however, this abundance of academics should make it apparent that the numbers which make an enclosed communal social life possible are unmistakably present. The intellectual world, furthermore, because of its wide array of different occupational specializations, is more like a loose network of subgroups with varying degrees of articulated social relations between them than a tightly integrated enclave. People in the theater, for instance—playrights, directors, and actors—form a closely knit group, as do those in the dance, in the visual arts, and so on. Even college professors (though this varies considerably with the personality of the individual) in the larger universities are likely to form a large part of their friendships along departmental or divisional lines.

As we pointed out earlier, any subsociety is likely to be composed of numerous subcommunities, each geographically located in a particular area, whose personnel are interchangeable. Therefore, the geographical dispersion of intellectuals by no means argues against the existence of an intellectual community. Furthermore, the abundant reading which intellectuals engage in, either as a part of their occupational role or their avocational interests, tends to create a common framework of leadership, reference groups, and conventions of discourse. For instance, most intellectuals read what is, in effect, the national newspaper of the intellectuals—*The New York Times;* they read it selectively but they read it either daily or Sunday, and they have some idea from the Book Review of what books are being written, from the drama section of what plays are being produced, from the music section of what orchestras, conductors, artists, and ensembles are appearing in New York, and from the news section, of what the current serious national and

3. Seymour Martin Lipset, "American Intellectuals: Their Politics and Status," *Daedalus, Journal of the American Academy of Arts and Sciences,* Summer, 1959, pp. 470-72.
4. Lipset, op. cit., p. 470.

international events and controversies may be. The magazines on their coffee tables, apart from the professional journals they read, are likely to be selected, according to taste and interest, from *Harper's, The Atlantic Monthly, The New Yorker, The Reporter, Commentary, The Saturday Review, Daedalus, Consumer Reports*, the literary quarterlies, and a few others. If they have a television set ("for the children") they turn it on, themselves, only rarely to watch Leonard Bernstein, the Play of the Week, or the contemporary equivalent of Omnibus. If they are musically inclined, they will turn on their Hi-Fi sets to listen to solid classical music, either in orchestral or chamber music form, or to good jazz, or to both, but to nothing in between. They buy and read, if somewhat harriedly, books, not only in their professional fields, but also of a general nature such as biography, history, and analyses of current events. In other words, they bypass to a very large degree the popular culture which makes up the mass communications stimuli received with bemused attention, although somewhat selectively according to social class, by the rest of American society. I have argued elsewhere that, from the point of view of status position and the ordinary amenities of life style, the intellectuals fall within the ranks of the upper-middle class.[5] Even so, their basic frame of reference, outside these ordinary amenities, is likely to be not the frame of reference of the other members of the upper-middle class, but that which is peculiar to them as intellectuals. Thus, when intellectuals meet, they recognize each other and can communicate easily with one another, just as a lower-middle-class white Protestant non-intellectual, to take just one of a number of possible examples, recognizes and speaks with confidence and an awareness of common assumptions to another person who shares both his ethnic and his class background.

Intellectuals, of course, like other individuals have ethnic backgrounds and some of them do not venture beyond the ethnic fold. The man of ideas and the arts is a Negro, a Jew, an Irish or Italian Catholic, or something else.[6] As the culturally assimilating forces of the American social class system exert pressures which bring him into contact with persons of different ethnic but the same social class position, the containing walls of ethnic communality are threatened—but not necessarily broken. The intellectual, because his interests are sharper and

5. Gordon, "Social Class and American Intellectuals," op. cit.
6. The discussion and typology contained in the following few paragraphs is taken, mostly verbatim, from my article, "Social Class and American Intellectuals," op. cit. (by permission).

rarer, simply faces this conflict in a more acute form than do others. On the basis of his resolution of the conflict and the personality style which significantly influences it, we may distinguish three "ideal types" of response to the dual pressures of ethnicity and intellectualism. The representatives of these three types may be called "the actively ethnic intellectual," "the passively ethnic intellectual," and "the marginally ethnic intellectual."

The "actively ethnic intellectual" remains within his ethnic group and focuses his intellectual interests precisely on his ethnicity. He is the cultural historian of the group, the theologian, the communal leader, the apologist, the scholar of its art, its music, and its literature. While he maintains a respectable acquaintanceship with the broader ideological currents and events around him, his primary interests and passions are reserved for the racial, religious, or nationality background ethos in which he considers his roots to be firmly placed. His is a confident approach, and he appears to be spared many of the problems of marginality. He may be a white Protestant as well as a member of a minority, since white Protestants are simply the largest American ethnic group.

The "passively ethnic intellectual" is the second distinguishable type. Finding it easier, safer, or more in line with his personality style, this individual remains predominantly within the subsocietal boundaries of his ethnic group and social class. If he is a Negro, most of his friends may be intellectuals but they will also be Negroes. If he is a Jew, he confines his friendships primarily to other Jewish intellectuals. While his interests are mostly of the broader, nonethnic variety, he gratifies them within the borders of ethnic communality. Occasionally, he looks wistfully beyond the ethnic boundaries at other intellectuals but he is not moved, or not able, to cross these boundaries in any substantial sense.

The "marginally ethnic intellectual" is, from our point of view, the most interesting and the most significant type. It is he who enters and makes up the intellectual subsociety. As the appellation indicates, he wears his ethnicity lightly, if not in his own eyes at least in the eyes of the world. Whatever his social psychology, he finds ethnic communality unsatisfactory and takes his friends, and probably even his spouse, where he finds them, so long as they share his fascination with Kafka and his passion for Heinrich Schuetz. To other, more conventional ethnics he is very occasionally a traitor, sometimes a snob, not infrequently, in Lewin's term, a "leader from the periphery." Mostly they let him alone; if he is successful, they will claim him—and he will be pleased by their claim.

In the absence of relevant research, it is impossible at this time to specify the relative numerical strength of these three types of intellectuals either as a whole or in relationship to particular ethnic groups. We would hypothesize that Type 1 is numerically small but relatively stable in proportion to the size of the ethnic group; that Type 2 is larger in numbers but tends to be unstable in size and composition as the resources of the ethnic community are increasingly perceived by the intellectually inclined ethnic group member as inadequate for his needs. According to this hypothesis, then, Type 3, the "marginally ethnic intellectual," is the numerically largest category and the one which constantly expands in size, forging along with its numerical increase, the structure of the intellectual subsociety.

Empirical data which would either verify or disprove our hypothesis concerning the existence of an intellectual subsociety are scarce. Seeman, in a largely qualitative study of forty assistant professors in a midwestern university, found that his respondents, in discussing themselves and their role as intellectuals, used the language and mechanisms which frequently characterize the responses of ethnic minority groups in self-discussion. While the language and mechanisms alluded to were negatively oriented toward the image of intellectuals, and while, overt acceptance of intellectual status was rare, it is possible to infer from the protocol materials presented a covert awareness of both intellectual group identity and a subjective feeling of alienation from the broader society.[7]

Survey data from a study by Hajda of over 2000 native-born graduate students in twenty-five American universities bear somewhat more directly on our hypothesis.[8] Of the sample, 47 per cent defined themselves as intellectuals—that is, answered in the affirmative to the question: "Do you think of yourself as an 'intellectual' "? This proportion rose to 53 per cent of the students in the humanities and 51 per cent of those in the social sciences. About two-thirds of the entire student group felt alienated from the larger society (alienation being measured by an index based on responses to a series of questions dealing with how the students felt in the presence of non-academic people). Thus,

7. Melvin Seeman, "The Intellectual and the Language of Minorities," *American Journal of Sociology*, Vol. 64, No. 1 (July 1958), pp. 25-35.
8. Jan Hajda, "Alienation and Integration of Student Intellectuals," *American Sociological Review*, Vol. 26, No. 5 (October 1961), pp. 758-77.

while Hajda's data do not suggest that all graduate students are either self-defined intellectuals or feel estranged from the larger society (or that alienation is ever complete), the percentages in each category are noticeably large. Moreover, another of Hajda's findings, namely that "alienation, coupled with intellectual orientation, is generally characteristic of those who expect to stay in the academic world after graduation,"[9] bears even more suggestively on the validity of our hypothesis of the existence of an intellectual subsociety. Furthermore, this investigator's description of the sociological profile of the alienated intellectual indicates the minimization of structural affiliation with the institutions and organizations of the larger society which is characteristic of this group: "The alienated intellectuals among graduate students are persons committed more or less exclusively to the academic community. They are most prone to regard the larger society as anti-intellectual; to have no religious affiliation, or merely formal church membership; to have less intense attachment to their parental families than other students; to have few if any friends from high school days. Their personal career is marked by dissent from religious traditions in which they were reared and by a history of conflict with parental authority. The only non-academic organization that sometimes commands their loyalty is a liberal political movement."[10] In this last connection, a finding of Lazarsfeld and Thielens in their study of the reactions of a national cross-section of nearly 2500 college teachers in the social sciences to the pressures for ideological conformity in the decade following World War II deserves mention. In answer to the question, "Are the people you see the most of socially mainly from your department, from the faculty generally, or from the community?" 62 per cent reported that their main social contacts were confined to the university faculty. This figure rises to above 70 per cent for faculty members in the more distinguished and prestigeful colleges and universities.[11]

A final piece of evidence—of a highly qualitative nature, to be sure —may be cited from the pages of *Commentary*, the monthly magazine of high intellectual distinction published by the American Jewish Committee. In the spring of 1961, the editors of this periodical published a symposium on the theme of "Jewishness and the Younger Intellectuals." The symposium consisted of the replies of thirty-one American

9. Ibid., p. 772.
10. Ibid., p. 775.
11. Paul F. Lazarsfeld and Wagner Thielens, Jr., *The Academic Mind*, Glencoe, Ill., The Free Press, 1958, pp. 31-2.

intellectuals of Jewish birth, none of them over the age of forty and most of them under thirty-five, to a series of questions dealing with their attitudes toward a series of issues relating to Jewish culture and the Jewish community in America.[12] Their replies, while highly varied and complex, as might be expected from a group of this nature, revealed an overwhelming estrangement from the ideologies, issues, and concerns of Jewish communal life in America. The anguished and angry "letters to the editor" received from a number of Jewish communal representatives and published in subsequent issues of the magazine[13] testified to their perception of this estrangement and their negative evaluation of it.

In short, empirical evidence of the existence of an intellectual subsociety in America is in short supply, indicating the need for research focused directly on the hypothesis. However, much of that evidence which does exist suggests that the outlines of such a subsociety have begun to take shape in the United States.

12. "A Symposium: Jewishness and the Younger Intellectuals," *Commentary*, April 1961, pp. 306-59.
13. See the "Letters From Readers" column in the June and July 1961 issues of *Commentary*.
This is not to say that the symposium contributors disclaimed having been influenced by Jewish culture. But their interpretation of Jewish culture tended to be in the direction of emphasizing the universalistic prophetic tradition of social justice rather than those elements of the cultural heritage which foster specific ethnic concerns.

14. The Intellectual Subsociety Hypothesis: An Empirical Test

CHARLES H. ANDERSON

In a recent book on ethnic communality in America, Milton Gordon outlined an "intellectual subsociety hypothesis" in which it was argued that intellectuals in the United States do not fit the contours of the sociological mold cast by the forces of race, religion, and national origin in contemporary group life. Gordon contended that "intellectuals in the United States interact in such patterned ways as to form at least the elementary structure of a subsociety of their own, and . . . this subsociety is the only one in American life in which people of different ethnic backgrounds interact in primary group relations with considerable frequency and with relative comfort and ease."[1] Stated otherwise, intellectuals often find life within the ethnic fold unsatisfactory and transcend the boundaries of their respective ethnic groups to form collectively a transethnic subsociety.[2] Thus, Gordon hypothesized that there is emerging in this country a social stratum of intellectuals, a stratum within which ethnic backgrounds are superseded and no marked ethnic divisions (unlike other strata with their ethnic subgroups) are revealed. This ethnically neutral subsociety may not, of course, embrace all intellectuals. Some may prefer ethnic solidarity in the mainstream society or with other intellectuals of a similar ethnic background.

The impetus for an ethnically undivided subsociety of intellectuals is provided by shared ideational interests of such intensity as to overcome background variables: Gordon notes that ". . . in the situation of men and women coming together, because of an overriding common interest in ideas, the creative arts, and mutual professional concerns, we find the clas-

1. Milton M. Gordon, *Assimilation in American Life: The Role of Race, Religion, and National Origin* (New York: Oxford University Press, 1964), p. 224.
2. It is the nature of a subsociety to provide its members with a context for the realization of the majority of their primary social relationships, chiefly those found in the family, the clique, and the club.

sic sociological enemy of ethnic parochialism."[3] Involvement in the realm
of ideas becomes the pivot of commonality rather than ancestry or socio-
religious heritage.

Intellectuals are defined by Gordon as "persons who have a serious and
relatively informed interest in ideas and the arts. They are people for
whom ideas, concepts, literature, music, painting, the dance have intrinsic
meaning—are part of the social psychological atmosphere which one
breathes."[4] Or, in the words of Deutsch, an intellectual is "a person
who takes a wide range of abstract symbols and ideas seriously, and who
does so in relation to a wide range of topics outside his immediate field of
specialization."[5]

What available empirical evidence is there in the current literature
which might substantiate the intellectual subsociety hypothesis? Evidence
is, in fact, very meager and inferential. Seeman found that college professors tended to use the language and mechanisms which frequently characterize minority groups.[6] A study by Hajda of data gathered on graduate
students disclosed that those with intellectual self-conceptions felt more
estranged from the larger society than other graduate students.[7] Lazarsfeld
and Thielens reported that about two-thirds of the college professors ques-
tioned during their research confined their main social contacts to other
academics.[8] Wilensky and Ladinsky discovered that professors in their
sample were significantly more likely to find their three closest friends
among members of their own profession than were samples of lawyers and
engineers.[9] Academics' identification with their profession was also much
stronger than was that of either lawyers or engineers. And Bensman has
pointed out that professional classical musicians tend to restrict primary
relationships to music colleagues.[10]

3. Gordon, *op. cit.*, p. 58.
4. Milton M. Gordon, "Social Class and American Intellectuals," *American Association of University Professors Bulletin*, 40: 517-28 (Spring, 1954).
5. Karl W. Deutsch, "Comments on American Intellectuals," *Daedalus*, 88: 488-91
(Summer, 1959).
6. Melvin Seeman, "The Intellectual and the Language of the Minorities," *American
Journal of Sociology*, 64 : 25-35 (July, 1958).
7. Jan Hajda, "Alienation and Integration of Student Intellectuals," *American Sociological Review*, 26: 758-77 (July, 1958).
8. Paul F. Lazarsfeld and Wagner Thielens, Jr., *The Academic Mind* (Glencoe, Ill.:
The Free Press, 1958).
9. Harold L. Wilensky and Jack Ladinsky, "From Religious Community to Occupational Group: Structural Assimilation among Professors, Lawyers, and Engineers,"
American Sociological Review, 3 : 544, 548 (August, 1967).
10. Joseph Bensman, "Classical Music and the Status Game," *Trans-Action*, 4: 54-
59 (Sept., 1967). It is entirely possible that there are nonintellectual occupational

Although these findings point in the direction of a potential intellectual stratum, there have been no direct investigations of the role of the ethnic factor in intellectual life.[11] We may conceive of a social stratum of persons formed on intellectual criteria, but which also contains ethnic cleavages similar to those found in the larger society.

This paper attempts to deal directly—in an exploratory fashion—with certain variables which might be considered basic to any verification of the intellectual subsociety hypothesis, focusing primarily upon the ethnic dimension and secondarily upon the class factor.

Procedures

Interviews were conducted with 36 college and university professors of white Protestant background and 25 of Jewish background representing the arts and science faculties of three non-sectarian liberal arts colleges and a state university in Massachusetts. Academics of Catholic background were to be studied later.* Respondents were selected for interview by means of a random sampling procedure which stratified them (disproportionately) on the basis of religious background. The interviews were carried out during the summer and fall of 1965 and ranged from one to two hours in length.

The interview schedule contained a combination of structured and semi-structured items which provided both quantifiable and qualitative re-

---

groups which are also social groups, such as the case of the printers in *Union Democracy*. See S. M. Lipset, Martin A. Trow, and James S. Coleman, *Union Democracy* New York: Doubleday, 1963).

11. Wilensky and Ladinsky discovered that 41 per cent of 68 professors at a state university (a majority of Protestant background) reported strong religious identifications, whereas over 70 per cent of lawyers and engineers did so; however, 84 per cent of predominantly Catholic academics at a church school were strong in religious identification. In the same study, it was found that the state university professors found significantly fewer of their three closest friends from among co-religionists than did lawyers, engineers, and church university professors. In all groups but the state university academics, "religion is far stronger than occupation . . . as a basis for social ties" (*op. cit.*, pp. 544, 548, 557). It is plain from these results that the Catholic intellectual or academician warrants separate attention, and that we cannot generalize regarding intellectuals of other groups on the basis of our findings on intellectuals of Protestant and Jewish backgrounds. Regarding Jews, Kramer and Leventman, and Gans noted the relative indifference with which the intellectuals in their samples looked upon ethnicity, but they did not deal much further with the issue. See Judith R. Kramer and Seymour Leventman, *Children of the Gilded Ghetto* (New Haven, Conn.: Yale Univ. Press, 1961); Herbert Gans, "The Origin and Growth of a Jewish Community in the Suburbs," in Marshall Sklare, ed., *The Jews: Social Patterns of an American Group* (Glencoe, Ill.: Free Press, 1958).

* See Murray's papers in Chapters 15 and 17.

sponses, the latter being of particular value in view of the rather small sample size. A wide range of questions pertaining to ethnic participation and identification were asked, including recall questions dealing with the respondents' parents and with their own past. Religious background of close and of general friends,[12] formal ethnic group memberships, attitudes toward intermarriage, children's ethnic status, ethnic self-identification, and the perceived role of ethnicity in the academic and intellectual world were among the variables studied which related directly to the prominence of the ethnic factor. Further class-linked questions were directed at the occupation of close and general friends,[13] organization and club life, and attitudes toward the existence of an intellectual stratum.

Academics were selected as subjects partially because of previous studies which found many academics to possess the traits incorporated in the definitions of an intellectual given above.[14] Furthermore, Coser's contention that "academic intellectuals . . . are numerically and strategically the most important group among contemporary intellectuals" can scarcely be challenged.[15] Inasmuch as the intellectual subsociety hypothesis does not refer to entire occupational groups as such but to a collectivity of individuals representing a number of different occupations, it might be expected that if such an hypothesis is tenable there would be within an occupation differences between the intellectual and the nonintellectual, including the academic, on various relevant dependent variables. Answers to the question, "Do you think of yourself as an intellectual?" provided a basis for comparisons within the Protestant (21 affirmatives, 15 negatives) and Jewish (18 affirmatives, 7 negatives) groups. This subjective dimension of intellectual self-identification found significant correlation with a six-item media behavior scale which included the extent and type of newspaper ex-

12. Close and general friends were defined for the respondents in the following way: "By general friends I mean people who are more than mere acquaintances, people whom you do things with or socialize with occasionally, people with whom you are at ease. By close friends I mean people whom you see socially very often and are very comfortable with."

13. Questions which required respondents to state the number of close and general friendships which cut across particular ethnic or occupational lines were phrased in terms of a seven-point scale: All—Most—Majority—Half—Less than Half—Few—None. "Less than half" is a relatively awkward scale component, but if it is understood to indicate a numerical space between "half" and "few," there should be no difficulty in its interpretation. It was so explained to the respondents.

14. See Joel E. Gerstle, "Leisure, Taste, and Occupational Milieu," in Erwin O. Smigel, ed., *Work and Leisure* (New Haven, Conn.: College and Univ. Press, 1963); Harold Wilensky, "Mass Society and Mass Culture," *American Sociological Review*, 29: 173-93 (April, 1964).

15. Lewis A. Coser, *Men of Ideas: A Sociologist's View* (New York: The Free Press, 1965), p. 249.

posure, the number of nonprofessional periodicals read regularly, the number of books read outside the area of professional specialization year-ly, the number of movies seen yearly (excluding those shown on televi-sion), the average number of artistic performances or shows (music, art, theatre, etc.) attended yearly, and the number of television hours logged weekly.[16] Using the point-biserial r measure of statistical association, we find that the coefficients of association between the six-item media behav-ior scale and intellectual self-identification are .66 for Protestants (p = .001) and .54 for Jews (p = .01). Intellectual self-identification thus seemed to offer a meaningful basis for making within-group comparisons.

The primary concern in an exploratory study of this nature, however, was with the shape of evidence as it emerged from the study and sample as a whole. The academic profession per se has been selected for study at this time because it represents the most conspicuous and easily reached of all potentially intellectual groupings. Ideally the problem would be ap-proached not along occupational lines at all, but through a study whose sample would cross-cut all sectors of a general population and which em-ployed a sophisticated index of intellectual behavior to arrive at classi-fications.

Finally, let me say something of the demographic characteristics of the sample. All respondents were white and all but four were native-born Americans; half of the Protestants and all of the Jews were raised in cities of more than 100,000 people; only four Protestants and three Jews came from the blue-collar families; half of the Protestants but four-fifths of the Jews were under 46 years of age; the spouses of all but seven held college degrees and twenty-three held advanced degrees.

The Ethnic Factor

Friendships. There were few traces of any personal preferences for an ethnically structured social life. The following remarks exemplified the attitudes of most respondents.

My attachments are to people whom I'm congenial with regardless of ethnic background.

---

16. The six items were each categorized and weighted in the following way (com-bined they form a 20-point scale): newspapers (none = 0, local only = 1, regional only = 2, national Sunday = 3, national daily and Sunday = 4); periodicals (none = 0, one =1, two = 2, three = 3, four or more = 4); books, movies, and artistic perform-ances each scored the same (none = 0, one to six = 1, seven to twelve = 2, over twelve = 3); television (over ten hours weekly = 0, six to ten = 1, less than six = 2, never = 3).

People in the academic world have more in common with one another than with people outside, regardless of religion. I'm not concerned with religious backgrounds. Intellectual interests are basic.

Religious background is inconsequential. The religious background of friends is a function of the setting I happen to be in at any given time.

Less typical was the following view expressed by a Jewish respondent:

Other things being equal, I might out of tribal loyalty first invite Jews to the house. But the fact of common religious background only facilitates meeting people. After that, friendship must be sustained by the person's own merits—which may belong to a Catholic, Protestant, or Jew.

Did the religious backgrounds of the respondents' friends parallel this attitudinal assimilation? The data in Table 1 answer this question in the affirmative. Forty-four per cent of the Jewish respondents reported that a majority of both general and close friends were of Protestant background, while only 8 per cent counted a majority of general Jewish friends and 12 per cent a majority of close Jewish friends. In contrast to this finding, several studies of Jews in the United States indicate that approximately four-fifths confine all or nearly all of their primary social relationships to other members of the Jewish group.[17] Catholic friendships were nearly as numerous in the Jewish sample as they were in the Protestant.

Among respondents of Protestant derivation, 53 per cent checked a scale item showing that they held more than a few general Jewish friends and 28 per cent showing that they held more than a few general Catholic friends. Forty-two per cent counted more than a few close Jewish friends and 34 per cent more than a few close Catholic friends. On the other hand, only 20 per cent found that all or most of their general friends were co-religionists and 30 per cent that all or most of their close friends were co-religionists.[18] Several respondents in both groups noted that they held friends among members of non-Western religions and of non-white groups.

17. See Kramer and Leventman, *op. cit.*, p. 175; Gans, *op. cit.*; John P. Dean, "Jewish Participation in the Life of Middle-Sized American Communities," in Sklare, *op. cit.*, pp. 311-12; Gerhard Lenski, *The Religious Factor* (Garden City, N.Y.: Doubleday, 1963), p. 39; and Benjamin Ringer *The Edge of Friendliness* (New York: Basic Books, Inc., 1968).

18. There is a dearth of hard data on the extent of white Protestant communality. Lenski reported that almost 40 per cent of the Protestants in his sample found all or nearly all of their close friends among fellow white Protestants (*op. cit.*, p. 39). See also C. H. Anderson, "Religious Communality Among White Protestants, Catholics, and Mormons," *Social Forces*, 46 (June, 1968) pp. 501-508. More than one-third of the Protestants displayed strong, and less than 30 per cent displayed weak, communality.

Two further observations might be made concerning the data in Table 1. First, there was only a slight discrepancy between the distribution of religious backgrounds of general and close friends. If ethnicity were very important, we would expect to find a more marked tendency toward closure at the level of close friends when compared to general friends. Second, the proportions of Protestant, Jewish, and Catholic backgrounds found in the primary groups of both Protestant and Jewish samples followed the same rough proportions of Protestant, Jewish, and Catholic backgrounds found in the sampling universe. This indicates that the importance of the objective situation far exceeded that of religion in the structuring of group life. Only a slight tendency toward ethnic preference existed.

In what way, if any, did intellectual self-conception modify the results pertaining to religious background of friends? As would be predicted, intellectual self-conception strengthened the hypothesis. For example, 57 per cent of the respondents of Protestant origin with an intellectual self-conception reported more than a few close Jewish friends, but only 20 per cent of the Protestants who eschewed intellectual self-identification did so ($p = .05$). And within the Jewish group, those who negated intellectual identity were more likely to count more than a few close Jewish associates than the self-defined intellectuals: only 17 per cent of the latter, but 71 per cent of the former, checked points higher on the scale than "few" for the number of close Jewish friends ($p = .05$).

In the Protestant sample, age was strongly related to the ethnic background of close friends. Only 20 per cent of the Protestants under 46 years of age held a majority of close Protestant associates, whereas 69 per cent of those 46 or over held a majority of co-religionists as close friends ($p = .01$). Conversely, while only 13 per cent of the older Protestant group reported more than a few close Jewish friends, fully 65 per cent of the younger group did so ($p = .01$). It should be recalled that the Jewish sample was as a whole much younger than the Protestant, a fact which probably accounts for the disparities between the Protestant age groups on religious backgrounds of friends: older Protestant academics have fewer Jewish peers than do their younger colleagues.

Most respondents perceived ethnicity to be a comparatively innocuous fact in the social life of the academic world, as is indicated by the following remarks.

From what I can see, there is little or no ethnic prejudice of any sort.

I live in a community of people where ethnic backgrounds have no real importance.

Most academics value individuals for what they are rather than in terms of their backgrounds.

Groups form around specific interests, and religious background lines are constantly cross-cut.

People who share cultural and intellectual interests are attracted to one another. It matters little who holds them.

In the academic world, there tends to be an ignoring of the religious question, not as an object of discussion, but as a functional matter. This situation is much different from the background in which I grew up.

There is much mixing and freedom of movement and mixing of religious backgrounds. Assimilation is in process here and in other areas where preoccupations center on other than background variables.

I know what it is to be identified as a Jew before I am identified as an individual. But the university setting seems to neutralize much of this and produce a common frame of reference.

However, there were a few who expressed an awareness of the presence of ethnic considerations.

As a Protestant I've noticed that Jews have an unmistakable affinity toward one another . . . things that the outsider is not aware of.

One cannot deny the role played by general cultural background in easing the creation of friendships. If I meet a Jew from New York we have a cultural image of things in common and these act as some of the building blocks of friendship.

The degree of communality differed markedly from that reported by respondents for their own parents and their preprofessional lives. Sixty-nine per cent of the Protestant respondents declared that their parents found all or most of their friends among other Protestants; similarly, 80 per cent of the parents of Jewish professors were reported to have all or most of their friends within the Jewish group. And while 61 per cent of the Protestants reported that all or most of their adolescent friends were Protestants, a mere 11 per cent did so at the graduate school level. Similarly, 80 per cent of the Jewish respondents recalled that a majority of their friends in adolescence were also Jewish, while only 8 per cent held a majority of Jewish friends in graduate school. Several respondents pointed out that graduate school seemed to mark a turning point in the salience of ethnicity.

It was at the graduate school stage that religious affiliation didn't seem to make any difference.

Religious backgrounds have never seemed important since graduate school. From graduate school days on, I've scarcely known the backgrounds of people.

At the undergraduate level, I stopped differentiating between Protestants and Catholics; at the graduate level between gentiles and Jews.

Intermarriage. Another indication of extensive interethnic association was the finding that 40 per cent of the Jewish respondents were intermarried. This stands in marked contrast to estimates of the intermarriage rate for the Jewish population in the United States. A Census Bureau survey, for example, placed it near 7 per cent.[19] *All* of the Jewish respondents declared that *both* of their parents were lifelong Jews. All of the intermarried Jewish respondents were among those who affirmed an intellectual self-concept and most met their spouses in graduate school, a fact which suggests that the finding of a high intermarriage rate in the Jewish sample is part of a larger configuration of factors basic to the verification of the intellectual subsociety hypothesis rather than an independent statistic. Only two Jewish respondents were averse to religious intermarriage; a lone Protestant was opposed. A Jewish respondent answered the question on intermarriage stance, "I don't really have any particular views about that. But my parents did. They were very concerned." By contrast, Kramer and Leventman discovered that about 70 per cent of the Jews in their community-wide sample were negatively adamant on the mixed marriage question,[20] while Broom and Glenn, on the basis of national poll data, reported that 43 per cent of Protestants would oppose intermarriage of a son or daughter to a Catholic.[21]

Ethnic Identification. In order to arrive at some estimate of the strength of ethnic identity, respondents were asked questions regarding self-identification and group membership. When those of Protestant derivation were asked, "Do you think of yourself as a Protestant?" 75 per cent replied yes; but when asked, "Do you think of yourself as a member of the Protestant group?" only 28 per cent answered positively. Although three-fourths identified themselves as Protestants, most did so in a nominal and perfunctory way:

In a very vague and general sense. On certain occasions such as when guests

19. See U.S. Bureau of Census, *Current Population Reports: Population Characteristics,* Series P-20, No. 79 (Feb. 2, 1958), Tables 6 and 7.

20. Kramer and Leventman, *op. cit.,* p. 181.

21. Leonard Broom and Norval Glenn, "Religious Differences in Reported Attitudes and Behavior," *Sociological Analysis.* 27 (Winter, 1965), pp. 187-209.

of another faith are over for dinner certain foods cannot be served. This is rare, since we have few orthodox friends of any faith.

The marks of a Protestant background and upbringing are apparent enough to me, but that's as far as it goes.

In a broad sense. For example, I felt more at home in Holland's churches than in Italy's cathedrals. I was raised in an anti-Catholic and anti-Jewish environment and experienced a strongly Protestant emphasis. Some remnants of identity hang on.

In a highly metaphysical sense. In the sense that I stand for basic principles of individual autonomy from institutional structures. All Jews, Catholics, and Protestants who are good friends of mine are "Protestants" in this sense.

Concerning the question on Protestant group membership, the modal response was, "I don't feel I belong much to it. It doesn't interest me." On the other hand, one response represented a small minority attitude: "I have a strong sense of Protestant group membership. I'm very self-consciously a Protestant, and I play an active role in the church."

Among those with Jewish origins, 92 per cent affirmed Jewish self-identity. The dimensions of identification were highly varied and too complex to attempt to analyze in detail here, but a few themes might be noted. Easily the most frequently mentioned type of Jewish identity concerned consciousness of a liberal-intellectual tradition. Thus:

I'm very Jewish in background, inclination, and ethnic identity. I'm happy to be a part of a long, liberal tradition and sound system of ethics.

I sustain ties with Jewish identity in some cultural aspects. I have an awareness of Jewish contributions to music, literature, and the emphasis on education.

In a cultural sense I have a Jewish identity such as with the respect for education and concern for social justice. The proportions of Jews making cultural contributions in literature, education, music, and so on, have been high, and these common elements and values are points of identification.

A second group of answers centered less on heavy aspects of Jewish tradition and more on general life styles and lighter customs. For example:

Culturally speaking, yes. I share an interest in some things having to do with Jewish customs, attitudes, foods, stories, and that sort of thing.

In a cultural sense. Certain elements I hold in common with other Jews. I regret not knowing more about Jewish culture. If one is French, he may desire a knowledge of French culture. Only in that sense.

In the sense of a cultural tradition—certain foods and attitudes relating back to a heritage from the old country.

I feel I should fulfill the duties of a cultural heritage. One may have loyalties to a class or region. Here it is just about the same.

A few traced an almost undefinable identity to the experience of being *raised* Jewish.

I think of myself as a Jew in a very personal way which relates closely to my position as a Jew in adolescence. Not in a religious or even cultural sense. It is almost inflectional—very difficult to define. But I do not have rapport with mainstream Judaism.

I'm identified by others as being Jewish. I've experienced resentment in my youth. Not so much cultural identification as identification with a minority. It's hard to define.

Closely related to the responses were those which made stronger and more explicit reference to identification with a (suffering) minority:

Historically, traditionally, and culturally I have a strong sense of identity. I'm looked upon by others as being a Jew. I have pride in how Jews have handled themselves in historical situations. I could never dissociate myself from a group which has suffered so much.

After what happened in Europe, it's important for me to identify, regardless of only formal obeisance to ceremony and ritual.

A final set of responses reflected only the most tenuous ethnic identification; they appeared often:

I think of myself as Jewish only in terms of accident of birth. There is no strong consciousness of tradition.

In terms of background only. No more than that.

I was born Jewish, brought up in the faith, and although not a believer, my religion is as good as any and I see no reason to change or deny my identity.

I have no idea of Jewish culture, identity, or roots. I've never really been concerned with it, or given it much thought.

Not unless Jews can be considered a race and that is doubtful. In no other way.

None of the above themes of Jewish identity would tend to create important social division in the academic world. Indeed, where Jewish identity is the strongest, i.e., the liberal-intellectual tradition, it is at one with the ethos of academia.

Though most Jewish respondents expressed links with a phenomenon broader than self-identity (in response to the question, "Do you think of yourself as a member of the Jewish group?"), none reported that they thought of themselves as being active members of a Jewish social community:

I do not participate in a self-conscious Jewish group. I'm outside such.

I do not think of myself as part of the Jewish group nor would they accept me. They consider me a lost brother.

I do not participate in the life of the Jewish community. But I do feel part of a secular history and cultural tradition.

I have not been since adolescence. I do not at present feel part of a larger Jewish social community.

I'm not a member of the local Jewish social community.

Most Jewish life styles would conflict with mine. I indulge too strongly in the intellectual life; I feel at home with the cultural and intellectual Jew.

Comparatively, Gans found that about four-fifths of the Jews in his study reported that they felt they belonged to a formal Jewish community.[22]

Only one Protestant and two Jews participated in specifically Protestant or Jewish secular organizations; and only 39 per cent of the Protestants and 8 per cent of the Jews held church or synagogue membership.[23]

Children. Slight concern was expressed over the religious or ethnic status of children. Although most Protestants had sent or intended to send their children to Sunday School, attitudes toward religious education were by and large indifferent:

She attends Sunday School. She may continue as long as she wants. It's up to her.

They attended Sunday School for a while, but it didn't take.

22. Gans, *op. cit.*, pp. 205-6.
23. In comparison, Dean found that 90 per cent of the Jews in a middle-sized New York community belonged to at least one Jewish organization (*op. cit.*, p. 305). For both Protestants and Jews in the general population, membership in church and synagogue is the rule rather than the exception, as it seems to be in the case of academics. See, for example, Bernard Lazerwitz, "Membership in Voluntary Associations and Frequency of Church Attendance," *Journal for the Scientific Study of Religion*, 2: 74-84 (Fall, 1962); Lenski, *op. cit.*, pp. 36, 45; Kramer and Leventman, *op. cit.*, p. 166; Dean, *op. cit.*, p. 305. In our own sample, 78 per cent of the Protestants' parents held church membership and 80 per cent of the Jews' parents belonged to a synagogue. For further discussion of academic irreligiosity see Fred Thalheimer, "Continuity and Change in Religiosity: A Study of Academicians," *Pacific Sociological Review*, 8: 101-8 (Fall, 1965).

Only 28 per cent of the Jewish respondents had provided or intended to provide their children with formal instruction in Judaism or Jewish traditions. Once more, this finding stands in sharp relief against a corresponding finding by Kramer and Leventman that fully 90 per cent of the Jewish parents in that study had their children scheduled for religious instruction, and 80 per cent hoped that their children would be confirmed or bar mitzvahed.[24] Three Jewish academics remarked:

I don't think there will be any religious instruction. There has been no demand from the children themselves. I see no reason why we should.

Probably some out of habit. My wife would be for it.

Our boy goes to Unitarian Sunday School. But that isn't religion.

An intermarried Jew had this to say: "I really see no need for our children to go in either direction. I can't see where it will be of great importance."

Neither group displayed any interest in the religious backgrounds of their children's friends, including those of dating age. To quote a Jewish professor: "I have never given it a thought. I know my boy has never given it a thought either."

The Class Factor

Next we briefly turn our attention to the other aspect of the intellectual subsociety hypothesis, i.e., "intellectuals in the United States interact in such patterned ways as to form at least the elementary structure of a subsociety of their own." It should be made clear that it is not being argued that intellectuals in this country form a unitary group. Rather, as Gordon states, "The intellectual world, because of its wide array of different occupational specializations, is more like a loose network of subgroups with varying degrees of articulated social relations between them than a tightly integrated enclave."[25] Parsons' remark that "the 'intellectual community' tends to lose its solidarity in the sense that 'everyone knows everyone else' " is, of course, true.[26] However, this does not preclude the possibility of a reference group of more general scope, or of there being a network of overlapping subcommunities strung out so as to form a potential social stratum within which social and geographical movement carries a person from one in-

---

24. Kramer and Leventman, *op. cit.*, p. 166.
25. Gordon, *Assimilation in American Life*, p. 225.
26. Talcott Parsons, "Comments on American Intellectuals," *Daedalus*, 88: 493-95 (Summer, 1959).

tellectual subcommunity to another (perhaps following, to a greater or lesser degree, various occupational channels).

In response to the question, "Do you think that there is an intellectual stratum or community in the United States?" 72 per cent of the Protestant and 88 per cent of the Jewish respondents answered positively (almost as many felt that they belonged to such a group). Among self-defined intellectuals, the verdict was nearly unanimous: 86 per cent for Protestants and 94 per cent for Jews. To quote several respondents on the subject:

It is more true now than thirty years ago. Society is more willing to identify an intellectual class and give it a certain amount of esteem.

Presently, there is a much clearer identification of an intellectual group, both by its members and society.

I definitely feel there is an intellectual community. It is classified by society as such as well as being self-defined. I would think of intellectuals as increasingly belonging to a group, a stratum, interested in particular things.

I feel that this is a group which in the 19th and first part of the 20th century was involved in a struggle to receive status and is now taking on a cohesiveness which it never had in the past.

A self-conscious intellectual group is present all right. It has splits, but exists as a group.

I believe there is such a group. It contains a certain kind of person. When one is thrown together with another person in a plane or bar or some other situation, you soon find out whether he has the view of an intellectual.

Definitely. People in this layer think, talk, and act on a different level. I mesh better with people of this kind, but not so well with others.

In contrast, there are these views:

There are professionals concerned with truth in their own field. I don't see it as a social stratum or class. They are spread in various occupations, and may or may not come together.

It is hard to know because of the limiting nature of life. We tend to underrate the intellectual concerns of people in other occupations such as engineering and business.

The responses as a whole, however, did not concur with Wilensky's observation that American intellectual life is characterized by a loss of sense of autonomy and intellectual community.[27]

27. Wilensky, *op. cit.*, p. 190.

We gain some idea of the extent of social enclosure from the occupational distribution of respondents' general and close friends (Table 2). Fifty-eight per cent of Protestants asserted that all or most of their general friends were academicians and 77 per cent that all or most of their close friends were from their profession. Comparable figures for the Jewish group were 64 and 68 per cent. Thirty-nine per cent of the Protestants and 52 per cent of the Jews reported having general friends among members of the nonacademic intellectual professions (illustrated by artist, editor, musician, and writer); corresponding figures for close friends were 23 and 40 per cent. In all, one-third of the respondents of Protestant background and half of the respondents of Jewish background could count no close associates outside one of the intellectual professions, including the academic. Nearly all of these individuals were self-defined intellectuals.

Primary interaction with members of one of the other upper white-collar occupations was limited. Considering close friends, we see that only 20 per cent of the Protestants and 16 per cent of the Jews checked a scale item higher than a few for an occupational category which included all other professions, higher administrative and managerial jobs, and business. As might be expected as a consequence of differences in objective class standing, social contact at the lower white-collar and blue-collar levels was negligible.

What influence did intellectual self-identification have on the occupational distribution of friends? Ninety per cent of the self-defined Protestant intellectuals reported that all or most of their close friends were academicians while only 60 per cent of the self-defined nonintellectuals did so (p = .05). Conversely, whereas only 5 per cent of the Protestants holding intellectual self-conceptions counted more than a few close friends among persons in upper white-collar positions, 40 per cent of the self-defined nonintellectuals checked higher scale items (p = .05). Similar differences were found within the Jewish sample.

Several self-defined intellectuals cited reasons for their limited social contact within the white-collar ranks:

I rub the wrong way with white collar people. I have nothing in common with the vast majority of people in these groups.

My friends are men whose lives are devoted to ideas and books. If I go home to the old neighborhood I run out of things to say and do with my old buddies; they talk about the stock market.

It's not snobbishness. Things just get tedious among most nonacademics. Four or five years spent developing your mind in graduate school and many more using it make it think in different channels.

I'm more comfortable with colleagues from the academic environment. I have nothing in common with people of the New York middle-class strata—Jewish or non-Jewish.

By way of comparison some of those who eschewed the intellectual self-concept pointed specifically to a frequency of, or preference for, white collar contacts:

We belong to the local temple and there are virtually no academic people in membership, so our friends connected with the temple are largely non-academic . . . an engineer, an accountant, and some businessmen.

Academics tend to become monotonous sometimes. We have a number of friends in the business and professional fields whom we find refreshing.

Younger respondents counted fewer nonacademic friends than their older colleagues. Among Protestants, three-fourths of those under 45 years of age reported that all or most of their general friends were academics, while only about one-third of those 45 or over did so ($p = .05$).

Excluding memberships in professional societies and in church and synagogue, we found that only 14 per cent of the Protestants and 16 per cent of the Jews belonged to more than one organization or club. It is noteworthy, however, that of the comparatively few formal memberships which were held by sample members, civil liberties, civil rights, and peace groups predominated among self-defined intellectuals, whereas local groups whose functions were largely social typified the memberships of the self-defined nonintellectuals.

Summary and Concluding Remarks

Gordon's hypothesis of a transethnic subsociety has been explored. Nearly all of the respondents asserted that ethnic background was not an important aspect of primary group choice. For both Protestant and Jewish samples, an extensive interchange of religious backgrounds in both general and close friendships was a behavioral corollary of the attitudinal assimilation. Self-defined intellectuals of both Protestant and Jewish backgrounds reported more extraethnic primary contact than did their self-defined nonintellectual colleagues. Most of the respondents considered the academic social world to be largely free of ethnic fractures, especially in comparison to other segments of society with which they were purportedly familar. Important differences existed between amounts of current extraethnic social contact and that reported by respondents for parents and for their own preprofessional pasts. Two-fifths of the Jewish sample were married to non-Jews; few respondents were opposed to intermarriage. Almost all respondents denied ethnic group membership in the concrete social sense, and their indifference to the ethnic strata of their children served to further document a high degree of defection or detachment from their original socioreligious groups.

Concerning the notion of a distinctive intellectual social stratum in the United States—the other component of the hypothesis under study —we learned that a substantial majority of both Protestants and Jews discerned its existence, with several commenting on its increasing visibility and heightened self-awareness. Friends came largely from the academic profession, even more among respondents with an intellectual self-conception and among the younger group. Finally, low rates of community organization and club memberships offered additional evidence of closure.

In brief, information gathered on 61 college and university professors suggests that intellectuals do in fact interact in patterned ways and that these patterns are largely undelineated by ethnic background. This preliminary evidence, then, confirms Gordon's hypothesis.

The fact that the study was conducted in an area of medium population density should not detract significantly from results which point in the direction of an intellectual social stratum. For although opportunities for more general upper white-collar contact may be greater in a large city, the proportion of available persons in nonacademic intellectual professions correspondingly increases, as no doubt does the proportion of intellectually oriented persons within other upper white-collar occupations themselves. What effect city size might have on the class factor is an empirical question which can be answered only by further research. However, the fact that none of the several respondents who had lived previously as academics in major urban areas could recall that occupation of friends had ever varied noticeably from the present situation would seem to indicate that population size is of secondary importance when compared to cultural proclivities.

The much larger proportion of Jews residing in metropolitan areas raises the further question as to how such greater ethnic availability would affect the amount of Jewish-gentile contact among academics or intellectuals. I suspect, again on the basis of respondents' recall data and related comments, that results would not point to any real ethnic communality on the part of Jewish academics or intellectuals, but rather, like the findings of this study, would reflect the relative proportions of academics or intellectuals of each ethnic group present, for alienation from middle-class Jewry was marked.

The necessity for further studies dealing with samples large enough to impose more rigorous controls is obvious. Further studies should seek to make direct comparisons between academic or intellectual professions and a general population sample,[28] or even better, to dispense with occupational categories altogether and analyze the relationship between intellectual orientation and interethnic contact.

Three final points. First, it is interesting to note that if a transethnic subsociety does indeed exist in America, the classical notion of the direction of assimilation from ethnic minority to majority (white Protestant) must be revised for intellectuals to read from ethnic group (minority or majority) to nonethnic group. There would be no ethnically dominant intellectual group into which members of ethnic minorities are assimilated, for ethnicity has been eradicated as a viable fact.[29] It would be "a subsociety of marginals." The intellectual subsociety would always expand at the cost of some ethnic group and to the aggrandizement of none. It is conceivable, however, that an intellectual subsociety of this nature might be a way station for eventual assimilation into white Protestant group life for the children and grandchildren of non-Protestant members. Or, future generations—Protestant and non-Protestant—may return to the ethnic groups of their ancestors. Yet, interviews with this group of academics—particularly the self-identifying intellectuals and the intermarried—left me with the impression that ethnic socialization of children would be much too vacuous to see the offspring's family of procreation return to the ethnic fold. The ethnic status of spouses also poses an interesting question, one which nothing in our data can directly answer. We might note, however, that only three spouses held religious memberships in the Jewish sample, that derelict ethnic socialization of children reflects negatively upon the spouse's own ethnic interest, and that clique life in

28. Since this writing, I have made such a comparison in "Religious Communality Among Academics," *Journal for the Scientific Study of Religion*, 7 (Spring, 1968), pp. 87-96.

29. One might plausibly argue that if there is a "direction" to the assimilation among intellectuals, it is more "toward" the Jewish group than the representatives of the dominant white Protestant society.

the middle classes tends to be heterosexual—all of which hint at weak ethnic communalism on the part of spouse as well as respondent.

Second, I must caution that this study has dealt basically with the private lives of academics and intellectuals. Because intellectuals may constitute a social stratum in the sense of primary networks of social relationships, one should not interpret this as some would as a withdrawal from social responsibility or as a declaration of superiority. Academicians and intellectuals, in both their writings and their actions, have recently demonstrated an unprecedented concern with and involvement in (though perhaps not nearly as much as they could or should and perhaps often in misguided ways) the problems which beset our society. And if academics and intellectuals prefer the company of other academics and intellectuals in their primary group life, this is no more an indication of superiority or snobbery than it is for blue-collar workers to prefer the company of other blue-collar workers instead of salesmen and clerks, or vice versa. Certainly there could be few non-intellectuals who would themselves be offended in status terms.

Finally, one might ask, if an intellectual subsociety of this kind is now taking shape, where has it been in the past? A plausible answer is that the intellectual professions—especially that of college teaching— have only recently emerged as open, burgeoning occupational categories capable of reaching the proportions of a stratum, and until recently they have been monopolized by white Protestants. The fairly recent influx of large numbers of Jews and Catholics into college and university teaching has enormously multiplied the opportunities for intergroup contact. Hence, where there was once a small number of disparate and isolated marginal men, there can now flourish a subsociety composed of such marginals.

15. Catholic Academicians and the Intellectual Subsociety Hypothesis

In the last two decades a considerable amount of empirical research has focused upon the changing social structure of American Catholicism.[1] Observations have been made that Catholics are upwardly mobile in the class structure, that they probably are marrying Protestants and Jews at a slightly increasing rate, and that they have been culturally assimilated to a substantial degree. But this does not mean that Catholic "separatism" no longer exists to any appreciable extent. Catholic communal ties remain vital and are of some consequence for American Catholics in shaping their fundamental social relationships and self-identity.[2]

Most of the sociological research that has focused on either the acculturation of American Catholics or the existing social structural separation of American Catholics from others in the society has neglected one interesting segment of Catholicism in the United States—the Catholic intellectuals. A question can be raised as to whether these intellectuals constitute a significant exception to the pattern of social and psychological separation shared to an important degree by ither Catholics. This question is particularly salient in light of recent evidence which supports Milton Gordon's hypothesis concerning the existence of an in-

---

1. See, for example, the following studies: Joseph H. Fichter, *Social Relations in the Urban Parish* (Chicago: University of Chicago Press, 1954); Joseph H. Fichter, *Religion as an Occupation* (Notre Dame, Indiana: University of Notre Dame Press, 1961); John J. Kane, "The Social Structure of American Catholics," *American Catholic Sociological Review*, XVI (March, 1955), 23-30; and Joseph B. Schuyler, *Northern Parish* (Chicago: Loyola University Press, 1960).

2. See, for example, Milton M. Gordon, *Assimilation in American Life* (New York: Oxford University Press, 1964) and Paul R. Wozniak, "Assimilation into Pan-Catholicism: A Sociological Study of Structural Assimilation among Catholic National Origin Groups" (unpublished Ph.D. dissertation, University of Massachusetts, 1967).

tellectual subsociety that in terms of primary group relationships is not founded upon traditional ethnic distinctions.[3]

But where are the Catholic intellectuals located in relation to this subsociety?. Empirical evidence is somewhat tenuous. In a comparison of a predominantly Protestant faculty at a state university with teachers at a Catholic college, Wilensky and Ladinsky found that the Catholic college teachers were significantly more likely to (1) identify closely with their religious group and (2) limit their three closest friendships to other Catholics. The professors at the Catholic institution "display more involvement in the religious community, which acts to moderate both their professionalism and their participation in the occupational community."[4] Other writers suggest a similar pattern. John Donovan, Thomas O'Dea, James Trent, and Daniel Callahan have implied that there exists a separation in attitude or behavior of the Catholic intellectual from the mainstream of American intellectual life.[5] Callahan writes that "as the Catholic intellectual tries to work his way out of the ghetto there is little ground on which to build. Like all newcomers to any established society, he is neither fully at home in the newworld nor happy with the narrow world he is trying to move beyond."[6] He states further that "no one has yet shown how a separate system of higher education, scholarly journals, publishing houses, and intellectual societies can overcome separation and cease to hinder assimilation."[7]

But sociologist Andrew Greeley contends that Catholic scholars are not insulated from non-Catholic intellectuals. He states:

The Catholic intellectual . . . likes to think of himself as torn between the demands of his intellectual concerns and the polity if not the dogma of his re-

3. See Gordon, pp. 224-232; Charles H. Anderson, "The Intellectual Subsociety: An Empirical Test of the Intellectual Subsociety Hypothesis" (unpublished Ph.D. dissertation, University of Massachusetts, 1966); Harold L. Wilensky and Jack Ladinsky, "From Religious Community to Occupational Group: Structural Assimilation Among Professors, Lawyers, and Engineers," *American Sociological Review*, XXXII (August, 1967), 548.

4. Wilensky and Ladinsky, p. 549.

5. John D. Donovan, *The Academic Man in the Catholic College* (New York: Sheed and Ward, 1964); Thomas F. O'Dea, *American Catholic Dilemma* (New York, Sheed and Ward, 1958); James W. Trent, "Progress and Anxiety," in a symposium entitled "Catholic Intellectual Life," *Commonweal*, LXXXI (October 2, 1964), 40-42; Daniel Callahan, *The New Church: Essays in Catholic Reform* (New York: Charles Scribner's Sons, 1966), pp. 3-10.

6. Callahan, p. 6.

7. *Ibid.*, p. 5.

ligion. . . . I find myself often growing impatient with the pose of alienation cultivated by a good number of Catholic intellectuals.[8]

Data that have been gathered on 1961 college graduates lend some empirical support to Greeley's position, at least with respect to the emerging generation of scholars.[9] But Greeley's findings offer no explicit information on the presence or absence of structural separation between Catholic and non-Catholic intellectuals.

Thus, the question raised above remains unanswered: Where does the Catholic intellectual stand in relation to his non-Catholic counterpart? Is he insulated from the mainstream of American intellectual life, or is he located within the boundaries of a subsociety of intellectuals that is not based upon ethnic criteria? This study provides some empirical data on the question. Specifically, the study involved an examination of the following hypothesis:

Catholic intellectuals, in terms of primary group relationships, organizational participation, self-identification, and life style, are structurally within the boundaries of a subsociety composed of intellectuals and based upon non-ethnic criteria.

Confirmation of the hypothesis would give further empirical support to Gordon's hypothesis that there exists today in American society an intellectual subsociety that is not grounded in ethnic distinctions.

Research Procedure

The necessary data were gathered by means of sixty interviews conducted during the summer and fall of 1967 among Catholic faculty members holding the ranks of assistant, associate, and full professor in the arts and science programs at selected Catholic and nonsectarian colleges and universities.[10] A total of thirty interviews were conducted

8. Andrew M. Greeley, "Anything But Marginal," in *Generation of the Third Eye*, ed. by Daniel Callahan (New York: Sheed and Ward, 1965), pp. 80 and 86.

9. Andrew M. Greeley, *Religion and Career* (New York: Sheed and Ward, 1963), pp. 49-55. See, also, his "The Religious Behavior of Graduate Students," *Journal for the Scientific Study of Religion*, V (Fall, 1965), 34-40.

10. The term "Catholic faculty member" in this paper refers to any college teacher, excluding clergy and other members of religious orders, who was at the time of the study or previously had been a member of the Roman Catholic Church. Such factors as "orthodoxy in religious beliefs," "extent of participation in church activities," or "degree of commitment to Roman Catholicism" were not considered in selecting members of the samples. These criteria, however, were used in the attempt to determine the existence of different types of Catholic intellectuals.

among randomly selected lay professors at a Catholic liberal arts college and a Catholic university, both located in a metropolitan area in eastern New England. An additional thirty interviews were conducted among randomly selected teachers at three private nonsectarian liberal arts colleges and a public university in western New England.[11] By interviewing professors at a public university, private nonsectarian men's and women's liberal arts colleges, a coeducational Catholic liberal arts college, and a Catholic university, an attempt was made to include in the samples diverse elements of the research universe.

The study centered upon intellectuals within the academic community. Obviously, not all academicians are intellectuals, nor are all intellectuals academicians. But the college campus is nonetheless a logical site for examining the intellectual subsociety hypothesis. A methodological concern in the study, then, was to distinguish in each of the samples between the intellectuals and the nonintellectuals.

In order to differentiate between these two groupings, an index based upon the definitions of an intellectual put forth by Deutsch, Gordon, and Nettl was used.[12] These writers, among others, consider the distinguishing mark of the intellectual to be the broad scope of his interests; he is one whose concerns extend beyond the more narrow boundaries of his own field of specialization and involve the quality of life. It would be reasonable, then, to expect that his exposure to, and preferences in, the media and the performing arts would differ, by definition, from the pattern for nonintellectuals. Accordingly, a media exposure index, devised by Charles Anderson in his research among intellectuals of Protestant and Jewish background, was used to distinguish the intellectuals from the nonintellectuals. The index taps preference in reading, viewing, and "cultural activities."[13]

Finally, before discussing the findings, a word on sample characteristics. All but four respondents were native-born Americans. Two-thirds

11. For a detailed discussion of the methodology of the study, see John D. Murray, "The American Catholic Intellectual: An Empirical Test of the Intellectual Subsociety Hypothesis" (unpublished Ph.D. dissertation, University of Massachusetts, 1969), pp. 12-20.

12. See Karl Deutsch, "Comments on American Intellectuals: Their Politics and Status," Daedalus, LXXXVIII (Summer, 1959), 489; J. P. Nettl, "Are Intellectuals Obsolete?" The Nation, CCVI (March 4, 1968), 301; Milton M. Gordon, "Social Class and American Intellectuals," American Association of University Professors Bulletin, XL (Winter, 1954-55), 518-519.

13. For a discussion of this index, see Chapter 17. See also Murray, "The American Catholic Intellectual: An Empirical Test of the Intellectual Subsociety Hypothesis," pp. 18-20.

of the Catholic college sample and half the teachers at the nonsectarian colleges were born and raised in New England, close to half of each in cities of over 100,000 population. The socio-economic backgrounds of the two groups were similar: both tended to be lower white-collar in origin, although almost a third of the non-Catholic college faculty members were products of professional families. Over half of the Catholic college teachers were over forty-five years old, compared with only one-fifth of the second sample.

The data on the educational backgrounds of the respondents accent some interesting differences between the two samples. Approximately half of the teachers in each sample were products of Catholic grammar schools, and a slight decline was evident in each sample in the number attending Catholic secondary schools. A striking difference between the samples emerged, however, in the type of college attended. Slightly over half (seventeen) of the teachers in the Catholic college sample received their B.A. degree from Catholic colleges, whereas only seven of the teachers at the non-Catholic colleges were products of Catholic colleges. Similar distinctions issue from the data on graduate education. Forty-seven percent of the M.A. holders among the Catholic college teachers received their degree from Catholic graduate schools; only one member of the other sample did so. Furthermore, nearly a fourth of the Catholic college teachers who held the doctorate received their degrees from Catholic schools, while none of the second sample members received his Ph.D. from a Catholic institution.

Primary Relationships: The Occupational Factor

I have suggested that Catholic intellectuals, if they are part of a subsociety of intellectuals, should have among other characteristics a substantial amount of primary contact restricted to other intellectuals. Moreover, common ideational interests rather than ethnic identity should serve as the basis for these relationships. Before examining the ethnic data, however, I shall delineate the friendship patterns of respondents in terms of occupation.

Friendship ties. A clear majority of both samples indicated a tendency to limit close friendships primarily to fellow academicians.[14]

14. The respondents were asked to distinguish between close and general friends. General friends were defined as "people who are more than mere acquaintances, people with whom you socialize or do things occasionally, people with whom you are at ease." Close friends were described as "people whom you see socially very often and are very comfortable with."

Table 1.

Occupation of Close and General Friends of Catholic Academicians

Number of Friends	Close Friends						General Friends					
	Academic		NAI[a]		UWC[b]		Academic		NAI[a]		UWC[b]	
	%	(N)	%	(N)	%	(N)	%	(N)	%	(N)	%	(N)
Catholic College Academicians												
All or nearly all	57	(17)	0	(0)	0	(0)	50	(15)	0	(0)	0	(0)
Majority	23	(7)	0	(0)	0	(0)	17	(5)	0	(0)	0	(0)
Half	0	(0)	0	(0)	13	(4)	13	(4)	0	(0)	17	(5)
Less than half	10	(3)	10	(3)	20	(6)	7	(2)	7	(2)	10	(3)
Few	7	(2)	17	(5)	47	(14)	10	(3)	33	(10)	60	(8)
None	3	(1)	73	(22)	20	(6)	3	(1)	60	(18)	13	(4)
Total	100	(30)	100	(30)	100	(30)	100	(30)	100	(30)	100	(30)
Non-Catholic College Academicians												
All or nearly all	50	(15)	0	(0)	0	(0)	60	(18)	0	(0)	0	(0)
Majority	20	(6)	0	(0)	0	(0)	13	(4)	0	(0)	0	(0)
Half	7	(2)	3	(1)	13	(4)	20	(6)	3	(1)	13	(4)
Less than half	13	(4)	17	(5)	23	(7)	7	(2)	3	(1)	20	(6)
Few	7	(2)	20	(6)	40	(12)	0	(0)	37	(11)	43	(13)
None	3	(1)	60	(18)	23	(7)	0	(0)	57	(17)	23	(7)
Total	100	(30)	100	(30)	99	(30)	100	(30)	100	(30)	99	(30)

[a] Nonacademic intellectuals   [b] Upper white-collar

Table 1 indicates that 80 percent of the Catholic college teachers and 70 percent of the professors at the nonsectarian institutions maintained a majority of their close friendships with other college teachers.[15] In both their close and general friendships, few of the respondents had predominantly nonacademic ties. As two teachers said:

It's a matter of convenience and interests. You develop friendships among the people you see constantly. It stands to reason then that most of my friends are colleagues. We have things to talk about.

My close friends I see almost every day? Most of them are from the department. I've been teaching here for eight years and have come to know a few people here very well. They're congenial. . . .

Several respondents were quick to point out that, although they did have one or more close friends who were nonacademicians, these friends were involved in an intellectual style of life, that is, they were engaged in writing or the arts on a full-time basis outside an academic setting. Indeed, 27 percent of the teachers in the Catholic college sample and 40 percent of the non-Catholic college sample stated that at least a few of their close friends were "nonacademic intellectuals." There was minimal primary contact with other upper white-collar professionals and businessmen, and as one might expect, primary ties with lower status white-collar and blue-collar workers were negligible. However, while these sixty Catholic professors, overall, did emphasize academic ties in their primary relationships, they were less likely than Protestant and Jewish college teachers (See Chapter 14) to restrict their social contacts to those working in an intellectual setting (differences were negligible, however, when only intellectuals are considered).

In both samples of Catholic professors, it was the *younger* faculty members who were more likely to limit "all or nearly all" of their primary contacts to other faculty.[16] Among the teachers at the Catholic

15. A 7-point scale was used to determine the extent of primary relationships established across both occupational and ethnic lines. The respondents were asked to indicate how many of their close and general friends were, for example, college teachers. The scale showing number of friends consisted of the following intervals: all, nearly all, more than half, half, less than half, few, and none.

16. Distinctions were made in both samples between "younger" and "older" groupings. In the sample of Catholic college teachers, the cutting point was between "under 45 years of age" and "45 years and older." This resulted in fourteen "younger" and sixteen "older" professors. The non-Catholic college teachers, overall, were a younger group. Accordingly, to obtain approximately equal groupings the cutting point was between "under 40 years of age" and "40 years and older." However, even with the lower cutting point, the second sample resulted in an unequal distribution of eighteen "younger" and twelve "older" respondents.

colleges 71 percent of those under forty-five years of age said that "all or nearly all" of their close friends were academicians; for those forty-five years of age and older the figure dropped to 44 percent. In the sample of teachers at the non-Catholic colleges a similar pattern existed: 61 percent of the younger but only 33 percent of the older faculty stated that "all or nearly all" of their close friends were college teachers.

Moreover, the intellectually oriented group in each sample was more likely than the nonintellectuals to choose friends from academia: 75 percent of the teachers at the Catholic colleges who were classified as intellectuals stated that all or nearly all of their close friends were colleagues, compared to only 44 percent of the nonintellectuals. Data for the teachers at the non-Catholic schools pointed in the same direction. Also, in both samples the intellectuals were much more likely than the nonintellectuals to experience primary contact with persons engaged in writing or the arts on a full-time basis outside of an academic setting.

Organizational participation. An analysis of the respondents' involvement in various types of nonprofessional organizations indicates that the Catholic professors, intellectual as well as nonintellectual, experienced minimal contact with nonacademicians through membership in voluntary associations. A majority in each sample belonged to no civic or nonprofessional organizations; only one-fourth of the Catholic college teachers and one-tenth of the second sample held membership in more than one such association. Typically, the question of involvement in nonprofessional organizations and civic activities elicited such comments as the following: "Financial support and little else"; "I've signed petitions and ads for the *Times*, and that's about it"; "I just don't have the time."

Unless they resided in academic or highly professional neighborhoods, few respondents expressed close ties with any of their neighbors. One respondent, not atypical, described his neighborhood situation graphically:

I've lived here for eight years, but I've established no real ties with the neighbors. I suppose we have little in common, but I'm a fairly outgoing person—I make friends easily. But not here—there's an aloofness—not on my part— but theirs. I think the people here are somewhat suspicious of me and my family because I'm a teacher. Perhaps they think I'm a subversive. The area is really quite anti-intellectual.

In summary, the data on friendship ties, organizational participation, and neighborhood contacts clearly indicate a strong tendency toward occupational closure in the primary relationships of the sixty Catholic professors. The most consequential finding concerns the extent to which the intellectuals in each sample tended to restrict their friendship ties to colleagues and others engaged in writing and the arts. Thus, the data give support to one aspect of the intellectual subsociety hypothesis. This hypothesis, however, involves more than simply occupational or class restrictions on the primary ties of intellectuals. More important is the extent of ethnic assimilation. Perhaps Catholic academics restrict their primary ties to other Catholics within the academic world just as Catholic nonacademics tend to do in the larger nonacademics society.

Primary Relationships: The Ethnic Factor

Friendship Ties. Among 70 percent of the teachers at the Catholic colleges and 80 percent of the faculty at the nonsectarian colleges, religious criteria were viewed as irrelevant in the choice of friends. The following responses convey the tone of their comments:

Life is short. You have time to cultivate just so many friends, and these you treasure. You can't afford to allow man-made barriers like religion to keep people from one another. A person's particular religious tag certainly wouldn't put me off at all. . . .

I find religion frightfully interesting. It's the focus of my intellectual concerns. I imagine I would respond openly to persons with a similar intellectual orientation. . . . A person's religious background, however, would be of absolutely no significance in determining whether we would or would not become friends.

The actual social contact data on the friendship ties of the thirty academicians at the nonsectarian colleges support this pattern of attitudinal assimilation. As Table 2 indicates, only two of thirty noted that a majority of their close friends were Catholics, while a striking 60 percent had few or no close Catholic friends. A similar pattern describes general friendship ties. But a sharply different situation was evident in the sample of teachers from the Catholic colleges. Two-thirds of the respondents reported that a majority of their close friends were Catholic. In fact, for nearly half of the sample "all or nearly all" close friends were Catholics. A greater number of non-Catholics were included among general friends, but even here the Catholic college sample, in comparison with the nonsectarian sample, tended toward ethnic closure in friendship ties.

But the data must be examined further. The possibility of a person of Catholic background including a substantial number of non-Catholics among his close friends depends, in part, on the Catholic's having access to a situation in which stable associations with non-Catholics may be established. Clearly, Catholics teaching at Catholic colleges have *less opportunity* to associate with non-Catholic academicians than do Catholics teaching at nonsectarian colleges. Four-fifths of the professors at the Catholic colleges did, in fact, trace the ethnic imbalance of their primary ties directly to the opportunity structure, that is, teaching at a college with a predominately Catholic faculty. But why did they choose to teach at a Catholic college? Was it due to an explicit decision to be associated closely with the Catholic community? When asked, 80 percent said it was simply a matter of accepting the best job offer received. Several felt that as products of Catholic graduate schools, they had no choice but to teach at a Catholic college. As one respondent said, "Things may be different today, but until quite recently a graduate degree from a Catholic school meant a lifetime of teaching at Catholic colleges. There was very little chance of teaching elsewhere."

Because the sample of teachers from Catholic colleges was disproportionately older than the sample of professors from the nonsectarian institutions, a question may be raised as to whether age might also help explain the divergent distributions of Catholic friendships in the two samples. Were the younger teachers less likely than the older ones to exhibit ethnic closure in their primary relationships? The data suggest this to be true only of the nonsectarian college sample, where 78 percent of the younger and 58 percent of the older professors indicated that "less than half" of their close friends were Catholics. But among Catholic college faculty members, nearly two-thirds of the younger in comparison with less than one-third of the older professors said that "all or nearly all" of their close friends were Catholics. These findings for the Catholic college sample, of course, are consistent with the previous finding that the younger professors at the Catholic colleges were more likely than their older colleagues to tend toward *occupational* closure in their primary relationships and thus were exposed to more Catholic academics.

The above data are particularly important because they indicate that in the Catholic college sample the younger age grouping, which was slightly more likely to include a greater percentage of intellectuals,

Table 2.

Close and General Catholic Friends of Catholic Academicians

Number of Friends	Close Friends		General Friends	
	%	(N)	%	(N)
Catholic College Academicians				
All	17	(5)	0	(0)
Nearly all	30	(9)	23	(7)
Majority	20	(6)	27	(8)
Half	23	(7)	33	(10)
Less than half	10	(3)	10	(3)
Few	0	(0)	7	(2)
None	0	(0)	0	(0)
Total	100	(30)	100	(30)
Non-Catholic College Academicians				
All	0	(0)	0	(0)
Nearly all	7	(2)	7	(2)
Majority	0	(0)	3	(1)
Half	10	(3)	3	(1)
Less than half	13	(4)	53	(16)
Few	33	(10)	33	(10)
None	37	(11)	0	(0)
Total	100	(30)	99	(30)

actually was considerably more likely to be ethnically enclosed in primary relationships. This suggests a *reversal* of the assimilation thesis.
Specifically, in the sample of teachers from the Catholic colleges, 58
percent of the intellectuals in comparison with only 39 percent of the
nonintellectuals did indicate that "all or nearly all" of their close
friends were Catholic. On the other hand, in the non-Catholic college
sample only 8 percent of the intellectuals versus 47 percent of the nonintellectuals said that "half or more" of their close friends were Catholic; the data for the nonsectarian college sample, in other words, support the assimilation hypothesis.

It should be recalled that a substantial majority of the Catholic college faculty members attributed the ethnic imbalance of their friendship ties to the opportunity structure, that is, to a teaching situation
in which there existed minimal opportunity for developing primary
relationships with non-Catholics. This at least partially explains why

at the Catholic colleges the intellectuals, and the younger ones in particular, displayed such relatively extensive ethnic closure in their
friendship ties; they were more occupationally enclosed in their primary relationships than were their nonintellectually oriented colleagues. Yet, a basic question remains unanswered: Was the comparatively greater ethnic involvement of the Catholic college professors, and
especially the intellectuals, limited to their friendship ties, or did they,
in fact, actually display a more *all-inclusive* pattern of participation
in Catholic communal life? If the Catholic college intellectuals did, in
fact, exhibit a comparatively strong overall communal orientation, then
the pattern of structural separation in friendship ties discussed above
could be traced to *more* than simply limitations in the opportunity
structure. Rather, this pattern of ethnic enclosure in primary relationships would be viewed as part of a larger profile of a basically communal life style for the Catholic college intellectuals. An index of religious communality was constructed to answer this and related questions.

Religious Communality. The concept of religious communality refers
to the degree of social structural and attitudinal involvement along
intrareligious lines. People exhibit a religiously communal life-style to
the extent that they are oriented toward their own religious group in their
social interaction and self-identification. Conversely, to the extent that
people enter into religiously heterogeneous groups and are not oriented
toward their religious heritage in their self-identification, they manifest a religiously assimilated life-style. "Religious communality" and
"religious assimilation" are, thus, at opposite ends of a continuum that
has its theoretical grounding point in Gordon's assimilation
paradigm.[17]

In order to locate on this continuum the relative positions of, first,
the two samples in general and, second, the intellectual group within
each sample, a 10-point index of religious communality was devised.[18]
The index was structured upon the following five items: (1) the
number of the respondent's close friends who were Catholics; (2) the
number of Catholic-sponsored social groups in which the respondent
held membership; (3) the frequency with which the respondent attended Catholic church services; (4) the strength of the respondent's

17. Gordon, *Assimilation in American Life*, p. 71.
18. The communality index stems from a similar index developed by Charles Anderson. See his "Religious Communality Among White Protestants, Catholics, and
Mormons," *Social Forces*, XLVI (June, 1968), 501-508.

identification with other Catholics, based upon the respondent's self-rating; and (5) the respondent's attitude toward Catholic interreligious marriage.[19] At the polar extremes, respondents who indicated that nearly all of their close friends were Catholics, belonged to some Catholic social groups, attended religious services regularly, perceived a strong bond with other Catholics, and strongly disapproved of interreligious marriage would logically be considered as communally oriented persons. Conversely, those academicians·who included few Catholics among their close friends, failed to hold membership in any Catholic social organizations, rarely attended religious services, expressed weak identification with other Catholics, and did not object to the interreligious marriage of Catholics would, obviously, not be considered as communally oriented individuals. Rather, they might well be treated as being religiously assimilated, that is, as persons who manifest neither structural nor attitudinal enclosure in regard to the religious factor.

As the previous data on friendships might indicate, the Catholic college academicians were significantly more communally oriented than the teachers at the non-Catholic institutions. Fifty-seven percent of the Catholic college sample in comparison with only 27 percent of the nonsectarian college sample scored "high" in religious communality. And, again, within the sample of Catholic college academicians it was the younger teachers who were more communally enclosed; 71 percent of the younger faculty members compared to 44 percent of the older teachers scored high in communalism. In line with the subsosociety hypothesis, however, in the nonsectarian college sample a majority of both age groups scored "low," and the younger teachers were less likely to exhibit a communal orientation.

What influence did the intellectual orientation of respondents have

19. These five items were weighted as follows:
     (1) number of close friends who are Catholic: all or nearly all = 2; majority or half = 1; less than half = 0
     (2) number of Catholic social groups: two or more = 2; one = 1; none = 0
     (3) frequency of church attendance: weekly = 2; less, but at least once a month = 1; less = 0
     (4) self-rating of identification with other Catholics: very strong or strong = 2; moderate = 1; weak or not at all = 0
     (5) attitude toward intermarriage: strongly opposed = 2; mildly disapprove = 1; no objection = 0
     Those scoring 6 or higher on this 10-point scale were considered as being "high" in religious communality; those scoring 5 or lower were considered as being "low" in religious communality.

upon their religious communal orientation? In the Catholic college sample there was no difference between the intellectual and the nonintellectual groups; over half of each displayed a strong communal orientation. However, in the sample of academicians from non-Catholic colleges, the intellectuals were significantly *less* likely than the nonintellectuals to score "high" in religious communality (8 versus 41 percent, respectively).

In brief, the Catholic college professors tended to contradict the assimilation hypothesis not only in their primary relationships but in the larger sphere of ethnic communalism as well. On the other hand, the nonsectarian Catholic academics did conform to the notion of an ethnically neutral intellectual subsociety as reflected in their relative estrangement from the Catholic community.

Pre-Academic Influences. To what extent can the differences in religious communalism among members of the two samples be traced to differences in their early religious socialization experiences in family and peer group?

Neither the respondents' own early religious activity nor their parents' communal involvement and religious orientation evidently had any discernable influence on the professors' current religious communality. However, the religious composition of friendship ties during high school and college years was influential in shaping current religious communalism, *but only among professors at the Catholic colleges.* For example, 71 percent of the Catholic college academics who indicated that "all or nearly all" of their close adolescent friends were Catholics currently rated high in religious communalism, in camparison with 44 percent who had fewer adolescent Catholic friends.

In the nonsectarian sample, however, the communally oriented teachers were no more likely than their noncommunally oriented colleagues to be products of ethnically insulated backgrounds. How, then, can we account for differences in their communal orientation? It was noted earlier that communally oriented respondents in the nonsectarian college sample tended to be older and less intellectually oriented than the "assimilated" respondents. The latter, more often the younger and intellectually oriented faculty members, typically embarked on their educational careers in a non-Catholic college environment during the recent past at a time in which the academic profession had become considerably more fluid and more ethnically diverse than it previously had been. Consequently, they may well have become more psychologically attuned to a trans-ethnic social world and, at the same time, developed intellectual interests which led them into mixed groups with limited ethnic character.

Participation in the Intellectual Community

Specifically, to what extent did the respondents actually perceive the existence of a pan-ethnic intellectual social world and see themselves as part of an intellectual community or stratum? Over four-fifths of both samples responded affirmatively to the question, "Do you think there is an intellectual group as such in the United States—a distinct intellectual social world?" In both samples, an affirmative answer was virtually unanimous among those respondents who were defined as intellectuals. The following comments of several professors typify a majority of the responses:

In the Europe of the past, the intellectual elite was a part of the rigid class system. Today in the United States there is a new type of intellectual grouping no longer identified by traditional factors. They come out of different ethnic and religious groups. You would find a variety of these groups in cities like Boston and New York.

It is a group of people whose professional and nonprofessional concerns center on art, writing, creating, and teaching. It is hard to say whether a single national group exists. There are so many colleges which serve as eddys, as circles of intellectuals, but I imagine membership overlaps considerably.

Yes, a group composed of individuals who, in view of their education and ability, consistently see the underlying significance of things. They associate with one another.

Intellectuals form a group whose members seek one another out for exchange purposes, and they are uncomfortable with people with whom they are not in "sympathy."

When the respondents were asked whether they *considered themselves to be a part* of this intellectual group or community, a significant difference became evident between the two samples. Forty-seven percent of the Catholic college teachers in comparison with 67 percent of the nonsectarian college faculty members perceived themselves to be members of this group. One of the Catholic college teachers explained his nonmembership in the intellectual community in decidedly forceful language:

I, and most but certainly not all Catholic college teachers, do not have that broad cultural background that, according to the rules, decides who is and who is not a member of the intellectual community. The rules of the game are decided by the New York literary people—Podhoretz, Trilling, the *New York Review* crowd. These people have a genius at a broad approach to human behavior and ideas. Ethnically, the tone is Jewish. . . .

In both samples it was the intellectuals who were most likely to see themselves as participants in an intellectual group. This was particularly true of the non-Catholic college sample, where 85 percent of the intellectuals (67 percent for the Catholic colleges) affirmed membership in an intellectual community.

Only half of each sample felt that the academic world was basically free of ethnic prejudice. Somewhat surprisingly, it was the intellectuals in both samples, but especially those at the non-Catholic colleges, who were most likely to detect at least a moderate amount of prejudice on the college campus. In the non-Catholic college sample, 77 percent of the intellectuals in comparison with 29 percent of their nonintellectually oriented colleagues felt that the academic world was *not* basically free of ethnic prejudice.

In both samples those respondents who felt that the academic community was not free of ethnic prejudice overwhelmingly traced this prejudice to what they considered the antireligious atmosphere of the intellectual world. The following comments of several nonsectarian college intellectuals convey the tone of many responses:

There's a lingering antireligious hostility among intellectuals over thirty, and it's still quite strong. Unfortunately, most who are in power are over thirty years old.

It's very concealed, because the expression of this prejudice is considered bad taste. However, certain indications in social communication show that many intellectuals don't know what religion is all about.

There is a noticeable amount of antireligious feeling in the academic world, but this antireligious stance is shifting away from outright hostility to simply an unconcern. Certainly the academic community is more free of prejudice than any other segment of the society, primarily because it's made up of Jews and other secular humanists.

Very few respondents, however, felt that there was any actual religious discrimination in the academic world. As one teacher said: "It's not a matter of overt discrimination or prejudice against Catholics or any other religious believers. It's more an antireligious tone in the academic community. Religion is simply not considered a respectable intellectual pursuit."

Summary and Conclusions

Essentially, this research has involved an examination of the hypothesis that Catholic intellectuals are participants in an ethnically neutral subsociety of intellectuals. The data suggest that a significant number of the respondents did exhibit a behavioral and attitudinal pattern that supports the hypothesis in question, and by implication the findings give support to the more general hypothesis concerning the existence today of an intellectual subsociety in the United States. Yet the comparatively strong communal orientation of the Catholic college faculty members, especially the intellectuals, was in contradiction to the hypothesis. Nevertheless, these same Catholic college intellectuals did tend to see themselves as participants in an ethnically neutral subsociety of intellectuals. Overall, the intellectuals in the Catholic college sample tended to conform to Gordon's "passively-ethnic intellectual" type—one who "remains predominantly within the subsocietal boundaries of his ethnic group. . . . If he is a Negro, most of his friends may be intellectuals but they will also be Negroes. If he is a Jew, he confines his friendships primarily to other Jewish intellectuals."[20] And, as we have found, if he is a Catholic, he finds most of his friends among other Catholic intellectuals. The comparatively strong communal orientation of many young intellectuals at the Catholic colleges was a particularly interesting finding. They are, perhaps, part of what is often referred to as a "new breed" of Catholics—young, educated Catholics who direct their insight and talents toward improving the quality of life within the Catholic community.

On the other hand, the nonsectarian college intellectuals conform to Gordon's "marginally ethnic intellectual" type. In Gordon's words, "It is he who enters and makes up the intellectual subsociety . . . he wears his ethnicity lightly, if not in his own eyes at least in the eyes of the world. Whatever his social psychology, he finds ethnic communality unsatisfactory and takes his friends . . . where he finds them. . . ."[21] In the non-Catholic college sample, the "marginally ethnic intellectual" was likely to be a relatively young man who, while not rejecting Catholicism, had moved well beyond the provincial boundaries of the Catholic community in forming both his friendships and his attitudes.

---

20. Gordon, *Assimilation in American Life*, p. 228.
21. *Ibid.*

16. The Socialization of Jews into the Academic Subculture

ALLAN MAZUR

The intent of this paper is to describe the socialization of a population of Jewish social scientists. I am particularly concerned with the description and explanation of their "assimilated" ethnicity—their ethnic attitudes, behaviors and self concept notions.

Traditional approaches to socialization attribute most variation in adult personality, including ethnicity, to variation in childhood socialization. Since the present subjects were studied as adults, it was difficult to obtain much accurate detailed data on their early childhood experiences. Therefore, as a practical matter, the usual emphasis on childhood has been minimized here, and the focus is on socialization later in life, mainly the influence of the wife and the effect of participating in the academic subculture. These results should clarify some of the basic processes of adult socialization.

The Study Population

The study population was defined to be the male Jewish faculty members of social science departments at Harvard, Brandeis, and Boston universities. A faculty member was considered Jewish if one or more personal acquaintances specified with a high degree of certainty that he had Jewish antecedents, and the faculty member himself did not deny having Jewish antecedents.

Jewish men constituted 31 percent of the selected departments at Harvard, 57 percent at Brandeis, and 40 percent at Boston University. Cooperation of the population was very high, and 92 percent of those who were in the Boston area at the time of the study were interviewed. (I interviewed 83 percent of the Harvard group, 100 percent of the Brandeis group, and 95 percent of the B.U. group.) There were 63 interviews in all.

Interviews were usually held informally in the subject's offce or home. They averaged about one and one-half hours in duration. The interview consisted of open and closed questions about the subject's family and childhood, and about his current ethnic attitudes and behaviors. Answers to the open-ended questions were tape recorded.

Childhood Socialization

As a group, the subjects are relatively uncommitted to the Jewish religion. Traditional notions of socialization suggest that the roots of this lack of commitment may be found in early childhood. It is clear that the family of orientation sets the ethnic basis for further development. If ethnicity is at all significant to the family, the child learns about it quickly. Hartley, Rosenbaum and Schwartz (1948) found that over two-thirds of a sample of New York Jewish children, aged four and one-half to ten and one-half, gave ethnic responses to questions about being Jewish. Radke, Trager and Davis (1949) compared five- to eight-year-old children from the major religions and found that 71 percent of the Jews had specific or extensive knowledge about being Jewish. The comparable percentages for Protestant and Catholic children, when asked about their own groups, were 25 percent and 51 percent respectively. Pettigrew (1964) reports a corresponding racial awareness in very young Negro children.

If the early childhood experiences of the social scientists were characteristically different from the early experiences of most other American Jews, then this might explain the academicians' lack of commitment. Do the social scientists come from a special subset of the population, or are their family backgrounds typical? During the same period in which this study was conducted, Axelrod (1967) surveyed the general Jewish population of Greater Boston, including the areas of Harvard, Brandeis and Boston universities, thereby providing a better than usual basis for comparison. Using all available information, it was possible to compare the social scientists with a larger Jewish population on cultural characteristics of the childhood home (i.e., first, second, or third generation American, or European; family derived from eastern or western Europe); whether childhood was spent in an urban setting, and if so, in a largely Jewish neighborhood; occupational and educational background of the father; religious denominational affiliation of the parents; and degree of formal religious education as a child. The subject population is similar to the general American Jewish population on all of these indicators but two. A somewhat large proportion of the social scientists (19 percent) are foreign born, and the parents of the social scientists were somewhat less affiliated with a formal denomination of Judaism than parents in the general population.

About 89 percent of American Jews are descended from immigrants who come to the United States from eastern Europe near the beginning of this century. These immigrants settled in the large cities of the northeast quarter of the country, forming Jewish, working-class (and later, middle class) neighborhoods. The result was a fairly homogeneous Jewish subculture, and Jewish children encountered many similar experiences as a result of growing up in that subculture. Individual families varied substantially in their degree of participation in the subculture; most were near the mainstream, but many others were more assimilated and therefore peripheral to the Jewish subculture. It would seem reasonable to expect that adults whose childhood was spent in mainstream families would be more involved in religious and other ethnic activities than those who came from peripheral families. Therefore, a simple four item Guttman scale of Childhood Socialization (CS) was constructed to indicate the degree to which a subject's family of orientation participated in the Jewish subculture. The items were based on: the proportion of the parents' friends who were Jewish; the perceived importance of "being Jewish" and marrying a Jew to the parents; the observance of kosher dietary laws in the home; and parents' attendance at religious services. A CS score of 4 indicated that the family was at the mainstream of the subculture, and 0 indicated the periphery.[1]

A similar four item Guttman scale was constructed to measure the subjects' *present* degree of participation in the Jewish subculture.[2] The Pearson product-moment correlation between the two scales is .36. The

1. Given the difficulties that an adult has in recalling childhood, a special effort was made to use items which would be relatively easy to remember accurately. The scale appeared quite reasonable to sociologists familiar with Jewish culture, and it was sufficiently general that it was used as an indicator of childhood socialization for the twelve foreign-born subjects as well as for the American-born. The scale had a reproducibility of .98 (Torgerson, 1958: 318-319). The distribution of subjects at each CS score was 13 at 4, 24 at 3, 14 at 2, 7 at 1, and 5 at 0. The CS scale correlated very well with several additional indicators of mainstream participation in the subculture. All indications are that it is quite accurate. Complete details are available in Mazur (1969: 72-76).

2. Because the social scientists as a group currently participate much less in the Jewish subculture than their parents did, it was necessary to modify the scale, particularly the cutting points for each item, in order to distribute the subjects over the full range of scores. The distribution of subjects at each score on this modified scale was 3 at 4, 14 at 3, 13 at 2, 22 at 1, and 11 at 0. Reproducibility was .98. This scale correlated very well with several additional indicators of mainstream participation in the

existence of this relationship is hardly surprising, since it corresponds so well with common notions of the importance of childhood in determining adult behavior. Perhaps the most striking aspect of the correlation is that it is not higher. If the indicator scales were of low quality, then their intrinsic error could explain the low correlation, but the scales are quite reliable by customary standards.[1,2] The accuracy of the CS scale is perhaps best demonstrated by its very strong correlation with the percentage of subjects who have married Gentile wives. (Table 1) Childhood socialization in the mainstream appears to make marriage to a Gentile very unlikely, while socialization at the periphery gives just the opposite effect.

A man's wife is usually his major social influence after marriage, and also for some period before marriage. Therefore, while the fact that a man marries a Jewish or Gentile wife is interesting as an *effect* of his childhood socialization, the ethnicity of his wife may be more significant as a *cause* of his adult socialization. The influence of the wife in shaping her husband's ethnicity will be examined in the next section.

The Influence of Later Primary Relationships

Social influence from outside the family usually begins when the

Table 1.

Percentage of Subjects (Who Are or Have Been Married)
Who Have Married Gentile Wives.

CS Score	Percent of Subjects Who Have Married Gentile Wives
4 (= mainstream) (n = 10)	10%
3 (22)	32%
2 (14)	43%
1-0 (= periphery) (11)	73%

subculture, so it seems to be quite accurate. Details are available in Mazur (1969: 77-81).

child enters school at about the age of five. Student peers quickly become a major determiner of behavior and attitudes. American Jewish students frequently find themselves in two separate student groups because they typically attend some sort of religious school in addition to public school. Five-sixths of the American-born respondents attended some sort of formal Jewish school—usually for an afternoon chedar—from the age of nine until Bar Mitzvah at age 13. Bernard Rosen's (1965) study of Jewish adolescents points out the force of peer relationships formed during this period:

The effect of peer group pressures upon the adolescent's religiosity could be seen in the high degree of similarity of religious convictions, conduct and self-evaluation among clique members. We found, also, that when the adolescent deviated from the parental religious pattern, he tended to conform to the peer group's norms. Sometimes the adolescent was caught between the cross-pressures of conflicting family and peer group expectations. When this occurred, and it did in a number of cases as regards the use of *kosher* food, it was the peer group which most often succeeded in determining the adolescent's behavior (Rosen, 1965: 200).

The influence of adolescent peers is somewhat mediated by the family, since the child still lives at home. But entry into college is usually a major breaking point (Thalheimer, 1965). Not only is the freshman entering a new peer group and a new cultural environment, but he is simultaneously being removed from the influence of his family. This break is most marked when the student lives at school, but even a commuting freshman finds himself relatively removed from his family environment.

The student cultural climate is a characteristic of the individual school (Sanford, 1962: 463-530). Some colleges have quite intellectual orientations. Other schools, for example in the Ivy League, might value the genteel behavior of the upper middle class WASP. In either case, the prevailing values often conflict with the Jewish mainstream. The student might escape the influence of the cultural climate by isolating himself in a clique, such as a social fraternity. If the clique's values differ from the values of the undergraduate climate, the student will be shielded. But very often the clique effect is to exaggerate the prevailing value system. For example, one subject had been an undergraduate at an Ivy League school and belonged to a "Jewish fraternity which partly prided itself in being non-Jewish in culture." The members of the fraternity were very Ivy oriented and were not "New York Jew types."

This orientation carried through in the subject's detached description and evaluation of a Jewish caricature:

[There] is a sort of aggressiveness that's too obvious. There's nothing wrong with ambition and achievement, but my view of the Jews is that many of them do this much too obviously. It's a matter of style. I have nothing against setting high goals for oneself—and usually in terms of paths chosen—but they do seem to lack a style, if I can put it that way, which is appealing to me (#55).

By way of contrast, another subject, who had spent much of his student and faculty career at very non-Ivy universities in New York City, described Jewish aggressiveness in rather admirable terms:

In discussion situations Jews are much more likely to be aggressively vociferous in, say, discussing issues. . . . For example, at State University you hire a lot of assistant professors. The Gentile assistant professors were always clearly an outgroup, even with the Gentile senior staff. They were quiet; they didn't say anything; you didn't know they existed. Some guy would show up—some Jew from the East—and the first department meeting some issue would come up and he'd give a 15 minute—he'd tell exactly what he thought about the thing and pay no attention to the fact that he was . . . a junior man on the staff, and that it might not be proper for him to behave this way the first time. And yet I don't think it had the effect, at least in that context, of alienating people. It was the other guys who suffered—that is, the Gentiles. They might be bright, but nobody would know it. They wouldn't talk up (#45).

But whatever the specific culture at a college, it was usually at variance with the Jewish mainstream, and this influence, coupled with the reduced influence of the family, almost invariably led subjects to reduced participation in certain aspects of Jewish ethnic behavior. Pork would be eaten for the first time, or attendance at High Holiday services would be dropped, or the student would stop fasting on Yom Kippur. Many subjects never did follow all of these practices, and many who did dropped some before college, but whatever the state of Jewish participation in high school, it was predictably less in college and in graduate school.

There were only two groups of exceptions to this general rule. First, there were the very few subjects whose early socialization included so few Jewish characteristics that there was nothing to drop. Second were the few subjects who maintained a high level of religious observance through college, apparently reinforced by very strong primary group religious influence during this period. Of the thirteen subjects with the highest Childhood Socialization score (CS = 4), only two maintained their level of religious practice through school. One of these went to

college at a Jewish seminary, and he maintained his permanent residence with his Orthodox religious family. Clearly, prevailing social
pressure was into the Jewish mainstream. The second subject who
maintained his initially high level of religious observance lived at
home with his Orthodox family through college until the age of 25. He
had been a Hebrew college student in his teens (beyond the usual retirement at the age of 13), and so his school peers were largely of the
Jewish mainstream. It seems probable that these primary group influences countered the university's secularizing effect.

It appears that high school and college are periods of homogeniza-
tion during which students become more similar in their ethnicity regardless of their family backgrounds. While there are certainly limits
to this uniformity, the trend is strong enough for us to raise a question
about the basis of the earlier mentioned positive correlation between
childhood socialization (CS) and adult participation in the ethnic subculture. Is a mainstream childhood socialization strong enough to
withstand the effects of high school and college apostasy and lead directly to a relatively high participation in Jewish culture as an adult?
Or is some additional mediating factor necessary to return the apostate
to the direction of the mainstream?

This study will not provide definitive answers to these questions,
but at least one related point is quite clear. Childhood socialization
is very influential in the selection of a wife. Table 1 shows the percentage of subjects (who are or have been married) who have married
Gentile wives, by subject's CS. The relationship is very strong; the more
mainstream the childhood socialization, the less likelihood of a Gentile
wife.

There are undoubtedly several factors contributing to this relationship. By definition of the CS scale, parents of the more mainstream
children are more concerned that they marry Jews, and so these parents
can be expected to exert pressure in that direction. Again by definition
of the CS scale, mainstream children came into contact with a relatively
larger number of Jews, and this increased the probability that dates and
mates would be Jewish. Also, we might expect that mainstream children would be more likely to prefer a Jewish spouse over a Gentile, although any such tendency would probably be mitigated during the
high school and college periods.

Attitudes on intermarriage were measured with the question, How
much are you concerned that the person your child would marry be
Jewish? The percentages of subjects who indicated some such concern

are displayed in Table 2 as a function of CS, and wife's ethnic group. There is an extremely strong tendency for subjects with Jewish wives to prefer Jewish spouses for their children, while subjects with Gentile wives show no such preference. The most obvious explanation for this relation is that people who believe in intermarriage before marriage intermarry, while people who don't believe in it before marriage do not intermarry. This would explain Table 2 quite well.

But there is another equally good explanation. Ethnicity is largely influenced by primary social relationships. Since the most primary adult relationship is between husband and wife, we can expect very great mutual influence within a married couple. In general, a Jewish wife will be a pro-Jewish ethnic influence, and a Gentile wife would be an anti-Jewish ethnic influence, although there are certainly exceptions. Table 2 could also be explained as the *result* of marrying a Jew or a Gentile, rather than the cause of it. Very likely both explanations are true.

Recall that a modified form of the CS scale was used to measure the subjects' *present* participation in the Jewish subculture. Table 3 shows the percentage of subjects who scored above the median on this modified scale, as a function of wife's ethnic group and subject's CS score. The wife's ethnic group is a much stronger predictor of the husband's

Table 2.

Percentage of Subjects (Who Are Currently Married) Who Indicated Some Concern That the Person Their Child Marries Should Be Jewish.

		Wife's Ethnic Group		CS
		Jewish	Gentile	Marginals:
				CS
	4-3 (mainstream)	52%	0% *	45%
		(n = 23)	(6)	(29)
CS Score:				
	0-2 (periphery)	70% *	8% *	35%
		(10)	(13)	(23)
	Wife Marginals:	61%	5%	40%
		(33)	(19)	(52)

* Information not available for one subject in this category.

present participation in the Jewish subculture than is his CS score. Wife's ethnic group was also a stronger predictor than CS in Table 2. This suggests that the present influence of the wife might be a more important determiner of adult ethnicity than the childhood socialization of the past.

The same suggestion may be drawn from Table 4, where subjects' "Jewish Emotional Involvement" score is the dependent variable. (This score is based on three interview questions which asked the subject if he had any emotional feelings of vicarious identity, pride, or shame with respect to other Jews. The higher the score, the more emotional involvement the subject has with other Jews.)[3]

High emotional involvement is related to having a Jewish wife. CS appears to have no effect on emotional involvement at all. This comparison again suggests that the influence of the wife might have a greater effect on her husband's ethnicity than the influence of his childhood socialization.

Although the data presented here are quite consistent with the explanation that the wife's ethnicity determines her husband's ethnicity, they are also consistent with the explanation that the husband and wife

Table 3.

Perecntage of Subjects (Who Are Currently Married)
Above the Median In Participation In the Mainstream Culture,
As A Function of Childhood Socialization (CS) and
Wife's Ethnic Group.

		Wife's Ethnic Group		CS Marginals:
		Jewish	Gentile	
CS Score:	4-3 (mainstream)	61% (n = 23)	29% (7)	53% (30)
	0-2 (periphery)	64% (11)	7% (14)	32% (25)
	Wife Marginals:	62% (34)	14% (21)	44% (55)

3. Details are available in Mazur (1969: 107-110).

Table 4.

Percentage of Subjects (Who Are Currently Married)
Above the Median In Jewish Emotional Involvement,
As A Function of Childhood Socialization (CS) and
Wife's Ethnic Group.

| | | Wife's Ethnic Group | | CS Marginals: |
		Jewish	Gentile	
CS Score:	4-3 (mainstream)	48% (n = 23)	28% (7)	43% (30)
	0-2 (periphery)	55% (11)	36% (14)	44% (25)
Wife Marginals:		50% (34)	33% (21)	44% (55)

simply choose each other on the basis of having similar ethnic attitudes. It would be pointless here to argue whether a Gentile wife is
the cause or effect of minimal ethnicity in the husband; it is usually a
chicken and egg situation. Both are true. A man with minimal ethnicity
is more likely to marry a non-Jewish wife, but a Gentile wife rein-
forces any tendency toward minimal ethnicity. The comments of several respondents emphasize the wife's influence as a major determiner
of husband's ethnicity:

> Subject: I think if I had married a Jewish girl for whom it was very
> important, it wouldn't have been important to me to *not* be ritu-
> alistically Jewish, and I would have been perfectly happy to
> have a kosher home, if it had been important to, say, my wife
> (#63).

> Subject: My wife's influence keeps up our religious practices.... Her
> maintaining a kosher home is simply a cultural lag from her
> parents. That's what she had known, and she maintains it....
> I started attending High Holiday services when I got married.
> I never did when I was single (#70).

> Interviewer: What is the nature of the attraction of the Unitarian church
> for you?

> Subject: It's less of that than it is a feeling that it's good if kids have a

religious education, and Unitarian makes as much sense as anything else. . . . If my wife were Jewish [instead of Unitarian], my kids could go to Reform [Jewish] Sunday school (#76).

Of course the husband-wife social influence is mutual. We might note Newcomb's (1958) study of college girls who picked up very liberal New Deal political views at Bennington College in the 1930's. A recent followup study of those girls (Newcomb et al., 1967) showed that they maintained or dropped those attitudes after college depending on whether or not they had social support—mainly from their husbands—over the ensuing years. The Bennington girls run parallel to the social scientists. Both had a particular type of childhood socialization: one into political conservatism, and one into Judaism. Both went through a resocialization in the new environments they encountered as students: one reformed political views, and one reformed ethnicity. Both tended to marry spouses generally in agreement with their new attitudes. Both received reinforcement and reshaping from their spouses. In those cases where spouses differed on these attitudes at marriage, the couple appear to have reshaped each other into a mutual conformity.

The influence of the wife, and other primary relationships, is only one of at least two agents of adult socialization. A second agent, to be considered now, is the diffuse social influence of the cultural environment.

The Effect of the Academic Subculture

The simple conceptualization of adult socialization used here assumes that it is analytically meaningful to separate the influence of primary relationships from the effect of the larger diffuse cultural environment. I recognize, of course, that much of the effect of the culture is transmitted through primary relationships, and also that much of the tone of a primary relationship is set by the cultural context. Nevertheless, for analytical purposes it is useful to separate the two. The previous section was concerned with primary influences. This section will focus on the socializing effects of the subculture of the academic community.

The Intellectual Subsociety

The subjects not only work in the academic milieu, but their friendships and associations usually come from this community. Therefore, even though they derive from backgrounds that are fairly representative of American Jewry, we would expect that the similarity of their adult subcultural environment will lead to a certain homogeneity, or at least convergence, of their self concepts and behavior. This assumes, of course, that the academic community does indeed constitute a relatively homogeneous cultural environment.

Milton Gordon (1964) has hypothesized that the intellectuals in the United States, who are largely located in the academic community, "interact in such patterned ways as to form at least the elementary structure of a subsociety of their own"; and that within this academic community the typical intellectual "finds ethnic communality unsatisfactory and takes his friends, and probably even his spouse, where he finds them" (Gordon, 1964: 224-232; see Chapter 13). Anderson's (1968) study of college professors has provided some empirical support for this position—"that intellectuals do in fact interact in patterned ways and that these patterns are largely undelineated by ethnic background" (Anderson, 1968: 225; see Chapter 14).

Gordon's general discussion refers to several values that are particularly stressed in the intellectual subsociety. Six of these, which are of particular concern here, are: (1) dissent from formal religious traditions; (2) disapproval of ethnic clannishness or exclusiveness,[4] and neutral or favorable attitudes toward interethnic intermarriage; (3) minimal affiliation with organizations of the larger society; (4) dissociation, and even alienation, from the concerns and attitudes of the larger society; (5) intellectuality and emphasis on the virtues of learning—not as a means of obtaining status, but as an elaboration and extension of ideas; and (6) concern with liberal politics, social ethics and social justice—particularly in the areas of interethnic harmony and integration (Gordon, 1964: 224-232, 255).

The Brandeis Environment

The Brandeis interviews indicate that that school's social scientists are much more secular and universalistic than one might initially assume, given that the school was founded under Jewish auspices:

There seems to be a selection of Jews here such that a lot of the people in this department probably rebelled against the Jew as businessman, the Jew as operator, certain kinds of financier. What is predominantly here is the Jew as intellectual, radical and cultural. . . . And I think that everyone approves of that

4. It appears that this value may be changing. Intellectuals seem to look on ethnic exclusiveness, at least among blacks and other underprivileged minorities, more favorably than in the past.

so it's a very comfortable environment. . . . So, it's that part of the Jewish world which you probably take pride in. Yet no one goes to temple or things of this sort. I don't think anyone observes (#62).

This alienation and separation from American Jewish middle class materialistic attitudes is quite in keeping with intellectual value (4)—dissociation from the larger society. This sort of alienation was reported by a majority of all respondents, but was particularly strong at Brandeis with 70 percent of the subjects giving alienated responses as opposed to only 48 percent and 53 percent at B.U. and Harvard respectively. This alienation was very clearly not against all things traditionally Jewish, but mainly against the Americanized middle class.

Well I suppose I feel most alienated not from the European-born pushcart peddlers in New York City—I don't feel as alienated from them as I do from American-born Jews who have been to college, who live in the suburbs, who are fairly well-to-do, and who are afraid to let go. . . . It's interesting. I never thought of that before, but I feel less alienated from the Yiddish-speaking pushcart peddler than I do from people who are closer to me (#66).

Only seven respondents in the whole sample mentioned any sort of alienation from the ultra-orthodox.

At Brandeis, this anti-middle class orientation takes on much more specificity than at the other schools. It focuses on the administration officers—who are viewed as "businessmen," "operators," and "financiers"—and wealthy Jewish donors to the school, whose conspicuous consumption is epitomized by placing their obviously Jewish names on all the Brandeis buildings. These names are a source of irritation and/or embarrassment to many of the faculty. Some of the subjects simply state that the Jewish names on university buildings sound very odd and funny. Others are concerned with more subtle nuances:

I: Why is it, for example, that you would object to the Fishbein Social Science Center but not the Brown Social Science Center?

S: Oh [not] . . . because of the Jewish names. No, that isn't what bothers me. What does bother me is, for example, if it were just called the Brown Social Science Center, the Fishbein Social Science Center—that would be fine. But why does it have to be the Morris and Sara Fishbein—You know what I mean?

I: You mean the elaboration?

S: Yes. Why can't it just be called the Fishbein Social Science Center? Now this isn't so terrible, but sometimes it is amusing (#36).

The Brandeis faculty orientation can be viewed as an extremely functional adaptation to a potentially conflicting situation. Such close association with a Jewish institution is difficult to resolve in terms of ego's intellectual set of values. It would be cognitively dissonant to disapprove of ethnic communalism and institutional affiliation while at the same time being intimately associated with an ethnic institution. However, by a strict compartmentalization of Jews into "them" (the materialistic, the professionals, the new-rich, the Brandeis administration) and "us" (the Jewish intellectual, the ultra-liberal, the Brandeis faculty), it is possible for the individual to very completely dissociate his self concept from most of those characteristics of the ethnic community that are so distasteful. Academics at B.U. and Harvard are not so closely associated with Jewish communalism, and therefore are not under as great pressure to dissociate themselves from the Jewish community, and therefore do not manifest the extremes of Jewish middle class alienation found at Brandeis. That there is a need for some sort of adaptation is very clear; one-quarter of the Brandeis respondents reported some reluctance to affiliate with a Jewish school when they were initially deciding to come. However, in almost all cases, they have adapted and now feel very comfortable in the environment. The general tendency is to view the Jewishness of the environment in a warm and humorous (and perhaps tension-reducing) manner:

For my first luncheon here . . . I came . . . and on the menu . . . was corned beef and potato *lotkes* with sour cream. It wasn't kosher, but you knew you were eating Jewish. It was very good, and I had finished the meal and was talking to one of the faculty and looked at the dessert menu of which there were about ten or eleven, and the waitress asked me if I wanted one, and I said, "no." And she looked down and said, "Come on, this one—". And I said, "No, I'm really trying to diet," and she said, "Ach, a little dessert—what will it matter?" (#85).

In sum, then, we can characterize the Brandeis academic environment as intellectual with a strong Jewish ethical, but secular, flavor, and strong alienation from the Jewish middle class. The Boston University environment is perhaps more closely associated with the American middle class orientation. (One B.U. professor, when asked if he felt alienated from any aspect of American Judaism, responded: "I feel right in the mainstream. . . . I'm a middle class, suburban, professional Jew, and we're the majority" (#70). Harvard fits the intellectual pattern without any of the particular flavor of Brandeis. But all three schools are representative of Gordon's intellectual subsociety, though in widely varying degrees. Each has an intellectual value orientation relative to the larger American society.

Anti-Ethnic Effects of the Intellectual Environment

An individual's ethnicity will be largely determined by his cultural environment. Given the prevailing values of that environment, he will eclectically "pick and choose" those aspects of his ethnicity which would be positively valued and will integrate them into his personality. Those ethnic aspects which would be negatively valued will be discarded.

The Gordon-Anderson observations that the intellectual's behavior is largely undelineated by his ethnic background (Gordon, 1964; Anderson, 1968) follows immediately from this conceptual framework. The first three of the set of six intellectual values previously listed—those against formal religious traditions, ethnic exclusiveness, and organizational affiliation—would have the effect of dissociating the intellectual from most of those self concept and behavorial manifestations which characterize normal ethnic group behavior. A comparison of Jewish attitudes and practices of the social scientists and the Greater Boston Jewish population (from Axelrod et al., 1967) shows that there are very great differences between these groups, and that these differences are completely consistent with the intellectual's emphasis on these three values. (see Table 5).

The Jewish academic's lack of concern with religious and communal aspects of Judaism is hardly a surprising finding. Any number of recent observers have commented on this point. But the situation is usually far overstated. For example, Milton Konvitz, in commenting on the Jewish intellectuals at American universities, has written, "Most of them . . . are Jews only in the sense that they had Jewish parents. They have evaded or escaped from the Jewish community and have no Jewish ties or loyalties" (Konvitz, 1964: 15). The data in Table 5 show this to be a gross exaggeration. Even Gordon's picture of ethnic irrelevancy in the intellectual subsociety (1964: 224-232) seems overstated—at least in the Greater Boston academic community. Ethnicity is certainly not irrelevant. Eighty-eight percent of the Boston area social scientists reported that, of the friends who come to their home, at least half are Jewish. This finding is partially accounted for by the high incidence of Jews in the departments under study. Clearly, even non-Jews in these

Table 5.

*Anti-Ethnic Effect of the
Values of the Intellectual Subculture.*

Value:	Specific Indicators:	Greater Boston Jewry	Percent of Respondents in Each Group:			
			Social Scientists (n = 63)	B.U. Only (21)	Harvard Only (19)	Brandeis Only (23)
1) Dissent from formal religious traditions.	Identification with a formal denomination of Judaism:	85%	16%	24%	17%	9%
	Sabbath candles in the home:	62%	18%	29%	11%	9%
	Attends High Holiday services or more:	77%	27%	43%	21%	17%
	Participates in a Passover seder:	87%	59%	71%	58%	48%
2) Disapproval of ethnic clannishness or exclusiveness.	Intermarried:	7%*	38%*	22%*	50%*	40%*
	Expressed concern about intermarriage:	70%	47%	48%	56%	40%
3) Minimal organizational affiliation.	Belongs to at least one Jewish organization:	50%	13%	14%	16%	9%
	Is a member of a synagogue or temple:	53%	17%	38%	11%	4%

* These percentages represent only the married respondents. Contrary to all the other listed indicators, we would expect the so-cial scientists to score higher on this indicator than the Greater Boston Jewish population.

departments would be expected to have a very large number of Jewish friends. But even controlling for this, 54 percent of the respondents reported that the Jewish portion of their friends was greater than the Jewish portion of their department, while only 8% reported the Jewish portion of their friends was lower. While it may be true that Jewish academics associate more with non-Jewish academics than with Jewish non-academics, other things being equal, there is still some sort of friendship selection of Jews over Gentiles.

Pro-Ethnic Effects of the Environment

I have argued so far that the individual's ethnicity will be shaped largely by the prevailing values of his social environment, and that therefore, given the values of the intellectual social environment, there is a clear tendency for the academic to dissociate himself from the religious and communal aspects of his ethnic group. This has been widely interpreted as a total detachment from the ethnic group. But if the formulation presented here is correct, and if there are certain aspects of Jewish ethnicity which are quite consistent with the prevailing values of the academic's social environment, then we would expect a corresponding attachment to his ethnic group. In the case of the Jewish intellectual, there are at least two such ethnic aspects which are very highly compatible with his intellectual value system—the tradition of Jewish learning and intellectual preeminence; and the tradition of Jewish liberal social ethics and social justice. If we have argued that the Jewish intellectual will negatively evaluate the religious and communal aspects, and reject these from his own ethnicity, then we must also argue that he will positively evaluate the intellectual and ethical aspects of Judaism and integrate these into his ethnic self.

This very positive association with notions of Jewish intellectuality and social ethics pervades the large bulk of the interviews. For example, the following sorts of responses were very often given when subjects were asked to describe in general their feelings about being Jewish:

... I think that I do feel a certain pride in Jewish accomplishments of an intellectual and moral nature ... (#66).

... [B]eing an intellectual is also, in part, being a Jew, and being a Jew is in part being an intellectual, and so on ... I feel good about the fact that I belong to a group, or a sub-group, or what have you, that has this kind of positive orientation toward the world, toward people, toward relationships. ... That the orientation has been constructive—that it has been respect and dignity for the human being, rather than other things which seem to be so prevalent to-day (#68).

I think my own sense of Jewish history and culture has played an important part in shaping my life, and that a great deal of my political conceptions—I'm far more politically than I am religiously active—far more active in left-wing than in Jewish circles. I think that the values of biblical Judaism—especially prophetic Judaism—which I learned as a child—were very important to me in determining my political life. . . . It's very easy to feel just the kind of extraordinary pride in very recent cultural and intellectual achievements of Jews, and to identify with that whole group of Jewish intellectuals (#77).

I think to me it means some of these positive, intellectual, liberal, human qualities. I think the Jews, more so than most other recognizable groups, have, to me, the virtues which mankind needs. . . . I'm proud to be affiliated and to demonstrate in my own life these same qualities (#70).

It's very hard to separate being a Jew from the things one learns as a child so that to me, more than the real religious element about which I knew some, but I wasn't really involved in, is the ethical element—the way of life, the values. I remember when I was a kid being told that I was named for a person on my mother's side who had been the scholar of, wherever they lived. . . . The rabbis would appeal to him and so on. Well, this made about as much impression as, you know—. Of late I've suddenly remembered this because, Lord knows, the last thing I ever intended to be was a scholar. . . . But I realize now that this might be related to it (#78).

In order to objectively demonstrate this high tendency to positively associate with Jewish intellectuality, respondents were asked if they had any pride in intellectual achievements of the Jews. Seventy-six percent reported some positive level of personal pride in Jewish intellectual achievements (see Table 6).

Unfortunately, a similar convenient indicator of positive association with the Jewish tradition of social ethics was not available. However, it was possible to construct a satisfactory indicator by coding the answers to four open-ended interview questions for positive mention of specifically Jewish aspects of social ethics, social justice, and humanitarianism. The four questions were: (1) Could you describe in general your feelings about being Jewish? (2) In what sense, if any, do you consider yourself a religious Jew? (3) Do you think that the existence of the Jews as a separate group has been in any sense good or bad for the rest of mankind? Why? (4) Are there any characteristics of American Jews that you would consider good or bad by some reasonable criterion?

Table 6.

*Pro-Ethnic Effect of Two of the Values of the
Intellectual Subculture*

Value:	Specific Indicators:	Percent of Respondents in Each Group:			
		Social Scientists (n = 63)	B.U. Only (21)	Harvard Only (19)	Brandeis Only (23)
5) Intellectuality and the virtues of learning.	Reports pride in intellectual achievements of Jews:	76%	86%	68%	74%
6) Concern with liberal politics and social ethics.	Positive mention of Jewish social ethics and morality in open-ended answers to four questions:	49%	67%	31%	48%

Forty-nine percent of all respondents made at least one positive reference to Jewish social ethics or liberal politics or humanism in the open-ended responses to these questions. This figure is an underestimate, because subjects who did not make a positive response in the very limited portion of the interview that was coded here, did frequently make such a comment elsewhere in the interview. This indicator shows a high evaluation on the tradition of Jewish social ethics, liberality, humanism and morality. In contrast, only 22 percent made a similar positive mention of religious aspects or religious contributions of Judaism.

The picture of Jewish social scientists drawn from Table 6 alone shows attachment to their ethnicity, just as the picture drawn from Table 5 alone shows detachment. While it certainly seems reasonable to characterize the group as being relatively unconcerned with ethnic characteristics, the degree of attachment or detachment to any given aspect of the ethnicity appears to be largely determined by its consistency or inconsistency with the prevailing values of the cultural environment.[5]

5. Tables 5 and 6 show consistent differences between the three schools. The Boston University faculty, which was earlier characterized as being in a less "intellectual" social environment than the other two faculties, deviates least from the attitudes and behaviors of the Greater Boston Jewish population. This consistent pattern

Conclusions

The data presented here confirm the common observation that Jewish academicians—at least those in the social sciences—are relatively uncommitted to the Jewish religion, compared to the general Jewish population. However, their lack of religious commitment does not jus- tify the stereotype of the Jewish intellectual as being totally detached from ethnic group concerns. Rather, the ethnicity of this group is an eclectic one, conforming to the general values of the academic commu- nity. For example, most academics disdain restricted, parochial behav- ior, and so the Jewish academic disdains, and dissociates himself from, Jewish clannishness. On the other hand, most academics value intel- lectuality, and so the Jewish academic is proud of the Jewish intellec- tual tradition. Ethnicity, viewed in this eclectic manner, is a very strong characteristic of many of the present subjects.

The shaping process of the academic subculture appears to be medi- ated by the social influence of the subjects' wives. The ethnicity of a subject's wife, in conjunction with an indicator of the subject's child- hood socialization into the Jewish ethnic subculture, provides a rather good prediction of the subject's present degree of participation and emotional involvement in Jewish ethnic activities.

This paper assumes that it is analytically meaningful to separate the social influence of primary relations (particularly the wife) from the influence of the larger, diffuse cultural environment. This is clearly an over-simplification, but it has the advantage of simplifying the analysis. Both the primary influence of the wife, and the diffuse in- fluence of the academic subculture, considered separately, show their effects on the ethnicity of the subjects. Presumably, they may reinforce each other, contradict each other, or be quite independent of each other, depending on the values of the subculture and the primary relations. In the present case, the separate effects of the wife and the academic subculture appear to be additive, as indicated in Table 7. Participation

suggests that the social scientists are not only influenced by the general value orien- tation of the academic community, but that the specific climate of each school has its own special effect. Further examination indicates that this is not the case, however. At Boston University, 76% of the married social scientists had Jewish wives, where- as at Brandeis only 55%, and at Harvard only 54% of the married subjects had Jewish wives. The variation between schools is satisfactorily explained by assuming that a Jewish wife will influence her husband toward the mainstream, and the dispropor- tionately large number of Jewish wives at Boston University accounts for that school's relative nearness to the mainstream. Statistical details are presented in Mazur (1969: 126-133). Note, however, that even Boston University differs substantially from the Greater Boston Jewish population.

Table 7.

*Interaction of the Academic Subculture, The Influence
of the Wife, and Childhood Socialization (CS).*

| | | Percentage of Respondents in Each Group: The Academic Subculture | | | |
| | | Jewish Wife | | Gentile Wife | |
Indicator:	Greater Boston Jewry	CS = 4-3 (mainstream) (n = 23)	CS = 0-2 (periphery) (7)	CS = 4-3 (mainstream) (11)	CS = 0-2. (periphery) (14)
Denomination:	85%	22%	36%	0%	0%
Sabbath candles:	62%	33%	18%	0%	0%
High holidays:	77%	43%	27%	29%	0%
Seder:	87%	78%	64%	43%	14%
Concern about intermarriage:	70%	57%	70%	0%	8%
Belong to a Jewish organization:	50%	26%	0%	14%	0%
Temple member:	53%	30%	18%	0%	0%
Pride in Jewish intellect:	—	87%	91%	57%	50%

in the academic community appears to be a sufficient condition to remove most subjects from the Jewish mainstream. A gentile wife moves
a subject even further from the mainstream; a Jewish wife moves a
subject somewhat closer. However, even subjects with Jewish wives
show less involvement in the mainstream than the Boston non-academic population.

There is a tendency for the social scientists to have parents who are
less affiliated with a formal denomination of Judaism than the general
Jewish population. This suggests that some of the social scientists have
been "assimilated" since childhood. This reasoning could be extended
to suggest that the academic subculture really has no socialization effect at all; the academic community simply recruits Jews who are minimally concerned with their ethnicity. There are two problems with that
argument, however. First, two-thirds of the subjects did have parents
who were affiliated with a formal denomination of Judaism. In fact,
over one-third of the subjects' parents were Orthodox Jews. Yet even

the subjects with the most mainstream childhoods are now dissociated from the mainstream, relative to the larger Jewish population (see Table 7). Second, if the academic subculture had no socializing effect, and if the social scientists were assimilated before they first entered the academic community as university students, then it would be hard to explain why so many of them (76 percent) take personal pride in the intellectual achievements of other Jews. Therefore, it seems much more reasonable to assume that both effects are operating. The academic life seems to have a special attraction for Jews from minimally religious homes, *and* the academic subculture shapes the ethnicity of those who participate in it.

We have a similar situation in considering the effect of the wife, or of any other primary relationship. An individual clearly tends to pick his friends, and his wife, from those whose attitudes and behaviors are similar to his own. But the close association which then ensues has the effect of *increasing* the similarity. Newcomb (1967) has demonstrated just this sort of effect in his study of the political attitudes of married couples.

It should be clear by now that an adult's ethnicity cannot be understood simply on the basis of his childhood socialization. The traditional notions of the importance of early experiences are not helpful here. Most of the findings of this paper are consistent with the assumption that childhood socialization experiences do *not* determine adult ethnicity. All of the data tables show that an adult's ethnicity is more closely related to his adult social influences than his childhood influences. *His earlier influences may be most relevant in determining what his adult influences will be, rather than in directly shaping his ethnicity.* Subjects' childhood socialization, as measured by the CS score, was only weakly related to several measures of adult ethnicity, but it was very strongly related to his choice of wife—Jewish or Gentile.[6] The mere fact of being raised as a Jew appears to bias one toward entry into the academic subculture, since 40 percent of the faculty of the departments used in this study were Jewish, while only about 3 percent of the population of the United States are Jews. An individual's early socialization biases him toward one sort of social setting or another. Once in that setting, the setting itself may influence the individual's subsequent socialization more directly than his earlier experiences.

6. I am assuming that the ethnicity of a subject's wife is not in itself a strong measure of his own ethnicity.

Bibliography

Anderson, Charles. 1968. "The Intellectual Subsociety Hypothesis: An Empirical Test." *The Sociological Quarterly* 9 (April): 210-227.

Axelrod, Morris, Floyd Fowler, Jr., and Arnold Gurin. 1967. *A Community Survey for Long Range Planning: A Study of the Jewish Population of Greater Boston.* Boston: Combined Jewish Philanthropies of Greater Boston.

Gordon, Milton. 1964. *Assimilation in American Life: The Role of Race, Religion, and National Origins.* New York: Oxford University Press.

Hartley, E., M. Rosenbaum and S. Schwartz. 1948. "Children's Perceptions of Ethnic Group Membership." *Journal of Psychology* 26: 387-398.

Konvitz, Milton. 1964. "The Jewish Intellectual, the University and the Jewish Community," in *The Jewish Intellectual, The University and The Jewish Community.* Washington, D.C.: B'nai B'rith Hillel Foundations: 7-20.

Mazur, Allan. 1969. "Resocialized Ethnicity: A Study of Jewish Social Scientists." Unpublished Ph.D. dissertation. Baltimore: Johns Hopkins University.

Newcomb, Theodore. 1958. "Attitude Development as a Function of Reference Groups," Pp. 265-275 in E. Maccoby, T. Newcomb, and E. Hartley (eds.), *Readings in Social Psychology.* New York: Holt, Rinehart and Winston.

Newcomb, Theodore, Kathryn Koenig, Richard Flacks, and Donald Warwick. 1967. *Persistence and Change: Bennington College and Its Students After Twenty-Five Years.* New York: Wiley.

Pettigrew, Thomas. 1964. *A Profile of the Negro American.* Princeton: Van Nostrand.

Radke, M., H. Trager and H. Davis. 1949. "Social Perceptions and Attitudes of Children." *Genetic Psychology Monographs* 40: 327-447.

Rosen, Bernard. 1965. *Adolescence and Religion.* Cambridge, Mass.: Schenkman.

Sanford, Nevitt (ed.). 1962. *The American College,* New York: Wiley.

Thalheimer, Fred. 1965. "Continuity and Change in Religiosity: A Study of Academicians." *The Pacific Sociological Review* 8: 101-108.

Torgerson, Warren. 1958. *Theory and Methods of Scaling.* New York: Wiley.

17. Religious Orthodoxy among Catholic Academicians

JOHN D. MURRAY

A rather widespread image of the academic life suggests that college professors are less traditional in their religious attitudes than persons who do not function in an intellectual milieu. In the words of one writer, commenting on this apparent religious heterodoxy of academics:

Among the academic professions . . . one of the most ancient and ardently taught occupational norms is the obligation to question, to suspend belief in received knowledge. Moreover, . . . many scholars . . . have applied this institutionalized rule of doubt in their examination of religious as well as secular questions, leading some of them partially or completely to abandon traditional religious beliefs and practices.[1]

Some empirical support for this assumption that academicians are less traditional than the general public in their religious beliefs has been offered by Thalheimer in a study of West Coast state university professors.[2]

Some would explain the relatively low orthodoxy of professors in terms of an asserted incompatibility between the values implicit in a religious orientation and those inherent in the scientific outlook that underlies much contemporary scholarship. In commenting on the impact of this incompatibility of religious and scientific values, Stark writes: "Implicit in any discussion of value conflicts is the assumption that contradictory values cannot be readily held . . . and hence, that the adoption of one means the non-adoption of the other."[3]

1. Fred Thalheimer, "Continuity and Change in Religiosity: A Study of Academicians," *Pacific Sociological Review*, VIII (Fall, 1965), 101-102.
2. *Ibid.*, pp. 101-108.
3. Rodney Stark, "On the Incompatibility of Religion and Science: A Survey of American Graduate Students," *Journal for the Scientific Study of Religion*, III (Fall,

This raises some questions concerning the religious orientation of Catholic academicians, particularly those teaching at Catholic colleges. Existing data suggest that Catholic college teachers are more communally involved than non-Catholic professors.[4] Is this comparatively strong communal orientation associated with a pattern of traditionalism in religious attitudes, or are Catholic college teachers, like Thalheimer's state university sample, relatively heterodox in their religious outlook?

Furthermore, do differences in religious beliefs and attitudes exist between Catholics teaching at Catholic colleges and Catholics on the faculties of nonsectarian institutions? In a comparison of a sample of teachers from Catholic colleges with a sample of Catholic professors from non-sectarian colleges, the Catholic college faculty members evinced the greater religious communality.[5] Do parallel differences exist in religious orthodoxy?

A final question concerns Catholic intellectuals within the academic world. Are they more unconventional in their religious attitudes than Catholic nonintellectuals, as suggested in the judgment of Stark, cited above? And do differences in religious beliefs exist between Catholic intellectuals on Catholic college faculties and their religious counterparts at non-sectarian colleges and universities? This paper is an attempt to suggest answers to this question and those raised above.

Research Procedure

The data for exploring these questions are based on a study of Cath-

---

1963), 5. Stark's conclusions were based on data on the religious orientation of graduate students. Furthermore, Hadja found that graduate students who were self-defined intellectuals were less religiously involved than other graduate students. See Jan Hajda, "Alienation and Integration of Student Intellectuals," *American Sociological Review*, XXVI (October, 1961), 759-777. However, Greeley's data on Catholic graduate students suggest that a religious commitment and an intellectual orientation are not mutually exclusive. He found that church-going Catholic graduate students were as likely as non-religious students to plan academic careers and value creativity and were more likely to consider themselves intellectuals. See Andrew M. Greeley, "The Religious Behavior of Graduate Students," *Journal for the Scientific Study of Religion*, V (Fall, 1965), 34-40. See also Andrew M. Greeley, *Religion and Career* (New York: Sheed and Ward, 1963), pp. 49-55.

4. See Chapter 15. See also Harold W. Wilensky and Jack Ladinsky, "From Religious Community to Occupational Group: Structural Assimilation among Professors, Lawyers, and Engineers," *American Sociological Review*, XXXII (August, 1967), 549; John D. Murray, "The American Catholic Intellectual: An Empirical Test of the Intellectual Subsociety Hypothesis," unpublished Ph.D. dissertation, University of Massachusetts, 1969, pp. 50-83.

5. See Chapter 15.

olics holding the rank of assistant, associate, or full professor in the
arts and science programs of Catholic and non-Catholic colleges and
universities. Thirty interviews were conducted with a randomly selected sample of teachers from a Catholic liberal arts college and a Catholic university. An additional thirty interviews took place with a random sample of Catholic faculty members from three private nonsectarian liberal arts colleges and a public university. All interviews
were conducted in New England during the summer and fall of 1967.[6]

Intellectual identification. In each sample distinctions were made between intellectuals and nonintellectuals. Based initially on the rationale
that a distinguishing mark of the intellectual is the broad scope of his
nonprofessional interests, an index composed of the following six
items was used to differentiate between intellectuals and nonintellectuals: type of newspaper exposure, number of regularly-read nonprofessional periodicals, number of nonprofessional books read annually,
television viewing habits, number of motion pictures viewed annually,
and extensiveness of attendance at the performing arts and other cultural activities.[7]

Obviously, there are difficulties involved in defining intellectuals
by means of this index. It clearly does not tap all that is involved in
being an intellectual. However, if we assume that, at minimum, the
horizons of the academic intellectual extend beyond the narrow boundaries of his own field of professional specialization and involve the
quality of life, then we could reasonably expect certain patterns to exist
in his preferences in the media and performing arts—patterns that
would distinguish the intellectual in the academic life from his nonintellectually oriented colleagues. The logic of the media exposure scale
is, thus, clear. Its empirical validity was tested by means of the point
bi-serial measure of association with an alternative index of intellectual orientation, that of intellectual self-identification.[8]

6. For a more complete discussion of sample characteristics, see Chapter 15.
7. For a further discussion of this index of intellectuality, see Murray, *op. cit.*, pp.
17-20.
8. The correlation between the index of intellectual self-identification and the
media exposure index was statistically significant for both samples. The point bi-
serial measure of association between the two scales produced correlation coefficients
of .38 for the Catholic college sample (p = .05) and .44 for the sample of teachers at
non-Catholic institutions (p = .02). Obviously, discrepancies do exist between the
scores on the two scales for some of the subjects. It is important to stress, however,
that those individuals who scored "high" on the media exposure index also conceived
of themselves as intellectuals. This convergence between the two indices is expressed
by the fact that eleven out of twelve teachers at the Catholic colleges and eleven out

Religious communality. The concept of religious communality refers to the degree of intrareligious enclosure in social interaction and attitude. Individuals exhibit a religiously communal life style to the extent that they are oriented toward their co-religionists in their primary relationships and self-identification. The degree of religious communality of each respondent was determined by an index based upon the following five items: the proportion of close friends who are Catholic, the number of Catholic-sponsored social groups in which membership is held, frequency of church attendance, strength of identification with the Catholic community, and attitude toward interreligious marriage.[9]

Religious orthodoxy. In a period of widespread and deeply rooted religious ferment, when traditional theological distinctions and doctrinal interpretations are in a state of flux, it is singularly difficult to arrive at a workable and meaningful definition of "religious orthodoxy." It is possible, of course, to define orthodoxy simply as the acceptance of doctrines "held to be vitally true by the dominant section in a church or other body of religious believers."[10] But in the Christian churches today, and perhaps most notably in the Roman Catholic Church, the religious leaders and theologians are engaged in fundamental debate over the validity and relevance of traditional dogmatic teachings. When customary theological interpretations are in a process of radical change, it obviously becomes extremely difficult for the theologian to define the "approved" or "true" or "orthodox" beliefs of a religious organization which is very much involved in this process of change. Moreover, it becomes difficult for the social scientist to gauge the "orthodoxy" of members of such an organization.

The task of the social scientist is compounded, even during periods of relative religious stability, when the group whose beliefs he is attempting to investigate is assumed to be somewhat sophisticated theologically, or is at least aware of the complexity inherent in certain theological issues. The recent work of Charles Glock and Rodney Stark illustrates this problem.[11] They have devised a four-item index

---

of thirteen non-Catholic college faculty members who scored "high" in the media exposure scale also viewed themselves as intellectuals. This consideration reinforced the research strategy of placing primary emphasis on the media exposure index in the analysis of the data.

9. See Chapter 15 for a further discussion of this index. See also Murray *op. cit.*, pp. 66-69.

10. E. Royston Pike, *Encyclopedia of Religion and Religions* (New York: Meridian Books, 1958), p. 285.

11. Rodney Stark and Charles Y. Glock, *American Piety* (Berkeley: University of California Press, 1968).

to be used in measuring the religious orthodoxy of persons from a Christian background. But the index is structured in such a way that many, perhaps most, mainstream Christian theologians would be classified as religiously unorthodox in terms of the measures used in the index.[12] Furthermore, any layman who was even moderately aware of the theological undercurrents within Christianity during the last several decades would probably have difficulty in achieving a "high" orthodoxy score. A basic problem with this index, as well as with some other indices of religious orthodoxy, is that they actually come closer to tapping the intellectually simplistic religious beliefs of Christian fundamentalism rather than the "orthodoxy" of contemporary mainstream Christianity.

Because of the complexity involved in attempting to accurately measure the religious orthodoxy of the teachers in this study, it was decided simply to ask each respondent a series of open-ended questions on a variety of theological issues. A judgment was made as to whether a given response to a particular question tended toward a more traditional or "conservative," position or toward a more untraditional, or "liberal," position. What is important in these data is not a particular response to a single question but, rather, overall trends in the data that are suggestive of different patterns in religious beliefs and attitudes among the respondents. No attempt was made to assess the actual religious "orthodoxy" of the respondents.

Religious Beliefs

In a series of questions on religious beliefs, the respondents were asked, first, whether they agreed with the following traditional interpretation of the nature of religious belief: "Religious belief is an assent to a set of eternally valid, that is, unchanging truths." The Catholic college professors were slightly more likely than the non-sectarian college academicians to express general agreement with the statement (77 percent and 63 percent, respectively). When comparisons were made between those scoring "high" and "low" in religious communality, little difference was found between the two groups in the Catholic college sample. In the non-Catholic college sample, however, a

---

12. The four items in the index measure the respondent's belief in the following: (1) a personal God, (2) the divinity of Christ, (3) the actual occurrence of biblical miracles, and (4) the existence of devils. One point is given for each item in which the respondent expresses firm belief; a score of zero is given for each item in which the respondent expresses disbelief or even doubt. "High" orthodoxy indicates a total score of three or four; "low" orthodoxy indicates a total score of one or two.

significant difference existed between those exhibiting a "high" and "low" communal orientation; 75 percent of the former and only 32 percent of the latter expressed definite agreement with the statement (p = .05).

But it was the comparisons between the intellectuals and the non-intellectuals that produced the most interesting differences. In the Catholic college sample, only 17 percent of the intellectuals in comparison with 72 percent of the nonintellectuals indicated unqualified acceptance of the statement (p = .01). The corresponding figures for the second sample (23 percent and 59 percent, respectively; p = .10) showed a similar, though less striking, pattern. The following responses to the above definition of religious belief distinguish clearly between the intellectuals and the nonintellectuals.

Nonintellectuals

The statement accurately expresses what religious belief is all about—a response to an unchanging truth.

There have been many changes in church structure which I guess I have to accept. But doctrine never really changes. Only the words used to express the doctrine change.

Dogma never changes, because what is true cannot change. Sometimes what appears to be a truth may only be a working hypothesis which will be supplanted later.

Intellectuals

This statement is an accurate expression of the traditional Catholic position. I would disagree with the statement and all of the assumptions that underlie it.

Religious belief is simply an attitude toward self and others based on transcendence. This statement inhibits a vital religious life.

Belief is far more dynamic than this. Every individual is in a constant state of development, and, as he changes, his understanding of God and other religious concepts change. Religious truth is an evolving truth.

Thus, in both samples those respondents who were defined as intellectuals were significantly less likely than the non-intellectuals to interpret the nature of religious belief in the context of traditional Catholic theology, that is, as an assent by the individual to a set of immutable truths. Rather, the intellectuals tended to define the meaning of religious belief in the contemporary context of relativism and evolution.

Differences in religious orientation similar to the above pattern were

evident in responses to questions concerned with belief in God, Jesus
Christ, and the traditional teaching of the Roman Catholic Church on
the morality of birth control. In regard to belief in God, the respondents were asked the following question: "Do you believe in God as
He has been expounded traditionally by the Roman Catholic Church,
that is, as God the Father in the Trinity?" A majority of both samples
(67 percent of the Catholic college academicians and 60 percent of the
non-Catholic college academicians) answered affirmatively and without qualification.[13] When comparisons were made between those scoring
high and low in communalism, here, as in the question concerning the
nature of religious belief, the communally oriented teachers at the non-
Catholic colleges were most likely to hold a traditional position; 88 percent answered "yes" to the question on belief in God. Conversely, the
nonsectarian college faculty members who scored low in communality
were least likely to hold a traditional position; 50 percent answered the
question positively (p = .10). The corresponding figures for the Catholic
college sample were 71 percent and 62 percent, respectively. Furthermore,
the intellectuals in both samples were significantly less likely than the
nonintellectuals to express belief in a traditional conception of God. In
the Catholic college sample, 42 percent of the intellectuals in comparison
with 83 percent of the nonintellectuals answered "yes" to the question
(p = .05). The corresponding figures for the second sample were 31
percent and 82 percent (p = .01).

When asked the question, "Who is Jesus Christ?," 77 percent of
the teachers at the Catholic colleges and 67 percent of the teachers at
the nonsectarian colleges referred to the traditional Christian teaching
on the divinity of Christ.[14] Here again, the communally oriented
teachers at the non-Catholic colleges were most likely to express traditional beliefs concerning Jesus Christ, whereas their noncommunally
oriented colleagues were least likely to adhere to a traditional position
(88 percent and 59 percent, respectively). The corresponding figures for
the Catholic college sample were 76 percent and 77 percent, indicating
no difference between the communally oriented and noncommunally
oriented respondents. As with the previous questions on religious

13. In comparison, only 47 percent of the college teachers in Thalheimer's sample
held to a traditional conception of God. See Thalheimer, p. 104.
14. In a sample of 545 Roman Catholics in twenty-one northern California par-
ishes, Stark and Glock found that 86 percent of the Catholics expressed unqualified
belief in the divinity of Jesus Christ, and an additional 8 percent, while expressing
some doubts, felt that the doctrine was basically true. See Stark and Glock, *American
Piety*, p. 13.

belief, so here also were the intellectuals in both samples less likely than their colleagues to adhere to a traditional theological conception. In the Catholic college sample, only 42 percent of the intellectuals in comparison with all of the nonintellectuals expressed a belief that Jesus Christ was the Son of God. The corresponding figures for the second sample were 54 percent and 76 percent.

The patterns present in the above data on religious beliefs were also evident in the respondents' attitudes toward the traditional opposition of the Roman Catholic Church to the use of chemical and mechanical means of birth prevention.[15] While a minority of both samples (30 percent of the Catholic college teachers and 7 percent of the nonsectarian college teachers) felt that any modification in the official teaching of the Church was impossible, 43 percent of the Catholic college academicians and 50 percent of the teachers at the non-Catholic colleges expressed the attitude that the issue had already been decided in favor of "individual conscience." They believed that a decision on the morality of various methods of birth control was to be made by the married couples involved rather than by church authorities. As one respondent said: "As a result of the intolerable discontinuity between what has been said and what has been done, the issue has already been resolved in favor of individual conscience."

In following the patterns evident in the previous questions on religious beliefs, the respondents in the non-Catholic college sample who scored "high" on the communality index were the least likely group to feel that a decision on the use of birth control devices was to be left to the individual; in fact, none of them, in comparison with 68 percent of their noncommunally oriented colleagues, expressed such a position. The corresponding figures for the Catholic college sample were 39 percent and 62 percent, respectively (p = .10). And in both samples, the intellectuals were more likely than their nonintellectually oriented colleagues to reject the traditional Roman Catholic teaching on birth prevention. In the Catholic college sample 58 percent of the intellectuals and 33 percent of the nonintellectuals felt that questions concerning the morality of using various birth control devices were to be decided by the married couple directly involved. The respective figures for the non-Catholic college sample were 77 percent and 29 percent (p = .05).

15. The respondents were asked to comment on statements made in 1966 and 1967 by Pope Paul VI in which the Pope expressed his opposition to theologians who were arguing for the necessity of a modification in the Church's teaching on birth control.

The following responses accent the difference in the religious orientation of the intellectuals and the nonintellectuals with regard to the question of birth control:

Nonintellectuals

The Church has taught that any method outside of abstinence or rhythm is immoral. I don't see how this can possibly be changed.

The Pope has taken the proper posture. Within the Natural Law theory, the pill could be made acceptable, but I do not see how any other method could become authorized.

I really don't see the Church's opposition to artificial birth control as the terrible problem many people make it out to be. In the long run, they'll come up with an effective method for Catholics. Possibly some pill will be okayed, but nothing else.

Intellectuals

The Pope is answering politically to this issue. He will change. You can't reverse intellectual currents by fiat.

The pattern is already clear. First, the pill will be admitted, and later the whole Natural Law framework will go. The Council killed it, but the Pope has not caught up with the decisions of the Council.

The traditional teaching is as dead as anything could be. The Natural Law props for the Church's position are gone. The issue has already been resolved.

In summary, the data on religious beliefs show that the differences between the Catholics teaching at Catholic colleges and those teaching at non-sectarian institutions were insignificant; overall, the Catholic college faculty members were only slightly more traditional in their religious thinking. Interestingly, although religious communality revealed no association with religious "orthodoxy" in the Catholic college sample (with the exception of the birth control issue), the communally-oriented faculty at the non-sectarian colleges were far more likely than their noncommunal colleagues to hold to a traditional theological position. But the most significant findings involve the intellectuals. The respondents' intellectual orientation (as measured by the media exposure index) was strongly associated with overall theological position. The intellectuals at both the Catholic and the non-Catholic colleges were markedly less likely than their nonintellectual colleagues to express a traditional theological orientation. But it should be emphasized that these findings *do not mean that the intellectuals were less "religiously oriented" or less "orthodox," as such.* Perhaps what the data most clearly suggest is that these Catholic intellectuals simply were more aware of, and in agreement with, contemporary theological currents within the Church.[16]

Perspectives on Problem Areas Within the Church

In addition to the questions on basic religious beliefs, the respondents were asked a series of questions concerned with the problems currently facing the Catholic Church. These open-ended questions dealt with the respondents' attitudes on (1) the role and functioning of authority in the Church, (2) the respondents' relationships with clergymen, (3) the perception of anti-intellectualism within the Church, and (4) perspectives on the multifaceted changes occurring today within the Church.

Exactly half of each sample was explicitly critical of some aspect of the authority structure of the Catholic Church. Furthermore, it was the intellectual group in each sample which was most likely to voice criticism of church authority. Among the Catholic college teachers, 67 percent of the intellectuals and 33 percent of the nonintellectuals indicated objection to some aspect of authority within the Church (p = .10). The figures for the non-Catholic college sample were 77 percent and 24 percent, respectively (p = .01). The following comments convey effectively the difference between the two groupings:

Nonintellectuals

The purpose of authority in the Church is the same as authority anywhere—to interpret and enforce. Enforce is an odd word to use, but it's necessary.

16. It should be noted here that the intellectuals were relatively active churchgoers. In the Catholic college sample 82 percent of the intellectuals and 89 percent of the nonintellectuals attended church every week. The corresponding figures for the non-Catholic college sample were considerably lower; 62 percent of the intellectuals and 76 percent of the nonintellectuals participated in services weekly. However, the differences between the two samples declined sharply when comparisons were made between respondents who attended church at least twice a month. Here, 92 percent of the intellectuals and 94 percent of the nonintellectuals at the Catholic colleges were "frequent" if not "regular" churchgoers; the figures for the second sample were 85 percent and 88 percent, respectively.

What is perhaps most immediately significant in these findings is the comparatively high percentage of teachers in both samples who did attend weekly religious services. Thalheimer found that only 19 percent of his large sample of West Coast academicians attended church every week (Thalheimer, p. 103). And in Anderson's study of college teachers, it was found that only 31 percent of the Protestant faculty members and a negligible number of Jewish professors participated in religious services on either a weekly or at least a "frequent" basis. Furthermore, Stark and Glock found that 70 percent of a national sample of Catholics attended church services at least once a week (Stark and Glock, *American Piety*, pp. 85-86). Overall, then, the Catholic academicians in both samples were indeed quite active churchgoers.

Authority is necessary within the Church. Without authority the Church would be seriously impaired in its operation.

Authority is necessary for clarification and explanation. If I have a question on science, I consult an expert. The same thing applies to religious questions.

The hierarchy and authority are necessary for the preservation of unity and the upholding of doctrine. The major problem within the Church today is the rejection of authority by self-righteous theologians who are proclaiming the new gospel of freedom without regard to the consequences.

Intellectuals

The purpose of authority should be to legitimize some kind of belief structure. But these are words. There's been far too much authority in the Church.

The role of authority should be maintenance of the religious and moral heritage of the Church, an institution of long and revered history. But there has to be a considerable loosening up of the hierarchy's autocratic control.

Authority is a very complex concept. In the Catholic Church it is a patriarchal system that derives from the Jewish conception of God. It has not been particularly beneficial to the Church throughout its history.

In this century the hierarchy has been concerned with power and regulation and its continued existence and competitive survival. It should have provided moral leadership for the world, but it has failed tragically in its prophetic role.

The striking differences in attitude between the intellectuals and the nonintellectuals evident in the above data also characterized, although to a somewhat lesser extent, the responses to the following question: "How would you describe the relationship that exists between you and the Catholic clergy?" The split between the intellectuals and the nonintellectuals was particularly evident in the non-Catholic college sample: 77 percent of the intellectuals in comparison with only 29 percent of their nonintellectually oriented colleagues described their relations with clergymen in less than positive terms ($p = .05$). One teacher responded caustically: "I'm embarrassed in the presence of the Catholic clergy in this area. I know very well what they expect of me as an intellectual, and I feel they appreciate my friendship for very expedient reasons." More typical of the intellectuals' responses, however, was the comment: "Our relations are quite correct but not intimate." In the Catholic college sample, the difference between the intellectuals and the nonintellectuals, although not statistically significant, pointed in a direction similar to that of the non-Catholic college sample; two-thirds of the intellectuals and half of the nonintellectuals perceived a gap in their relations with clergymen. Many of the Catholic college intellectuals were particularly critical of their clerical colleagues rather than the parish clergy. As one of these professors said: "Many of them are scared of me because of my writing. The younger clergy are more sympathetic, but I would not say they are among my close friends." Another respondent was more emphatic: "When you work so closely with clergy on a so-called equal basis, and see so much pettiness and professional inadequacy covered up, and so much crass immorality, then you begin to wonder about a great many things. If you can teach in a Catholic college and keep your faith, you have a very strong faith."

Several of the Catholic college teachers were quick to state that the attitudes of the Catholic clergy and, in particular, the hierarchy were responsible for an undercurrent of anti-intellectualism within the American Catholic Church. Actually, 73 percent of the Catholic college sample in comparison with 47 percent of the non-Catholic college sample felt that there existed an observable amount of anti-intellectualism within the American Church (p = .01). Furthermore, 43 percent of the first sample and 27 percent of the second sample expressed the belief that this anti-intellectualism was "substantial." It was the intellectuals in both samples who were most likely to perceive a considerable amount of anti-intellectualism in the Church in the United States. This was particularly evident in the non-Catholic college sample, where 54 percent of the intellectuals in comparison with 6 percent of the nonintellectuals expressed this attitude (p = .01). The corresponding figures for the Catholic college sample were 58 percent and 33 percent.

An interesting difference was observed among those respondents who did perceive a substantial amount of anti-intellectualism within the American Church. In the Catholic college sample the source of the anti-intellectualism over-whelmingly was traced to the clergy and the hierarchy. The nonsectarian college teachers, however, found this anti-intellectualism rooted primarily not within the clergy but, rather, within the Catholic population as a whole. Compare the following sets of responses:

Catholic College Respondents

Intellectualism implies investigation and search for truth. Most problems are complex. They are either insoluable or at least do not lend themselves to easy solutions. But the clergy rely on black and white terms when dealing with religious issues.

Among the still-frightened clergy there is an intense anti-intellectualism. It's bred in the seminaries. Among Catholics as a whole—they constitute a most nonhomogeneous group. It depends on their social class.

One example of this anti-intellectualism is the Catholic hierarchy's patronizing attitude toward the laity. They felt until recent years that the laity could not think correctly.

It's not primarily in the Church populace as a whole but, rather, in the clergy —particularly in the colleges. They are afraid they may lose control of "their" institutions.

Non-Catholic College Respondents

The anti-intellectualism in the Church is merely a reflection of the American culture.

It's a very implicit anti-intellectualism. It's an attitudinal assumption on the part of the average churchgoer: Do not question it; it shakes everything up.

The anti-intellectualism of the Catholic Church in this country is depressing evidence that the Church has assimilated and accommodated itself to American society and culture with extraordinary success and completeness.

This anti-intellectualism comes from a huge mass of the American Catholic population that has a limited educational and cultural background and views with alarm anything outside a narrow structure of ideas. This is changing now.

Frequently encountered in the often intensely negative criticism of the functioning of the institutional Church was an attitude of guarded optimism on the part of respondents. The critics at both the Catholic and the non-Catholic colleges often qualified their at-times-biting commentary with such phrases as: "It's improving now"; "Things are beginning to change"; and "There's reason to be somewhat optimistic." Nowhere was this optimism over currents of change more evident than in the responses to an open-ended question concerned with the academicians' reaction to the changes introduced by the Second Vatican Council. Eighteen of the Catholic college teachers and twenty-one of the non-sectarian college teachers were explicitly positive in their reactions to the Vatican Council. As one respondent said: "The changes are fantastically revolutionary. The Church is being thrown into chaos and uncertainty, causing much insecurity. But chaos and uncertainty are not too high a price to pay for the enormous progress that's being made." Another commented: "This is a radical revolution—the fastest in the Church's history—even faster than the Protestant Reformation. It's a sign that the Church is very healthy today. But this good health will continue only if the reform keeps coming quickly."

Not all of the teachers were optimistic, however, over the current period of change in the Church. Seven respondents in each sample—only one of whom was defined as an intellectual—felt that the Council had proceeded too far in altering traditional teachings and structures within the Church. In the words of one teacher: "The reformers will accomplish from within the Church what has not been accomplished by forces outside the Church for 2,000 years: they will ultimately destroy it." Another commented: "It has been an aesthetic disaster. We are cheapening our liturgy and using appeals to the masses. I find it all very undignified."

At the other extreme, negative reactions to the Council's activity were expressed by another seven respondents—all of whom were defined as intellectuals—who felt that the process of change was too limited in scope. One teacher said: "I think of the changes as a desperate rearguard activity. They are not significant and not renewal." Another commented: "The Council's activity was superficial. There has been no real transformation of institutional structure or parish life, and there is the continued maintenance of a set of rigid, irrational dogmas." But this same respondent, in a note of optimism that characterized the majority of both samples, added: "Perhaps they didn't realize what they were doing, because there is now underway a widespread theological revolution which will have doctrinal ramifications in the future. They're beginning to confront the great discrepancy that exists between what people say they believe and what they do believe." Thus, in the data on reactions to changes in the Catholic Church, as elsewhere in this paper, the voices found to be most critical of traditionalism in the Church were those of the intellectuals.

Summary and Conclusions

The findings on basic religious beliefs and on attitudes toward selected problem areas within the Church indicate little difference between the Catholic college and non-Catholic college samples. But rather significant distinctions were found to exist between the intellectually oriented and the nonintellectually oriented faculty members in each sample. Consistently, the intellectuals at both the Catholic and the non-Catholic colleges were less traditional in their overall theological position than were their nonintellectually oriented colleagues. Furthermore, the intellectuals were considerably more critical of the authority structure in the Church, the role traditionally associated with Catholic clergymen, and the pace of institutional change within the Church.

Again, however, these findings should not be interpreted to mean that the intellectuals in the study were not "religious" or had disassociated themselves from the Church. Actually, the intellectuals in both samples were comparatively active churchgoers. What the data on religious beliefs may well indicate, as has been mentioned, is that the apparent heterodoxy of the intellectuals points to an awareness on their part of current theological trends and controversies within the Church. Certainly their comments did indicate an intellectual concern with both theological issues and structural problems facing the Church at the present time. On this level, then, it could be argued that they are, overall, more "religiously involved" than their nonintellectually oriented colleagues. It appears, then, that the data give little support to the argument of those writers who feel that religious belief is psychologically incompatible with an intellectual orientation. Evidently, the intellectually oriented teachers in this study found little conflict between religious values and scholarly commitment, at least on an operational level.

Admittedly, the data are, at times, highly qualitative, and they are certainly more suggestive than demonstrative. A more precise measure of religious orthodoxy undoubtedly would have strengthened the conclusions which can be drawn from the data. Such an index was not used simply because of the problems involved in constructing a valid index of religious orthodoxy at a time when traditionally "orthodox" doctrines are undergoing redefinition. In much of Christianity today, and certainly within Roman Catholic Christianity, the definition of "orthodoxy" is obscure, on both a conceptual and an operational level. And the application of existing indices of religious orthodoxy to a group of respondents assumed to be reasonably sophisticated theologically would not appear to resolve this problem.

VII

WORK AS POLITICAL RESPONSIBILITY

Academics are predominant among the "cultural workmen," as Mills calls intellectuals in his essay on the cultural default. Scholars, using a liberal rhetoric and allusions to an end of ideology, Mills charges, often conceal their conservative default, that is, their uncritical acceptance of official definitions of world reality. "What scientist," Mills asks, "can claim to be a part of the legacy of science and yet remain a hired technician of the military machine?" Not all cultural workmen have defaulted politically, however; a number of intellectuals have been involved in the critique of entrenched power and have proposed alternatives to existing structures.

Chomsky discusses some consequences for foreign policy that have stemmed from the cultural default. Perhaps the distortions of fact by bureaucratic intellectuals, as noted by Chomsky, arise from an inability of some academic intellectuals, when on the payroll of vested economic interests, to remain committed to the Jeffersonian ideal, cited by Roszak, of unmasking monopolies of honor, wealth, and power. The scholarly service of exposing, argues Roszak, has been neglected in favor of the utilitarian service of indiscriminately adapting "to every demand that monied interests and the general public could imagine making."

The extent to which many academics have responded favorably to the demands of monied military-industrial interests has been rather well documented, underneath the often flamboyant rhetoric, by today's student radicals. And, as Horowitz notes, the professorial response, with few exceptions, has been one of criticism rather than defense of these students. Horowitz describes a group that has been particularly severe in its criticism of the student left—the liberal academic establishment—and he explores the reasons for the professors' lack of confidence in the behavior and attitudes of the rebellious students and the students' mistrust of their professors.

Like their vociferous student critics, professors must select from a hierarchy of values to guide their behavior, for, ultimately, decisions cannot be based simply on fact. Lippman expects from academics not only unbiased inquiry but also commitment to a set of values that would continually reshape and redirect knowledge for wise, just, and humane uses. Only then, Lippman believes, can the academic community meet its responsibility of filling the spiritual and intellectual void caused by the dissolution of the ancestral order.

18.   The Cultural Default

C. WRIGHT MILLS

Intellectuals are now living in a world that drifts and is being thrust toward World War III. Both the drift and the thrust depend upon ideas: upon definitions of world reality and upon the acceptability of policies and lack of policies among elites, publics and masses. Intellectuals deal with ideas—with recollections of the past, definitions of the present, and images of possible futures. By intellectuals I mean scientists and artists, ministers and scholars; I mean those who represent the human intellect; those who are part of the great discourse of reason and inquiry, of sensibility and imagination that in the West began in Jerusalem and Athens and Rome, and that has been going on intermittently ever since. They are the organized memory of mankind, and such cultural apparatus as it has they create and they maintain. If they write, paint, speak, if they create and distribute images and ideas, their work is publicly relevant. In so far as it is attended to, it focuses the views of men; and it distracts attention from that which it ignores. It justifies authority or criticizes it.

Other men can feel that their power to reason, their skills to investigate, their ability to find out are inadequate to the situations they confront; they can feel that they are not expected to confront them. But intellectuals cannot. So long as they are intellectuals, they must reason and investigate and, with their passion to know, they must confront the situations of all men everywhere. That he expects this of himself is the mark of the intellectual as a type of social and moral creature. That he is alienated is another way of saying that he is capable of transcending drift, that he is capable of being man on his own.

Other men can mutter, with much justification, that they find nowhere to draw the line, to speak the emphatic "No." But it is the political and the intellectual job of the intellectual to draw just that line, to say the "No" loudly and clearly.

What scientist can claim to be part of the legacy of science and yet remain a hired technician of the military machine?

What man of God can claim to partake of the Holy Spirit, to know the life of Jesus, to grasp the meaning of that Sunday phrase "the brotherhood of man"—and yet sanction the insensibility, the immorality, the spiritual irresponsibility of the Caesars of our time?

What Western scholar can claim to be part of the big discourse of reason and yet retreat to formal trivialities and exact nonsense, in a world in which reason and freedom are being held in contempt, being smashed, being allowed to fade out of the human condition?

The answer to all these questions, if we remain generous in our conception of "cultural workmen," is quite plain: Very many scientists, very many preachers, very many intellectuals, are in default.

Scientists become subordinated parts of the Science Machines of over-developed nations; these machines have become essential parts of the apparatus of war; that apparatus is now among the prime causes of war; without scientists it could not be developed and maintained. Thus do scientists become helpful and indispensable technicians of the thrust toward war.

Preachers, rabbis, priests—standing in the religious default—allow immorality to find support in religion; they use religion to cloak and to support impersonal, wholesale murder—and the preparation for it. They condone the intent to murder millions of people by clean-cut young men flying and aiming intricate machineries toward Euro-Asia, zeroing in on cities full of human beings—young men who, two years before, were begging their fathers for the use of the family car for a Saturday-night date.

Intellectuals accept without scrutiny official definitions of world reality. Some of the best of them allow themselves to be trapped by the politics of anti-Stalinism, which has been a main passageway from the political thirties to the intellectual default of our apolitical time. They live and work in a benumbing society without living and working in protest and in tension with its moral and cultural insensibilities. They use the liberal rhetoric to cover the conservative default. They do not make available the knowledge and the sensibility required by publics, if publics are to hold responsible those who make decisions "in the name of the nation." They do not set forth reasons for human anger and give to it suitable targets.

1

Many intellectual fashions stand in the way of a release of the imagination—about the cold war, about the politics of peace, about any new beginnings at home and abroad. One such fashion is the sophisticated weariness of many NATO intellectuals with what they call "ideology" and their proclamation of "the end of ideology." So far as I know, this began in the mid-fifties, in intellectual circles more or less associated with the Congress for Cultural Freedom and the magazine *Encounter*, and now many take it up as a posture and as an unexamined slogan.

Smug conservatives, tired liberals and disillusioned radicals have carried on a kind of discourse in which issues are blurred and potential debate muted, the sickness of complacency prevails and reasoning collapses into reasonableness. Not liberalism as a political philosophy, but the liberal rhetoric is the common denominator of this approved style. Its sophistication is of tone rather than of ideas. The disclosure of fact—set forth in a bright-faced or a dead-pan manner—is the rule. The facts are duly weighed, carefully balanced, always hedged. Their power to outrage, their power to enlighten politically, their power to aid decision, even their power to clarify some specific situation—all that is blunted or destroyed.

Arguments of a displeasing kind and facts contrary to the general view are ignored by the more naïve celebrants of complacency. By the more wary they are duly recognized but neither connected with one another nor related to any general view. They are acknowledged in a scattered way but never put together: to do so is to risk being called, curiously enough, "one-sided" in one's observations and reflections.

Above all, there is a refusal to relate these isolated facts and fragmentary comments to the institutions of society, and to their changes. So there is no understanding of the structural realities which such facts might reveal, the longer trends of which they might be tokens. In brief: in this style, facts and ideas are isolated, and so the real questions are not even raised; the analysis of the meanings of facts not even begun.

Underneath this style of observation and comment there is the assumption that in the West there are no real issues or even problems of great seriousness left. That, in the end, is why it is a posture of "false consciousness": it stands in the way of considering with any chance of success what may be happening in the world.

First and above all, it does rest upon a simple provinciality. If the phrase "the end of ideology" has any meaning at all, it pertains to self-selected circles of intellectuals in the richer countries of the world. It is in fact merely their own self-image. The total population of these countries is a fraction of mankind; the period during which such a view has been assumed is very short indeed. To speak in such terms of much of

Latin America, Africa, Asia, the Soviet bloc, is ludicrous. It is a consensus of provincials about their own immediate and provincial position.

Second, "the end of ideology" is of course itself an ideology—a fragmentary one, to be sure, and perhaps more a posture. The end of ideology is in reality the ideology of an ending—the ending of political reflection itself as a public fact. It serves as a weary know-it-all justification, by tone of voice rather than by explicit argument, of the cultural and political defaults of the NATO intellectuals.

But the most important thing about all this is that it *is* merely a fashion. And fashions change. Already there are signs that the "end of ideology" fashion is on the way out. It is on the way out because it stands for the refusal to work out an explicit political philosophy, and alert men everywhere today feel the need of a political philosophy.

I.   It is surely obvious that any significant political reflection is *ideological:* in its terms policies, institutions, men of power are criticized or approved. In this respect, the "end of ideology" stands, negatively, for the attempt to withdraw oneself and one's work from political relevance; positively, it is an ideology of political complacency, and therefore comfortable for many writers who acquiesce in, or wish to justify, the status quo. But in addition to ideology, political philosophies also require attention to theories of society, history and human nature; to agencies of historical change; and to ideals.

II.   So far as orienting *theories* of society and of history are concerned, "the end of ideology" rests upon a fetish of empiricism: more academically, upon a pretentious methodology used to state trivialities about unimportant social areas; more essayistically, upon a naïve journalistic empiricism—which I have already characterized above—and upon a cultural gossip in which "answers" to the vital and pivotal issues are merely assumed. Thus does political bias masquerade as epistemological excellence, and there are no orienting theories.

III.   So far as *historic agencies of change* are concerned, the "end of ideology" rests upon an identity of such agencies with going institutions—perhaps upon their piecemeal reform, but never upon the search for agencies that might be used or that might themselves make for a structural change of society.

IV.   So far as political and human *ideals* are concerned, the "end of ideology" stands for a denial of their relevance—merely to hold such ideals seriously is, in this view, "utopian."

The practitioners of the "end of ideology" are left, it seems to me,

with a style of pseudo-sophisticated comment, along with a mutual cele-
bration of one another's "sober studies." Among them and for them
there are no real debates and no real issues. Their pessimism is part of
the fact, which they do not have the courage to assert, that in all truth
they see no way out.

Perhaps, given our task, we ought simply to ignore these historical
provincials, and their several fashions which have already come and
gone during our own short lifetime. We cannot altogether do so because
the terms they use, the feelings and the denial of feelings they embody,
stand in the way of our efforts to communicate. In the meantime, every
day about 3 o'clock in the afternoon, when our energies are beginning
to go, with Melville we exclaim: "O, Time! Cash! Patience!"

2

The withdrawal of cultural workmen from politics, in America especially, is part of the international default, which is both cultural and
political, of the Western world today. The young complacents of America, the tired old fighters, the smug liberals, the shrill ladies of jingoist
culture—they are all quite free. Nobody locks them up. Nobody has to.
They are locking themselves up—the shrill and angry ones in the to-
tality of their own parochial anger, the smug and complacent ones in
their own unimaginative ambitions. They do not examine the U.S.A. as
an overdeveloped society full of ugly waste and the deadening of human sensibility, honoring ignorance and the cheerful robot, pronounc-
ing the barren doctrine and submitting gladly, even with eagerness, to
the uneasy fun of a leisureless and emptying existence. Is not all this—
our intellectual condition—among the main points our friends in Poland and Hungary, in the Soviet Union and in Yugoslavia, ought to
grasp about the United States in the middle of the twentieth century?
In this time of total war and of official absurdity, should not the intellectual communities of the West decide again what they are about?

Not all cultural workmen have gone the way of official conformity
and intellectual default. Many, in fact, are now beginning to withdraw
from the rigid military definitions of the meaning of their scientific and
cultural work; they are beginning to transcend the nationalist
boundaries of the contemporary mind. The meetings of scientists from
both sides, arranged by Cyrus Eaton, are such a sign; the intellectual opposition to the Teller propaganda is another. There are many others.
Not all scientists identify science as a technological Second Coming.
Not all preachers are presenting arms. Not all of them are able to com-

fort themselves with that sophisticated variety of theology which tells us that sin is very serious indeed, probably even original; and that accordingly we should repent mightily as we bomb. The theological tranquillizers do not quiet all urges to moral passion that Christians and humanists feel.

Among cultural workmen there is an underground revulsion from official idiocy; there is an urge to speak as cultural workmen, as scientists and scholars, as designers and ministers, to act as definers of the human condition.

Western intellectuals should remember with humility, even with shame, that the first significant crack in the cold-war front was not made by those who enjoy the formal freedom of the Western democracies, but by the men who run the risk of being shot, imprisoned, driven to become nervous caricatures of human beings. The first significant cracks in the intellectual cold war came in the Communist world, after the death of Stalin. They were made not only by politicians but by professors, not only by factory workers but by writers, not only by the established but by students. They were made in Poland and Hungary and Yugoslavia, and they are still being made there. I know they are weak beginnings; that they falter and stumble. But talking in Warsaw and Zagreb and Vienna with some of those who have made the cultural break, I have seen the fingers of such men for two hours at a time continuously breaking up matchsticks on the table before them as they talk of possible new meanings of Marxism, as they try honestly to define the new beginnings in Eastern Europe after the death of Stalin. I have seen the strain and courage, and now in the inner forum of myself those Poles and Hungarians and Yugoslavs are included. I can no longer write seriously of social and political reality without writing to them as well as to the comfortable and the safe. I can no longer write seriously without feeling contempt for the different professors and smug editors of the overdeveloped societies in the West who so fearlessly fight the cold war, and for the cultural bureaucrats and hacks, the intellectual thugs of the official line who have so readily abdicated the intellect in the Soviet bloc. I can no longer write with moral surety unless I know that they will understand where I stand—and I think this means unless they know I have feelings of equal contempt for both leading types of underdeveloped cultural workmen of the overdeveloped countries of the world.

This is a time, I am contending, when the power of the intellectual has become potentially very great indeed. Surely there will be little disagreement among sane men that these powers are urgently needed in the construction of peaceful human societies. There is less "necessity" for more military emphasis on missiles than for moral and political imagination. There is less "need" for more Science in education than for more education in the uses of science. It is less "realistic" to spend more money on arms than to stop at once—and, if must be, unilaterally—all preparation of World War III. There is no other realism, no other necessity, no other need. If they do not mean these things, necessity and need and realism are merely the desperate slogans of the morally crippled.

War is not inevitable today; it is, immediately, the result of nationalist definitions of world reality, of dogmatic reliance upon military endeavor as the major or even the only means of solving the explosive social problems of this epoch of despair and terror. And because this is now so, to cultivate moral sensibility and to make it knowledgeable is the strategic task of those intellectuals who would be at peace. They *should* debate short-run and immediate policies, but, even more, they should confront the whole attitude toward war, they should teach new views of it, and on this basis they should criticize current policies and decisions.

Every time intellectuals have the chance to speak yet do not speak, they join the forces that train men not to be able to think and imagine and feel in morally and politically adequate ways. When they do not demand that the secrecy that makes elite decisions absolute and unchallengeable be removed, they too are part of the passive conspiracy to kill off public scrutiny. When they do not speak, when they do not demand, when they do not think and feel and act as intellectuals—and so as public men—they too contribute to the moral paralysis, the intellectual rigidity, that now grip both leaders and led around the world.

19. The Responsibility of Intellectuals

NOAM CHOMSKY

Twenty years ago, Dwight Macdonald published a series of articles in
Politics on the responsibilities of peoples, and specifically, the responsibility of intellectuals. I read them as an undergraduate, in the years
just after the war, and had occasion to read them again a few months
ago. They seem to me to have lost none of their power of persuasiveness.
Macdonald is concerned with the question of war guilt. He asks the question: To what extent were the German or Japanese people responsible
for the atrocities committed by their governments? And, quite properly,
he turns the question back to us: To what extent are the British or American people responsible for the vicious terror bombings of civilians, per-
fected as a technique of warfare by the Western democracies and reaching their culmination in Hiroshima and Nagasaki, surely among the
most unspeakable crimes in history? To an undergraduate in 1945-1946
—to anyone whose political and moral consciousness had been formed
by the horrors of the 1930s, by the war in Ethiopia, the Russian purge,
the "China incident," the Spanish Civil War, the Nazi atrocities, the
Western reaction to these events and, in part, complicity in them—these
questions had particular significance and poignancy.

With respect to the responsibility of intellectuals, there are still other,
equally disturbing questions. Intellectuals are in a position to expose
the lies of governments, to analyze actions according to their causes and
motives and often hidden intentions. In the Western world
at least, they have the power that comes from political liberty, from access to information and freedom of expression. For a privileged minority, Western democracy provides the leisure, the facilities, and the training to seek the truth lying hidden behind the veil of distortion
and misrepresentation, ideology, and class interest through which the

This is a revised version of a talk given at Harvard and published in *Mosaic*,
June 1966. It appeared in substantially this form in the *New York Review of Books*,
February 23, 1967. The present version is reprinted from Theodore Roszak, ed., *The
Dissenting Academy* (New York, Pantheon Books, 1968).

events of current history are presented to us. The responsibilities of intellectuals, then, are much deeper than what Macdonald calls the "responsibility of peoples," given the unique privileges that intellectuals enjoy.

The issues that Macdonald raised are as pertinent today as they were twenty years ago. We can hardly avoid asking ourselves to what extent the American people bear responsibility for the savage American assault on a largely helpless rural population in Vietnam, still another atrocity in what Asians see as the "Vasco da Gama era" of world history. As for those of us who stood by in silence and apathy as this catastrophe slowly took shape over the past dozen years, on what page of history do we find our proper place? Only the most insensible can escape these questions. I want to return to them, later on, after a few scattered remarks about the responsibility of intellectuals and how, in practice, they go about meeting this responsibility in the mid-1960s.

It is the responsibility of intellectuals to speak the truth and to expose lies. This, at least, may seem enough of a truism to pass without comment. Not so, however. For the modern intellectual, it is not at all obvious. Thus we have Martin Heidegger writing, in a pro-Hitler declaration of 1933, that "truth is the revelation of that which makes a people certain, clear, and strong in its action and knowledge"; it is only this kind of "truth" that one has a responsibility to speak. Americans tend to be more forthright. When Arthur Schlesinger was asked by the *New York Times*, in November 1965, to explain the contradiction between his published account of the Bay of Pigs incident and the story he had given the press at the time of the attack, he simply remarked that he had lied; and a few days later, he went on to compliment the *Times* for also having suppressed information on the planned invasion, in "the national interest," as this was defined by the group of arrogant and deluded men of whom Schlesinger gives such a flattering portrait in his recent account of the Kennedy administration. It is of no particular interest that one man is quite happy to lie in behalf of a cause which he knows to be unjust; but it is significant that such events provoke so little response in the intellectual community—no feeling, for example, that there is something strange in the offer of a major chair in humanities to a historian who feels it to be his duty to persuade the world that an American-sponsored invasion of a nearby country is nothing of the sort. And what of the incredible sequence of lies on the part of our government and its spokesmen concerning such matters as negotiations in Vietnam? The facts are known to all who care to know. The press, foreign and domestic, has presented documentation to refute each false-hood as it appears. But the power of the government propaganda appara-tus is such that the citizen who does not undertake a research project on the subject can hardly hope to confront government pronouncements with fact.[1]

The deceit and distortion surrounding the American invasion of Vietnam are by now so familiar that they have lost their power to shock. It is therefore well to recall that although new levels of cynicism are constantly being reached, their clear antecedents were accepted at home with quiet toleration. It is a useful exercise to compare government state-ments at the time of the invasion of Guatemela in 1954 with Eisen-hower's admission—to be more accurate, his boast—a decade later that American planes were sent "to help the invaders."[2] Nor is it only in mo-ments of crisis that duplicity is considered perfectly in order. "New Frontiersmen," for example, have scarcely distinguished themselves by a passionate concern for historical accuracy, even when they are not be-ing called upon to provide a "propaganda cover" for ongoing actions. For example, Arthur Schlesinger describes the bombing of North Viet-nam and the massive escalation of military commitment in early 1965 as based on a "perfectly rational argument": ". . . so long as the Viet-cong thought they were going to win the war, they obviously would not

1. Such a rsearch project has now been undertaken and published as a "Citizens' White Paper": F. Schurmann, P. D. Scott, and R. Zelnik, *The Politics of Escalation in Vietnam* (New York, Fawcett World Library, and Boston, Beacon Press, 1966). For further evidence of American rejection of United Nations initiatives for diplomatic settlement, just prior to the major escalation of February 1965, see Mario Rossi, "The US Rebuff to U Thant," *New York Review of Books*, November 17, 1966. See also Theodore Draper, "How Not To Negotiate," *New York Review of Books*, May 4, 1967. There is further documentary evidence of NLF attempts to establish a coalition gov-ernment and to neutralize the area, all rejected by the United States and its Saigon ally, in Douglas Pike, *Viet Cong* (Cambridge, Mass., The M.I.T. Press, 1966). In reading material of this latter sort one must be especially careful to distinguish between the evidence presented and the "conclusions" that are asserted, for reasons noted briefly below. . . .

It is interesting to see the first, somewhat oblique published reactions to *The Politics of Escalation* by those who defend our right to conquer South Vietnam and institute a government of our choice. For example, Robert Scalapino (*New York Times Magazine*, December 11, 1966) argues that the thesis of the book implies that our leaders are "diabolical." Since no right-thinking person can believe this, the thesis is refuted. To assume otherwise would betray "irresponsibility," in a unique sense of this term—a sense that gives an ironic twist to the title of this chapter. He goes on to point out the alleged central weakness in the argument of the book, namely, the failure to per-ceive that a serious attempt on our part to pursue the possibilities for a diplomatic settlement would have been interpreted by our adversaries as a sign of weakness.

2. *New York Times*, October 14, 1965.

be interested in any kind of negotiated settlement."[3] The date is important. Had the statement been made six months earlier, one could attribute it to ignorance. But this statement appeared after months of front-page news reports detailing the United Nations, North Vietnamese, and Soviet initiatives that preceded the February 1965 escalation and that, in fact, continued for several weeks after the bombing began, after months of soul-searching by Washington correspondents who were trying desperately to find some mitigating circumstances for the startling deception that had been revealed. (Chalmers Roberts, for example, wrote with unconscious irony that late February 1965 "hardly seemed to Washington to be a propitious moment for negotiations [since] Mr. Johnson . . . had just ordered the first bombing of North Vietnam in an effort to bring Hanoi to a conference table where bargaining chips on both sides would be more closely matched."[4]) Coming at this moment, Schlesinger's statement is less an example of deceit than of contempt—contempt for an audience that can be expected to tolerate such behavior with silence, if not approval.[5]

To turn to someone closer to the actual formation and implementation of policy, consider some of the reflections of Walt Rostow, a man who, according to Schlesinger, brought a "spacious historical view" to the conduct of foreign affairs in the Kennedy administration.[6] According to his analysis, the guerrilla warfare in Indochina in 1946 was

3. *Ibid.*, February 6, 1966.
4. *Boston Globe*, November 19, 1965.
5. At other times, Schlesinger does indeed display admirable scholarly caution. For example, in his introduction to *The Politics of Escalation* he admits that there may have been "flickers of interest in negotiations" on the part of Hanoi. As to the administration's lies about negotiations and its repeated actions undercutting tentative initiatives towards negotiations, he comments only that the authors may have underestimated military necessity and that future historians may prove them wrong. This caution and detachment must be compared with Schlesinger's attitude towards renewed study of the origins of the Cold War: in a letter to the *New York Review of Books*, October 20, 1966, he remarked that it is time to "blow the whistle" on revisionist attempts to show that the Cold War may have been the consequence of something more than mere Communist belligerence. We are to believe, then, that the relatively straightforward matter of the origins of the Cold War is settled beyond discussion, whereas the much more complex issue of why the United States shies away from a negotiated settlement in Vietnam must be left to future historians to ponder.

It is useful to bear in mind that the United States government itself is on occasion much less diffident in explaining why it refuses to contemplate a meaningful negotiated settlement. As is freely admitted, this solution would leave it without power to control the situation. . . .

6. Arthur M. Schlesinger, Jr., *A Thousand Days: John F. Kennedy in the White House* (Boston, Houghton Mifflin Company, 1965), p. 421.

launched by Stalin,[7] and Hanoi initiated the guerrilla war against South Vietnam in 1958 (*The View from the Seventh Floor*, pp. 39 and 152). Similarly, the Communist planners probed the "free world spectrum of defense" in Northern Azerbaijan and Greece (where Stalin "supported substantial guerrilla warfare"—*ibid.*, pp. 36 and 148), operating from plans carefully laid in 1945. And in Central Europe, the Soviet Union was not "prepared to accept a solution which would remove the dangerous tensions from Central Europe at the risk of even slowly staged corrosion of communism in East Germany" (*ibid.*, p. 156).

It is interesting to compare these observations with studies by scholars actually concerned with historical events. The remark about Stalin's initiating the first Vietnamese war in 1946 does not even merit refutation. As to Hanoi's purported initiative of 1958, the situation is more clouded. But even government sources[8] concede that in 1959 Hanoi received the first direct reports of what Diem referred to[9] as his own Algerian war, and that only after this did they lay their plans to involve themselves in this struggle. In fact, in December 1958 Hanoi made another of its many attempts—rebuffed once again by Saigon and the United States—to establish diplomatic and commercial relations with the Saigon government on the basis of the status quo.[10] Rostow offers no evidence of Stalin's support for the Greek guerrillas: in fact, though the historical record is far from clear, it seems that Stalin was by no means pleased with the adventurism of the Greek guerrillas, who, from

7. Walt W. Rostow, *The View from the Seventh Floor* (New York, Harper & Row, Publishers, 1964), p. 149. See also his *United States in the World Arena* (New York, Harper & Row, Publishers, 1960), p. 244: "Stalin, exploiting the disruption and weakness of the postwar world, pressed out from the expanded base he had won during the Second World War in an effort to gain the balance of power in Eurasia . . . turning to the East, to back Mao and to enflame the North Korean and Indochinese Communists. . . ."

8. For example, the article by CIA analyst George Carver, "The Faceless Viet Cong," in *Foreign Affairs*, Vol. 44 (April 1966), pp. 347-72. . . .

9. Cf. Jean Lacouture, *Vietnam: Between Two Truces* (New York, Random House, 1966), p. 21. Diem's analysis of the situation was shared by Western observers at the time. See, for example, the comments of William Henderson, Far Eastern specialist and executive, Council on Foreign Relations, in Richard W. Lindholm, ed., *Vietnam: The First Five Years* (East Lansing, Michigan State University Press, 1959). He notes "the growing alienation of the intelligentsia," "the renewal of armed dissidence in the South," the fact that "security has noticeably deteriorated in the last two years," all as a result of Diem's "grim dictatorship," and predicts "a steady worsening of the political climate in free Vietnam, culminating in unforeseen disasters."

10. See Bernard Fall, "Vietnam in the Balance," *Foreign Affairs*, Vol. 45 (October 1966), pp. 1-18.

his point of view, were upsetting the satisfactory postwar imperialist settlement.[11]

Rostow's remarks about Germany are more interesting still. He does not see fit to mention, for example, the Russian notes of March-April 1952, which proposed unification of Germany under internationally supervised elections, with withdrawal of all troops within a year, *if* there was a guarantee that a reunified Germany would not be permitted to join a Western military alliance.[12] And he has also momentarily forgotten his own characterization of the strategy of the Truman and Eisenhower administrations: "to avoid any serious negotiation with the Soviet Union until the West could confront Moscow with German rearmament within an organized European framework, as a *fait accompli*"[13]—to be sure, in defiance of the Potsdam agreements.

11. Stalin was pleased neither by the Titoist tendencies inside the Greek Communist party nor by the possibility that a Balkan federation might develop under Titoist leadership. It is nevertheless conceivable that Stalin supported the Greek guerrillas at some stage of the rebellion, in spite of the difficulty in obtaining firm documentary evidence. Needless to say, no elaborate study is necessary to document the British or American role in this civil conflict, from late 1944. See D. G. Kousoulas, *The Price of Freedom* (Syracuse, N.Y., Syracuse University Press, 1953), and *Revolution and Defeat* (New York, Oxford University Press, 1965), for serious study of these events from a strongly anti-Communist point of view.

12. For a detailed account, see James Warburg, *Germany: Key to Peace* (Cambridge, Mass., Harvard University Press, 1953), pp. 189f. Warburg concludes that apparently "the Kremlin was now prepared to accept the creation of an All-German democracy in the Western sense of that word," whereas the Western powers, in their response, "frankly admitted their plan 'to secure the participation of Germany in a purely defensive European community'" (i.e. NATO).

13. *The United States in the World Arena*, pp. 344-45. Incidentally, those who quite rightly deplore the brutal suppression of the Eastern German and Hungarian revolutions would do well to remember that these scandalous events might have been avoided had the United States been willing to consider proposals for neutralization of Central Europe. Some of George Kennan's recent statements provide interesting commentary on this matter, for example, his comments on the falsity, from the outset, of the assumption that the USSR intended to attack or intimidate by force the Western half of the continent and that it was deterred by American force, and his remarks on the sterility and general absurdity of the demand for unilateral Soviet withdrawal from East Germany together with "the inclusion of a united Germany as a major component in a Western defense system based primarily on nuclear weaponry" (Edward Reed, ed., *Peace on Earth* [New York, Pocket Books, 1965]).

It is worth noting that historical fantasy of the sort illustrated in Rostow's remarks has become a regular State Department specialty. Thus we have Thomas Mann justifying our Dominican intervention as a response to actions of the "Sino-Soviet military bloc." Or, to take a more considered statement, we have William Bundy's analysis of stages of development of Communist ideology in his Pomona College address, February 12, 1966, in which he characterizes the Soviet Union in the 1920s and early 1930s as "in a highly militant and aggressive phase." What is frightening about fantasy, as distinct from outright falsification, is the possibility that it may be sincere and may actually serve as the basis for formation of policy.

But most interesting of all is Rostow's reference to Iran. The facts are
that there was a Russian attempt to impose by force a pro-Soviet government in Northern Azerbaijan that would grant the Soviet Union access to Iranian oil. This was rebuffed by superior Anglo-American force
in 1946, at which point the more powerful imperialism obtained full
rights to Iranian oil for itself, with the installation of a pro-Western government. We recall what happened when, for a brief period in the early
1950s, the only Iranian government with something of a popular base
experimented with the curious idea that Iranian oil should belong to the
Iranians. What is interesting, however, is the description of Northern
Azerbaijan as part of "the free world spectrum of defense." It is pointless, by now, to comment on the debasement of the phrase "free world."
But by what law of nature does Iran, with its resources, fall within Western dominion? The bland assumption that it does is most revealing of deep-seated attitudes towards the conduct of foreign affairs.

In addition to this growing lack of concern for truth, we find, in recent statements, a real or feigned naiveté with regard to American actions that reaches startling proportions. For example, Arthur Schlesinger
has recently characterized our Vietnamese policies of 1954 as "part of
our general program of international goodwill."[14] Unless intended as
irony, this remark shows either a colossal cynicism or an inability, on a
scale that defies comment, to comprehend elementary phenomena of contemporary history. Similarly, what is one to make of the testimony of
Thomas Schelling before the House Foreign Affairs Committee, January 27, 1966, in which he discusses the two great dangers if all Asia
"goes Communist"?[15] First, this would exclude "the United States and
what we call Western civilization from a large part of the world that is
poor and colored and potentially hostile." Second, "a country like the
United States probably cannot maintain self-confidence if just about the
greatest thing it ever attempted, namely to create the basis for decency
and prosperity and democratic government in the underdeveloped
world, had to be acknowledged as a failure or as an attempt that we
wouldn't try again." It surpasses belief that a person with even minimal
acquaintance with the record of American foreign policy could produce
such statements.

It surpasses belief, that is, unless we look at the matter from a more
historical point of view, and place such statements in the context of the

14. *New York Times*, February 6, 1966.
15. *United States Policy Toward Asia*, Hearings before the Subcommittee on the
Far East and the Pacific of the Committee on Foreign Affairs, House of Representatives
(Washington, Government Printing Office, 1966), p. 89.

hypocritical moralism of the past; for example, of Woodrow Wilson, who was going to teach the Latin Americans the art of good government, and who wrote (1902) that it is "our peculiar duty" to teach colonial peoples "order and self-control ... [and] ... the drill and habit of law and obedience." Or of the missionaries of the 1840s, who described the hideous and degrading opium wars as "the result of a great design of Providence to make the wickedness of men subserve his purposes of mercy toward China, in breaking through her wall of exclusion, and bringing the empire into more immediate contact with western and Christian nations." Or, to approach the present, of A. A. Berle, who, in commenting on the Dominican intervention, has the impertinence to attribute the problems of the Caribbean countries to imperialism—*Russian* imperialism.[16]

As a final example of this failure of skepticism, consider the remarks of Henry Kissinger in concluding his presentation in a Harvard-Oxford television debate on American Vietnam policies. He observed, rather sadly, that what disturbs him most is that others question not our judgment but our motives—a remarkable comment on the part of one whose professional concern is political analysis, that is, analysis of the actions of governments in terms of motives that are unexpressed in official propaganda and perhaps only dimly perceived by those whose acts they govern. No one would be disturbed by an analysis of the political behavior of Russians, French, or Tanzanians, questioning their motives and interpreting their actions in terms of long-range interests, perhaps well concealed behind official rhetoric. But it is an article of faith that American motives are pure and not subject to analysis (see note 1). Although it is nothing new in American intellectual history—or, for that matter, in the general history of imperialist apologia—this innocence becomes increasingly distasteful as the power it serves grows more dominant in world affairs and more capable, therefore, of the unconstrained viciousness that the mass media present to us each day. We are hardly the first power in history to combine material interests, great technological capacity, and an utter disregard for the suffering and misery of the lower orders. The long tradition of naiveté and self-righteousness that disfigures our intellectual history, however, must serve as a warning to the Third

16. *New York Times Book Review*, November 20, 1966. Such comments call to mind the remarkable spectacle of President Kennedy counseling Cheddi Jagan on the dangers of entering into a trading relationship "which brought a country into a condition of economic dependence." The reference, of course, is to the dangers in commercial relations with the Soviet Union. See Schlesinger, *A Thousand Days*, p. 776.

World, if such a warning is needed, as to how our protestations of sincerity and benign intent are to be interpreted.

The basic assumptions of the "New Frontiersmen" should be pondered carefully by those who look forward to the involvement of academic intellectuals in politics. For example, I have referred to Arthur Schlesinger's objections to the Bay of Pigs invasion, but the reference was imprecise. True, he felt that it was a "terrible idea," but "not because the notion of sponsoring an exile attempt to overthrow Castro seemed intolerable in itself." Such a reaction would be the merest sentimentality, unthinkable to a tough-minded realist. The difficulty, rather, was that it seemed unlikely that the deception could succeed. The operation, in his view, was ill-conceived but not otherwise objectionable.[17] In a similar vein, Schlesinger quotes with approval Kennedy's "realistic" assessment of the situation resulting from Trujillo's assassination: "There are three possibilities in descending order of preference: a decent democratic regime, a continuation of the Trujillo regime or a Castro regime. We ought to aim at the first, but we really can't renounce the second until we are sure that we can avoid the third."[18] The reason why the third possibility is so intolerable is explained a few pages later: "Communist success in Latin America would deal a much harder blow to the power and influence of the United States." Of course, we can never really be sure of avoiding the third possibility; therefore, in practice, we will always settle for the second, as we are now doing in Brazil and Argentina, for example.[19]

Or consider Walt Rostow's views on American policy in Asia.[20] The basis on which we must build this policy is that "we are openly threatened and we feel menaced by Communist China." To prove that we are menaced is of course unnecessary, and the matter receives no attention; it is enough that we feel menaced. Our policy must be based on our national heritage and our national interests. Our national heritage is briefly outlined in the following terms: "Throughout the nineteenth century, in good conscience Americans could devote themselves to the extension of both their principles and their power on this continent," making use of "the somewhat elastic concept of the Monroe doc-

17. *A Thousand Days*, p. 252.
18. *Ibid.*, p. 769.
19. Though this too is imprecise. One must recall the real character of the Trujillo regime to appreciate the full cynicism of Kennedy's "realistic" analysis.
20. Walt W. Rostow and R. W. Hatch, *An American Policy in Asia* (New York, Technology Press and John Wiley & Sons, Inc., 1955).

trine" and, of course, extending "the American interest to Alaska and the mid-Pacific islands. . . . Both our insistence on unconditional surrender and the idea of post-war occupation . . . represented the formulation of American security interests in Europe and Asia." So much for our heritage. As to our interests, the matter is equally simple. Fundamental is our "profound interest that societies abroad develop and strengthen those elements in their respective cultures that elevate and protect the dignity of the individual against the state." At the same time, we must counter the "ideological threat," namely "the possibility that the Chinese Communists can prove to Asians by progress in China that Communist methods are better and faster than democratic methods." Nothing is said about those people in Asian cultures to whom our "conception of the proper relation of the individual to the state" may not be the uniquely important value, people who might, for example, be concerned with preserving the "dignity of the individual" against concentrations of foreign or domestic capital, or against semifeudal structures (such as Trujillo-type dictatorships) introduced or kept in power by American arms. All of this is flavored with allusions to "our religious and ethical value systems" and to our "diffuse and complex concepts" which are to the Asian mind "so much more difficult to grasp" than Marxist dogma, and are so "disturbing to some Asians" because of "their very lack of dogmatism."

Such intellectual contributions as these suggest the need for a correction to De Gaulle's remark, in his memoirs, about the American "will to power, cloaking itself in idealism." By now, this will to power is not so much cloaked in idealism as it is drowned in fatuity. And academic intellectuals have made their unique contribution to this sorry picture.

20. On Academic Delinquency

THEODORE ROSZAK

There was a time when men of intellect described the purpose of their lives in ways that stirred the souls of the noble and chilled the blood of the base . . .

If those of us who teach in the universities today were to observe this fact, how many of our students would believe or understand us? And of those who did believe and understand, how many would have learned what they knew from the lessons and examples we have set for them?

"Dare to know!" So Kant defined the function of intellect in a day which pursued the critical examination of life and society neither as an amusing pastime nor as a lucrative career, but rather as an act of defiance and of risk. It was a day in which men of intellect carried banners as if to battle and on them inscribed mottoes of impudent and hazardous intention. "Everything," Diderot insisted, "must be examined, everything must be shaken up, without exception and without circumspection." And *"écrasez l'infâme!"* Voltaire commanded. These were marked men and they knew it. With Jefferson, their intellectuality was an oath sworn upon an altar against enemies who were many and mighty. Denouncing the *Encyclopédie* on the eve of its suppression, the Attorney General of France drew the line between official authority and the free intellect with menacing precision.

Society, Religion, and the State present themselves today at the tribunal of justice in order to submit their complaints. . . . Impiety walks with head held high. . . . Humanity shudders, the citizenry is alarmed. . . .

It is with grief that we are forced to say it: can one conceal from oneself that there is a project formed, a Society organized, to propagate materialism, to destroy Religion, to inspire a spirit of independence, and to nourish the corruption of morals? . . .[1]

1. Arthur M. Wilson, *Diderot: The Testing Years* (New York, Oxford University Press, 1957), p. 333.

But the great project went forward nonetheless, though its authors were driven to desperation and ruin.

That was one age . . . and this is another. And what are the imperatives our students would find inscribed upon their teachers' lives? "Secure the grant!" "Update the bibliography!" "Publish or perish!" The academic life may be busy and anxious, but it is the business and anxiety of careerist competition that fills it, not that of a dangerous venture. So it is by and large outside the boundaries of the academic profession that our students must look for the defiant minds of the time.

But then let us admit that the academy has very rarely been a place of daring. One might perhaps count on the fingers of one hand the eras in which the university has been anything better than the handmaiden of official society: the social club of ruling elites, the training school of whatever functionaries the status quo required. The great minds of the Enlightenment—and especially the French *philosophes*—were not, of course, academics. They preferred to think of themselves as "men of letters." Most contemporary studies identify them by the more generic and free-wheeling term "intellectuals": non-university-related thinkers and writers. The distinction is historically correct, but too often it becomes, for the academic, a convenient moral barricade. "*They* were intellectuals; *I* am an academic. *Theirs* is not *my* tradition. *Their* ideals place no claim upon *me*." But why weren't the *philosophes* university men? Because the universities of their day proved to be inhospitable to the most advanced, critical thought of the time. Important intellectual history *had* to be made outside the oppressive environment of the academic establishment. The *philosophes* were no academics, because to be an academic in their age required that one be a petty and irrelevant mind, thus a "safe" mind from the viewpoint of the authorities. The contemporary academic who connects himself with the tradition such minds represent, claims a pedigree that is historically legitimate but not, alas, ethically ennobling.

The American university has been no exception to the historical rule. It has offered its academics little opportunity to disconnect from this dismal tradition of official conformity. No doubt if Jefferson had had his way, things would have been different. For Jefferson, the purpose of the academy—as he outlined it in his plans for the University of Virginia—was to exercise an independent criticism of those forces of church or state which "fear every change, as endangering the comforts they now hold." The university was to "unmask their usurpation, and monopolies of honors, wealth, and power."[2] But Jefferson's influence was limited to one school and to his own lifetime. While his controversial ideals of nonsectarianism and the teaching of practical knowledge were eventually picked up later in the nineteenth century by the great state universities, his ideal of independent criticism never proved acceptable to the forces of church, state, or corporate wealth which were to dominate the funding of higher education.

Interestingly enough, it was, in the early nineteenth century as it is now, very largely the students who exercised initiative in demanding that a critical social relevance should be an integral part of their education. The medium which the students chose for this objective was the extracurricular literary (or debating) societies. These societies, which sprang up in the wake of the Revolution, were by far the most vital element in American education through the first third of the nineteenth century. Their purpose was to study and debate the issues of the day, very much in the tradition of the *philosophes*.

... the propagation of dogma was not the purpose of the literary societies. They, instead, respected reason, nurtured intellect, and subjected much that was established to scrutiny and debate. . . .[3]

The clubs also served to bring controversial speakers to the campus (like Rufus Choate and Ralph Waldo Emerson; the latter was frequently denied the use of college buildings on campuses where he spoke), produced literary magazines, and assembled the best libraries of current literature available.[4] As one might imagine, the clubs were never well accepted by college authorities.

But with the weakening of the debate tradition (mainly before the advance of the fraternities) it is only at exceptional schools like the early Oberlin that we find the ideal of dissent being honored. Oberlin was consecrated from its beginning to an activist Christianity that rapidly led to a dissenting position on the issue of slavery. The resistance of the campus and the students to the often violent dislike of the

2. From Jefferson's Education Bill of 1779. For a study of Jefferson's theories see Roy J. Honeywell, *The Educational Work of Thomas Jefferson* (New York, Russell & Russell Publishers, 1964).

3. Frederick Rudolph, *The American College and University* (New York, Vintage Books, 1965), p. 141.

4. On the literary clubs, see H. D. Sheldon, *Student Life and Customs* (New York, D. Appleton & Co., 1901).

surrounding community was quite heroic.[5] But by the end of the century, when the modern academic establishment had fully "arrived," the closest any of the major universities cared to come to exercising an independent critical function was in providing expert advice to state legislative committees and personnel for the regulatory agencies that were becoming a feature of industrial America. The University of Wisconsin probably went furthest in formulating this type of service into a doctrine—especially during the presidency of Charles Van Hise. But even at Wisconsin, the administration decided to put the patriotic screws on once the First World War began: expert criticism, yes; radical dissent, no.

Since that time American higher education has been dominated by and divided between traditions that have had nothing to do with the socially aggressive inquisitiveness which Voltaire and Jefferson took to be the essential feature of intellect. This is not to say the dominant traditions have been totally lacking in a certain initial worthiness of intention. But despite that intention, they have corupted fast, mainly because they have insisted on evaluating the academic, not as a whole personality, but rather as the receptacle of specialized and seemingly detachable talents. But as Socrates long ago warned the Sophists, to partition the personality is the first step away from wisdom. To isolate any human skill (as the Sophists isolated the skill of rhetoric), to cultivate and assess it apart from the total person in whom it resides, is to trivialize the skill and diminish the person.

The traditions of higher education I speak of here may be called those of "service" and "scholarship." "Service" is that catchphrase which designates a peculiarly American interpretation of the higher learning. The ideal was most clearly embodied in the Morrill Land Grant Act of 1862, which declared that the American public universities should be an integral part of the community and serve its needs. There was—and still is—an obvious democratic idealism about this conception of the university. But how was "service to the community" to be construed? The question is a classic one and it was raised by Socrates:

To which sort of treatment of our city do you urge me? Is it to combat the Athenians until they become as virtuous as possible, prescribing for them like a physician; or is it to be their servant and cater to their pleasure?

5. J. H. Fairchild's historical account of this period at Oberlin appears in Richard Hofstadter and Wilson Smith, eds., *American Higher Education: A Documentary History* (Chicago, University of Chicago Press, 1961), Vol. 1, pp. 419-25.

Inevitably, the administrative and financial forces that came to govern American higher education chose to be catered to, not combatted. And so service came to mean the indiscriminate adaptation of the university to every demand that monied interests and the general public could imagine making. It meant, for example, offering "professional study" and even baccalaureates in boy-scouting, fire insurance, home economics, and hotel management. (Such were available—even from schools of the caliber of Cornell, Chicago, and Wisconsin.) It meant, in brief, cloaking in all the glamour and prestige of the higher learning whatever form of low-level training or ordinary entertainment the "community" felt it "needed."

But at the same time that the university was being turned into an emporium of marketable skills, other Americans were discovering a very different and very exciting vision of the higher learning. These were the young scholars and scientists who, in the immediate post-Civil War period, began flocking to the German universities, there to experience the intellectual vitality of the lecture method, the seminar, the laboratory, the rigorous Teutonic ideal of *Wissenschaft*. Here, they felt certain, they had found what higher education was all about—or *ought* to be all about. The German university was the academic New Jerusalem, and they brought home its style and standards like exotic treasure.

Nietzsche, far more perceptive than the German or American scholars of his day, could discern the dross beneath the treasure and he raised one of his typically abrasive questions.

Now Pascal thinks that men pursue their business and their sciences with such single-mindedness in order to escape the most important questions which every moment of loneliness and true leisure would urge upon them—questions concerning the Why, Whence, and Whither of life. But curiously enough, not even the most obvious question occurs to our scholars: what benefit their labor, their haste, and their painful ecstasies can possibly have? . . . But if, as men of science, you go about science in the same manner in which workers go about tasks which life's daily necessities impose upon them, then what is to become of a culture condemned to await the hour of its birth and its salvation amidst this excited, breathless, aimless, fidgeting infatuation with science and learning?[6]

But who was there to ponder such questions a century ago? The "service station" ideal of education was rapidly vulgarizing the Ameri-

6. Quoted in Frederic Lilge. *The Abuse of Learning: The Failure of the German University* (New York, The Macmillan Company, 1948), pp. 92-93.

can university, and the German-bred scholars and scientists of that generation (they were to become the creators of the graduate school, of aristocratic scholarly communities like Johns Hopkins and Clark, and of the American learned societies) had their hands full with fighting the philistine. The battle was—originally—a real one and the lines were militantly drawn. Thorstein Veblen, offering the classic statement of the academicians' position in his *The Higher Learning in America*, plumped for a standard by which only the original Johns Hopkins would ever have qualified as a true "university."

The conflict between service and scholarship in higher education, between the technician and the academic, was not destined to be resolved wholly in favor of either side—at least not at the vast majority of America's more important state and private universities. Instead the conflict has gradually worked itself into an impasse. And, in a typically "pragmatic" American way, the impasse has been given a name and has become a substitute for a solution. The name is "the multiversity": the school which teaches, in Robert Hutchins' words, "anything we can get anybody to pay for." Including, let it be said, valid subjects. For if the "service station" conception of higher education has survived and, indeed, prospered over the past three generations, the dedicated scholar has at least managed to carve out a fortified niche for himself in the busy labyrinth of the contemporary campus. Such was the compromise the scholar and the liberally educated intellectual finally settled for in the major state and private universities. In the graduate school, in the colleges of arts and letters, in their portion of the general education requirements, the academics have achieved a kind of disgruntled coexistence with the home economists, the educationists, the engineers, the business administrators, and the vast contingent of those who train and entertain in the guise of educating.[7]

This turn-of-the-century quarrel between competing elite and vulgar conceptions of higher education has continued to smolder in the multiversities—but rather at the level of a peeve than a real issue. Nevertheless, it continues to structure much of whatever small amount of discussion transpires in the schools about the ideals of education—as well as a much greater amount of intramural politics on the campuses. The proponents of the multiversity parade the "democracy" of their

7. Laurence R. Veysey has done a very thorough job of describing this historic clash of educational ideals—which he describes as a three-cornered struggle between "utility," "research," and "liberal culture." See his recent study, *The Emergence of the American University* (Chicago, University of Chicago Press, 1965).

ideal; the scholars proudly champion the aristocratic virtues of pure intellect. But the truth is that their dialogue has become a corrupted one, a debate between half-men who have lost touch with the essential meaning of both "democracy" and "intellect" and who are equally guilty of a cultural default that transcends the comprehension of both.

For where, at last, have these two supposedly irreconcilable traditions led American higher education? On the one hand, the ideal of service has matured into a collaboration between the universities, the coporate world, and the government, so indiscriminate that the American warfare state has had no greater difficulty finding academic hirelings for any project—bar none—than its totalitarian opposite numbers. Ranking physicists and engineers at the "best schools" unquestioningly pursue classified research in the refinement of the thermonuclear arsenal (schools like MIT and the University of California-Berkeley derive a major part of their budget from "service" of this kind). Biologists at the University of Pennsylvania work under secret contracts to develop chemical-biological weaponry.[8] As part of the Army's Project Camelot, leading social scientists have pooled their expertise in order to help the American military plan counterinsurgency activities in Latin America.[9] In order to provide the United States Information Agency and the military with cold-war propaganda of a scholarly cut, the University of Southern California sets up, with the generous support of a radical right-wing industrialist, a Research Institute on Communist Strategy and Propaganda.[10]

And so on. And so on.

A full listing of such activities—including the prestigious employment academics have sought at military think-tanks like the RAND Corporation—could go on for dozens of pages. And it would have to

8. This project, called quaintly enough the "Institute of Cooperative Research," has been discontinued as of the fall of 1966 in the face of faculty protest. But how did it get on campus in the first place? And how much of a "victory" is it when Penn's president explains the discontinuation on the grounds that the project "is no longer needed"? See New York Times, August 12, 1966, p. 4; August 14, 1966, IV, 9.

9. On Project Camelot, which has been metamorphosed under pressure of criticism into the Army's Special Activities Group, see Senator William Fulbright's remarks in the Congressional Record—Senate, 89th Cong., 1st Sess., August 25, 1965, pp. 20905–6. For a series of critical articles covering the project, see also the Weekly Magazine (published by the University of California Daily Californian, Berkeley) for November 25, December 7, 1965; February 24, 1966. But also see W. J. Goode's letter to the American Sociologist, November 1966, pp. 255-57, for a defense (an unsuccessful one, I think) of the project.

10. See Gladwin Hill's report in the New York Times, September 15, 1963, p. 118.

include the government's use of scholarly "names" like Arthur Schlesinger, Jr., for the purpose of authoring cover stories in support of policies secretly devised for the most cynical and unworthy purposes. But the picture is clear enough: in the name of service (and of course in return for handsome fees and cushy appointments) universities and university men have been prepared to collaborate in genocide, espionage, deceit, and all the corruptions our government's sense of omnipotence has led us to. "Service," by becoming a blanket willingness to do whatever society will pay for, has led the university to surrender the indispensable characteristic of wisdom: moral discrimination. So it is that the multiversity progressively comes to resemble nothing so much as the highly refined, all-purpose brothel Jean Genet describes in his play *The Balcony*.

21. Young Radicals and Professorial Critics

IRVING LOUIS HOROWITZ

While there has been a great deal of analysis of student riots, unrest and regimentation on American campuses, there have been stunningly few defenses of this unrest from the adult portion of the university community. Instead, professors have been publishing articles, and with increasing frequency, criticizing the current wave of student rebellion. The most serious of these academic critics include figures like Diana Trilling, Irving Howe, Seymour Martin Lipset, and Lewis Feuer.

This professorial response deserves to be examined in its own turn, but first a sociological appraisal of the critics themselves might be made.

The characteristics shared by these people are (1) they are all in their forties and fifties; (2) they are professional liberals; (3) their material usually appears in "traditional" socialist magazines; (4) their critiques invariably contain strong allusions to the '30s and the struggles between the Communist and the anti-Communist left; and finally (5) each of them appears to have a vested interest in academic liberalism as the quintessence of campus politics.

Interestingly enough, serious adult defenses of student unrest usually stem from non-academic, or at best, marginal academic sources. The names that most readily come to mind are Hal Draper, a librarian in Berkeley; Norman Mailer, the novelist; and Paul Goodman, one of the few practicing "free-wheeling" and unattached intellectuals in the United States. Others who have been relatively sympathetic to the student cause, such as Herbert Marcuse and Noam Chomsky, while philosophically instrumental in motivating the youth rebellion (despite the sharpest possible ideological differences between the two), in practice have found themselves at radical variance with student aims and ambitions, at least as those aims and ambitions were exercised by student militants at Columbia University and San Francisco State College. On the other hand, someone like Amitai Etzioni (his clear sympathies with the students notwithstanding) has been more involved in the adjudication of student-administration conflict than with either active participation in the rebellion or theoretical justification for such uprisings.

One might consider the low degree of faculty support for the current wave of student rebellion part of a self-fulfilling prophecy by which students define themselves over and against their professors in the same general terms that faculty members often define themselves over and against university administrators. The student militants tend to see the professorial Estate not as one of genteel marginality in the social whirl, but as a tawdry and organic involvement in the social world. Students' rhetoric indicates that they consider their professors economically and politically powerful rather than what they are in fact—economically and politically impotent.

There are other aspects to the students' self-definition of the situation, but in each case these would be typical of any student subculture. We are concerned with the political aspects of the situation. It is clear that this generation has the time and the affluence to see itself as a social subclass having permanent political and social aims, even though the state of being a student is transitional.

However, the main purpose of these remarks is not to define origins of the student initiative, but to characterize the faculty academic response. There are two main aspects of this reponse.

First, nearly every old liberal critic of the New Left has had a strong commitment in the past generation which included a struggle against the old left, or at the very least a traumatic confrontation that led to an abandonment of old allegiances.

Second, each of the main professorial critics deals with the New Left very much as if it is a continuation of the old left instead of as it perceives itself—in sharp dichotomy with what came before. Indeed, the critics have portrayed the left as a continuum, while students have presented the new wave of radicalism as highly discrete and separable from previous areas of student struggles.

Third, it is characteristic of the professional professoriate to confront the imperfections and vagaries of student action with the perfections of history and doctrine. Nearly every critique has made the absence of a program on the part of the new student left a central point, and accused radicals of a lack of concrete goals. In point of fact this criticism is largely justified, although reasons for the absence of specific goals are rarely discussed. Rather than fault the students, perhaps the answers are to be found in the betrayal of socialism and in the failure to present an economic alternative that is more viable or at least more morally worthwhile than the capitalist system which Soviet socialism seeks to displace. This, combined with the behavior of the Soviet Union as a national state rather than as a member of the international socialist community, has made the formation of New Left goals an exceedingly difficult chore. Instead of working out parameters of a future society, the old professorial left has been content to criticize, while the new student left remained content with not stipulating its goals.

There are obvious tactical advantages to having ambiguously defined goals. The network of recruitment can be cast much wider, while chances for polemical falling out among the dedicated are greatly restricted. And, a point easily overlooked, the new student left is remarkably sensitive to the totalitarian ideological styles of the old left. In the very act of rejecting specific socialist goals there is also a rejection of totalitarian ideologies.

However, the New Left has replaced demands for complete ideological consistency with demands for absolute adherence to a style of living. As might be expected of any group devoted to "total" change of existing society, the new student left requires a maximum commitment of its followers, but in terms of life-style rather than of ideology. While a variety of beliefs is acceptable, what counts is the way supporters act rather than what they profess. The new student left demands consistency of action rather than in verbiage.

Their peculiar brand of totalitarianism creates its own typology of problems. An almost pathological fear of "selling out" to the system precludes involvement in positions of institutional power, indeed, in most forms of legitimate occupation. In demanding maintenance of an uncompromising life-style, the New Left excludes the possibility that its advocates may become gradualists, but it also provides slender moral basis for radical politics beyond student days and no means of extending student power concepts into society in general. In short, the reason many top professorial critics find the new student left either feeble or foolish is perhaps the greatest single source of its strength; its refusal to be categorized or criticized.

Professorial critics such as Trilling frequently criticize the New Left for acting as a moralizing group rather than a political force. They note that student rebels rarely link the struggle to the quality of their instruction, but concern themselves with the control of the institutional mechanism. However, why this should be considered nonpolitical is difficult to appreciate. After all, the question of control is eminently moral. It appears that the old left always considered the university as a liberalizing or radicalizing agency rather than as a conservatizing agency. And it is the propensity of the university to "lock in" students that is clearly perceived by many members of the New Left as the central weakness in the current round of confrontations.

Other detractors who have felt the predominant character of the student rebellion to be moral rather than political have been concerned with the size rather than the character of unrest. Lipset in particular has insisted that although students succeeded in playing a significant role in the civil rights struggles of an earlier period, and in focusing attention on the higher educational bureaucracy, the recent student movement has not succeeded in mobilizing a really significant segment of the student population. While there are obvious problems in defining just what constitutes a "significant segment" of any population, it is clear that Lipset has become so enamored of electoral processes as to forget his revolutionary history. For in the process of rapid social change, population clusters of three to ten percent—the estimated size of the core and periphery of student rebels—have been significantly able to achieve their goals of either shutting down or transforming university life. At peak points, not organization membership but mass student participation has most frequently determined the success of a student uprising. Only if "politics" is defined in narrow electoral terms, or student government terms, can the character of the present movement be described as non-political in character.

Why should there be not only a crisis of university education but a crisis within the university, a lack of professorial confidence in radical student behavior? What should immediately be appreciated is that generational factors are relatively constant. When students were politically quiescent, the professoriate condemned them for being a "silent generation"; now that the student population has become politically alert and demanding, the professoriate condemns them either on tactical grounds or for lacking the requisite calm and judiciousness needed in public affairs. Thus, the sharpness of the current critique may also be viewed as a function of the generation gap.

Three additional answers come readily to mind, although it is difficult to say which is the most important single factor.

In the first place, for the old professoriate, going to college or going to the university was a chance for achievement, for moving beyond the occupational and prestige levels of the parent generation. But now the very same process, magnified and massified, has become a *familial obligation* rather than as an *individual choice*. The growth of the university in the quarter of a century since the end of World War II from a community of one million to a community of more than eight million, indicates this radical shift from the special favored position of higher education to its general acceptance as a requisite for "life."

Confusion on the part of the professoriate arises. There is an incredulous disbelief that, given such a vast set of opportunities, students would rebel. In fact, the rebellion is not so much against the opportunities gained by going to college but about the lack of options available to those who choose not to go to college. The "credential society" sharply curtails possibilities of real achievement without a college degree. There is a real concerted effort—if one can say anyone acts in concert—among families, friends, and draft boards to insure male university attendance. For the families of girls, nearly the same amount of pressure is applied in order to insure a proper locale for meeting the prospective "right" husband. The weight of middle-class familial expectations looms far larger as a factor in student rebellion than it could when going to college itself represented a rebellion against lower-class wishes.

In this respect, the acute ambivalence of many Negro students becomes clearer. Although they clearly share with the professoriate an appreciation of upward mobility and increasing life chances, they also share with the student radicals a genuine concern for the bureaucratic anti-democratic spirit of university hierarchies—a phenomenon they come into contact with simply by virtue of their racial position in American society.

The old professoriate was touched by the fear of failure, but the new student radical is touched by the guilt of success. The natural history of moving from college radicalism to occupational conservatism is a *rite du passage* gone through by nearly every member of the professorial Estate. Many look back to radical pasts. Few can claim radical commitments in the present, and fewer still have any prospects for a radical future. Precisely such an assault on the natural history of political socialization—from radicalism to conservatism in four easy years—has been made by the New Left in common with such radical regimes as Maoist Communism in China. It is not the nature of their respective political systems that links the Red Guards and the student radicals in America, but rather their shared apprehension of being overtaken by middle-generational conservatism, or as it is sometimes known, right-wing socialism. In this sense every professorial attack on the student radical movement serves as a negative reinforcement precisely because of this gap between generational ideologies.

A second new element in the present situation, one that certainly separates the old professorial critics from the new student movement, is the infusion on campus of new ethnic groups, such as Negroes, Puerto Ricans, and Mexican-Americans. Such groups share with the working-class in general a far different attitude toward higher education than older ethnic groups, such as the Jews and other European immigrants from relatively well-developed economic regions. They share a functional rather than reverential view of the educational process. The idea of a liberal arts education has become subverted in some measure by the idea of application. The demand for relevance as an ethnic demand is at its core an insistence upon occupational specificity, to assure for oneself a meaningful role in society.

Too often the position of minorities such as Negroes in college has been interpreted in simplistic terms. It is assumed that either they want to be fully integrated into the American system of higher education, or that they are in rebellion against that system on ideological grounds. Rather, it might be that their vision of college education is functional rather than ideological, occupational rather than professional. These differences create unspoken and unmentioned tensions that may appear as a struggle between campus blacks and campus whites, when in fact the struggle could better be conceptualized as concerning the nature of the liberal arts university *per se*.

The attitude of the old professoriate toward the black students is quite instructive. It is perhaps best summed up by Irving Howe in a recent essay. As a representative of a significant ideological wing of professorial liberalism, Howe shares with his colleagues a belief in the desirability and attainability of egalitarian goals for the Negro students. But he perceives of these goals only in traditional terms of integration and participation. As long as demands are made for equity, and for greater attention to the economic and intellectual needs of minority groups in American society, these minority demands elicit the wholehearted support of the professoriate.

When demands are made for separatism, such as radical demands for separate black housing to offset the effects of fraternity segregation policies, or for separate black studies institutions to offset ongoing Establishment institutions dedicated to the study of East African Affairs, Russian Affairs, and so on, the attitude toward the "extremist" demands of the black students becomes increasingly hostile and negative. In other words, when the radical student movement permeates and links up with the black student organizations, the special place of Negroes in American society is overlooked and the special value of going to college resurrected.

Black student demands for separateness and para-university structure do pose serious challenges to the traditional norms of academic freedom. They also raise the specter of the "Balkanization" of higher education. While today the demand is for a black study group, tomorrow there can be the same type of demand for a Polish or Irish study group. The role of ideology and racial parity can in this way blunt the edge of universal criteria for the training of people, criteria which are historically linked to the autonomous functioning of the university.

However, this danger duly noted, the fact is that the Negro is only replicating the practices now extant in higher education. For years academia countenanced the separatism foisted upon the community by the fraternity and sorority system. Only at this time, belatedly and without much feeling, has this WASPish system of old student power opened itself to the demands of minority groups. There was no hue and cry of factionalism or separatism when fraternities first established their exclusionary policies. The fragmentation and even polarization of American university campuses has been going on for quite some time. The multiplication of institutions and agencies on American campuses having policy implications without potential theoretical spinoffs is too well known to require further detailed commentary. Everything from the Institute for Defense Analysis to police "science" training centers has become standard university fare. In point of fact, the whole foreign area studies programming and military training programs have institutionalized separatism at every level of university life—the movement towards cross-fertilization of ideas and interdisciplinary research notwithstanding.

While criticisms directed at the Negro groups are abstractly well taken, and obviously are presented with the telling force of logic, the same kind of logic was never applied by professorial critics in an earlier age when the institutionalization of separatism and particularism initiated by the World War and the Cold War arose. Thus it is that the professional ideology of the established professoriate, now firmly linked to the medieval mythology of university autonomy, finds itself unwanted by the New Left and unappreciated by the black militants. In its self-righteous reconstruction of the past it is simply out-of-tune—with the history that was, or the utopia that is becoming.

This has agonizing consequences, since at times the traditional definition of the university, and such concepts as academic freedom, are contradicted by the demands for black control of certain parts of the educational curriculum. The struggle becomes one of autonomy at the level of student control versus integrity at the level of intellectual performance. And as in all real struggles, the problem is choosing between alternative goods. What is entailed is a radical departure from traditional, professional concepts of the purpose of a university. Little wonder that the older professorial educationalists invariably attack the new student left for being oblivious to the nature of the university! But the student radical response is that the classic system of higher learning in America is often more mythic than real. The role of military contract work, the place of large-scale business enterprise in defining curriculum, and the role of government *per se* in determining the upper limits of university experimentation, has finally made obsolete certain inherited standards of academic freedom. The struggle of student rebels has thus shifted from one of academic freedom to one of organizational control. This in itself should be a sobering indication that we have reached a new stage in the maturation of higher education in American life.

The third and final point is that professorial opposition to student radicalism stems in part from the retreat of liberalism from the prosaic political arena to the academic realm. The university has become the organic and natural expression of classical liberalism, the resting home of ex-presidents and future-advisors. The anti-intellectualism and the fanaticism of students perceived in this context seem to present the same sort of threat to liberal values in the current generation as the threat represented by the political right thirty years ago. The rhetoric of fanaticism of the new student left tends to be confused with that of the old anti-student right and to be seen as a common assault on living the life of reason and living the life of shared judgment and experience—reason being equated with professionalism. The angularity and sharpness of struggle is thus a consequence of the social victimization of students, rather than a general consequence of the social malaise in this country.

The transition of the university from a conservative force to the university as a liberal force emerged gradually. It took place as a result of the exhaustion of the conservative upper classes of the Eastern seaboard, and the Latinist conservative curriculum which prevailed in the trolley-car colleges. The older conservatism was unable to service a modern technological society, even though it may remain operational in the realm of political struggles. Liberalism in its new form never announced its ideology, but rather became important in the university context as a by-product for the needed expertise of the institution. The liberal persuasion assumed control from the conservatives on the American academic campuses not as a fighting creed but as a genteel by-product of its presumed technological proficiency.

The high irony is that the classical liberal in his form as the modern

professorial educationalist has become obligated to defend all kinds of
federal programs for social welfare and for international domination,
again as a by-product of the continuing need for expertise. In this way
the professional liberalism that stands in such marked contrast to the
student ideology on American campuses has become an enemy to the
new student radicals. It is these liberals who now see the role of the university as something other than a technical *tour de force* and an institution that needs to be defended—from students rather than from administrators.

22. The University

WALTER LIPPMANN

I am free of the obligation to offer solutions of the problems which occupy so much of the time of the governing authorities in the academic world: how to raise money, how to appease the alumni, how to get around the trustees, the state legislatures, the foundations and the Pentagon, how to ingratiate themselves with the chamber of commerce, the board of trade, and the clergy, how to tranquilize the egos of the faculty, how to deal with the students in their academic lives, their ideological lives, and their sexual lives, how to be cheerful and good fellows with the excessively inquiring reporters. About all of these preoccupations I shall have nothing to say. This leaves open to me the broad, unrestricted field of the human condition and what the universities ought to be doing for it and about it.

The proposition with which I am starting is that as men become modern men, they are emancipated and thus deprived of the guidance and support of traditional and customary authority. Because of this, there has fallen to the universities a unique, indispensable and capital function in the intellectual and spiritual life of modern society. I do not say that the universities today are prepared to perform this spiritual and intellectual function. What I do say is that a way will have to be found to perform these functions if the pursuit of the good life, to which this country is committed, is to continue and to be successful.

For modern men are living today amidst the consequences of emancipation from established authority. The dream of Franklin and Jefferson, as Mr. James A. Perkins describes it in his recent Stafford Little Lecture, was of "an open society, free of both ecclesiastical and civil control, with little to fear from the uninhibited search for truth and for experiments in the application of truth." The preponderant majority of our people in America today have arrived at such an open society. They have found, I submit, that as they are emancipated from established authority they are not successfully equipped to deal with the problems of American society and of their private lives. They are left with the feeling that there is a vacuum within them, a vacuum where there were the signs and guide posts of an ancestral order, where there used to be ecclesiastical and civil authority, where there was certainty, custom, usage and social status, and a fixed way of life. One of the great phenomena of the human condition in the modern age is the dissolution of the ancestral order, the erosion of established authority; and having lost the light and the leading, the guidance and the support, the discipline that the ancestral order provided, modern men are haunted by a feeling of being lost and adrift, without purpose and meaning in the conduct of their lives. The thesis which I am putting to you is that the modern void, which results from the vast and intricate process of emancipation and rationalization, must be filled, and that the universities must fill the void because they alone can fill it.

It is a high destiny. But it must be accepted and it must be realized.

Before we can proceed, we must ask ourselves why, in the quest of a good life in a good society, we now turn to the universities rather than, let us say, to the churches or the government. We do that because the behavior of man depends ultimately on what he believes to be true, to be true about the nature of man and the universe in which he lives, to be true about man's destiny in historical time, to be true about the nature of good and evil and how to know the difference, to be true about the way to ascertain and to recognize the truth and to distinguish it from error.

In other times and in other places, the possessors and guardians of true knowledge have been held to be the appointed spokesmen of a universal and indisputable tradition and of divine revelation. In the Western society to which we belong the traditional guardians and spokesmen of true knowledge have in varying degrees lost or renounced their titles to speak with complete authority. The hierarchy of priests, the dynasties of rulers, the courtiers, the civil servants and the commissars have to give way . . . and there is left as the court of last resort when the truth is at issue, "the ancient and universal company of scholars."

Having said this, I have not forgotten how often the professors have been proved to be wrong, how often the academic judgment has been confounded by some solitary thinker or artist, how often original and innovating men have been rejected by the universities, only to be accepted and celebrated after they are dead. The universal company of scholars is not an infallible court of last resort. Not in the least. On the contrary, it is an axiom of modern thought that the very process of thinking evolves. In human affairs nothing is infallible, absolute and everlasting. There are no courts which can anticipate fully the course of events. There are none which can take account of the unpredictability of genius. Nevertheless, in the modern world there exists no court which is less fallible than the company of scholars, when we are in the field of truth and error.

This court, this universal company of scholars, comprises all who study and teach in all the universities and institutes of the world. The colleagues of each scholar are his peers, those who have qualified themselves in mastering and obeying the criteria by which, in a field of knowledge, truth and error are judged.

The company of scholars is all over the globe, and its members are duty-bound to hear one another.

Insofar as the communication among them is adequate, so that a physicist in California is aware of the experiments and citicisms of a physicist in Peking, there exists the best possible insurance available to mortal men against the parochialism, the stuffiness and the dogmatism which are the chronic diseases of academies.

There Is No Other Court

I have said enough, I hope, to reassure anyone who might think that I am glorifying the professors and attributing to them more power and authority than they are entitled to have. I do not mean to do that. I have had my share of controversies with a good many professors. What I do say is that the community of professors is, in the modern world, the best available source of guidance and authority in the field of knowledge. There is no other court to which men can turn and find what they once found in tradition and in custom, in ecclesiastical and civil authority. Because modern man in his search for truth has turned away from kings, priests, commissars and bureaucrats, he is left, for better or worse, with the professors.

And while we must treat the verdicts of the prcfessors with a vigilant skepticism, they do have a certain authority. It comes from the fact that they have vowed to accept the discipline of scholarship and to seek the truth by using the best intellectual methods at the time known to contemporary men.

To make sure that I am not overstating my thesis, let me repeat. The community of scholars is the court of last resort in those fields of inquiry and knowledge about which scholars, as scholars, are concerned.

Thus, if a professor is charged with the murder of his colleague, the court of last resort is not the faculty of his university or the faculties of all the universities. It is the judiciary of the state in which he lives. For the scholar is a scholar only part of the time and in part of his activity. In the role of murderer he is outside the field of scholarship.

But if a professor is alleged to have murdered his colleague a hundred years ago, as in the case of Professor Webster at Harvard, the court of last resort *today* about his guilt or innocence a century ago is not the judiciary of Massachusetts. It is the historians who have studied the evidence now available and have been confronted with the findings of all the historians who have read the history of the case. After a hundred years, no one is more qualified than are the historians to judge the case.

Reflecting on this we come close, I think, to the essential principle of academic freedom. In his relations with the laws of the land, a professor is as subject as any other man to the laws against murder, robbery, cheating on the income tax, driving his automobile recklessly. The laws for him, as for all other men, are what the law-enforcing authorities say they are. The professor has no special privileges and no special immunity.

But in the field of truth and error about the nature of things, and of the history and future of the universe and of man, the state and its officials have no jurisdiction. When the scholar finds that two and two make four, no policeman, no judge, no governor, no legislator, no trustee, no rich alumnus, has any right to ordain that two and two make five. Only other scholars who have gone through a mathematical training equivalent to his, and are in one way or another qualified as his peers, can challenge his findings that two and two make four. Here, it is the community of scholars who are the court of last resort.

It follows that they are the court of last resort in determining the qualifications of admission to the community of scholars—that is to say, the criteria of appointment and the license to teach. No criterion can be recognized which starts somewhere else than in the canons of scholarship and scientific research. No criterion is valid here because it emanates from the chamber of commerce, or the trade union council, or the American Legion, or the clergy, or the newspapers, or the Americans for Democratic Action, or the John Birch Society or any political party. The selection and the tenure of the members of the community of scholars is subject to the criterion that scholars shall be free of any control except a stern duty to bear faithful allegiance to the truth they are appointed to seek.

A judgment as to whether a scholar has been faithful is one that only his peers can render. The supreme sin of a scholar, *qua* scholar, is to lie, not about where he spent the previous weekend, but about whether two and two make four.

Truth for Its Own Sake

If we say that the vocation of the scholar is to seek the truth, it follows, I submit, that he must seek the truth for the simple purpose of knowing the truth. The search for truth proceeds best if it is inspired by wonder and curiosity, if, that is to say, it is disinterested—if the scholar disregards all secondary considerations of how his knowledge may be applied, how it can be sold, whether it is useful, whether it is good or bad, respectable, fashionable, moral, popular and patriotic, whether it will work or whether it will make men happier or unhappier, whether it is agreeable or disagreeable, whether it is likely to win him a promotion or a prize or a decoration, whether it will get a good vote in the Gallup poll. Genius is most likely to expand the limits of our knowledge, on which all the applied sciences depend, when it works in a condition of total unconcern with the consequences of its own findings.

Believing this, I hold that the university must have at its core a sanctuary for excellence, where the climate is favorable to the pursuit of truth for its own sake. In our conglomerate and swarming society, the last best hopes of mankind lie in what is done, and in what example is set, in these sanctuaries.

I do not think of them as monastic establishments shut off from the struggles and strains of the human condition. I think of them as societies of fellows within the great corporate institutions that our universities have become, as societies where the relatively few who can pursue truth disinterestedly will find the support and sustaining fellowship of their peers.

Since man's whole knowledge of things is not inherited and must be acquired anew by every generation, there is in every human society a culture, a tradition of the true and the false, the right and the wrong, of the good which is desirable and the bad which is to be avoided. This culture is rooted in the accepted version of the nature of things and of man's destiny. The accepted version evolves and the encyclopedias become outdated and have to be revised.

Since the prevailing tradition rests on the prevailing science, it follows that modern men must look to the company of scholars in the universities to guard and to preserve, to refine and enrich the tradition of civility. They have to revise the curricula of studies and the encyclopedias of knowledge.

This does not mean, of course, that the scientists and the scholars are to be regarded, much less are to regard themselves, as a mysterious elite of the initiated who can lay down the law of right and wrong, of good and evil, in human affairs. It does mean that insofar as religion, government, art and personal living assume or imply that this or that is true or false, they are subject to the criticism and judgment of the company of scholars. The prevailing and accepted science of the time is the root from which grow the creations of poets and artists, of saints and prophets and heroes. The science of an age is the material with which inspiration and genius create.

I am more than a little concerned as I proceed, that you will think that I am erecting a very high tower on a very small base, that I am nominating the professors to carry too great a responsibility. All I can say is that the human condition in the modern age brings us to what I have been talking about. The dissolution of the ancestral order and the dethronement of usage and authority in modern society have left us dependent upon man's ability to understand and govern his own fate. Necessarily, therefore, we are in a high degree dependent upon the men whose lives are committed to the pursuit of truth.

The responsibility may be too great for the professors to carry. But somehow—since the responsibility must be met—we shall have to learn to find men who will tell us how to find the professors who can carry the responsibility. And if we are ever to find them, we must begin by realizing the need to find them. If they cannot be found, modern man is indeed adrift on a trackless sea.

So, I venture to proceed. There is still something more, still another great function which the universities and their scholars cannot neglect, indeed cannot escape.

For there is more to the task of learning than to discover more and more truths than have ever been known before. That something more, which may mark the difference between mediocrity and excellence, is the practice of a kind of alchemy, the creative function of transmuting knowledge into wisdom.

Wisdom, says the Oxford English Dictionary, is "the capacity of judging rightly in matters relating to life and conduct." It is "soundness of judgment in choice of means and ends." The development of the capacity of judging rightly is something different from, and in some ways much more than, the capacity to know the truth in any particular field of knowledge, or to have mastered the art of applying this knowledge to some desired end. The capacity to judge rightly in a choice of both means and ends cuts across the specialties and the technologies, and it is, I dare to say, the hallmark of a liberal, as distinguished from a utilitarian or vocational, education.

We may say, I think, that knowledge is made into wisdom when what is true about the nature of things is reshaped to the human scale and oriented to the human understanding, to human need and to human hope. As this is done, the findings of scientists and scholars are transformed into the humanities, and the materials for a liberal education begin to appear.

The universities, therefore, are not only the depositories of wisdom. They are also laboratories where alchemists work, whose function it is to transmute knowledge into human wisdom. If the scholars do this, insofar as they do this, they transcend the sterile controversies about the two cultures, the scientific and the humanistic, and they learn to transcend the intellectual puzzle about specialism and generalism. For knowledge transmuted into wisdom places the sciences and the humanities within one universe of discourse.

Usable Knowledge

Can it be done? There is no need to doubt that it can be done. The most revolutionary of all the intellectual achievements of the modern age has been man's increasing mastery of the art of discovery and invention. The reshaping and reorientation of knowledge, so that it is humanly accessible and viable, is the task of philosophers, of the masterminds in the special fields of learning, of the advanced students in the field of education, and of the great teachers themselves. It would be a feeble kind of defeatism to think that man, who is penetrating the secrets of matter and of life itself, is unable to make usable the knowledge he is able to acquire.

A liberal education is concerned with what Plato calls the "royal science," the science that needs to be possessed by the rulers of the state. The education of a prince who is destined to be the king has from time immemorial been the primary function of education. Now that we live in a time when, as Huey Long truly said, every man is a king, it is still the prime function of education to instruct and to train the future rulers of the state.

It cannot be said that there exists as yet an adequate royal science. It is the task of the scholars to invent and compile the royal science of the modern age, a science which can in some measure be absorbed by all who vote, and can educate the comparatively few who will actually govern.

The heart of this science will be a presentation of the history and the practice of judging rightly in a choice of means and ends. Such a body of wisdom must be composed and compiled and made communicable, if the supreme teaching function of the institutions of learning is to be successful. This is their necessary business if they are to be more than laboratories of research, institutes of technology and vocational centers for careers.

For they cannot neglect the highest function of education which is the education of the rulers of the state. Quite evidently, it is not easy to discover what should be taught to the future rulers of a modern state, how they are to be made to acquire that capacity of judging rightly, which is the essence of wisdom. We are only at the frontier of modern, democratic education, within sight of the promised land. Those who come after us will have to make, out of the accumulating knowledge of the specialists, a body of available and usable wisdom. The political scientists and the educators of the coming times will have to explore what is as yet a largely unknown continent—this royal science for our age. They will have to extract from the infinite complexity of knowledge what it is that the rulers of the state need to know.

Quite evidently, the ruler of a state, the President of the United States for example, cannot master all the branches of knowledge which bear on the decisions he must make. Yet he must have enough knowledge of a kind which will enable him to judge rightly whose judgment among the specialists he should decide to accept. He must learn the art, which is not described in the textbooks as yet, of listening to experts and seeing through them and around them. The educators of the future will have to extract from the whole body of nuclear science, for example, what it is that the President and the Congress and the leaders of public opinion need to know about nuclear science and the behavior of great powers when they are confronted, let us say, with a treaty prohibiting the testing of nuclear weapons. Out of these extracts from the body of knowledge, the educators must design the curriculum of our own royal science.

I have been meditating out loud about one central theme: that in the modern age, as the ancestral order of usage and authority dissolves, there exists a spiritual and intellectual vacuum of discipline and guidance which, in the last analysis, can be filled only by the universal company of scholars, supported and protected and encouraged by their universities.